ADAM AND EVE IN
SEVENTEENTH-CENTURY THOUGHT

This book offers a fascinating account of the central myth of Western culture – the story of Adam and Eve in the Garden of Eden. Philip Almond examines the way in which the gaps, hints, and allusions within this biblical story were filled out in seventeenth-century English thought. At this time, the Bible formed a fundamental basis for studies in all subjects, and influenced greatly the way that people understood the world. Drawing extensively on primary sources, he covers subjects as diverse as theology, history, philosophy, botany, language, anthropology, geology, vegetarianism, and women. He demonstrates the way in which the story of Adam and Eve was the fulcrum around which moved lively discussions on topics such as the place and nature of Paradise, the date of creation, the nature of Adamic language, the origins of the American Indians, agrarian communism, and the necessity and meaning of love, labour, and marriage.

PHILIP C. ALMOND is Professor of Studies in Religion at the University of Queensland and a Fellow of the Australian Academy of the Humanities. He is the author of many articles and a number of books, including *Mystical Experience and Religious Doctrine* (1982), *The British Discovery of Buddhism* (1988), *Heretic and Hero: Muhammad and the Victorians* (1989), and *Heaven and Hell in Enlightenment England* (1994).

ADAM AND EVE IN SEVENTEENTH-CENTURY THOUGHT

PHILIP C. ALMOND

CAMBRIDGE
UNIVERSITY PRESS

CAMBRIDGE UNIVERSITY PRESS
Cambridge, New York, Melbourne, Madrid, Cape Town, Singapore, São Paulo, Delhi

Cambridge University Press
The Edinburgh Building, Cambridge CB2 8RU, UK

Published in the United States of America by Cambridge University Press, New York

www.cambridge.org
Information on this title: www.cambridge.org/9780521660761

First published 1999
This digitally printed version 2008

A catalogue record for this publication is available from the British Library

Library of Congress Cataloguing in Publication data

Almond, Philip C.
Adam and Eve in seventeenth-century thought / Philip C. Almond.
p. cm.
Includes bibliographical references and index.
ISBN 0 521 66076 9
1. Adam (Biblical figure) 2. Eve (Biblical figure) 3. Eden –
History of doctrines – 17th century. 4. England – Intellectual life –
17th century. 5. Bible. O.T. Genesis I–III – Influence.
I. Title.
BS580.A4A55 1999
222'.1106'09032 – dc21 99–10370 CIP

ISBN 978-0-521-66076-1 hardback
ISBN 978-0-521-09084-1 paperback

To Tennyson K. Almond

Contents

Acknowledgements

For the past fifteen years, the Department of Studies in Religion at the University of Queensland has provided a stimulating context in which to teach and to pursue research. I owe debts of gratitude to many of my friends and colleagues. For many stimulating conversations, I am once again indebted to my friend Associate Professor Peter Harrison. I continue to be grateful for long friendships with my colleagues Associate Professor Ed Conrad and Professor Michael Lattke. And my friend Natalie Bell has been a continuing source of support and encouragement for which I am very grateful. The original stimulus for this work came from Professor Paul Morris of the Victoria University of Wellington, New Zealand, and I thank him for it.

I owe debts of gratitude also to the University of Queensland for supporting this research with a Special Study Program in England, and to the Australian Research Council, who provided funds for teaching relief in 1997, during which this work was written. I am very much aware too of the many scholars who have laboured in this particular garden before, and I hope I have used the fruits of their labours carefully and wisely.

This book is dedicated, with love and gratitude, to my father.

Introduction

In Paradise, then, man lived as he desired so long as he desired what God had commanded. He lived in the enjoyment of God, and was good by God's goodness; he lived without any want, and had it in his power so to live eternally. He had food that he might not hunger, drink that he might not thirst, the tree of life that old age might not waste him. There was in his body no corruption, nor seed of corruption, which could produce in him any unpleasant sensation. He feared no inward disease, no outward accident. Soundest health blessed his body, absolute tranquillity his soul. As in Paradise there was no excessive heat or cold, so its inhabitants were exempt from the vicissitudes of fear and desire. No sadness of any kind was there, nor any foolish joy . . . The honest love of husband and wife made a sure harmony between them. Body and spirit worked harmoniously together, and the commandment was kept without labor. No languor made their leisure wearisome; no sleepiness interrupted their desire to labor.

Augustine, *City of God*, 14.26

This book is about the central myth of Western culture – the story of the creation of Adam and Eve, of the Garden of Eden, of mysterious trees of life and the knowledge of good and evil, of a talking snake, of temptation, of nakedness shamed and shame clothed, of loss and expulsion. It occupies only some fifty-five verses in the Book of Genesis. But it is the foundation upon which, endlessly interpreted and elaborated, Christian men and women have built their various understandings of the human condition for the last two thousand years.

For the better part of this period, the story of Adam and Eve in the Garden of Eden was understood as an historical account of how things were in the beginning, as the opening scene in the great drama of redemption which shaped the Christian understanding of history. But it functioned as myth, for it presented a story which enabled its readers to construct accounts of the relations between men and women,

between God and humanity, and between God, nature, and humankind. It gave answers to the questions of suffering, pain, and death. It
legitimised particular authorities and institutions. And it explained the
nature of humans in their present physical, moral, social, and political
conditions. Thus, it provided the key to interpreting the nature of the
present in terms of an ideal past to which all were temporally linked,
though one from which all were separated by the cataclysmic event of
the Fall, at least until such time as Eden would be restored and Paradise regained, for some in the inner life of every individual, for most at
the end of time.

Provided the key to interpreting the nature of the present

In seventeenth-century England, the Bible was central to all intellectual endeavours. As Christopher Hill has pointed out, 'by the mid-
seventeenth century English men and women had experienced a quarter of a millennium of emphasis on the sovereignty of the Scriptures as
the unique source of divine wisdom on all subjects . . .'[1] And it was the
myth of Eden that shaped seventeenth-century understandings of why
things were the way they were, in the light of how they ought ideally to
have been.

This work will examine the way in which the gaps, hints, and
allusions within the biblical story of Adam and Eve in the Garden of
Eden were filled out in seventeenth-century English thought. It will give
a picture not only of the multiple mainstream theological and philosophical readings of the Edenic tradition, but also of the various and
varied radical and sectarian understandings of it.

In the modern West, the story of Adam and Eve no longer functions
mythologically, although it still features inchoately in contemporary
debates on animal rights, on the environment, on the relation between
the sexes, on the status of women – if only among the theologically
inclined. But the story of Adam and Eve was seminal for all aspects of
seventeenth-century cultural life. It had to be read, and by all, not
merely by theologians. For it was the focus of heated debates on
democracy versus monarchy, on nakedness, on richness of apparel and
the use of cosmetics, on androgyny, on sexual libertinism, on the nature
of marriage, and on polygamy. It was the fulcrum around which moved
excited discussions on the place of Paradise, on the date of creation, on
the nature of the Adamic language, on the identity of the forbidden
fruit, on the provenance of the American Indians, on vegetarianism, on
the stature and longevity of prediluvian people, on levelling and agrar-

---

[1] Christopher Hill, *The English Bible and the Seventeenth-Century Revolution* (London, 1994), p. 18.

ian communism, on herpetology, on the delights of gardening and fruit-growing, and on the necessity and meaning of labour.

So this book also explores the meanings of the story of the Garden of Eden in non-theological works – from books of history, natural history, political theory, and natural philosophy to writings on gardening, anthropology, fashions, language, travel, vegetarianism, anatomy, women, other worlds, botany, and geology.

Readers of this book will recognise the debt I owe to the work of Keith Thomas and Christopher Hill. But my approach has also been influenced by that of Robert Darnton. For I have been concerned to attempt to capture some of the otherness of the seventeenth century through its many and varied readings of the story of Adam and Eve, to try, in his terms, to clear the way through a foreign mental world. To this end, I have explored much strange and unfamiliar territory. As a history of the reading of the biblical story of Adam and Eve in the seventeenth century, I hope it makes a useful contribution to the history of the Western reception of the biblical text. As a description of the seventeenth century's many imaginings about the life of Adam and Eve in the Garden of Eden, I hope it may bring new insights into our understanding of a century which, in marked contrast to our own, still lived and breathed and had its being in a very different mental world, inspired by the Bible.

CHAPTER I

The origin of man

(AB)ORIGINAL ANDROGYNES

So God created man in his *own* image, in the image of God created he him; male and female created he them. Genesis 1.27

All the *Australians* are of both Sexes, or Hermaphrodites, and if it happens that a child is born but of one, they strangle him as a Monster. Gabriel de Foigny (1676)

Gabriel de Foigny was a defrocked Franciscan monk and a man in constant revolt against the sexual and moral restrictions of church and state. In 1676, he wrote *A New Discovery of Terra Incognita Australis*, a work which purported to be the story of the shipwrecked explorer James Sadeur, cast up on the shores of the Great South Land, there to remain for twenty-five years.

Australia was certainly *Terra Incognita*. A French map of Australia published in Melchissedec Thevenot's *Relations de divers voyages curieux* in 1663 outlined the northern, western, and part of the southern coasts, but little more.[1] Europeans who landed were unimpressed. In 1605, Captain William Jansz had found only wilderness and wild, cruel black savages. In 1644, Abel Tasman found only black and 'naked beach-roving wretches, destitute even of rice . . . miserably poor, and in many places of a very bad disposition'.[2] In 1688, the English buccaneer William Dampier imagined the inhabitants, whom he saw as little better than brutes:

The inhabitants of this country are the miserablest people in the World. The *Hodmadods* [Hottentots] of *Monomatapa*, though a nasty people, yet for wealth are Gentlemen to these . . . and setting aside their humane shape, they differ but little from Brutes. They are tall, strait-bodied, and thin, with small long Limbs. They

---

[1] See Robert Clancy, *The Mapping of Terra Australis* (Macquarie Park, New South Wales, 1995), p. 82.
[2] Quoted by Robert Hughes, *The Fatal Shore* (London, 1987), p. 48.

have great Heads, round Foreheads, and great Brows. Their Eye-lids are always half closed, to keep the Flies out of their Eyes . . . therefore they cannot see far . . .[3]

This was not the Australia or the Australians of the imagination of Gabriel de Foigny. His was an antipodean Paradise, where food and drink was abundant, and 'where every one may eat and drink his fill, with the greatest Pleasure in the World, without being obliged, either to Till the Earth, or cultivate any Trees'.[4] Its inhabitants lived in a perpetual springtime, the trees in fruit and flower all year round, exempt from illness not least because of their vegetarian diet. 'Their admirable temperance, and the goodness of their Fruits upon which they live', he wrote, 'maintains them in such a frame of health, as is never interrupted by any sickness.'[5] All things were held in common, all lived together in peace and harmony, and no thought was taken for the morrow: 'their manner of living thus may pass for a *Perfect Image of the State that man at first enjoyed in Paradise*'[6] and a far cry from the mores of Foigny's native France. In short, they were not fallen.

Like their Edenic counterparts, the Australians went naked, but unlike them they were hermaphrodites, yet eight feet tall, red-skinned (like Adam), with black beards and hair. Foigny's ideal humans were non-sexual. Children grew within them like fruit upon trees, for sexual generation was seen as bestial: 'we are intire Men', declared Sadeur's informer, 'wherefore we live without being sensible of any of these Animal Ardours one for another, and we cannot bear them spoke of without horror: Our Love has nothing Carnall, nor Brutall in it . . .'[7]

Not so much a nostalgia for how we once were, Foigny dreamt of a distant present, of an alternative humanity, created three thousand years before that of his European forebears. He envisaged himself as the progeny of a primal act of intercourse between a woman and a serpent. Thus was produced the first European man and woman, full of malice, bestiality, and brutality. It was a brutishness he was on occasion embarrassedly aware of before his antipodean other. In his own eyes, he was the ignoble savage.

To Foigny, original androgyny was the ideal, and the fall of European humanity was a fall into sexual difference, physical and cultural. The dominance of men over women was, as a consequence, an unnatural state, 'the effect of an odious Tyranny, than a Legitimate Authority',[8]

[3] John Masefield (ed.), *Dampier's Voyages* (London, 1906), i.350–1, quoted *ibid.*, p. 48.
[4] Gabriel de Foigny, *A New Discovery of Terra Incognita Australis* (London, 1693), p. 135.
[5] *Ibid.*, p. 88. [6] *Ibid.*, p. 76. [7] *Ibid.*, p. 70. [8] *Ibid.*, p. 72.

dom. of one
man over
woman
= bestial

and the dominance of one man over another was an unnatural descent to the bestial.[9]

The biblical phrase 'male and female created he them' was certainly conducive to an interpretation that both male and female natures were included in the original human. And the creation of woman from the substance of man, that is from Adam's rib, could also be seen as supportive of an originally androgynous creature. As John Cleveland *hermaphrodite* wrote in his poem 'Upon an Hermophrodite',

Adam

> Adam, till his rib was lost,
> Had both sexes thus engrossed,
> When Providence our Sire did Cleave
> And out of Adam carved Eve.[10]

For the puritan Richard Franck, Adam contained both male and female natures. Adam 'steer'd both Sexes in one bottome', he wrote.[11] 'Male and Female God created them', he declared, 'so that both Sexes liv'd under one Species; and *Adam* in appearance was then Hermaphrodite, because having both Natures and Similitudes in himself.'[12]

Franck was influenced by both hermetic and rabbinic writings, in both of which the androgynous original featured. The hermetic *Poimandres* saw the primal man as bisexual 'as his Father is bisexual'.[13] The shift in Genesis 1.27 from 'created man' to 'created he them' had led some rabbis to conclude that Adam and Eve were originally one. Thus, for example, in the *Bereshith Rabbah*, 'R. Jeremiah b. Leazar said: When the Holy One, blessed be He, created Adam, He created him an hermaphrodite . . .'– here in the sense of Siamese twins.[14] As Thomas Burnet put it in *Archiologiae Philosophicae* in 1692, the rabbis say 'the first Man had two Bodies, the one Male and the other Female whose sides stuck together, or (as some will have it) their Backs; that God cut them asunder, and having thus cloven *Eve* from *Adam*, gave her to him for a Wife'.[15] In the Nag Hammadi texts *The Apocalypse of Adam* and *The Gospel of Philip*, Adam was an androgynous being whose separation from Eve is repaired in the coming of Christ.[16]

---

[9] See *ibid.*, p. 77. See also J. Max Patrick, 'A Consideration of *La Terre australe connue* by Gabriel de Foigny', *PMLA* 61 (1946), pp. 739–51.

[10] Brian Morris and Eleanor Withington (eds.), *The Poems of John Cleveland* (Oxford, 1967), p. 10.

[11] Richard Franck, *A Philosophical treatise of the original and production of things* (London, 1687), p. 144.

[12] *Ibid.*, p. 143.   [13] J. M. Evans, *'Paradise Lost' and the Genesis Tradition* (Oxford, 1968), p. 67.

[14] H. Freedman and M. Simon (eds.), *Midrash Rabbah* (London, 1939), i.54.

[15] Charles Blount, *The Oracles of Reason* (London, 1693), p. 34. This work contains a translation of chs 7 and 8 of Burnet's *Archiologiae Philosophicae.*

[16] See David L. Jeffrey, *A Dictionary of Biblical Tradition in English Literature* (Grand Rapids, Michigan, 1992), p. 17.

The shift from singular to plural in Genesis 1.27 had led Philo and later Origen to conclude that the original man was androgynous, and that the division of man into a male and female was a later stage in creation.[17] Their influence was significant among Renaissance Platonists.[18] They were aware too of Plato's account of the original androgynes in his *Symposium*.[19] These influences all flowed through into the seventeenth century. Indeed, an androgynous original is implicit in all those seventeenth-century metaphorical interpretations of the Fall in which the higher masculine faculties are seduced by the lower feminine ones.[20]

Thomas Browne was uninterested in metaphorical interpretations of the Genesis text. 'Whether the temptation of the man by the woman, bee not the seduction of the rational, and higher parts, by the inferiour and feminine faculties: or whether the Tree in the middest of the garden, were not that part in the centre of the body, on which was afterward the appointment of Circumcision in males, we leave it unto the Thalmudist' he declared in *Pseudodoxia Epidemica*.[21]

Browne was certainly with the majority in believing the issue of the first man's being literally an hermaphrodite not worthy of serious study.[22] The Anglican divine Andrew Willet, for example, in *Hexapla in Genesin* in 1595 rejected the androgynous interpretation of Genesis 1.27: 'And Moses saith, hee created *them male and female*, not *created him*: contrarie to the conceit of Plato, and some Hebrewes, which thinke that Adam was at the first created both a man and a woman and afterwards diuided in twaine.'[23] The puritan George Hughes agreed. Genesis 1.27, he declared, means 'one man and one woman; no hermaphrodite as some wicked Jewes glosse. Nor multitude of these sexes as in other creatures, but one man and one woman . . .'[24] In 1674, the by then excommunicated Sir John Pettus relied upon the divine injunction to be fruitful and multiply in Genesis 1.28 to suggest the impossibility of an original hermaphrodite: 'whoever consults rightly with Physicks', he wrote, 'will find almost an impossibility in that Conceit [of hermaphroditism], for the intent of Male and Female was propogation, which would rather be hindred then advanced by such improbable

[17] See Edgar Wind, *Pagan Mysteries in the Renaissance* (London, 1968), pp. 212–14.
[18] See Edgar Wind, 'The Revival of Origen', in Dorothy Milner (ed.), *Studies in Art and Literature for Belle da Costa Greene* (Princeton, 1954).   [19] See *Symposium*, 189D, 191D.
[20] See ch. 6, 'The Fall', below.
[21] Thomas Browne, *Pseudodoxia Epidemica*, (ed. Robin Robbins. (Oxford, 1981), 1.1.
[22] See *ibid.*, 3.12.   [23] Andrew Willet, *Hexapla in Genesin* (London, 1608), p. 16.
[24] George Hughes, *An Analytical Exposition of the Whole first Book of Moses, called Genesis* (London, 1672), p. 10. See also Edward Leigh, *A Systeme or Bodie of Divinitie* (London, 1662), p. 359.

Copulation, where the Agent and Patient must at one time naturally have a mutual operation or desire with each other . . .'[25]

Thomas Laqueur has argued that in the Renaissance and early-modern periods there were not two sexes opposed in various ways. Rather, 'there was but one sex whose more perfect exemplars were easily deemed males at birth and whose decidedly less perfect ones were labeled female. The modern question, about the "real" sex of a person, made no sense in this period, not because two sexes were mixed but because there was only one to pick from and it had to be shared by everyone'.[26] Sex was then much less related to anatomy. And for those equally both male and female in terms of their sexual organs, the choice of sex and gender was a social and legal one. As Ambroise Paré put it in *Des monstres et prodiges* in 1573, 'both the ancient and modern laws have obliged and still oblige these [hermaphrodites] . . . to choose which sex organs they wish to use, and they are forbidden on pain of death to use any but those they will have chosen'.[27] So the notion of an original hermaphrodite was less problematic in the early-modern period because it was less oppositional. On the other hand, the hermaphrodite *was* a monster or prodigy, a sign of the wrath of God, or at least a point of departure for moral observations on human sin. To John-Francis Senault, for example, nature 'goes astray for sports sake, and for her pastime commits faults, yea her disorders are oft-times usefull to us; she produceth Monsters to fore-shew things to come, and goes out of her ordinary course to advertize us of Gods anger. Thus we may observe that in all ages, the birth of Monsters have been followed with some disasters.'[28] So in spite of Foigny's presentation of the paradisal Australian androgyne, and of androgynous readings of the biblical text by Platonists, hermeticists, and Gnostics, the hermaphroditic Adam was never likely to become a mainstream exemplar of the innocent primal human.[29]

[25] John Pettus, *Volatiles from the History of Adam and Eve* (London, 1674), p. 79.

[26] Thomas Laqueur, *Making Sex: Body and Gender from the Greeks to Freud* (Cambridge, Massachusetts, 1992), p. 124. This claim of Laqueur's is a large one and no doubt will need refining. For a critique, see Katharine Park and Robert M. Nye, 'Destiny Is Anatomy', *New Republic*, January 31, 1991, pp. 53–7. See also Katharine Park, 'The Rediscovery of the Clitoris', in D. Hillman and Carla Mazzio (eds.), *The Body in Parts: Fantasies of Corporeality in Early Modern Europe* (New York, 1977), pp. 171–93.

[27] Janis L. Pallister (trans.), Ambroise Paré, *On Monsters and Marvels* (Chicago, 1982), p. 27. See also Thomas Laqueur, *Making Sex*, p. 277 n. 20.

[28] John-Francis Senault, *Man become Guilty, or the Corruption of Nature by Sinne* (London, 1650), p. 378.

[29] The original androgyne has recently been revisited in the work of the feminist theologian Phyllis Trible, there to argue against the creation of man first (and therefore superior) and woman second (and therefore inferior): 'the earth creature is not the male; it is not "the first man"'. See *God and the Rhetoric of Sexuality* (Philadelphia, 1978), p. 80.

ANTHROPOMORPHITES AND IMAGES OF GOD

And God said, Let us make man in our image, after our likeness.

Genesis 1.26

God is a single person in form of a man, a spiritual person, and no bigger in compass than a man, and he was so from eternity, even of the same stature as the first *Adam* was, therefore said to be made ni [*sic*] the image and likeness of God.   Lodowick Muggleton (1668)

That man was made in the image of God and that therefore God was shaped in the form of a man was a view more often railed against than accepted. In his *Gangraena* in 1646, Thomas Edwards included two anthropomorphite errors. One was the view that God's image was the human face and countenance, 'and every wicked man hath therefore Gods image as well as good men'.[30] I can find no seventeenth-century sectarian who believed this. The other was that 'God the Creator beareth the same form in shape and person which man hath.'[31] And this was a view held in the seventeenth century, notably by the founders of the sect of the Muggletonians, John Reeve and Lodowick Muggleton. For them God was not merely spiritually in the form of a man but physically, though gloriously so, a man of medium stature: 'the glorious body of the everliving God be very flesh and bone, yet you may understand, that its clearer then Cristal, brighter then the Sun, swifter then thought, yea and infinitely more softer then Doun, and sweeter then Roses'.[32]

The devil too was of a male form, capable of seducing and impregnating Eve and siring Cain. The serpent was 'more amiable or glorious in the form of his person to the outward appearance of *Eves* eyes, then the Person of the man *Adam* was'. The serpent overcame Eve, entered into her womb, and there 'was changed from his spirituality, and immediately he quickned in her pure undefiled seed; wherefore she being now naked from her former pure created Virginity, presently she is full of natural lust after her innocent Husband, that had no desire to a woman at all . . .'[33] In contrast to the traditional interpretation where the devil

what!?!

---

[30] Thomas Edwards, *Gangraena* (London, 1646), i.24.   [31] *Ibid.*, iii.2.

[32] John Reeve and Lodowick Muggleton, *A Divine Looking-Glass* (London, 1661), p. 77. See also Christopher Hill, Barry Reay, and William Lamont, *The World of the Muggletonians* (London, 1983), p. 25.

[33] John Reeve and Lodowick Muggleton, *A Transcendent Spiritual Treatise* (London, 1652), p. 20. See also Lodowick Muggleton, *A True Interpretation of the Eleventh Chapter of the Revelation of St John* (London, 1662), pp. 10 and 14, where the Tree of Life symbolically equals God in the form of a man, and the Tree of the Knowledge of Good and Evil the devil in the form of a man.

metaphorically enters into the serpent, here the serpent – the angelical dragon cast down from heaven to earth – in the form of a man enters literally into Eve. In a similar way, God was later to enter the Virgin Mary.

It is unlikely that Edwards was aware of the unusual combination of commonsense materialism and bizarre spirituality in the teachings of Reeve and Muggleton. They became active only in the late 1640s, and only in 1652 did they come to believe that they were the last two witnesses of the Spirit referred to in Revelation 11.3. Rather, Edwards and others were looking back to the anthropomorphites of the early Christian centuries. *Gangraena* refers, for example, to the Audiani who were fourth-century followers of a sect founded by Audius, were separated from the church on the grounds of the worldliness of the clergy, and were noted otherwise only for their belief in the bodily form of God.

Nicholas Gibbens (the elder) of Dorsetshire used Audius as a plank in his Protestant criticism of the idolatry of the Church of Rome, in spite of the fact that he drew his information on Audius from the works on heresies by Epiphanius and Augustine. Audius, he declared, supposed the image of God to be in the figure of the body which

the fathers of the Church of Rome, are content to like of and to defend: in whose Churches, Chappels, and places of deuotion, it is euery where to finde, the image of God the Father depictured on their walles . . . in the figure of a man.[34]

In his commentary on Genesis, Calvin had put it simply: 'The *Anthropomorphites* were too gross in seeking this resemblance in the human body; let that reverie therefore remain entombed.'[35] God has no bodily shape or composition, declared Sir Walter Raleigh, 'an errour of the *Anthropomorphite*'.[36] In 1615 Elnathan Parr, then rector of Palgrave in Suffolk, declared the bodily form to be most beautiful, yet no part of the image of God, though he rather puzzlingly went on to say that 'the woman was made as well, according to the Image of God: though in regard of the subication of the woman to the man, it more excellently, in that, appeares in the man'.[37] Similarly, Peter Heylyn in *Cosmographie*,

---

[34] Nicholas Gibbens, *Qvestions and Dispvtations concerning the Holy Scriptvre* (London, 1601), p. 32. See also Edward Leigh, *A Systeme or Bodie of Divinitie*, p. 498; Thomas Cooper, *A Briefe Exposition* (London, 1573), sig. M.2.r.; and M. Archibald Simson, *Heptameron* (Saint Andrews, 1621), p. 29.
[35] John King (trans.), *Commentaries on the First Book of Moses called Genesis by John Calvin* (Grand Rapids, Michigan, 1984), i.94.
[36] Walter Raleigh, *The History of the World* (London, 1614), p. 24.
[37] Elnathan Parr, *The Grounds of Divinitie* (London, 1615), p. 119.

while admiring the body's gallant composition and erected structure, did not see it as God's image.[38] In a collection of sermons in 1679, Robert South, rector of Islip in Oxfordshire, summed up the opinion of most about the anthropomorphites: 'they are too ridiculous to deserve a confutation'.[39] Most conveniently forgot that God was often depicted corporeally in the Old Testament, and notably so in the early chapters of Genesis, and that this merited explanation.

[handwritten margin note: Corporeal God of OT]

While it appeared simple to suggest in what God's image did not consist, it was much more difficult to determine just what it did consist in. All were agreed that, if it were not located in the body, it was to be found in the psychological faculties. As Arnold Williams has said, 'Almost every faculty of man appears to have been thought by someone to be the image of God in man.'[40] But as he goes on to point out, the image of God was most often found in man's dominion over the creatures and in reason as the ground of this. This was an Augustinian position, and for Augustine a matter of opposing the anthropomorphites. In *Against the Manichees*, he wrote:

Let them know, nonetheless, that the spiritual believers in the Catholic teaching do not believe that God is limited by a bodily shape. When man is said to have been made to the image of God, these words refer to the interior man, where reason and intellect reside. From these man also has power over the fish of the sea and the birds of heaven and all cattle and wild animals and all the earth and all reptiles which creep upon the earth. For when God said, 'Let us make man to our image and likeness', he immediately added, 'And let him have power over the fish of the sea and the birds of heaven', and the rest, so that we might understand that man is said to have been made to the image of God, not on account of his body, but on account of that power by which he surpasses the cattle. For all the other animals are subject to man, not by reason of the body, but by reason of the intellect which we have and they do not have.[41]

Despite variation in the understanding of what was to be defined as 'intellect', the Augustinian position was to dominate the seventeenth century. The manifestations of the intellectual image of God could be multiple. Nicholas Gibbens found the image of God in the soul by virtue of its reason, knowledge, wisdom, and memory, in righteousness,

[38] Peter Heylyn, *Cosmographie in foure Bookes* (London, 1666), p. 4. See also John Pettus, *Volatiles from the History of Adam and Eve*, p. 78.

[39] Robert South, *Sermons preached Upon Several Occasions* (Oxford, 1679), p. 147.

[40] Arnold Williams, *The Common Expositor* (Chapel Hill, North Carolina, 1948), p. 73.

[41] Augustine, *Against the Manichees*, 1.17.28, in Ronald J. Teske (trans.), *Saint Augustine on Genesis* (Washington, D.C., 1991), p. 76. See also Augustine, 1.32.47, in Vernon J. Bourke (trans.), *Saint Augustine: Confessions* (Washington, D.C., 1953), p. 452.

holiness, and free will, and in nobility, 'whereby hee was more excellent than all creatures: and also in dominion, wherebye he had the rule of all creatures . . .'[42] Alexander Ross, in 1626, saw it reflected in man's soul, life, sense, reason, and power over all creatures.[43] In *Annotations upon the Holy Bible,* the biblical commentator Matthew Poole remarked that it was in the whole man, though principally in the soul. And like Augustine, who found the image of man in that which distinguished him from the animals, it was not only in the soul but also in his unique erect stature, 'which is set towards Heaven, when other Creatures by their down looks shew the lowness and meanness of their nature.'[44]

In the popular and vernacular theology of English seventeenth-century writers, there were not the fine distinctions to be found as are elaborated by Arnold Williams in his account of the image of God in the sixteenth- and early-seventeenth-century commentaries on Genesis. But the Augustinian view that it was to be found in the three faculties of the memory, the will, and the understanding (or minor variations on this theme) was not uncommon.

Although Calvin had rejected Augustine's view that it was to be found in the understanding, intellect, will, and memory, and in man's dominion over all things,[45] Martin Luther had accepted it, as he had Augustine's view that Adam's external perfections mirrored his internal ones. To his internal perfections, wrote Luther, 'was added a power of body, and of all his limbs, so beautiful and so excellent that therein he surpassed all other animate natural creatures'.[46] Following Augustine and Luther, Thomas Milles envisaged the image of God in the understanding, will, and memory of the soul.[47]

A threefold image in man was popular not least because it reflected the threefold nature of the divine. As Giovanno Loredano succinctly put it in 1659, 'in Man only and in no other creatures, is seen the image of the holy Trinity; namely in the Memory, in the Understanding, and in the Will'.[48] Samuel Purchas spoke of the soul as a 'representation and modell of the glorious Trinitie in incomprehensible Vnitie'.[49] Other threesomes

[42] Nicholas Gibbens, *Qvestions and Dispvtations concerning the Holy Scriptvre*, p. 35.
[43] See Alexander Ross, *An Exposition on the Fovrteene first Chapters of Genesis* (London, 1626), p. 22.
[44] Matthew Poole, *Annotations upon the Holy Bible* (London, 1696), sig. B.2.r. See also Augustine, *Against the Manichees*, 1.17.28.
[45] See Henry Beveridge (trans.), John Calvin, *Institutes of the Christian Religion* (London, 1953), i.165.
[46] Henry Cole (trans.), *The Creation: A Commentary by Martin Luther* (Edinburgh, 1858), p. 89.
[47] Thomas Milles, *The treasurie of auncient and moderne times* (London, 1613–19), i.18.
[48] Giovanno Loredano, *The Life of Adam* (London, 1659), p. 4. See also Henry Ainsworth, *Annotations Upon the first book of Moses called Genesis* (London, 1616), sig. B.1.v.
[49] Samuel Purchas, *Microcosmus: or the historie of man* (London, 1619), pp. 119–20.

were also popular. John Milton in *Christian Doctrine* spoke of man's being originally endowed with natural wisdom, holiness, and righteousness.[50] John Donne made three trinities in man: mind, will, and understanding; power, knowledge, and goodness; nature, grace, and goodness.[51] And Elnathan Parr found it partly in the immortality of the soul and partly in man's dominion over the creatures, but 'principally in the gifts of his minde, knowledge, holinesse, and righteousness'.[52]

A crucial question was the extent to which the image of God had been destroyed by the Fall. For Augustine, as for Luther, the image of God was wholly lost. And although it is a matter of much controversy, in spite of some suggestions in Calvin that the supernatural gifts are lost and the natural retained, theological consistency can only be maintained if we read Calvin, like Augustine and Luther, as asserting the effacement of the image of God and not merely its defacement.[53]

The Catholic position was that although the supernatural gifts such as grace and virtue were lost, the natural gifts such as reason and domination over animals were not lost. This Catholic position was endorsed, probably unwittingly, by Walter Raleigh, who had taken it directly from the Catholic commentator Benedictus Pererius.[54] According to Raleigh,

the image of God, in man, may be taken two waies; for either it is considered, according to naturall gifts, and consisteth therein: namely to haue a reasonable and vnderstanding nature &c. and in this sense, the image of God is no more lost by sinne, then the very reasonable or vnderstanding, &c. is lost: (for sinne doth not abolish and take away these natural gifts), or, the image of God is considered, according to supernaturall gifts, namely, of diuine grace, and heauenly glorie, which is indeede the perfection and accomplishment of the naturall image, and this manner of similitude and image of god, is wholly blotted out and destroyed by sinne.[55]

This position was followed too by John Salkeld in 1617. Although he had by then formally reneged on his Catholicism, he was still committed to

[50] See Don M. Wolfe (ed.), *The Complete Prose Works of John Milton* (New Haven, 1973), vi.324.
[51] See Arnold Williams, *The Common Expositor*, p. 74.
[52] Elnathan Parr, *The Grounds of Divinitie*, p. 118.
[53] See, especially on this issue in Calvinist theology, Mary Potter Engel, *John Calvin's Perspectival Theology* (Atlanta, Georgia, 1988). She adopts a perspectival approach to Calvin with a view to showing in this instance that Calvin can be read coherently as seeing the image of God as both effaced and defaced, in contrast to, for example, T. F. Torrance's argument in *Calvin's Doctrine of Man* (London, 1952) that the doctrine of justification by faith and Calvin's doctrine of election point to the defacement of the image of God after the Fall. Arnold Williams in *The Common Expositor*, p. 75 n. 33, suggests that Calvin holds to a defacement theory.
[54] So Arnold Williams, *The Common Expositor*, p. 75.
[55] Walter Raleigh, *The History of the World*, p. 27.

its distinction of the image of God into the lost supernatural gifts first infused into the soul of Adam, and its natural faculties, 'though not in the same perfection, which shee possessed before, but rather much defaced, blemished, and deformed'.[56] Alexander Ross in *An Exposition on the Fovrteene first chapters of Genesis* in 1626 recognised both alternatives, though he was committed to neither. Thus he wrote, 'If wee take his Image for that righteousnesse wherein *Adam* was created, then we say, that Gods Image was abolished by sinne; but if by the Image of God, we vnderstand mans reasonable soule with the faculties thereof, then his Image is not vtterly abolished, but defaced by sin.'[57]

The Catholic division of the image of God was occasionally rejected by the denial of the natural faculties as being part of the divine image. Andrew Willet, for example, saw the image of God as altogether effaced by the Fall, its re-creation in the present the consequence of grace: 'This image then consisteth', he wrote, 'not so much in the substance of the soul, or in the naturall faculties thereof, as of vnderstanding, free will, memorie, but in the knowledge and illumination, holines and iustice of the soul, which are now wrought in man by grace, and then giuen by creation.'[58] John Swan in *Specvlvm Mundi* followed Willet verbatim and went on to point out that, since 'the substance of the reasonable soul, with the naturall faculties and powers thereof are not lost',[59] these cannot have formed part of the original image.

There was however virtually universal agreement that the plural personal pronoun in 'Let us make man' referred to the divine Trinity. No commentator accepted the Jewish position that this was a conversation between God and his angels.[60] Thus, for example, Nicholas Gibbens declared that it did not refer to the angels, 'as the Iewes affirme, for he vsed none of their Helpe in mans creation, neither did he create man after the image of Angels but of *Elohim*, of God himselfe'.[61] Only a few believed that by 'us' was intended royalty. Lodowick Muggleton and John Reeve were two. Just as a king uses the plural, they wrote, so 'likewise when the King of Glory was moved to create a thing of

[56] John Salkeld, *A Treatise of Paradise* (London, 1617), p. 112.
[57] Alexander Ross, *An Exposition on the Fovrteene first chapters of Genesis*, pp. 23–4. See also Henry Ainsworth, *Annotations Upon the first book of Moses called Genesis*, sig. H.3.r–v.
[58] Andrew Willet, *Hexapla in Genesin*, p. 15.
[59] John Swan, *Specvlvm Mundi* (Cambridge, 1635), p. 500.
[60] See J. M. Evans, *'Paradise Lost' and the Genesis Tradition*, p. 40.
[61] Nicholas Gibbens, *Qvestions and Dispvtations concerning the Holy Scriptvre*, p. 30. See also Gervase Babington, *Certaine Plaine, briefe, and comfortable Notes vpon euerie Chapter of Genesis* (London, 1592), sig. B.I.V.

concernment, from his spiritual privy Councel'.[62] John Salkeld was another. As he was later to be imprisoned during the Revolution for his royalist sympathies, this interpretation is perhaps not surprising.[63] Matthew Poole saw it merely as an invention of later times.[64] Most simply declared 'us' to refer to the Trinity. Giovanno Loredano was typical: 'Here his divine Majesty, by this verb plurall . . . expressed the high Mystery of the Holy Trinity.'[65]

ADAM EMBODIED

> And the Lord God formed man of the dust of the ground, and breathed into his nostrils the breath of life; and man became a living soul. And the Lord God planted a garden eastward in Eden; and there he put the man whom he had formed.   Genesis 2.7–8

The Hebrew text suggests that Adam was not a paradisal creation. Rather he was placed there after having been created elsewhere. Andrew Willet was rare in rejecting the belief that Adam was created outside of Paradise.[66] Most seventeenth-century commentators accepted his extra-paradisal origins. A few hazarded guesses at where he might have been made. In 1612, the rabbinical scholar Hugh Broughton conjectured that it was 'Vpon *Mount Moriah*, which is a mountaine adioyning to the gates of the Garden of *Eden* . . .'[67] A year earlier, Anthony Munday had suggested that it was 'in the *Damascene* territory situate in *Syria* or in *Hebron*, according to the *Haebrues* Tradition'.[68]

However, in spite of the fact that there was a significant amount of debate focused on the location of Eden, there was little on the location of Adam's formation. Yet many did wrestle with its symbolic meaning. Gervase Babington, for example, saw it as symbolic of all of our eventual translations to a heavenly Paradise, that 'wee also shall bee remooued from the place where wee first tooke our beeing, to a place with our GOD,

---

[62] John Reeve and Lodowick Muggleton, *A Divine Looking-Glass*, p. 122.

[63] See John Salkeld, *A Treatise of Paradise*, p. 89. John Calvin had rejected both the Jewish and the royal plural positions. See John King (trans.), *Commentaries on the First Book of Moses*, i.92.

[64] See Matthew Poole, *Annotations upon the Holy Bible*, sig. B.2.r. See also George Hughes, *An Analytical Exposition of the Whole first Book of Moses, called Genesis*, p. 10.

[65] Giovanno Loredano, *The Life of Adam*, p. 3. See also John Swan, *Specvlvm Mundi*, p. 496; Henry Ainsworth, *Annotations Upon the first book of Moses called Genesis*, sig. B.I.v; and Andrew Willet, *Hexapla in Genesin*, p. 14.   [66] See Andrew Willet, *Hexapla in Genesin*, p. 32.

[67] Hugh Broughton, *Observations Upon the first ten fathers* (London, 1612), p. 17.

[68] Anthony Munday, *A Briefe Chronicle* (London, 1611), p. 2. Here he may have been following the popular compendium of Peter Comestor, the twelfth-century *Historia Scholastica*. See J. M. Evans, *'Paradise Lost' and the Genesis Tradition*, p. 168.

where we shall neuer take ending'.[69] John White in 1656 saw it as a sign
to us of a later placement in heaven, as a proof to Adam that he might
know how perfect Eden was, and so that he might realise that his
presence in Eden was a matter of grace and not of necessity.[70]

That Adam was created outside of Eden to remind him that he was
there as a privilege and not as a right was the dominant reading of
Genesis 2.7. It functioned therefore predominantly as a homily against
pride. This reading of it gained dominance in the seventeenth century,
not least because of its inclusion in Guillaume de Saluste, Sieur du
Bartas' *The Divine Weeks and Works*, arguably the most popular Renaissance poem:[71]

> Now heaven's eternall al-fore-seeing king,
> Who never rashly ordreth any thing
> Thought good that man (having yet spirits souns-stated)
> Should dwell els-where, then where he was created.
> That he might know, he did not hold this place
> By nature's right, but by meere gift and grace.
> That he should never tast fruits un-permitted,
> but keepe the sacred pledge to him committed.
> And dresse that parke which God, without all terme,
> On these conditions gave him as in farme.[72]

That it was Adam who was born outside of the Garden and Eve who
was born inside it was also to serve as a proto-feminist argument for the
superiority of Eve. But more of this anon.

In the Hebrew version of the creation story, 'adam is not used as a
proper name until Genesis 4.25, where Adam, for the first time as
'Adam', knows his wife.[73] The Septuagint first rendered 'adam as 'Adam'
in Genesis 2.16. The Latin Vulgate translates 'adam as a proper name for
the first time in Genesis 2.19 when the animals are brought before 'adam
to name them, and it is followed in this by the King James version.[74]

---

[69] Gervase Babington, *Certaine Plaine, briefe, and comfortable Notes pon euerie Chapter of Genesis*, sig. c.i.v.
[70] See John White, *A Commentary Upon the Three First Chapters of . . . Genesis* (London, 1656), ii. 54.
[71] So Arnold Williams, *The Common Expositor*, p. 27. He points out that there were, in all, twenty-two
   separate publications, in whole or in part.
[72] Susan Snyder (ed.), *The Divine Weeks and Works of Guillaume de Saluste Sieur du Bartas* (Oxford, 1979),
   i.324. See also John Salkeld, *A Treatise of Paradise*, p. 142; Alexander Ross, *An Exposition on the
   Fovrteene first Chapters of Genesis*, p. 44; Giovanno Loredano, *The Life of Adam*, p. 6; and Lancelot
   Andrewes, *Apospasmatia Sacra* (London, 1657), p. 160.
[73] In fact, this is the second time that the word 'adam is used without the definite article, the first
   being in Genesis 1.26. Here it is most feasibly translated 'man' or 'humankind', not 'Adam'.
[74] See David L. Jeffrey (ed.), *A Dictionary of Biblical Tradition in English Literature*, p. 15. Modern
   translations are as inconsistent in their use of 'adam' as their forebears. The American Standard
   Version and the Revised Standard Version use 'Adam' for the first time in Genesis 3.17; the New

Thus, Adam gains a personal identity in his first spoken words in differentiating himself from other creatures in the act of naming them.

Gabriel de Foigny had imagined his aboriginal Australians to be red-skinned. In this, whether consciously or not, he was following a long tradition that pictured the first man (*'adam*) as being made from earth (*'adamah*), which was red (from the verb root *'adom* – to be red). This was a connection originally suggested by the first-century Jewish historian Josephus in *Antiquities*, whence it influenced the commentators on Genesis.[75] It was a commonplace in the sixteenth and seventeenth centuries. In 'An Almond for a Parrat', Thomas Nashe put it simply: '*Adam* signifieth but red earth.'[76]

The significance of Adam's dusty constitution was a little more contested. Philo and the rabbis saw God as having chosen *pure* dust, thus emphasising man's position as the crown of creation.[77] John Pettus, for another, did not want man to be just another beast of the field since 'we are not like beasts or other Creatures in our Temperaments, they made of the ground, that is, of the *faeces* or dregs of the Earth, we of the Superficies (or of some peculiar *sanctify'd dust*)'.[78] And although he, like the plants, is made of dust, unlike them he is mobile.

Like Adam's creation outside of Eden, man's formation out of dust could be read metaphorically in a more earthy way. For it was a reminder of his humble status, and a warning against vanity. Adam's body, declared John Calvin, 'is saide to be of dust, and wanting sense, leaste any man should be delighted beyonde measure in his fleshe. For whatsoeuer he be that learneth not humilitie hereby, is more than senseless.'[79] John Donne reminded his listeners that we should not estimate ourselves so highly had we been in Paradise to see 'God take a piece of red earth, and make that wretched clod of contemptible earth into man . . .'[80] In a

English Bible and Today's English Version in Genesis 3.21; the New American Bible and the Jerusalem Bible (and the New Jerusalem Bible) at Genesis 4.25. See also *Encyclopaedia Judaica* (Jerusalem, 1971–2), ii.235–6.

75 See William Whiston (trans.), *The Works of Flavius Josephus* (London, 1825), i.43. See also Frank E. Robbins, *The Hexaemeral Literature: A Study of the Greek and Latin Commentaries on Genesis* (Chicago, 1912), p. 34.

76 Ronald B. McKerrow (ed.), *The Works of Thomas Nashe* (Oxford, 1968), p. 363. The attribution of 'An Almond for a Parrat' to Nashe is doubtful. See also Thomas Drant, *Two Sermons* (London, 1569), sig. I.2.r.

77 See Robert Graves and Raphael Patai, *Hebrew Myths: The Book of Genesis* (London, 1963), p. 63.

78 John Pettus, *Volatiles from the History of Adam and Eve*, pp. 22–3.

79 Thomas Tymme (trans.), *A Commentarie of John Caluine, vpon the First Booke of Moses* (London, 1578), p. 57. Quoted by Arnold Williams, *The Common Expositor*, p. 70.

80 Henry Alford (ed.), *The Works of John Donne D.D.* (London, 1839), i.315. Quoted in Arnold Williams, *The Common Expositor*, p. 70.

sermon against vanity in clothing preached before Elizabeth I and her
court at Windsor, Thomas Drant used the curse upon the serpent to
remind us of our humble beginnings. In the Book of Genesis, he wrote,

> the most base and contemptible Serpent, to fill yet more full of contempte, was
> enioyned to eate the dust of the earth. Such base dust as is driuen before the
> face of the winde, which the vngodly do licke, which the Serpent doth eate,
> euen such dust is *Adam*, such dust is man . . . [81]

John White reminded his readers that, although the outer form of the
body was comely, it was full of filthiness within, 'breeding and casting out
corruption every day, maintained by as base meanes as itself is Bread out
of the Earth and flesh of such Creatures, as in a few hours would turn into
stincking carrion; and cloathed with Skins or Excrements of Beasts and
worms, or Linnen out of the Earth as vile as either . . .'[82]

There was little concern, and little agreement, over the age of Adam
(and Eve) on the day of their creation. The Jewish commentators had
seen them as created at the age of twenty years. *Genesis Rabbah*, for
example, imagined them created 'fully developed' and as 'adults twenty
years of age'.[83] Sir Thomas Browne was aware of variations among
Christian commentators. 'Some Divines,' he wrote in *Religio Medici*,
'count *Adam* 30 yeares old at his creation, because they suppose him
created in the perfect age and stature of man.'[84] He does not make clear
why thirty years of age should be perfect, though it undoubtedly was
deemed so by virtue of its being around the traditional age of Jesus
during his ministry. The barrister William Austin agreed. In his book
Haec Homo, a work based on Henry Agrippa's *A Treatise of the nobilitie and
excellencye of womenkynde*, he wrote, '*Ish* and *Isha* were perfect *Man* and
woman; both for Age, Stature, and Health. For as *S. Augustine* holds, they
were created in that health, strength, and stature of body, which wee
attaine unto at thirty (our best age).' That they were near one age, with
the man a little older, he went on to say, was desirable in marriage.[85]
John Salkeld endorsed a range of thirty to fifty as expressing perfection.[86]

[81] Thomas Drant, *Two Sermons*, sig. I.2.v.

[82] John White, *A Commentary Upon the Three First Chapters of Genesis*, ii.28–9.

[83] *Genesis Rabbah* 14.7. See *Encyclopaedia Judaica*, p. 236. See also *Bereshith Rabbah*, in H. Freedman
and M. Simon (eds.), *Midrash Rabbah*, i.114. See also J. M. Evans, *'Paradise Lost' and the Genesis
Tradition*, p. 40.

[84] Thomas Browne, *Religio Medici* 1.39, in Geoffrey Keynes (ed.), *The Works of Thomas Browne*
(London, 1964).

[85] William Austin, *Haec Homo wherein the excellency of the Creation of Woman is described, By way of an Essaie*
(London, 1637), pp. 170–1.

[86] See John Salkeld, *A Treatise of Paradise*, p. 134.

In *Pseudodoxia Epidemica*, Thomas Browne also reported on those who were inclined to see Adam as the most long-lived of all men, on the ground that he was created at the perfect age, which was then fifty or sixty years, so that in terms of old age, if not in length of days, he surpassed Methusalah.[87] Andrew Willet, for example, believed that he was created at the age appropriate for generation in those years, namely about sixty-five years. This was the opinion of Pererius[88] and of George Hakewill, with whose work Browne was familiar. For Hakewill, 'the *first man* . . .'. was notwithstanding in number of yeares exceeded . . .'. by *Mathusalath* . . .'. except wee will adde unto *Adams* age threescore yeares, as some divines doe, upon a supposition that hee was created in the flower of mans age, agreeable to those times'.[89]

ANCIENT ANTEDILUVIANS

It was obvious to all readers of the text that the ancients before the Flood were said to live to extraordinary old ages. Adam lived for 930 years, Seth for 912 years, Methuselah for 969 years, and so on. And it was obvious too that, after the Flood, with the exception of Noah, who lived for 950 years (though he was by birth an antediluvian), the years of life were progressively shortened down to the psalmist's expectation of three score years and ten. To John Donne,

> There is not now that mankinde, which was then
> When as the Sunne, and man, did seeme to striue,
> (ioynt tenants of the world) who should suruiue.
> When Stag, and Rauen, and the long-liu'd tree,
> Compar'd with man, dy'de in minoritee.
> When, if a slow-pac'd starre had stolne away
> From the obseruers marking, he might stay
> Two or three hundred yeares to see't againe,
> And then make vp his obseruation plaine.[90]

The long lifespan of the patriarchs in the Genesis text was supported too by classical testimony. Josephus, for example, gave a list of authorities who saw the ancients as extremely long-lived.[91]

No one doubted that the Bible had got it right. So their longevity

---

[87] Thomas Browne, *Pseudodoxia Epidemica*, 7.3.

[88] See Arnold Williams, *The Common Expositor*, p. 80.

[89] George Hakewill, *An apologie or Declaration of the Power and Providence of God in the Government of the World* (Oxford, 1635), p. 173.

[90] Frank Manley (ed.), John Donne, *The Anniversaries* (Baltimore, 1963), pp. 70–1.

[91] See W. Whiston (trans.), *The Works of Josephus* (Peabody, Massachusetts, 1987), pp. 34–5.

required explanation. One explanation was that their lives were measured in years of shorter length. But it was difficult, on this account to put together the right combination of long life and early fatherhood. If we were to count one of our years as ten of theirs, as George Hakewill calculated,

> it will from thence follow that *Cain* and *Enoch* begat children when they were but sixe yeares old and an halfe, or seauen at most, for the *Scripture* tells us, that the one begat them when he was but sixty five yeares old, and the other at seventy: so that if ten of their yeares made but one of ours, it would consequently follow, that they begat children when they were yet but seven yeares of age.[92]

Thomas Burnet was later to point out that, if the lunar years understanding of patriarchal longevity is extended only until the Flood, then the post-diluvian fathers would be longer lived than those before the Flood – a conclusion with which no one would wish to concur.[93]

More generally, Hakewill also saw the increased longevity in the ancients as a consequence of the desirability of rapidly increasing knowledge in all the arts and sciences, a reason made popular by the Catholic Pererius, by the Protestant commentator David Pareus, and by Alexander Ross.[94]

An early scientific version of the common theory that the years then were lunar years, and therefore only one-twelfth as long as ours now, was offered by Robert Hooke, fellow of the Royal Society from 1663. In his *Discourse of Earthquakes*, a paper read to the Royal Society in 1668, he suggested that at the beginning of the world a revolution of the earth may have been much shorter than now, the world, like a rotating top, having slowed down through friction. Thus, he proposed, 'the long Lives of the Posterity of *Adam* before the Flood, might be of no greater duration then Mens Lives are ordinarily now; for though perhaps they might number more Revolutions of the Sun, or more Years than we can now, yet our few Years may comprehend as great a space of time . . .'[95] This was an interesting solution, but one which still failed to take account of the problem of juvenile parenting.

The majority of seventeenth-century commentators were inclined to accept the longevity of the patriarchs as literally true, to propose reasons

---

[92] George Hakewill, *An apologie*, p. 172. See Also Thomas Browne, *Pseudodoxia Epidemica*, 6.6; Walter Raleigh, *The History of the World*, p. 76; and Alexander Ross, *An Exposition on the Fovrteene first Chapters of Genesis*, p. 88.

[93] See Thomas Burnet, *The Sacred Theory of the Earth*, 2 vols. (London, 1722), i.303.

[94] See George Hakewill, *An apologie*, p. 42. See also Arnold Williams, *The Common Expositor*, p. 147; and Alexander Ross, *An Exposition on the Fovrteene first Chapters of Genesis*, p. 87.

[95] Richard S. Westfall (ed.), *The Posthumous Works of Robert Hooke* (New York, 1969), p. 322.

why it should have been so, and to conjecture about the causes for its having been so, at least until the Flood. Josephus had supposed that the reason for their having been given such long lives was to enhance learning in the fields of astronomy and astrology.[96] His account was well known in the seventeenth century. In 1607, Henrie Cuffe's *The Differences of the Ages of Mans Life* had paraphrased Josephus' account of the reason for, and his statement of the two causes of, the longevity of the ancients, namely virtue and better food.[97] Similarly, George Hakewill summarised Josephus: 'in regard of the excellent and profitable use of *Astronomy* and *Geometry* . . . *Almighty God* granted them a longer space of life, in as much as they could not well finde out the depth of those *Arts*, unless they lived six hundred yeares, for in that revolution of time, the *great yeare* comes about'.[98]

The longer lifespan of Adam gave him time too to teach from the perfection of his knowledge the maximum number of his posterity. To Alexander Ross, Adam had the desirable amount of time to teach his posterity of Creation, Paradise, and Fall.[99] Gervase Babington believed that the long life of the patriarchs generally was necessary 'for continuance of remembrance of matters, and deducing of them to posteritie the better'.[100]

The most important reason put forward was the necessity to populate the world quickly by the rapid propagation of humankind. As Michael Drayton wrote,

> Men then begot so soone, and got so long,
> That scarcely one a thousand men among,
> But he ten thousand in his time might see,
> That from his loynes deriu'd their Pedegree.[101]

Gervase Babington listed 'for the propagation of mankinde, so much the faster and more speedely', as one of his two main reasons for patriarchal longevity.[102] George Hakewill suggested that only by the long lives of

---

[96] W. Whiston, *The Works of Josephus*, pp. 34–5.

[97] Henrie Cuffe, *The Differences of the Ages of Mans Life* (London, 1607), pp. 88–9. I owe this reference to Frank N. Egerton, 'The Longevity of the Patriarchs', *Journal of the History of Ideas* 27 (1966), p. 578. There is no little irony in this book's having been published six years after the death of Cuffe at the untimely age of c. 38 years, having been executed for his support of the Earl of Essex. See also Christopher Heydon, *A Defence of Judiciall Astrologie* (Cambridge, 1603), p. 305.

[98] George Hakewill, *An apologie*, pp. 172–3.

[99] See Alexander Ross, *An Exposition on the Fovrteene first Chapters of Genesis*, p. 87.

[100] Gervase Babington, *Certaine Plaine, briefe, and comfortable Notes vpon euerie Chapter of Genesis*, sig. E.2.r.

[101] Michael Drayton, *The Muses Elizium lately discovered* (London, 1630), p. 90. See also Arnold Williams, *The Common Expositor*, p. 148. The notion was endorsed too by Pareus and Pererius.

[102] Gervase Babington, *Certaine Plaine, briefe, and comfortable Notes vpon euerie Chapter of Genesis*, sig. E.2.r. See also Alexander Ross, *An Exposition on the Fovrteene first Chapters of Genesis*, p. 87.

men could the necessary and rapid multiplication of humankind be effected.[103] It was an argument destined not to survive the middle of the eighteenth century. As Frank Egerton has shown, by then it was realised that the human reproductive potential was sufficient to have populated the earth before the Flood even if the expected human lifespan were only some sixty years, and there were suggestions that too much faith ought not to be put into the numerical data of ancient sources.[104]

Just as the Genesis text was silent on the reasons for the longevity of the patriarchs, it gave no information on the causes of antediluvian longevity or its post-diluvian decline. The commentators however were not reluctant to fill in the narrative gaps. One theological answer for its decline was an obvious possibility – sin. William Lawson, for example, declared that God had shortened their lives for sin by means of 'want of knowledge, evill government, riot, gluttony, drunkennesse, and . . .'. the encrease of the curse, our sins increasing in an iron and wicked age'.[105] And Walter Raleigh had surmised that, had it not been for Adam's sin, 'the liues of men on earth might haue continued double, treble, or quadruple to any of the longest times of the first age, as many learned men haue conceiued'.[106]

Allied with this was the suggestion that the longevity of the patriarchs was a matter of divine grace and not nature, a gift withdrawn after the Flood. George Hakewill, for example, admitted that men lived longer then than now, but that since the time of Moses the age of three score years and ten had been standard. The patriarchal lives were longer to establish population and to develop the arts and sciences. He ascribed this rather to '*extraordinary priviledge*, then to the *ordinary course of nature*'.[107] God subsequently withdrew the special privilege by which

hee fitted their *foode*, their *bodies*, and all other *necessaries* proportionable thereunto; as extraordinary carefulnesse and skilfulnesse in the moderation and choice of their diet, together with a singular knowledge in the vertue of *plants*, and *stones*, and *minerals*, and the like, as well as for the preservation of their health, as the curing of all kinde of diseases.[108]

For Hakewill, our lack of longevity, not so much the result of sin, was the consequence of God's withdrawing our original divinely infused knowledge.

[103] See George Hakewill, *An apologie*, p. 42. See also Thomas Browne, *Pseudodoxia Epidemica*, 6.6.
[104] See Frank N. Egerton, 'The Longevity of the Patriarchs', p. 583.
[105] William Lawson, *A New Orchard and Garden* (London, 1653), p. 84.
[106] Walter Raleigh, *The History of the World*, p. 135.   [107] George Hakewill, *An apologie*, p. 42.
[108] *Ibid.*, p. 173. See also Victor Harris, *All Coherence Gone* (London, 1966), p. 70.

If the distinction between grace and nature has become blurred in Hakewill, it remains crystal clear in Erasmus Warren. He saw Thomas Burnet's completely naturalistic explanation of the post-diluvian brevity of human life as an assault upon the very foundation of religion, an issue of 'whether some sacred and *revealed Truths*; or gay, but groundless *Philosophic Phancies*; shall be preferred'.[109] Longevity, he declared, was the work of providence and not of nature, not universal among all humans at that time, or to any animals. If longevity among humans had been universal, there would soon have been insufficient living space; and if longevity among animals too, the competition for resources would have been too great for humankind to survive.[110]

Erasmus Warren was in the minority. Most looked rather to natural causes for antediluvian longevity. To some it was the result of the perfection of Adam's body. Walter Raleigh, for example, saw the patriarchs as the perfect fruit of the most perfect man.[111] Alexander Ross pointed to the greater physical perfection of the ancients.[112] In 1640, the London schoolmaster Thomas Hayne in the second edition of *The General View of the Holy Scriptures* saw their longevity as the result of their proximity to Adam: 'these Fathers being so neere to *Adam* . . .'. may be thought to have bin endowed with a just temper of humours in their bodies, and due proportion in their complexions, and extraordinary strength'.[113]

Adam's knowledge and skill in herbs, fruits, and metals, passed on to his posterity, was often cited as the cause of their long lives. In 1674, for example, John Pettus remarked that the patriarchs 'were neerer to the original perfection wherein *Adam* was made, and knew the sanative virtues of all things; nor had they those temptations of Exorbitancies which grew up with the exuberancy of the world'.[114] John Evelyn in *Acetaria* in 1699 believed that we have hardly yet recovered the knowledge with which Adam was originally infused.[115]

All agreed it was not merely a matter of knowledge but of better food. Josephus' opinion that the ancients' food was fitter for the prolongation of life was well known.[116] Gervase Babington was typical: 'the fruites of

---

[109] Erasmus Warren, *Geologia: or, A Discourse concerning the Earth before the Deluge* (London, 1690), Epistle to the Reader.

[110] See *ibid.*, pp. 277–82.   [111] See Walter Raleigh, *The History of the World*, p. 76.

[112] Alexander Ross, *An Exposition on the Fovrteene first Chapters of Genesis*, p. 87.

[113] Thomas Hayne, *The General View of the Holy Scriptures* (London, 1640), pp. 48–9.

[114] John Pettus, *Volatiles from the History of Adam and Eve*, p. 172.

[115] See John Evelyn, *Acetaria: A Discourse of Sallets* (London, 1699), p. 128. See also Alexander Ross, *An Exposition on the Fovrteene first Chapters of Genesis*, p. 87.

[116] See W. Whiston, *The Works of Josephus*, p. 34.

the earth', he wrote, 'in their puritie, strength, and vertue, not corrupted as after the flud, and euer since still more and more, might be to them a true cause and a most forcible cause of good health, greater strength, and longer life, then euer since by nature could be'.[117] Even Hakewill, who thought longevity a matter more of grace than of nature, admitted that the food before the Flood 'may well be thought to have beene more *wholesome* and nutritive, and the Plants more *medicinall* . . .'[118]

The decline in longevity was also perceived within the context of a Renaissance pessimism about the world in general. Thus, for example, Sir Michael Scott saw the decline in our longevity after the Flood as a consequence of the general and progressive decay of the earth since then:

now in these barren and declining times of ours, as our old men want their reverence, so are they shortned in their age; our young men soone ripe, conclude, our old men soone rotten. For as the earth decayes in her fertility and power, not yeelding that vigor, vertue, and strength that formerly it hath to plants, hearbs, and vegetables, depriuing us thereby of many of our former benefits of health: all conspiring our brevity and ruine.[119]

Such Renaissance pessimism aside, there is something decidedly modern about the seventeenth century's embrace of the notion of a healthy diet of fruit and vegetables as the key to a long life. William Coles in his advocacy of the delights of gardening was firmly convinced of the relation of a vegetarian diet to long life and good health, citing the patriarchs as firm evidence of this.[120]

Virtually all commentators accepted, as we shall see in more detail later, that until the Fall, if not until the Deluge, humans were vegetarian. This too was seen as a cause of longevity, and meat-eating as a curtailer of man's life. To John Evelyn, children still run naturally to fruit, and would prefer it to meat, 'did not Custom prevail, even against the very Dictates of Nature'.[121] He was convinced that even after the Fall Adam and Eve retained a vegetarian diet. And he was persuaded

[117] Gervase Babington, *Certaine Plaine, briefe, and comfortable Notes vpon euerie Chapter of Genesis*, sig. E.2.r.
[118] George Hakewill, *An apologie*, p. 42. See also Alexander Ross, *An Exposition on the Fovrteene first Chapters of Genesis*, p. 87; Thomas Hayne, *The General View of the Holy Scriptures*, p. 49; and [William Basse], *A Helpe to Discovrse. Or a Miscelany of Merriment* (London, 1619), p. 237. The attribution of the last work to Basse is doubtful.
[119] Michael Scott, *The Philosophers Banqvet* (London, 1633), pp. 137–8.
[120] William Coles, *Adam in Eden* (London, 1657), Epistle to the Reader. See also Thomas Milles, *The treasurie of auncient and moderne times*, i.21.
[121] John Evelyn, *Acetaria*, p. 146.

that even in a post-diluvial world a diet of fruit and vegetables and simple drink would conduce to length of days.[122] Vegetarianism was natural:

Man by Nature was never made to be a *Carnivorous* Creature; nor is he arm'd at all for Prey and Rapin, with gag'd and pointed Teeth and crooked Claws, sharpned to rend and tear: But with gentle Hands to gather Fruit and Vegetables, and with Teeth to chew and eat them . . .[123]

In 1721, Eugenius Philalethes (Robert Samber) believed that a vegetarian diet would not only create the sort of longevity enjoyed by the patriarchs but would also be a counter against the plague. He saw meat as engendering noxious juices within the blood which, in warfare one with another, made the body a prey to the pestilence. 'I could wish', he wrote, 'that Man had kept up to Nature, and followed what the great Creator of all Things had prescribed to the Infant World, and had still fed on that innocent Food, the Fruits and Herbs of the Earth, and Milk, and the Golden Productions of the Industrious Bee.'[124]

In 1652, in the first work to bear the part title *A Physico-Theological Treatise*, Walter Charleton, physician to Charles I, saw one particular part of the diet of Adam and Eve as crucial to their longevity, namely the fruit of the Tree of Life. His was a proto-deistic approach to the matter of longevity. The degradation of the world as a consequence of sin was trodden upon only lightly. And the longevity of the patriarchs was explained biomedically: 'manifest it is that the *Tree of Life* was planted in Paradise to this purpose, that the fruit thereof being frequently eaten might *instaurate* the *vital Balsam* of man as fast as it suffered *exhaustion* from the depredatory operation of his *Implantate Spirit*, and by a continuall refocillation of impaired nature keep her up fresh and vigorous to longevity'.[125] He ignored the rather obvious objection that Adam and Eve and those that came after were denied access to the Tree of Life after their expulsion from the Garden.

If the seventeenth-century commentators accepted that brevity of life was caused by an undesirable diet, they believed too, like some in our period, that it was the consequence of a far too complex lifestyle. They looked back nostalgically to what they imagined was the simple Edenic life. Thus, the longevity of the ancients provided the opportunity for

---

[122] See *ibid.*, p. 144.
[123] *Ibid.*, p. 172. See also John Pettus, *Volatiles from the History of Adam and Eve*, p. 129.
[124] Eugenius Philalethes, *A Treatise of the Plague* (London, 1721), pp. 15–16.
[125] Walter Charleton, *The Darkness of Atheism dispelled by the Light of nature* (London, 1652), pp. 221–2.

homilies on the simple life. Sir Walter Raleigh compared the patriarchal times with 'the exceeding luxuriousnesse of this gluttonous age . . .'[126] Gervase Babington thought them less inclined to 'surfetting and fleshlye pleasures' than now, 'theyr mindes quieter from eating and gnawing cares, [and] the shortness of mans life: since iniquitie then being not so strong manye woes and vexations were vnfounde'.[127] Thomas Hayne reflected on the simple plain diet more common then than now, remarking that Adam 'would in all likelyhood be very cautious not to offend God, by delicious palats, and affectation of dainties'.[128]

The longevity of the patriarchs was caused too by the ideal climate in which they lived. William Basse in 1619 surmised that before the Flood the planets sent more benign influences into human bodies, leading to longer life, and there were not so many '*Meteors, Comets & Eclipses* seene, from which innumerable defects and diseases doe proceede'.[129] To John Evelyn, compared to the earth before the Flood, the earth had become 'a very Bog'. There was something in the air now, so to say, which conduced to a shorter life and moral contagion. But then, 'Men breath'd the pure *Paradisian* Air, sucking in a more *aethereal,* nourishing, and baulmy *Pabulum,* so foully vitiated now, thro the Intemperance, Luxury, and softer Education and Effeminacy of the Ages since'.[130]

It was Thomas Burnet in *The Sacred Theory of the Earth* who gave the most complex account and who made the first 'scientific' attempt to explain the decreased longevity of the post-diluvians on climatic grounds. Burnet was dissatisifed with all of the traditional explanations. He rejected the notion that their longevity was the result of their simple vegetarian diet and lifestyles. He disputed that it was due to the greater virtue of the fruits, herbs, and plants of those days. Rather he believed that the longevity of those days was the consequence of there then being over all the earth a perpetual equinox, or more particularly a perpetual spring, itself the result of the situation of the earth relative to the sun, 'which was direct, and not, as it is at present, inclin'd and oblique'.[131] Thus,

---

[126] Walter Raleigh, *The History of the World,* p. 77.
[127] Gervase Babington, *Certaine Plaine, briefe, and comfortable Notes vpon euerie Chapter of Genesis,* sig. E.2.r.
[128] Thomas Hayne, *The General View of the Holy Scriptures,* p. 49.
[129] [William Basse], *A Helpe to Discovrse,* pp. 236–7.
[130] John Evelyn, *Acetaria,* p. 125. See also Alexander Ross, *An Exposition on the Fovrteene first Chapters of Genesis,* p. 87; Gervase Babington, *Certaine Plaine, briefe, and comfortable Notes vpon euerie Chapter of Genesis,* sig. E.2.r.
[131] Thomas Burnet, *The Sacred Theory of the Earth* (London, 1965), p. 146.

all the parts of the year had one and the same tenour, face and temper; there was no Winter or Summer, Seed-time or Harvest, but a continual temperature of the Air and Verdure of the Earth. And this fully answers the first and fundamental character of the Golden Age and of *Paradise*; And what Antiquity, whether Heathen or Christian, hath spoken concerning that perpetual serenity and constant Spring that reign'd there, which in the one was accounted fabulous, and in the other hyperbolical, we see to have been really and Philosophically true.[132]

William Whiston, Isaac Newton's successor in the Lucasian Chair of Mathematics at Cambridge, disagreed with Burnet's assessment of a perpetual spring, on the ground that were the sun directly over against the earth, it would have been too hot at the equator and too cold at the poles to sustain human life. Like others, he saw the human body as more adaptable than its modern counterparts, the earth more fruitful, and men's vegetarian diets more suitable for longevity. But he did agree with Burnet that it was the climate of the earth that was crucial in the long lives of the ancients. The air was purer, thinner, and more homogeneous, and the earth watered not by showers but by 'gentle mists and vapours' ascending by day and descending by night.[133] According to Whiston, only after the Flood did the diurnal rotation of the earth begin, which distinguished the seasons and the earth into its (tropical and polar) zones and progressively shortened the lives of those who followed. But before then, 'The gentleness of Summer and Winter, with the easie and gradual coming on, and going off of the same Seasons, are but necessary in order to the very long lives of the *Antediluvians*.'[134]

MEN OF STATURE

As we have seen, John Salkeld believed that Adam and Eve were created at the perfect age, somewhere, he supposed, between thirty and fifty years. He believed too that Adam was of perfect stature: 'hee was created of the best stature, and proportion of all lineaments and members of his body, that euer man was, or shall be, our Sauiour onely excepted'.[135] He was clearly reluctant to specify just what this might have been. But he did reject the opinion that Adam and Eve had been giants. Rather, he declared, Adam must have been 'the greatest of human beings, not in quantitie but in qualitie; not in dimensions of body, but in beauty of body and soule; not in corporall extension, but in

---

[132] *Ibid.*, p. 147.   [133] William Whiston, *A New Theory of the Earth* (London, 1696), p. 183.
[134] *Ibid.*, p. 182.   [135] John Salkeld, *A Treatise of Paradise*, p. 135.

dignitie, prerogatiues, and all other excellencies, both corporall and
spirituall; because otherwise hee might rather seeme a monster in
regard of vs then a man'.[136]

It had been part of the amplification of the microcosmic nature of
Adam that some rabbinic texts saw him as having literally filled the
macrocosmic world too: 'Rab Judah said in Rab's name: The first man
reached from the one end of the world to the other . . . R. Eleazar said:
The first man reached from earth to heaven.'[137] It was a stature which,
according to Rabbi Aibu, Adam had lost at the Fall: 'On that occasion
Adam's stature was lessened and reduced to a hundred cubits.'[138]

Within the Christian tradition, though, the issue of Adam's giant
stature was more often related to the question of the place of Paradise,
specifically whether it was located across the ocean. For if it were so, our
first parents must have been of sufficient stature to have waded across or
stepped over the oceans. Andrew Willet was having none of it. 'But that
is a ridiculous conceit of Ioannes Lucidus . . .'. that Adam was the
biggest giant that euer was: and Moses Barcepha reporteth the like
fantasie of some that iudged Adam to be of that bigge stature, that he
could wade ouer the Ocean.'[139]

Walter Raleigh too had read the *De Paradiso* of the tenth-century
Bishop of Bethraman near Baghdad, Moses bar Cephas. It was probably from him that Raleigh knew of Athanasius and Cyril of Alexandria
as supporters of the giant Adam and Eve. And like Moses, he rejected it
as ridiculous: '*Adams* shinne-bones must haue contained a thousand
fadome . . . if he had foorded the Ocean.'[140]

It is worth noting however that Raleigh was willing to admit that
'those of the first age were of great stature'.[141] Giovanno Loredano
imagined Adam as a primeval body-builder: 'He was of very great
strength according to the Giant like stature he was of.'[142] Similarly,
wrote William Basse, the men of ancient times were of great age, great
size, large of stature, and mighty in strength.[143] Michael Drayton envisaged the men of old rather like antediluvian Tarzans of the jungle,
though more malign:

[136] *Ibid.*, pp. 134–5.
[137] *Sanhedrin* 38b. Quoted by J. M. Evans, *'Paradise Lost' and the Genesis Tradition*, p. 43.
[138] *S.S.Rab.* iii.7. Quoted in Evans, *'Paradise Lost'*, p. 51.
[139] Andrew Willet, *Hexapla in Genesin*, p. 32.
[140] Walter Raleigh, *The History of the World*, p. 43. See also Moses bar Cephas, *De Paradiso*, 14 (P.G.
    111.497–8); and Pierre Bayle, *Mr Bayle's Historical and Critical Dictionary* (London, 1734–8), i.103,
    who also cited Moses bar Cephas.
[141] Raleigh, *The History of the World*, p. 43.   [142] Giovanno Loredano, *The Life of Adam*, p. 83.
[143] See [William Basse], *A Helpe to Discovrse*, p. 161.

> Seauen hundred yeares, a mans age scarcely then,
> Of mighty size so were the long-liu'd men:
> The flesh of Lyons, and of Buls they tore,
> Whose skins those Gyants for their garments wore.[144]

In the first half of the seventeenth century, the image of the giants of those days, in contrast to whom, as Drayton put it, 'We are but Pygmeyes',[145] was intertwined with the belief in the progressive decay of the world since the Fall. John Donne's 'The first Anniversary' was influential:

> And as in lasting, so in length is man
> Contracted to an inch, who was a span.
> For had a man at first, in Forrests stray'd,
> Or shipwrack'd in the Sea, one would haue laid
> A wager that an Elephant, or Whale
> That met him, would not hastily assaile
> A thing so equall to him: now alas,
> The Fayries, and the Pigmies well may passe
> As credible; mankind decayes so soon,
> We're scarse our Fathers shadowes cast at noone.[146]

And for Donne, not only us but all creation was in decay, the world was spent: ''Tis all in pieces, all cohaerence gone.' [147]

That doyen of early-modern optimists George Hakewill not only rejected the theory of the progressive decay of the earth but also of the diminishing stature of men and women. While granting that there may have been giants in former times, he argued that any diminution in stature since was a matter of culture and not nature. And he looked to the 'savage races' for evidence of this:

> it may well bee that in these parts of the world where *luxury* hath crept in together with *Civility*, there may bee some diminution of *strength* and *stature* in regard of our *Ancestours*; yet if wee cast our eyes abroad upon those nations which still live according to *nature*, though in a fashion more rude and barbarous, wee shall finde by the relation of those that have lived among them, that they much exceede us in *stature* . . . which would argue, that if any decay bee, it is not *universall*, and consequently not *naturall*, but rather *adventitious* and *accidental*.[148]

Against Henrie Cuffe's suggestion that the progressive decline in longevity and stature was the result of the progressive corruption of human

---

[144] Michael Drayton, *The Muses Elizium*, p. 91.   [145] *Ibid.*, p. 103.
[146] Frank Manley (ed.), John Donne, *The Anniversaries*, p. 71.
[147] *Ibid.*, p. 73. See also Michael Scott, *The Philosophers Banqvet*, pp. 139 and 340, where 'we are scarce our fathers shadows caste at noone' is used.
[148] George Hakewill, *An apologie*, p. 209.

seed, he simply pointed to the evidence before his eyes that this was not the case: 'the contrary thereunto is manifested by daily experience, in as much as we often see feeble and sickely parents to beget strong and healthy, short to beget tall, and such as have dyed young, long lived children'.[149]

Still, if there were divisions over the stature of original humanity, over the uniqueness of human status there was little debate. There was a virtual consensus that the human was superior to the animal; indeed, that there was a qualitative distinction which separated humans from animals. But what constituted this superiority was less clear. That man was made in God's image was evident, but what this entailed was less so. Psychological features – speech, reason, free will, and moral responsibility – had their advocates. So too did physical features and, above all, man's erect stature. He was after all the king among the kings of beasts. As Peter Charron declared in 1608,

To small and particular roialties there belong certaine markes of Maiesty, as we see in the crowned Dolphin, the Crocadile, the Lion with his coller, the colour of his haire, and his eies; in the Eagle, the king of the Bees: so man the vniversall king of these lower parts walketh with an vpright countnance as a master in his house ruling, and by loue or force taming euery thing.[150]

That man's erect stature compared to the animals was the major physical sign of human superiority was virtually a commonplace of the Western tradition. Plato is probably the source for the notion that beasts look down but men look heavenward.[151] It was developed by Aristotle and put forward by Ovid in *Metamorphoses*:

> Thus, while the mute Creation downward bend
> Their Sight, and to their Earthy Mother tend,
> Man looks aloft; and with erected Eyes
> Beholds his own hereditary Skies.[152]

It was much repeated by the early fathers.[153] Augustine and Aquinas (somewhat anthropomorphically) saw man's erect stature as an aspect of the image of God in man.[154] And while Calvin saw the image of God in

---

[149] *Ibid.* See also Henrie Cuffe, *The Differences of the Ages of Mans Life*, pp. 84–5.
[150] Peter Charron, *Of Wisdome* (London, 1608), p. 9.   [151] *Timaeus*, 90A, 92Aff.
[152] Anon. (trans.), *Ovid's Metamorphoses* (London, 1717), p. 4.
[153] For a useful list of patristic citations, see C. A. Patrides, 'Renaissance Ideas on Man's Upright Form', *Journal of the History of Ideas* 19 (1958), p. 257; and Frank E. Robbins, *The Hexaemeral Literature*, p. 10.
[154] See Augustine, *Against the Manichees*, 1.17.28, in Ronald J. Teske (trans.), *Saint Augustine on Genesis*, p. 76; and Thomas Aquinas, *Summa Theologiae*, 1a.91.3, 6.

man as primarily spiritual, he did not vehemently oppose those who saw the image of God in man's looking heavenwards.[155] Like Calvin, John Milton too relied on Ovid. Raphael informs us of God's intentions for the sixth day:

> There wanted yet the Master work, the end
> Of all yet done; a Creature who not prone
> And Brute as other Creatures, but endu'd
> With Sanctity of Reason, might erect
> His Stature, and upright with Front serene
> Govern the rest, self-knowing . . . [156]

It was a moot point whether the erect stature of man was primarily intended to emphasise his difference from the beasts or to stress his heavenly origins. Thomas Milles, for example, saw erectness as intended 'Not so much for his dissimilitude from the brutish Beasts, who are crooked, bended and looking downe vpon Earth: as to mount vp his understanding, and eleuate his eyes vnto the Heavens, his originall, to contemplate there Diuine occasions, and permanent, leauing the Terrestrial as vaine.'[157]

For most these were two sides of the same coin. Of dust the body may have been, but its erectness signified its uniqueness. To Joseph Hall, Bishop of Exeter, 'lo, this heape of Earth hath an outward appearance to Heaven: other Creatures grovell downe to their earth, and have all their senses intent upon it; this is reared up towards Heaven . . .'[158] In 1626, Alexander Ross saw the uprightness of man as an advantage to his senses and to the use of his hands for working and not for walking, and so that 'he may behold heauen his country . . .'[159] William Perkins invented a physical cause for it: 'whereas all other creatures haue but foure muscles to turne their eyes round about, man hath a fifth to put his eyes vp to heauen-ward'.[160] Bishop Henrie King in 1627 saw our erect stature as a sign of our heavenly destination and of our divine origin. 'When other Creatures', he wrote,

in signe of Homage to the earth that bare them, decline downewards, and with deiected postures, confesse their whole Parentage to bee nothing else but Dust

[155] Henry Beveridge (trans.), John Calvin, *Institutes of the Christian Religion*, i.15.3. Calvin cited the lines above from Ovid's *Metamorphoses*.
[156] John Milton, *Paradise Lost* (Harmondsworth, 1989), 7.505–10.
[157] Thomas Milles, *The Treasurie of auncient and moderne times*, i.18–19.
[158] Joseph Hall, *The Works of Joseph Hall* (London, 1634), i.775.
[159] Alexander Ross, *An Exposition on the Fovrteene first Chapters of Genesis*, p. 36.
[160] William Perkins, *An Exposition of the Symbole or creede of the Apostles* (Cambridge, 1597), p. 122.

. . .'. Man, like a monument of Honour, like a Pillar or Pyramid, erected for the glorie of his Creatour, points vpward at Him.[161]

This commonplace of the early-modern period was opposed by only two persons, both of whom were physicians. So ingrained was the notion that the obvious was overlooked; but not by the physicians Walter Charleton and Thomas Browne. Charleton simply pointed to other upright creatures as evidence that human uniqueness could not consist in our erect stature:

Since many other Animals, as the *Penguin*, a kind of water fowle frequent upon the straights of Magellan; the devout insect of Province, or *Prega Dio*, the praying grasshopper, so called because for the most part found in an upright posture answerable to that of man, when his hands are elevated at his devotions; the *Bitour* [bittern], which my self hath sometimes observed standing upright as an arrow falne perpendicular, and his eyes so advanced, as to shoot their visual beams point blank at the zenith, or vertical point of heaven; all *Plane Fishes*, that have . . .'. their eyes placed in the uper side of their head, and so pointing directly upward . . .[162]

No doubt Charleton was dependent on Thomas Browne's *Pseudodoxia Epidemica*, first published in 1646. For against the uniqueness of man's erect posture, he too had pointed to the penguin, the praying mantis, plane fishes, and the bitour.[163] Still, if there were doubts expressed by a few about the pre-eminence of man's physical stature, on the predominance of his metaphysical status in the created world, all were agreed.

[161] Henrie King, *Two Sermons preached at White-Hall* (London, 1627), ii.11–12, quoted by C. A. Patrides, *Milton and the Christian Tradition* (Oxford, 1966), p. 49. See also John Swan, *Specvlvm Mundi*, p. 428; Thomas Heywood, *The Hierarchie of the blessed Angells* (London, 1635), p. 338; Thomas Robinson, *A Vindication* (London, 1709), pp. 80–1; Thomas Nabbes, *Microcosmus* (London, 1637), sig. c.2.r.; Thomas Adams, *Heaven and Earth Reconcil'd* (London, 1613), sig. E.2.v.; William Vaughan, *The Golden Groue* (London, 1600), sig. D.1.r.; Michael Scott, *The Philosophers Banqvet*, p. 12.
[162] Walter Charleton, *The Darkness of Atheism*, pp. 86–7.
[163] See Thomas Browne, *Pseudodoxia Epidemica*, 4.1.

CHAPTER 2

The perfection of man

THE CROWN OF CREATION

And God blessed them, and God said unto them, Be fruitful and
multiply, and replenish the earth, and subdue it: and have dominion over the fish of the sea, and over the fowl of the air, and over
every living thing that moveth upon the earth.   Genesis 1.28

To seventeenth-century readers of Genesis 1.28, its meaning was self-
evident. They read it through the Graeco-Christian acceptance of
human ascendancy.[1] According to this, human ascendancy and the
dominion of man over all nature was a central part of God's plan. Man
was the centrepiece of creation. 'Man, if we look to final causes, may be
regarded as the centre of the world', declared Francis Bacon, 'insomuch
that if man were taken away from the world, the rest would seem to be
all astray, without aim or purpose.'[2]

The central place of man in the universe was not the consequence
of the belief that the earth was the centre of the universe. Quite the
contrary. Arthur Lovejoy has shown that it was not the pre-Coperni-
can view of the universe which was fitted to give man a high sense of
his own importance and dignity. Rather the earth was the place far-
thest removed from the heavenly realms, a diabolocentric world with
hell at its centre.[3] The world received *its* status from its human occu-
pants: 'It was not the position of our planet in space, but the fact
that it alone was supposed to have an indigenous population of rational beings whose final destiny was not yet settled, that gave it its
unique status in the world and a unique share in the attention of

[1] See John Passmore, *Man's Responsibility for Nature* (London, 1974), p. 17. For a discussion of Genesis
1.28 up to the time of the Reformation, see Jeremy Cohen, *'Be Fertile and Increase, Fill the Earth and
Master It'* (Ithaca, New York, 1989).
[2] Quoted by Keith Thomas, *Man and the Natural World* (Harmondsworth, 1984), p. 18.
[3] See Philip C. Almond, *Heaven and Hell in Enlightenment England* (Cambridge, 1994).

33

Heaven.'[4] This is evidenced too in the belief that the punishment due to man for his sin was extended to the whole earth, and to the heavens. They too bear the consequences of human sin. 'Now I haue brought man to his graue', concluded Godfrey Goodman, 'and together with man the whole fabricke of nature . . . I haue cast the heauens and the earth vpon him, and together with man intombed the whole world.'[5]

To du Bartas, man was both viceroy and regent of this realm.[6] According to Thomas Milles, man was 'Maister of all the/ Beasts of the Earth, of the Waters, and of the Ayre, with all creatures to them belonging'.[7] Lancelot Andrewes called man that 'masterpiece of His works'.[8] For Charles Wolseley, he was king of the universe.[9] In a passage described by Clarence Glacken as the most masterly exposition of Christian belief in the dominance of man over nature, Sir Matthew Hale saw man as not only viceroy, the vicegerent of almighty God, but also as steward, bailiff, and farmer of the lower world:

In relation therefore to this inferiour World of Brutes and Vegetables, the End of Man's Creation was, that he should be the Vice-Roy of the great God of Heaven and Earth in this inferior World: his Steward, *Villicus*, Bayliff, or Farmer of this goodly Farm of the lower World, and reserved to himself the supreme Dominion, and the Tribute of Felicity, Obedience and Gratitude, as the greatest recognition or Rent for the same, making his Usufructuary of this inferior World to husband it and order it, and enjoy the Fruits thereof with sobriety, moderation, and thankfulness.

And hereby Man was invested with power, authority, right, dominion, trust, and care, to correct and abridge the excesses and cruelties of the fiercer Animals, to give protection and defence to the mansuete and useful, to preserve the species of divers Vegetables, to preserve them and others, to correct the redundance of unprofitable Vegetables, to preserve the face of the Earth in beauty, usefulness, and fruitfulness. And surely, as it was not below the Wisdom and Goodness of God to create the very Vegetable Nature, and render the Earth more beautiful and useful by it, so neither was it unbecoming the same Wisdom to ordain and constitute such a subordinate Superintendent over it, that might take an immediate care of it.

And certainly if we observe the special and peculiar accommodation and adaptation of Man, to the regiment and ordering of this lower World, we shall

---

[4] Arthur O. Lovejoy, *The Great Chain of Being* (New York, 1960), pp. 102–3.

[5] Godfrey Goodman, *The Fall of Man. Proved by Reason* (London, 1618), p. 386. See also Victor Harris, *All Coherence Gone*, for a detailed analysis of Goodman's work.

[6] See Susan Snyder (ed.), *The Divine Weeks and Works*, i.275, 289.

[7] Thomas Milles, *The treasuries of auncient and moderne times*, i.20.

[8] Quoted by Arnold Williams, *The Common Expositor*, p. 68.

[9] Charles Wolseley, *The Unreasonableness of Atheism* (London, 1669), p. 9.

have reason, even without Revelation, to conclude that this was one End of the Creation of Man, Namely, To be the Vice-gerent of Almighty God, in the subordinate Regiment especially of the Animal and Vegetable Provinces.[10]

This was a dominion which, despite diminishment, was to survive the Fall. And for Hale, even in a post-lapsarian world, the responsibilities laid upon man in Paradise to dress and keep the Garden remained paramount.

Matthew Hale was one seventeenth-century voice which counts against the influential view of Lynn White that the current ecological crisis is, at least in the main, the consequence of Western Christianity's understanding of the creation, and more specifically 'that no item in the physical creation had any purpose save to serve man's purposes'.[11] Matthew Hale's position is much more readily described as one of conservation and not exploitation.

Moreover, part of the motivation for the development of the sciences was to restore that which had been damaged by the Fall, and to return the earth to its primevally perfect state. Francis Bacon's programme was driven by the quest to restore to man his original domination over nature, and to return to the pure contact with nature and the knowledge which went with that which Adam had before the Fall. As Christopher Hill remarks, Bacon 'shared the hope of alchemists and magical writers, that the abundance of Eden might be recreated on earth, in Bacon's case by experiment, mechanical skill, and intense cooperative effort . . . Labour, the curse of fallen man, might be the means whereby he would rise again.'[12]

This was a hope shared by many of the new experimental philosophers. To Robert Hooke, for example, 'as at first, mankind fell by tasting of the forbidden Tree of Knowledge, so we, their Posterity, may be in part restor'd by the same way, not only by beholding and contemplating, but by tasting too those fruits of Natural Knowledge, that were never yet forbidden'.[13] To restore dominion over things was part of the charter of the Royal Society. Natural philosophy replicates the religion of Adam. As Sprat puts it in his *History of the Royal Society*, the experimental philosopher

[10] Matthew Hale, *The Primitive Origination of Mankind* (London, 1677), p. 370. Quoted by Clarence J. Glacken, *Traces on the Rhodian Shore* (Berkeley, California, 1973), p. 481.
[11] Lynn White, Jr, 'The Historical Roots of Our Ecologic Crisis', *Science* (New York) 155 (1967), p. 1205.
[12] Christopher Hill, *The World Turned Upside Down* (London, 1972), p. 131. See also Frances Yates, *The Rosicrucian Enlightenment* (London, 1972), p. 119.
[13] Robert Hooke, *Micrographia* (London, 1665), Preface.

l to admire the wonderful contrivance of the *Creation*; and so to apply,
t his praises aright: which no doubt, when they are offer'd up to *heven*
.... .mouth of one, who has well studied what he commends, will be more
suitable to the *Divine Nature*, than the blind applauses of the ignorant. This was
the first service, that *Adam* perform'd to his *Creator*, when he obey'd him in
mustring, and naming, and looking into the *Nature* of all the *Creatures*. This had
bin the only *religion*, if men had continued innocent in *Paradise*, and had not
wanted a redemption.[14]

John Passmore is right to point out that, in the case of Bacon (and,
one might add, of Hooke and Sprat), the effects of man's sin were
minimised, and there was a Pelagian optimism that man was able, by his
own efforts, to restore nature to its prelapsarian ideal, partially at least.
In his words, 'What sin had shattered, science could in large part
repair.'[15] In short, the image of God was not completely shattered in the
Fall. And man was, in spite of his earthy origins, the crown of creation.

The rabbinic tradition had seen man as poised between the animals
and the angels. In the *Genesis Rabbah*, for example, we read that man has
four angelic features: 'he stands upright, like the ministering angels; he
speaks, like the ministering angels; he understands, like the ministering
angels; and he sees, like the ministering angels'; and he has four brutish
features: 'he eats and drinks, like an animal; procreates, like an animal;
excretes, like an animal; and dies, like an animal'.[16]

That he was made a little lower than the angels and crowned with
glory and honour, as the psalmist sang, was a matter of much pride.[17] As
Hamlet declared, 'What a piece of work is man! how infinite in faculty!
in form and moving how express and admirable! in action how like an
angel! in apprehension how like a god! the beauty of the world! the
paragon of animals!'[18] But it was a matter for humility also. For it served
as a reminder of the vast number of grades of spiritual beings who were
superior to man. 'The principall use of considering these scales of
Creatures', wrote Sir William Petty in 1677, 'is to lett man see that
beneath God there may be millions of creatures superior unto man.
Wheras Hee generally taketh himself to be the chiefe and next to God;'
and it indicates that there are beings within 'the orbs of the fixed Starrs
. . . which do [more] incomparably excell man in the sense of dignity
and infirmity then man doth excell the vilest insect'.[19]

---

[14] Thomas Sprat, *The History of the Royal Society of London* (London, 1667), pp. 349–50.
[15] John Passmore, *Man's Responsibility for Nature*, p. 19.
[16] *Genesis Rabbah* viii.11. Quoted by J. M. Evans, *'Paradise Lost' and the Genesis Tradition*, p. 41.
[17] See Psalm 8.5.   [18] *Hamlet*, II, ii, 315–20.
[19] Quoted by Arthur O. Lovejoy, *The Great Chain of Being*, p. 190. See also John Weemse, *The Portraiture of the Image of God in Man* (London, 1627), p. 48.

For many, man's superior status was the consequence of his having been created last, on the sixth day. Thus, for example, Alexander Ross saw his being created last as emphasising that he was lord of all the other creatures. For him, there were seven grounds for man's superiority: his dominion over creatures, having Paradise prepared for him, his knowledge in naming the animals, his holiness, his innocency, his being created above the other creatures, and God's careful deliberation in creating him.[20] To Oswald Croll in 1657, man's being created last allowed God to express all the perfections in him of all that he had created before him.[21]

This was a common theme, and one that had found its classical statement in Gregory the Great in the sixth century.[22] In 1621, in *Microcosmus*, Peter Heylyn wrote of the lord of the soil who 'was created last of all as that creature to whose constitution the perfections of all the rest were vnited'. This epitome of the great volume of nature, he went on to say, 'borroweth from the Angels soule, from the brute Animals sense, from Plants life, from other creatures bignes . . .'[23] Similarly, Thomas Adams believed man was 'a sweet abstract or *compendium* of all *creatures* perfections', for he shared being with stones, life with plants, sense with beasts, and understanding with angels.[24] To William Basse, man was the epitome of all creatures:

for seuerall creatures liue in seuerall elements, as water-fowles and fishes in the water, Birds in the ayre, Beastes vpon the earth: But man enioyes all these . . . some creatures *are* onely, as *Starres*; some *are* and *liue*, as *Plants*; some *are, liue,* and haue *sense,* as *Beasts,* some *understanding,* as *Angels*: all these concurre in man . . . [25]

Even here, the recognition of man's superiority was tempered by a recognition that, unlike other animals, he was far more helpless at birth. In the words of Peter Heylyn, 'this great and mighty Prince, this general Lord of all the World, and the Creatures in it . . . doth come into the world in a worse condition, than any of the creatures which were made to serve him: naked, and impotent, and speechless, without use of reason; neither of power to help himself, or ask help of others'.[26]

[20] Alexander Ross, *An Exposition on the Fovrteene first Chapters of Genesis*, p. 21.
[21] See Oswald Croll, *Philosophy Reformed and Improved* (London, 1657), p. 55.
[22] Gregorius Magnus, *Hom. in Evan.* XXIX (P.L. 76, 1214A): 'Omnis enim creaturae aliquid habet homo. Homini namque commune esse cum lapidibis, vivere cum arboribus, sentire cum animalibus, intelligere cum angelis.' Quoted by Rudolf Allers, 'Microcosmus from Anaximandros to Paracelsus', *Traditio* 2 (1944), p. 345.
[23] Peter Heylyn, *Microcosmus* (London, 1621), p. 6. See also John Salkeld, *A Treatise of Paradise*, p. 85.
[24] Thomas Adams, *The Workes* (London, 1629), p. 1017.
[25] [William Basse], *A Helpe to Discovrse*, pp. 10–11.
[26] Peter Heylyn, *Cosmographie in foure Bookes*, p. 4.

The flawed nature of the crown of creation at his birth required some explanation. John-Francis Senault saw man's defencelessness at birth as an outcome of the Fall and an explanation of his adult attack upon nature: 'When he is grown great', he declared, 'he is bound to make war upon nature, to preserve himself; to unrobe beasts to cloth himself, he must use a kind of tyranny upon creatures, if he will free himself from the fury of the elements, and he hath so little credit in his dominions, that as he must tear up the earth for food, so must he strip beasts to clothe himself.'[27] Most were inclined to make a virtue out of our infantile helplessness. It was necessary, Walter Charleton observed, 'to the perfection and maturity of those noble organs, contrived for the administration of the mandates of that Empress, the *Cogitant Soul*.'[28] John Yates in 1622 saw our bodily vulnerability as an expression of our perfection. Our nakedness, he wrote, 'is more exquisitely made then any other, as may appear by the nakedness of it. For others that are clothed with feathers, and haires, &c. shew that they are fuller of excrements', though actually why so is not explained.[29] Andrew Willet saw it as a consequence of our perfect temperature, 'whereas other creatures, by reason of their grosse and cold humours doe growe ouer, beasts with haire, foules with feathers, fishes with scales'.[30]

The biblical evidence was read by many as suggestive of man as the crown of creation. But it was to classical sources, and most notably to the first-century BCE Roman architect Vitruvius, that many looked for the perfection of proportion that the first man must have literally embodied. Throughout the Renaissance, the *De Architectura* of Vitruvius was the chief source of knowledge about classical architecture, and consequently of the ideal human proportions delineated in this work: 'in the human body', wrote Vitruvius,

the central point is naturally the navel. For if a man be placed flat on his back, with his hands and feet extended, and a pair of compasses centred at his navel, the fingers and toes of his two hands and feet will touch the circumference of a circle described therefrom. And just as the human body yields a circular outline, so too a square figure may be found from it. For if we measure the distance from the soles of the feet to the top of the head, and then apply that measure to the outstretched arms, the breadth will be found to be the same as the height, as in the case of plane surfaces which are perfectly square.[31]

---

[27] John-Francis Senault, *Man become Guilty*, p. 297.
[28] Walter Charleton, *The Darkness of Atheism*, p. 93.
[29] John Yates, *A Modell of Divinitie* (London, 1622), p. 150.
[30] Andrew Willet, *Hexapla in Genesin*, p. 31.
[31] Morris Hicky Morgan (trans.), Vitruvius, *The Ten Books on Architecture* (New York, 1960), 3.1.3, p. 73.

Leonardo's drawing of around 1492, 'The Proportions of the Human Body', is the best-known of representations of Vitruvius' perfect proportions, Leonardo's writing on this sketch being a loose rendering of Vitruvius' words.[32]

It resonated still in seventeenth-century England. In 1615, for example, in his work on human anatomy, Helkiah Crooke, who as a fellow of the College of Physicians held the readership in anatomy in 1629 and was for a time physician to James I, followed Vitruvius in finding in the proportion of man's parts 'both a circular figure, which is of all other the most perfect; and also a square, which in the rest of the creatures you shall not observe'.[33] It was an image upon which John Pettus also drew in *Volatiles* in 1674: 'The Body of a Man or Woman being exactly extended makes a true Circle, by fixing the Center at the Navel, and the Circumference to touch the extreame points of the fingers and toes.'[34]

Intimately linked to the idea of man as the crown of creation was the imagining of him as 'a little world' who comprehended within himself all, or most of, the world around about him. This was a seventeenth-century commonplace. William Struther in 1629 spoke of it as an idea 'in all mens mouthes'.[35] However, the idea was elaborated at various levels of complexity. At its most simple, man was a microcosm because he shared in the characteristic features of other beings higher or lower than himself – rocks, plants, animals, angels – as we have seen above. He is a little world, declared Henry Ainsworth in 1616, 'for he hath in him the bewtie of things without life, even the cheifest [*sic*], as of the Sun, Moon and Starrs, &c . . . he hath growth as plants . . . sense and sensible properties with beasts . . . and wisdom with angels'.[36] To John Yates, man had the life of a plant and the senses of beasts, with the addition of reason, for 'God after he had drawne the large and reall map of the world, abridged it into this little table of Man, as *Dioptron Microcosmicum . . .*'[37]

In the big picture, man was a microcosm because he was the epitome of creation. John Calvin thought man was deservedly called a 'world in miniature' by the ancients, since he was 'a certain pre-eminent specimen of Divine wisdom, justice, and goodness . . .'[38] He was the epitome

---

[32] See for example Ludwig Goldscheider, *Leonardo: Paintings and Drawings* (London, 1959), pl. 30.
[33] Helkiah Crooke, *Microcosmographia* (London, 1615), p. 6.
[34] John Pettus, *Volatiles from the History of Adam and Eve*, p. 11.
[35] William Struther, *Christian Observations* (Edinburgh, 1629), p. 177. Quoted by C. A. Patrides, 'The Microcosm of Man: Some References to a Commonplace', *Notes and Queries* 7 (1960), p. 55. In this short article, Patrides gives a list of 55 references to the microcosm–macrocosm relationship in prose works.
[36] Henry Ainsworth, *Annotations Upon the first book of Moses called Genesis*, sig. B.I.V.
[37] John Yates, *A Modell of Divinitie*, p. 149.

of the whole world, declared Henrie Cuffe, and therefore 'is not vnfitly by the Learned, both *Diuines* and *Philosophers*, termed, the *Lesser world*'.[39] Man was the microcosm too because God repeated in man his creation of the universe. Thus, he was that which held creation together and links the opposites. Peter Charron explains,

> As a Summary recapitulation of all things, and an Epitome of the world, which is all in man, but gathered into a small volume, whereby he is called the little world, as the whole vniuers may be called the great man: as the tie and ligament of Angels and beasts, things heauenly and earthly spirituall and corporall: and in one word, as the last hand, the accomplishment, the perfection of the worke, the honour and miracle of nature.[40]

The microcosmic–macrocosmic relationship lent itself to an image in which, as Rudolf Allers writes, 'man is conceived as not only including the divers elements and natures of which the universe consists, but also their specific powers and mutual relations'.[41] Thus, the relationship between the little and large worlds represents a universal harmonious order, one which establishes the place of everything in the universe in terms of its correspondences with everything else. So for Walter Raleigh, for example, man is the microcosm, not only because he has an angelic, a rational, and a brutish nature, and not only because he is the bond between the brutish and the angelic, but also because each part of him has a macroscopic analogue: blood to waters and rivers, hair to grass, eyes to the light of the sun and the moon, the thoughts of the mind to the movement of the angels, souls to the image of God, and so on.[42] In a sermon entitled 'Mysticall Bedlam', Thomas Adams spoke of the relation between heaven and soul, earth and heart, liver and sea, brain and sun, the senses and the stars. Concerned as he was with the progressive decay of the macrocosm, the 'great man', its decline served as a pointer to the inevitable decay of the little world.[43] It was an image which appealed to the scientifically minded, for it did suggest that man could be constructed in terms of a mechanically understood universe. It appealed to the anatomist Helkiah Crooke, to whom we owe one of the more complex statements;[44] and to the Scottish natural historian John Jonston. In *An History of the Wonderful Things of Nature* in 1657, 'Man' formed one of the ten classes of natural things and the last to be

[38] John King (trans.), *Commentaries on the First Book of Moses*, p. 92.
[39] Henrie Cuffe, *The Differences of the Ages of Mans Life*, p. 1.   [40] Peter Charron, *Of Wisdome*, p. 8.
[41] Rudolf Allers, 'Microcosmus from Anaximandros to Paracelsus', p. 348.
[42] See Walter Raleigh, *The Works of Sir Walter Raleigh* (New York, 1829), ii.8.
[43] Thomas Adams, *The Workes*, p. 482.
[44] See Helkiah Crooke, *Mikrocosmographia*, 2nd edn (London, 1631), pp. 6–8. Quoted by C. A. Patrides, 'The Microcosm of Man', pp. 54–5.

discussed. Many of the variations on the theme of man as a microscosm were here ornately synthesised in a final elaborate expression:

in man as in the Centre, as in a knot, or little bundle, the original and seminary cause of all creatures lye bound up . . . Who sees not the sublunary part of the World, expressed in the lower belly? In it, are contained the parts that serve for nutrition, concoction, and procreation . . . Behold, the flowing marrow of the brain represents the moystning power of the Moon, the genital parts serve for *Venus*, the instruments of eloquence and comelinesse, do the office of witty *Mercury* . . . So the belly of Man is the Earth, fruitful of all fruits: the hollow vein, is the Mediterranean Sea; the Bladder the Western Sea, into which all the Rivers discharge themselves . . . Wherefore *Abdalas* the *Barbarian* said well, that the Body of Man is an admirable thing; and *Protagoras* call'd Man, *the measure of all things*, Theophrastus, *The pattern of the Universe and Epitome of the world*, Synesius, *The horizon of corporeal and incorporeal things.* And lastly, we may truly cry out with *Zoroastres, O Man! the workmanship of most powerful Nature*; for it is *the most artificiall Masterpiece of Gods hands.*[45]

MAN, SUPERMAN AND MASTERMIND

While most commentators were probably unaware of the Vitruvian proportions of the ideal man, there was no doubt that Adam and Eve were perfect human specimens. The indescribable beauty of Adam and Eve was part of the rabbinic tradition. Living things approached Adam in awe, mistaking him for the creator.[46] In tractate *Bava Batra*, we are told that all other people compared to Sarah are like apes compared to a man; and 'Sarah compared with Eve, is like an ape compared to a man, as was Eve compared to Adam.'[47]

The beauty of the original couple was part of the Christian tradition too. On rare occasions, Eve was considered to be more perfect than Adam. William Austin in his paean of praise of women praised her shape, colour, softness, roundness, and smoothness like '*polish't Ivory*'. Of all creatures, he declared, women were the true owners of beauty.[48] Generally no distinction was made between the beauty of Adam and Eve. Robert South pointed to Adam's erect stature, his majestic coun-

---

[45] John Jonston, *An History of the Wonderful Things of Nature* (London, 1657), pp. 308–9. Much of this passage loosely follows Helkiah Crooke, with whose *Microcosmographia* Jonston was probably familiar. For another summary, see Thomas C. Faulkner, Nicolas K. Kiessling, and Rhonda L. Blair (eds.), Robert Burton, *The Anatomy of Melancholy* (Oxford, 1989–), i.121–2. The issue of correspondence between the microcosm and the macrocosm, indeed of all things, is linked to the concept of signatures. See ch. 4, 'The Language of Adam', below.

[46] See Robert Graves and Raphael Patai, *Hebrew Myths*, p. 62.

[47] *Encyclopaedia Judaica*, ii.238. See also J. M. Evans, '*Paradise Lost' and the Rabbinic Tradition*, p. 41.

[48] William Austin, *Haec Homo*, p. 107.

tenance. With Adam, there was no need of cosmetics: 'with the lustre of a native beauty, that scorned the poor assistance of Art, or the attempts of Imitation'.[49] The absence of feathers, scales, and hairs was a sign of their perfection. In 1641, for example, George Walker extolled their nakedness: 'Their skin was not rough, over-growne with haire like beasts, nor with feathers like birds, nor with hard scales like fishes; but their skin, faire, white, and ruddie, was comely in itselfe, and beautifull to their own eyes.'[50] Jacob Boehme's English disciple Samuel Pordage imagined Adam as a superman, with strength sufficient to throw himself across the sea, or through the air, incapable of destruction.[51]

It was self-evident to all that men and women no longer, as individuals, replicated the perfection of Adam and Eve, nor men the Vitruvian ideal. In general this was seen as a change from perfect proportions. To Renaissance collectors of social diversity, uniformity was notably absent. As Margaret Hodgen has noted,

> every fardel of fashions, disclosed to the impatient European viewer a disconcerting array, in the one family of the children of God, of diverse institutions, diverse types of shelter and diet, diverse customs of dress . . . Nowhere in the behaviour of man, son of Adam and progeny of Noah, did there seem to be any tranquilizing uniformity.[52]

John Bulwer's work *Anthropometamorphosis* in 1650 was typical. This was an elaborate attempt to show 'historically', as its subtitle indicates, the degradation of the natural body and its ornamentation as a consequence of human interference: 'the mad and cruel Gallantry, Foolish Bravery, ridiculous Beauty, Filthy Finenesse, and loathsome Lovelinesse of Most Nations, Fashioning and altering their Bodies from the Mould intended by Nature'.[53] To him it was a matter of our defacing man according to our likeness.[54] But while Bulwer laid out in great detail his vast array of bodily types and ornament, he forewent any detail of what it originally was from which these many types deviated.

[49] Robert South, *Sermons Preached Upon Several Occasions*, p. 149.
[50] George Walker, *God made visible in His Workes* (London, 1641), p. 204. See also Elnathan Parr, *The Grounds of Divinitie*, p. 147.
[51] Samuel Pordage, *Mundorum Explicatio* (London, 1661), p. 59. This may have been written by Samuel or by his father, John Pordage, or jointly. On the Pordages, see Christopher Hill, *The Experience of Defeat* (London, 1984), pp. 220–42. For Luther on Adam's strength and 'telescopic vision', see William Hazlitt (trans.), *The Table Talk or Familiar Discourse of Martin Luther* (London, 1848), p. 57; and Henry Cole (trans.), *The Creation: A Commentary by Martin Luther*, pp. 89–90.
[52] Margaret T. Hodgen, *Early Anthropology in the Sixteenth and Seventeenth Centuries* (Philadelphia, 1964), p. 208.
[53] John Bulwer, *Anthropometamorphosis: Man transform'd; or the Artificial Changeling* (London, 1650).
[54] *Ibid.*, Epistle Dedicatory.

However that may be, for Bulwer the changes were a matter of human choice and not necessity. For others, there were significant changes to the human body as an immediate consequence of the Fall, and particularly to the sexual organs. To Samuel Pordage, for example, Adam in his perfect state would have procreated magically, and alone, and without the need of sexual organs, much like Foigny's Australians. Genitalia, both male and female, and human generation were a consequence of the Fall.[55] There is the suggestion in Elnathan Parr that, although humans were created with genitalia, these lost their physical perfection and their aesthetic appeal as a result of the Fall: 'Outwardly in their bodies, there was exceeding beauty, and perfection of all parts, so that there was no uncomeliness, no not in those members which after sinne natural shame, for their deformity, and unseemlinesse, teacheth us to couer.'[56] More generally, there was the recognition that, while sexual organs had physically survived the Fall in the state in which they had been created, our attitude to them had changed. That which Adam and Eve perceived as perfect is perceived by us as deformed. John White, for example, imagined Adam and Eve perfect in body, with no thoughts likely to cause them to blush, with the result that, 'though they had in their view those parts from which we turn away, and at the sight whereof usually inordinate lusts kindle in our hearts; yet it wrought no such effect in their hearts, nor had any appearance of deformity to them at all'.[57] Phillip Stubbes in 1583 hinted that, once sin was committed, their bodies became 'vncleane, filthy, lothsome, and deformed . . .'[58] And the Presbyterian (and almost parodically puritan) Thomas Hall in 1653 in a work subtitled *The Loathsomeness of Long Haire* cried out against exposing any part of the body: 'sinne hath so horribly stained and defiled our whole bodies, and covered them with shame, that if it were possible, and necessity would permit it, the whole body, both face and hands, should all be covered . . .'[59]

It was also virtually universal to depict Adam and Eve in a general form identical to their posterity, and notably with navels. John Dunton defended the practice in the 1690s in his *Athenian Gazette*, on the ground that, according to physicians, the use of the navel was not only to nourish the child but was 'of great use to the Intestines and Bowels after

[55] Samuel Pordage, *Mundorum Explicatio*, p. 62.
[56] Elnathan Parr, *The Grounds of Divinitie*, pp. 147–8.
[57] John White, *A Commentary Upon the Three First Chapters of Genesis*, ii.116.
[58] Phillip Stubbes, *The Anatomie of Abuses* (London, 1583), sig. c.4.v.
[59] Thomas Hall, *Comarum akosmia: The Loathsomeness of Long Haire* (London, 1653), pp. 109–10.

Delivery', and 'one of the great *Seats* of our strength'.[60] It was the physician in Thomas Browne who, fifty years earlier, was having none of primal navels. Although he knew of the depiction of navels in the works of both Michelangelo and Raphael, and in 'ordinary and stayned peeces', the perfection of the original pair would not allow of superfluous or useless parts: 'now the Navell being a part, not precedent, but subsequent unto generation, nativity, or parturition, it cannot be well imagined at the creation or extraordinary formation of Adam, who immediately issued from the Artifice of God; nor also that of Eve, who was not solemnly begotten, but suddenly framed, and anomalously proceeded from Adam'.[61] Similarly John Evelyn, in the introduction to his translation of Roland Freart's *Idea of the Perfection of Painting*, lamented the presence of anachronisms in works of art, amongst which he mentions those of Malvogius, 'who not only represents our first *Parents* with *Navils* upon their bellys, but has plac'd an *artificial* stone-Fountain carv'd with *imagerys* in the midst of his *Paradise*'.[62]

Among the perfections of Adam was his perfect knowledge. This was the ultimate source of his dominion over nature. And it was the source of inspiration for the new experimental philosophers. As Charles Webster writes, the final rewards for scientific efforts 'might be man's return from the suburbs into Paradise'.[63] To rediscover Adamic knowledge and to restore the original dominion over nature was at the core of Francis Bacon's programme: 'For man by the Fall fell at the same time from his state of innocency and from his dominion over creation. Both of these losses however can even in this life be in some part repaired; the former by religion and faith, the latter by arts and sciences.'[64] The physician Philip Barrough hoped through study and experiment to rediscover the means to the perfect health enjoyed by Adam and Eve in Paradise. Thus, in *The Method of Phisicke* in 1583 he wrote,

there is no meanes by which a man can approach neerer unto the perfection of that nature which he first enioyed, and then lost by his fall, then by the painfull indagation of the secretes of nature, or anie way, whereby he may more truely glorifie his maker, then in his life time with his tongue to communicate that

---

[60] John Dunton (ed.), *The Athenian Gazette* (London, 1691–7), vol. 2, q. 12, no. 1.

[61] Thomas Browne, *Pseudodoxia Epidemica*, 5.5. See also *Religio Medici*, 2.10.

[62] Roland Freart, *An Idea of the Perfection of Painting* (London, 1668), Epistle to the Reader. The reference is to Jan Mabuse, an early-sixteenth-century Flemish painter, who introduced the Italian Renaissance style to the Low Countries.

[63] Charles Webster, *The Great Instauration: Science, Medicine and Reform 1626–1660* (London, 1975), p. 326.

[64] Francis Bacon, *Novum Organum*, bk II, aphorism 52. Quoted *ibid.*, p. 324.

knowledge which he hath by his industrie achieued . . . And seeing there is nothing giuen vnto vs of God, more acceptable then the health of the bodie, howe honorable must we thinke of the meanes, by which it is continued and restored if it be lost.[65]

There is no suggestion in the Genesis text of Adam's encyclopedic knowledge. It is an imaginative construction based solely on the parading of the animals before Adam to be named and to help him find a mate. It is in effect an elaboration of the belief that his naming of them was no mere arbitrary act, but an expression of his innate knowledge of their essential natures. To that 'angel in the pulpit' Lancelot Andrewes, because Adam was *pater viventum*, he was implicitly *pater scientum*. In the first speech act of man, perfect knowledge was revealed. Adam was, he exclaimed,

the first that practised Contemplation, and the first that practised Eloqution . . . and the first . . . that gave proper, fit and significant names and words to express the natures of things, and hee was not only the father of all the liberal Sciences, but also of all mechanical Arts . . . by all which wee briefly see the perfection of his minde, and the excellency of his gifts with which he was endowed: So that *Adam* then must needes be granted to bee the first and chiefest Author of all Knowledge and Learning that ever since, in all ages of the world hath beene among men, for from him it was derived and spread abroad among his posterity, into all parts of the world.[66]

For some, Adam's knowledge was attributed to superior sensory powers. Joseph Glanvill, for example, believed that in Paradise our sensory powers were without blemish and infinitely more powerful than ours now. Adam had both telescopic and X-ray vision. '*Adam* needed no Spectacles. The acuteness of his natural Opticks . . . shewed him much of the Coelestial magnificence and bravery without a *Galileo's* tube . . . It may be he saw the motion of the bloud and spirits through the transparent skin, as we do the workings of those little industrious *Animals* through a hive of glasse.' [67]

But for most, unlike the new experimental philosophers, Adam's was not a knowledge gained by experiment. It was immediate and innate. Adam's knowledge was inbred by God, declared John Weemse in 1627.[68] To Henry Vane in 1655, he had an 'intuitive prospect into the nature of all visible and bodily things in their causes without being

[65] Philip Barrough, *The Method of Phisicke* (London, 1583), Preface.
[66] Lancelot Andrewes, *Apospasmatia Sacra*, p. 208.
[67] Joseph Glanvill, *The Vanity of Dogmatising* (London, 1661), pp. 5–6.
[68] John Weemse, *The Portraiture of the Image of God in Man*, p. 82.

beholding to the report given by his senses . . .'[69] John Parkinson in his gardening 'encyclopaedia' in 1629, put Adam's knowledge of the vegetable world down to God's having 'inspired him with the knowledge of all natural things', a knowledge he retained after the Fall.[70] To Giovanno Loredano, his knowledge was encyclopedic, 'perceiving himselfe to excell in beautie above all things created, with an infused knowledge that inabled him to understand all sciences; knowing perfectly the nature of all Plants, Stones, Herbs, and animalls; and understanding the vertue, and properties of the heavens, elements, and stars; perceiving himself, finally to have the scepter of dominion over all creatures . . .'[71]

Astronomy, natural history, medicine: these headed the lists of Adam's attainments. Christopher Heydon in 1603, for example, saw Adam and his posterity as addicted to astrology, enabling them to foresee the world's destruction.[72] In 1585, the Paracelsian Robert Bostocke saw Adam as the original chemical physician. To him, Copernicus and Paracelsus were the Luther and Calvin of natural philosophy, charged with the task of restoring the ancient medicine which had steadily deteriorated after the Fall until it reached the degradations of Galen.[73] The mere mention of gold, bdellium, and onyx in Genesis 2.11–12 was sufficient to provoke John Pettus into casting Adam as a miner and metallurgist; 'otherwise, why should it be made known to him, that the River Pison did encompass the Land of Havilah where Gold was, if Adam were not to wash and refine it from the less valuable Earth?'[74] John Parkinson saw Adam's knowledge as extending to which fruits and herbs were fit for food or medicine, use and pleasure.[75] Similarly, Thomas Milles believed he knew the virtues 'in all Hearbes, Plants, and Stones'.[76]

In *Adam in Eden* in 1657, William Coles produced a table of the appropriations which showed for which part of the body every plant was

[69] Henry Vane, *The Retired Mans Meditations* (London, 1655), p. 53.
[70] John Parkinson, *Paradisi in sole* (London, 1629), Epistle to the Reader. See also J.-B. van Helmont, *Oriatrike* (London, 1662), p. 711. This was a translation by J. Chandler of Helmont's *Ortus Medicinus* (Amsterdam, 1648).
[71] Giovanno Loredano, *The Life of Adam*, p. 10.
[72] Christopher Heydon, *A Defence of Judiciall Astrologie*, p. 305.
[73] See Robert Bostocke, *Auncient Phisicke* (London, 1585), sigs. c.8.v., h.7.v.; and Allen G. Debus, *The English Paracelsians* (London, 1965), p. 58.
[74] John Pettus, *Volatiles from the History of Adam and Eve*, sig. b.2.r. Quoted by Charles Webster, *The Great Instauration*, p. 326.
[75] John Parkinson, *Paradisi in sole*, Epistle to the Reader.
[76] Thomas Milles, *The treasurie of auncient and moderne times*, i.22.

medically useful, an exercise which led G. Wharton in his prefatory poem to hope for a restoration in part of 'what *Adam* knew before'.[77]

It was especially in the naming of the animals that not only was Adam's dominion over them demonstrated but his knowledge of their essential natures was shown. According to Robert Bostocke, Adam

> was indowed with singular knowledge, wisdom and light of nature, that as soone as he did behold any beast, he by & by did so exactly know all their natures, powers, properties and vertues that he gaue them names, apt, meete and agreeable to their natures and properties.[78]

'And thou their Natures know'st, and gav'st them Names', says Milton's Raphael to Adam.[79] Robert South was unimpressed with Aristotle. He was but the rubbish of an Adam, and Athens but the rudiments of Paradise. Adam was the philosopher par excellence for he knew innately the essences of things. 'He came into the world a Philosopher', he declared, 'which sufficiently appeared by his writing the Nature of things upon their Names. Study was not then a Duty, night watchings were needless; the light of Reason wanted not the assistance of a Candle . . . There was then no poring, no strugling with memory, no straining for invention . . .'[80]

To Alexander Ross, Adam's knowledge extended not only to things natural but also to matters supernatural.[81] Andrew Willet believed that, along with natural things, Adam knew of the Trinity and of Christ's future incarnation, though not of the fall of the angels.[82] Others were less sanguine. Benjamin Needler, for example, excluded Adam's knowing the decrees of God, the secret thoughts of men, the number of all individuals, the future, and the Fall.[83] Edward Reynolds accepted that Adam had a knowledge of God sufficient for communion with him, a moral knowledge to enable relationships with other men, and a natural knowledge, but denied to Adam any knowledge of the future and any insight into the thoughts of God and men.[84]

To some, it was important that Adam knew the means of salvation and was saved. Thus Adam was the first Christian. According to John Durye, in a sermon preached before the House of Commons in Novem-

[handwritten margin note: But that means he understood death]

---

[77] William Coles, *Adam in Eden*, prefatory poem.
[78] Robert Bostocke, *Auncient Phisicke*, sig. F.4.r–v.   [79] *Paradise Lost*, 7.494.
[80] Robert South, *Sermons Preached Upon Several Occasions*, pp. 127–9.
[81] See Alexander Ross, *An Exposition on the Fovrteene first Chapters of Genesis*, pp. 50–1.
[82] Andrew Willet, *Hexapla in Genesin*, p. 37.
[83] See Benjamin Needler, *Expository Notes* (London, 1655), p. 53.
[84] See Edward Reynolds, *A Treatise of the Passions* (London, 1640), p. 458.

ber 1645, God 'told *Adam* in plain tearms from the beginning, the end of
the whole work of our salvation, which is, that the *seed of the woman should
tread down the head of the Serpent*.[85] The prophecy in Genesis 3.15 that the
serpent (Satan) would be crushed by the seed of the woman was
generally interpreted within Protestantism as a reference to the incarnation of Christ yet to come.[86] And Adam's acceptance of this was
interpreted to mean not only that he was the first Christian but also the
first Protestant, for he was justified by faith alone. In the words of John
Lightfoot, '*Adam* apprehendeth and layeth hold upon the promise by
Faith, and in evidence of this his faith he called his wives name *Eve* or
Life, because shee was to be the mother of Christ according to the flesh,
by whom life should come; and of all beleevers that by faith should live
in him, for an outward syne and seale of this his faith.'[87]

This was an interpretation which had been supported by the re-
formers Henry Bullinger and Philipp Melancthon.[88] It went back to
Eusebius and the early Christian apologists.[89] To any Catholic accusations that Protestantism was a new religion, Protestants pointed to
Adam and the patriarchs as their founding fathers; and hence the title of
the 1624 edition of Bullinger's treatise, which had been first translated by
Miles Coverdale in 1541: 'Looke from Adam, and behold the Protestants
Faith and Religion, evidently proved out of the holy Scriptures against
all Atheists, Papists, loose Libertines, and Carnall Gospellers: and that
the Faith which they professe, hath continued from the beginning of the
world.'[90] Milton also accepted the Protestant interpretation of the seed
as Christ. The last two books of *Paradise Lost* culminate in Adam's
acknowledgement of the seed as 'his Redeemer ever blest'.[91]

On the issue of Adam's knowledge, the Genesis text itself gave little
information one way or another. Even seventeenth-century ingenuity
was often stretched in filling in the gaps in the story. But that we had lost
the perfect knowledge which was once naturally ours, all were agreed.
To Joseph Glanvill, our former understanding 'now lies groveling in this
lower region, muffled up in mists, and darkness'; ignorance was to be
recognised, uncertainty ought to rule, and to dogmatise was vain.[92]

---

[85] John Durye, *Israels Call to March Out of Babylon* (London, 1646), p. 4.
[86] Calvin however interpreted it of humanity in general. See John King (trans.), *Commentaries on the
First Book of Moses*, p. 167.
[87] John Lightfoot, *A few, and new observations upon the Booke of Genesis* (London, 1642), pp. 5–6.
[88] See for example Heinrich Bullinger, *The olde fayth* (London, 1641); and Philipp Melancthon, *The
iustification of man by faith only* (London, 1548).   [89] See Eusebius, *Ecclesiastical History*, 1.4.6.
[90] Heinrich Bullinger, *Looke from Adam* (London, 1624).   [91] *Paradise Lost*, 12.573.
[92] Joseph Glanvill, *The Vanity of Dogmatising*, p. 12.

OTHER MEN, OTHER ADAMS?

Gabriel de Foigny's antipodean Australians were not the descendants of Adam. According to him, they were created three thousand years before their European counterparts.[93] Foigny's pre-Adamic and non-Christian natural society was intended to provide a fictional yet forcible contrast between it and European Christian communities. His was the first intricate fictional account of a pre-Adamic race. But there were a number of speculations prior to his which were motivated by other reasons. Towards the end of the sixteenth century, Thomas Nashe wrote of those 'mathematitions abroad that will proove men before *Adam*; and they are harboured in high places, who will maintain it to the death, that there are no divels.'[94]

One such was the orientalist Jacob Palaeologus, a Greek resident in Prague. He had argued, around 1570, in a tract entitled *An omnes ab uno Adamo descenderit*, that Adam and Eve were not the ancestors of all people. The implication of this was that not all of mankind could therefore have inherited original sin, and that consequently the redemption of Christ was not universal. He drew this implication. The church drew another, namely that he was a heretic. He was arrested in 1581, tried, and executed in Rome four years later.[95]

From the time of the voyages of Columbus and Vespucci, there arose the question of the origin of the inhabitants of the New World and of how they fitted into the scheme of the Old. From early in the sixteenth century, there was a general agreement that the Indians were truly men (and women), but what kind of men was less than clear. Matthew Hale put the problem precisely in 1642:

the late Discovery of the vast Continent of *America* and Islands adjacent, which appears to be as populous with Men, and as well stored with Cattel almost as any part of *Europe*, *Asia*, or *Africa*, hath occasioned some difficulty and dispute touching the Traduction of all Mankind from the two common Parents supposed of all Mankind, namely *Adam* and *Eve*.[96]

One alternative was to endorse their separate origin. This solution was embraced by Paracelsus. The children of Adam, he surmised, did

---

[93] See Gabriel de Foigny, *A New Discovery of Terra Incognita Australis*, p. 119.

[94] Ronald B. McKerrow (ed.), 'Pierce Penilesse his supplication to the divell', *The Works of Thomas Nashe*, i.172.

[95] See George Hunston Williams, *The Radical Reformation* (London, 1962).

[96] Matthew Hale, *De origine gentium Americanarum* (Paris [?], 1642), p. 189. Translation by E. Goldsmid (Edinburgh, 1884). Quoted by James S. Slotkin, *Readings in Early Anthropology* (London, 1965), p. 182.

not inhabit the whole world. It was difficult for him to conceive that Adam's children had gone to the 'hidden islands'. One should consider, he wrote, 'that these people are from a different Adam'.[97] And he suggests too that the pygmies are not of Adamic descent. Having said all of which, Paracelsus went on to fudge the issue by suggesting that perhaps they were post-diluvians, in which case they would have fitted into the history of Genesis; or perhaps they lacked language and souls, and therefore, not being strictly human, the problem of their relation to the redemption effected by Jesus Christ would not arise.[98]

Giordano Bruno was moved to speculate on the possibly diverse origins not only of the Indians but of Africans, those which lie hidden in the caves of Neptune, pygmies, giants, and so on. He believed all of these could not be traced to the same descent, nor could they have sprung from the same progenitor. Following Jewish sources, he suggested that there may have been three original protoplasts, the father of the Jews and the two fathers of all other races. And he referred to the Chinese notion of three separate protoplasts some twenty thousand years before.[99] This raised too for him the question of the relationship of the biblical and other chronologies. In *The Expulsion of the Triumphant Beast*, he spoke of the tablets of Mercury, 'which reckon more than twenty thousand years', and of the New World, where 'they have memorials of ten thousand years and more'.[100] But he, like Paracelsus, did suggest that this evidence might be best dealt with by assuming that 'those of the new land are not of the human generation', though they resemble us in bodily shape and intelligence, or by making their years shorter.[101]

Giordano Bruno was in England from 1583 to 1585, and it was there that he wrote *The Expulsion of the Triumphant Beast*. Pre-Adamitism was in the air. Thomas Nashe thought unbelief was the largest religion in England, and that doubt about biblical chronology was a major facet of it. 'Impudently they persist in it', he lamented, 'that the late discouered

---

[97] Paracelsus, *Astronomia Magna* (1537–8), p. 35, in K. Sudhoff and W. Matteissen (eds.), *Werke* (Munich, 1992–3) (Abt. I), xii.1–144. Quoted by James S. Slotkin, *Readings in Early Anthropology*, p. 42.

[98] See Thomas Bendysche,'The History of Anthropology', *Memoirs Read before the Anthropological Society of London* 1 (1863–4), p. 354.

[99] See James Slotkin, *Readings in Early Anthropology*, p. 43.

[100] Arthur D. Imerti (ed. and trans.), Giordano Bruno, *The Expulsion of the Triumphant Beast* (New Brunswick, New Jersey, 1964), pp. 249–50. Imerti points out that this reference to the New World was inspired by accounts of the circular Aztec Calendar Stone after the conquest of what is now Mexico City in 1521. See p. 307 n. 52.

[101] *Ibid.*, p. 250.

Indians are able to shew antiquities thousands before *Adam*.'[102] When he spoke of pre-Adamite mathematicians, it was probably the mathematician Thomas Harriot to whom he was alluding. And part of the atheism of which the playwright Christopher Marlowe was accused was to have questioned biblical chronology, namely 'That the Indians and many Authors of antiquity haue assuredly writen of aboue 16 thousand yeares agone wheras Adam is proued to haue lived within 6 thousand yeares.'[103]

Belief in men before Adam was also to be found among the sectarians. As early as 1578, John Rogers in *The displaying of an horrible secte . . . naming themselves the Familie of Love* listed the belief that 'there was a worlde before Adams time, as there is now' among the fifty-three doctrines of Elizabethan Familists.[104] Over sixty years later, probably following Rogers, Ephraim Pagitt in *Heresiography* noted the existence of pre-Adamite beliefs among the Familists, and went on to specify a group in Amsterdam founded by Theodoret, a tailor.[105]

Pre-Adamitism was probably a not uncommon belief during the revolutionary period. It was motivated not so much by tales of the Indians or the Ethiopians, or by knowledge of other chronologies, but by a desire to replace the dominant readings of the Bible with more personal and individual ones. It was held, for example, by the Ranters. In 1651, John Holland in *The Smoke of the Bottomlesse Pit* spoke, probably correctly, of those Ranters who 'say the world was created long before the time the Scripture speaks of . . . they argue that there were at that time more people in the world then *Adam* and *Cain*, though we read of no more'.[106] And in 1660, Laurence Clarkson admitted that while he was a Ranter, he had lost his belief in the devil and his faith in God and the historicity of the Bible: 'I neither believed that *Adam* was the first Creature, but that there was a Creation before him, which world I thought was eternal.'[107] The Digger Gerrard Winstanley thought that the scriptures declared that there were men in the world before the time of Adam. This gave the key to interpreting the narrative metaphorically rather than literally. For him, the story of Adam was the story of all men: 'looke upon every man and woman in the world', he cried, 'that lives upon the objects of the creation, and not upon the spirit in the creation,

[102] Ronald B. McKerrow (ed.),'Christs Teares Over Iervsalem', *The Works of Thomas Nashe*, ii.116.
[103] Paul H. Kocher, *Christopher Marlowe* (New York, 1962), p. 34.
[104] John Rogers, *The displaying of an horrible secte* (London, 1578), n.p.
[105] Ephraim Pagitt, *Heresiography* (London, 1645), p. 86.
[106] John Holland, *The Smoke of the Bottomlesse Pit* (London, 1651), p. 4.
[107] Laurence Clarkson, *The Lost Sheep found* (London, 1660), pp. 32–3.

and they are but branches of the first man; and then put them all together into one lumpe, and they make up still but the first man perfect . . .'[108]

All these motivations for the belief in the existence of men before Adam, and consequently for a polygenetic account of the origins of the human race, were to come together in the work of Isaac La Peyrère.[109] In 1655, there appeared in Amsterdam a work entitled *Prae-Adamitae*, which was translated into English in the same year in the middle of the English Revolution. Taking into account internal evidence from the Bible, the chronological evidence from antiquity, and the data gathered from the voyages of discovery, La Peyrère was led inexorably to his conviction that there were men and women before Adam. Thus, as he wrote in the 'proeme' to *Theological Systeme upon that Presupposition that Men were before Adam*,

It is a natural suspition that the beginning of the world is not to be receiv'd according to that common beginning which is pitched in *Adam*, inherent in all men, who have but an ordinary knowledge in things: For that beginning seems enquirable, at a far greater distance, and from ages past very long before; both by the most ancient accounts of the *Chaldeans*, as also by the most ancient Records of the *Aegyptians*, *Aethiopians*, and *Scythians*, and by parts of the frame of the world newly discovered, as also from those unknown Countries, to which the *Hollanders* have sayled of late, the men of which, as is probable, did not descend from *Adam*.

I had this suspition also being a Child, when I heard or read the History of *Genesis*: Where Cain goes forth; where he kills his brother when they were in the field; doing it warily, like a thief least it should be discovered by any: Where he flies, where he fears punishment for the death of his Brother: Lastly, where he married a wife far from his Ancestors, and builds a City.[110]

It was however, according to him, his reading of verses 12–14 of the fifth chapter of Paul's Epistle to the Romans that convinced him of the truth of pre-Adamitism. The relevant verses read: 'As by one man sin entered into the world, and by sin, death: so likewise death had power over all men, because in him all men sinned. For till the time of the Law sin was in the world, but sin was not imputed, when the Law was not. But death reigned from Adam into Moses, even upon those who had not sinned according to the similitude of the transgression of Adam, who is the Type of the future.'[111] Richard Popkin usefully summarises La

[108] George H. Sabine (ed.), *The Works of Gerrard Winstanley* (Ithaca, New York), p. 118.
[109] I am particularly indebted in the following discussion to Richard Popkin's excellent history of the pre-Adamitic idea, *Isaac La Peyrère (1596–1676)* (Leiden, 1987).
[110] Isaac La Peyrère, *A Theological Systeme* (London, 1655), Proeme.
[111] Isaac La Peyrère, *Men before Adam* (London, 1656), pp. 1–2.

Peyrère's reading of this text: 'the crucial connection between Romans 5 and the pre-Adamite theory is that if Adam sinned in a morally meaningful sense, then there must have been an Adamic law according to which he sinned. If law began with Adam, then there must have been a lawless world before Adam, containing people.'[112]

Thus, unlike Foigny's antipodean Paradise, La Peyrère's original state of nature, like that of Hobbes, who may have influenced him, was nasty and brutish: 'they became evil, wicked, fornicators, avaricious, given to lewdness, full of envy and blood, brawlers, deceitfull, despightful, whisperers, back-biters, hatefull to God, contumelious, proud, arrogant, inventers of wickedness, disobedient to Parents, foolish, madd, without affection, truth, or compassion.'[113]

For La Peyrère, there were two creations, the creation of the Gentiles outlined in Genesis 1, and the creation of Adam the first Jew and his posterity in the subsequent several chapters. The Jews were elected by God and given an elected land, the extent of which, as Popkin points out, 'would please the most expansionist Israelis, and would horrify even the most pacific Arabs', running as it did from the Nile to the Euphrates and from the Mediterranean to the lower end of the Arabian Peninsula.[114] The Gentiles were later to be adopted into the family of the Jews through a mystical election.[115]

The men of the first creation, as detailed in Genesis 1, were created by the word of God. But Adam was created from the earth.[116] Thus, the Jews are a separate species of mankind: 'you shall finde', writes La Peyrère, 'the species of the Iews peculiarly made and formed by God in *Adam*; you shall finde the species of the Gentiles promiscuously created with the rest of the creatures in the same day of Creation . . .'[117] There were many species of Gentiles, often unknown to the Jews notably, 'those of *America*, the Southern, and the *Greenlanders*, and the rest, to which neither the Jew, nor the rest of the Gentiles as yet had accesse'.[118]

In Book 3, chapter 5, of *A Theological Systeme*, having shown to his satisfaction the biblical proof of men before Adam, La Peyrère turned to the pagan histories. Thus he pointed to the chronologies of the Chaldeans, the Egyptians, and the Greeks, and marshalled the evidence from the Mexican, Peruvian, and Chinese data. The length of the history of

[112] Richard H. Popkin, *Isaac La Peyrère*, p. 44.
[113] Isaac La Peyrère, *A Theological Systeme*, p. 38.
[114] Richard H. Popkin, *Isaac La Peyrère*, p. 46. *A Theological Systeme* contains a map of 'Terra Sancta' between pp. 78 and 79.
[115] See Isaac La Peyrère, *A Theological Systeme*, pp. 83–8.   [116] See *ibid.*, p. 112.
[117] *Ibid.*, p. 122.   [118] *Ibid.*, p. 124.

the Gentiles was also suggested to him by their wisdom, especially their knowledge of astronomy, astrology, theology, and magic, all of which must have been acquired over many ages before Adam. And there was no shortage of time in which such knowledge could have been gained, for, according to La Peyrère, to all intents and purposes the world had been in existence for an eternity before Adam.[119]

The standard answer to the last statement was that Adam knew everything and that he was therefore the source of the knowledge of the Gentiles. But for La Peyrère, while Adam had the potential to know all things, he had little chance of acquiring knowledge in the short time before the Fall.

All of this was to lead La Peyrère to his most contentious conclusion. For after an account of various discrepancies and inconsistencies in the biblical text, he declared that Moses was not the author of the first five books of the Old Testament. Moses, he suggested, copied from others, and his account was copied by his successors. Thus, 'I need not trouble the Reader much further, to prove a thing in it self sufficiently evident, that the first five books of the Bible were not written by *Moses*, as is thought. Nor need any one wonder after this, when he reads many things confus'd and out of order, obscure, deficient, many things omitted and misplaced, when they shall consider with themselves that they are a heap of Copie confusedly taken.'[120]

With his belief that the biblical story was the history of the Jews and not of all humankind, La Peyrère was obliged to reread the Bible as suggesting local rather than universal events. Thus, the darkness at the death of Christ was over Palestine only and not over the whole world; the star of Bethlehem was not a celestial star, but a localised burning flame visible only to the Magi; Isaiah turned back the shadow on the sundial of Ahaz, rather than the sun itself having been turned back (Isaiah 38.8), and so on. Most important, had the Noachide Flood been a universal event, pre-Adamites would all have been destroyed. Consequently, for La Peyrère, it can only have been a local flood, the Jews being destroyed and the men before Adam surviving it.

Much ingenuity had been utilised, and was yet to be, in demonstrating the origins of the American natives. Hugo Grotius, for example, had read an earlier version of La Peyrère's work, and attacked it. At the time of the publication of La Peyrère's work Grotius had recently died. Though unwilling to speak ill of the dead, La Peyrère set about nonetheless to refute Grotius' argument.

---

[119] See *ibid.*, pp. 260–1.   [120] *Ibid.*, p. 208.

According to Grotius, the American Indians were the remnants of Vikings who had settled in Greenland and thence went to America.[121] To La Peyrère, this was just fanciful speculation. He accepted that the Norwegians settled in Greenland and thence may have travelled to America, but in neither case, he argued, were they the first people in those lands. He cited the Greenland Chronicle to demonstrate that the Norwegians had fought the shepherd race, the Schlegringians, before colonising Greenland. Moreover, he wrote, when several Greenlanders were brought to Copenhagen, it was clear to all that in appearance, speech, and behaviour they were far removed from Scandinavians.[122]

All of La Peyrère's radical theories – his pre-Adamitism, his critique of the Bible, and his notion of the world's eternity – were located in the context of his philosemitic and Judeocentric vision of history. Richard Popkin sums up:

> those aspects of La Peyrère's theory that created the greatest impact in generating biblical criticism and the secular study of history, resulted from his attempt to buttress his visionary picture of what he thought was about to happen – the Recall of the Jews and the Coming of that Jewish Messiah. From this vision the rest followed. There were men before Adam, namely the Gentiles. The Bible was the accurate account of human history. However our copies were defective. And the Bible had to be interpreted in a localized Jewish way. And, finally, the world was eternal, and the Jewish part of it just a small finite portion. However through what is about to happen as the conclusion of Jewish history, everybody, pre-Adamite, Adamite and post-Adamite, will be saved.[123]

There was some support for La Peyrère's theory during the remainder of the seventeenth century. Charles Blount, for example, in a letter vindicating Thomas Burnet, is clearly relying upon La Peyrère in his discussion of the darkness at the Crucifixion, the Star of Bethlehem, the sundial of Ahaz, and pre-Adamitism. With reference to divine miracles, he wrote, 'there is often times great Errors committed in the manner of reading Scripture; as when that is taken in a general Sense, which ought to be particularly understood: As that of *Adam*, whom *Moses* made only to be the first Father of the *Jew*, whilst others Hyperbolically make him to be the first Father of all Men'.[124] Blount's use of La Peyrère was recognised by William Nicholls in 1696 in his dialogue between a philosopher and a believer. He himself was not averse to

---

[121] See J. S. Slotkin, *Readings in Early Anthropology*, pp. 97–8.
[122] See Isaac La Peyrère, *A Theological Systeme*, p. 280.
[123] Richard H. Popkin, *Isaac La Peyrère*, p. 53.
[124] Charles Blount, *The Miscellaneous Works of Charles Blount, Esq.* (London, 1695), p. 8. It is ironic, at least in part, that La Peyrère should be invoked in defence of Burnet, for central to Burnet's account of the origins of the earth is his conviction of the universality of the Flood.

placing La Peyrère's arguments in the mouth of his philosopher, if only to allow his believer to discredit them.[125]

Richard Popkin also gives us a detailed account of an eight-volume work which appeared in English in 1692 and was reissued at least thirty times in English up to 1801, namely *Letters Writ by a Turkish Spy, who lived five and forty years undiscover'd at Paris*. Although there is no evidence that its author (or authors) knew the work of La Peyrère, many of his themes are in evidence – pre-Adamitism, the eternity of the world, the appeal to alternative chronologies (interestingly, that of the Brahmans),[126] the inconsistencies in the biblical text, and the limited extent of the Flood, guaranteeing the survival of the alternative chronologies. Once all this was accepted, he claimed, we would see

> the Splendour of Historical Truth rising from the Orient, and gilding the Tops of those Mountains, which the Ignorance and Superstition of some, the Pride and Ambition of others, have raised to hinder our Prospect of the far-extended Ages of the primitive World. And without Rapture, or Hyperbole, I dare be bold to presage, That a little more knowledge in the Indian Language and Histories, will bring those Things to Light, which have been hid for many thousands of Years, from the greatest Part of Mankind.[127]

In 1695, an anonymous author penned his version of the polygenetic theory in *Two Essays sent in a Letter from Oxford to a Nobleman in London*. He argued that the cultural differences between the Old and New worlds were such as counted against the latter's having derived from the former. And the fauna of the New World, he maintained, was sufficiently dissimilar to that of the Old to suggest independent and autonomous beginnings. Thus, he wrote,

> The *West-Indies*, and the vast *Regions*, lately discovered towards the *South*, abound with such variety of Inhabitants, and New Animals, not known or ever seen in *Asia*, *Africa*, or *Europe*, that the *Origine* of them doth not appear so clear as some late *Writers* pretend . . . and their differences from all the rest of the *Globe*, in Manners, Languages, Habits, Religions, Diet, Arts, and Customs, as well as in their Quadrupeds, Birds, Serpents and Insects, render their Derivation very obscure, and their Origine uncertain, especially in the common way, and according to the vulgar Opinions of Planting all the Earth from one little Spot.[128]

As in La Peyrère, the difficulties in believing that all migration had occurred from one place were highlighted. Moreover, it was suggested,

---

[125] See William Nicholls, *A Conference with a Theist* (London, 1696).
[126] Interestingly, because this was a century prior to the Western decipherment of Sanskrit.
[127] Giovanni P. Marano, *Letters Writ by a Turkish Spy*, 13th edn (London 1973), viii.257–8. Quoted by Richard H. Popkin, *Isaac La Peyrère*, p. 120.
[128] L.P., *Two Essays sent in a Letter from Oxford to a Nobleman in London* (London, 1695), p. 16.

even if it could be shown that the Americas were at some time or other stocked from Norway, Tartary, China, the land of Jesse, or Africa, the existence of antipodeans cried out for explanation. 'I see no way at present', he concluded, 'to solve this new face of *Nature* by old Arguments fetch'd from *Eastern* rubbish, or Rabinical Weeds, unless some *New Philosopher* starts up with a fresh System; in the mean time let them all be *Aborigines*.'[129]

The cause of racial differences also created problems for the author of *Two Essays*. Unless all blacks and whites were contained within Adam and Eve like homunculi, he believed it impossible for all to be derived from one single male and female. Neither the sun nor the curse upon Ham could explain the 'Negroes':

> Not the First, because many other *Nations*, living under the same *Climates* and Heats, are never *Black*; as the *Abyssynes*, the *Siamites*, the *Brasilians*, *Peruvians*, &c. neither will any White ever become a *Black*, in *Guinea*, *Congo*, or *Angola*, though born there . . . Not the latter: for what Curse is change of Colour, that being only accidental to Beauty, which consists wholly in Proportion and Symmetry? The old *Statues* in black Marble, are as much, if not more, valued than those in *White*. Besides, the Curse upon *Cham*'s account must have turn'd many of the *Asiaticks*, and all the *Egyptians* into *Negroes*; for they were Curs'd more peculiarly than the *Western* remote Coasts of *Africa*.[130]

IN DEFENCE OF ADAM

Overall, the reaction to La Peyrère's work was negative, indeed hostile. A large number of books and pamphlets were printed to rebut his arguments. Richard Popkin lists around forty or so works in the eighty years following the publication of La Peyrère's views which were, in part or in whole, devoted to refuting his work.[131] Throughout the remainder of the seventeenth century, Don Cameron Allen informs us, 'his name is usually joined with those of Spinoza and Hobbes to make a triumvirate of devils incarnate in an age that knew Satans when it saw them'.[132] As for La Peyrère, in February 1656 he was carried off to gaol, whence he eventually abjured his Calvinism and his pre-Adamitism, returned to the Catholic fold, and spent the remaining years of his life in a monastery.

La Peyrère was a universalist who believed that ultimately all would be saved. In spite of later adaptations of pre-Adamitism which would

---

[129] *Ibid.*, p. 23. [130] *Ibid.*, pp. 27–8. [131] See Richard Popkin, *Isaac La Peyrère*, pp. 80–1.
[132] Don Cameron Allen, *The Legend of Noah* (Urbana, Illinois, 1949), p. 137. See p. 136 for a list of some seventeenth-century responses to La Peyrère.

equate men before Adam with non-Caucasians and Adamites with Caucasians, La Peyrère himself saw all people as biologically identical. But for a number of his contemporaries, views of his sort were seen as at least socially divisive in denying, as we might perhaps put it, our common humanity. Thus, for example, in 1625, the philosopher Nathanael Carpenter in his *Geography* mantained that Moses' motivation in writing his genealogical lists was so that all people would understand themselves to be descended from the same original, 'then which there is no greater meanes to conciliate and ioyne mens affections for mutuall amitie and conversation'.[133] Similarly, in 1656, the year of La Peyrère's *Men before Adam*, John White remarked in his commentary on Genesis that the reason for God's having created only one couple was to unite all men in love to one another so that 'we cannot shut up our bowels of compassion from any man, of what Nation or Kindred soever he be'.[134] Some forty years later, Richard Kidder, Bishop of Bath and Wells, suggested that the origin of all people was from one man to ensure that claims of racial superiority could not arise, that 'men might not boast and vaunt of their extraction and original . . . and that they might think themselves under an obligation to love and assist each other as proceeding from the same original and common parent'.[135]

A key response to the thesis of pre-Adamitism was offered by Matthew Hale in *The Primitive Origination of Mankind* in 1677. Don Cameron Allen suggests that La Peyrère's work was one of the reasons for Hale's book, since Hale was determined to show that the world is not very old, that the Flood was universal, and that America was settled by the descendants of Noah, all of which issues La Peyrère had resolved differently.[136]

To Matthew Hale, as to many others, the key issue in the debate between monogenesis and polygenesis was the American Indian. To repeat his words, 'The late Discovery of the vast Continent of *America* and Islands adjacent, which appears to be as populous with Men, and as well stored with Cattel almost as any part of *Europe*, *Asia*, or *Africa*, hath occasioned some difficulty and dispute touching the Traduction of all Mankind from the two common Parents supposed of all Mankind, namely *Adam* and *Eve*.'[137] And like others who were committed to the

---

[133] Nathanael Carpenter, *Geography Delineated Forth in Two Books* (Oxford, 1625), ii.207.
[134] John White, *A Commentary Upon the Three First Chapters of Genesis*, i.111.
[135] Richard Kidder, *A Commentary on the Five Books of Moses* (London, 1694), i.6.
[136] See Don Cameron Allen, *The Legend of Noah*, p. 137, n. 103.
[137] Matthew Hale, *De origine gentium Americanarum* (Paris [?], 1642), p. 189. Translation by E. Goldsmid (Edinburgh, 1884). Quoted by James S. Slotkin, *Readings in Early Anthropology* (London, 1965), p. 182.

biblical account, Hale could only argue that those of the New World had migrated from the Old World either by land or by sea (or both).[138] This left plenty of room for conjecture about their ultimate origins, whether from the Tartars, as Edward Brerewood, Johannes Laetius, and Paul Rycaut would have had it, from the Scandinavians of Grotius, the Phoenicians of Robertus Nortmannus, the Greeks of Hobbes, or the Jews of Manasseh ben Israel and Thomas Thorowgood.[139]

Those who were concerned to defend the biblical account needed also to explain the differences in colour among the descendants of Adam. In this case too, the consequences of the Genesis account argued against the ascribing to those of different skin colours any essential differences. Rather, all of us were originally white, and the variations in colour were ascribed to environmental factors. As Margaret Hodgen writes, 'The popularity of this theory helped to keep the Negro and other darker-skinned peoples theoretically in the family of Adam, thus upholding their dignity as human beings.'[140] Thus, for example, Thomas Robinson in *The Anatomy of the Earth* recognised that if blackness or whiteness were a matter of nature, this would call into question the Adamic origin of all. He thought it more probable that 'the different Soyls, or various Modifications of Matter in several parts of the World, produced Men of different Colours and Complexions'.[141] William Nicholls put the colour of the Ethiopian down in part to the intensity of the sun. But, following the ancient belief that the imagination of the mother could mould the nature of the foetus, he attributed a progressive darkening of the Ethiopians' skins to its becoming aesthetically more and more desirable. Thus, he explained,

in a Generation or two, that high degree of Tawniness became the nature, and from thence the Pride of the Inhabitants; the men began to value themselves chiefly upon this complexion, and the Women to affect them the better for it; from thence by the love to the Male so complexioned, the daily conversation with him and the affectation of his hew, there was caused a considerable Influence upon the *Foetus's* which the Females were pregnant with; so that, upon this account, the Children in *Aethiopia* became more and more black, according to the fancy of the Mother.[142]

[138] See *ibid.*, pp. 189, 196–7, 203.　　[139] See Don Cameron Allen, *The Legend of Noah*, ch. 6.
[140] Margaret T. Hodgen, *Early Anthropology in the Sixteenth and Seventeenth Centuries*, p. 214.
[141] Thomas Robinson, *The Anatomy of the Earth* (London, 1694), p. 4.
[142] William Nicholls, *A Conference with a Theist*, pp. 146–7. Only during the nineteenth century did the theory of maternal impressions as a factor in foetal formation begin to lose influence in European thought. The biblical source of its influence was the story of Jacob multiplying the herd of Laban. On the history of this theory, see J. W. Ballantyne, *Teratogenesis: An Inquiry into the Causes of Monstrosities* (Edinburgh, 1897).

To La Peyrère, both Adamites and pre-Adamites were in need of redemption, the former by virtue of the sin of Adam, the latter by virtue of their state of nature being an evil one. But pre-Adamitism did imply that the redemption wrought through Jesus Christ was applicable only to those Adamites infected with original sin. Thus, for example, Edward Stillingfleet recognised that La Peyrère's pre-Adamitism cast doubt both upon the veracity of the scriptures and upon the universal effects of the Fall of man. 'For as it is hard to conceive', he wrote, 'how the effects of Man's fall should extend to all Mankind, unless all Mankind were propogated from *Adam*; so it is inconceivable how the account of things given in Scripture should be true, if there were persons existent in the world long before *Adam* was.'[143]

ALIENS AND ADAM

The possibility of life elsewhere in the universe, and thus of the existence of non-Adamites, if not pre-Adamites, also raised the question of the universal redemptive significance of the work of Christ. It was a debate which was set in the context of the larger issue of the plurality of worlds.

The possibility of the plurality of worlds could be seen as one consequence of the principles of the divine plenitude and the divine omnipotence. To the Platonist Henry More in 1646, by then a convinced Copernican, just as the sun is the centre of our universe, so

> The skirts of his large Kingdome surely lie
> Near to the confines of some other worlds
> Whose Centres are the fixed starres on high,
> Bout which as their own proper Suns are hurld
> Joves, Earths, and Saturns; round on their own axes twurld.[144]

And for Henry More, these other worlds also contained other forms of life.

But the Copernican view of a sun-centred cosmos no doubt gave an added fillip to speculation about life on other planets and moons close to us, for if we were now more like the other planets and revolved around the sun, then they were more like us, and therefore contained other inhabitants. Robert Burton's argument is a common one:

[143] Edward Stillingfleet, *Origines Sacrae: or, A Rational Account of the Grounds of Natural and Revealed Religion*, 7th edn (Cambridge, 1702), p. 367.
[144] Henry More, *Democritus Platonissans, or, an Essay upon the Infinity of Worlds out of Platonick Principles* (Cambridge, 1646), st. 21–2.

hoc posito, to grant this their tenent of the earths motion: if the Earth move, it is a Planet, and shines to them in the *Moone*, and to the other Planitary inhabitants, as the *Moone* and they doe to us upon the Earth: but shine she doth, as *Galilie*, *Kepler*, and others prove, and then *per consequens*, the rest of the Planets are inhabited, as well as the *Moone* . . . Then (I say) the Earth and they be Planets alike, inhabited alike, moved about the Sunne, the common center of the World alike . . . [145]

Christian Huygens was one who believed that life on other planets was a consequence of the sun-centred view of Copernicus. But his speculation on the nature of such life proceeded essentially on the basis of the divine plenitude. Thus all animals and rational creatures would have senses like us. There would be the need for one to be head and sovereign over the rest. Just as on this earth, the study of nature and the improvement of the sciences separates us from other creatures, so too on other planets. Like us, the highest inhabitants of other planets would have hands, feet, and an upright stance, though in keeping with the greater size of some of the planets relative to earth, and particularly Jupiter and Saturn, such planetary beings may be of a greater stature than us. Like us, they enjoy social lives, live in houses, make music, contemplate the works of God, and so on. Thus, he inquired,

Now can any one look upon, and compare these Systems together, without being amazed at the vast Magnitude and noble attendance of these two Planets, in respect of this pitiful little Earth of ours? Or can they force themselves to think, that the wise Creator has so disposed of all his Plants and Animals here, has furnish'd and adorn'd this Spot only, and has left all those Worlds bare and destitute of Inhabitants, who might adore and worship him; or that those prodigious Bodies were made only to twinkle to, and be studied by some few perhaps of us poor fellows?[146]

Huygens was unusual in speculating in such detail on the nature of aliens. Matthew Hale thought that little would come of expending reason on such a matter.[147] Joseph Glanvill argued that, even though the details of life on other planets were unknown, this did not prejudice 'the *Hypothesis* of the *Moon's* being *habitable*; or the supposal of its being *actually inhabited*'.[148] John Dunton was willing to confess his ignorance of the knowledge, customs, laws, and manners of the inhabitants of the moon,

[145] Nicolas Kiessling, Thomas C. Faulkner, and Rhonda L. Blair (eds.), Robert Burton, *The Anatomy of Melancholy* (Oxford, 1990), ii.51–2.
[146] Christian Huygens, *The Celestial Worlds Discover'd* (London, 1698), p. 117.
[147] Matthew Hale, *The Primitive Origination of Mankind* (London 1676), p. 7.
[148] Joseph Glanvill, 'The Usefulness of Real Philosophy to Religion', *Essays on Several Important Subjects in Philosophy and Religion* (London, 1676), p. 37.

but had no qualms about admitting their existence.[149] But Huygens was not alone, at the end of the seventeenth century, in supporting the reality of extraterrestrials.

That other worlds were inhabited seemed an appropriate conclusion to draw, not only as a consequence of Copernicanism and/or classical understandings of plenitude, but also as an implication of a Christian natural theology focused on God's works in nature and not on the Bible. In a universe with plural worlds, the biblical history appeared too historically and geographically particular. As Stephen Dick remarks, the notion of the plurality of worlds 'provided better arguments for God's glory than did Scripture, revealing at the very least the inadequacy of Scripture alone'.[150] Thus, in 1691, for example, John Ray wrote of the received hypothesis that every star is a sun with planets 'in all likelyhood furnished with as great a variety of corporal Creatures animate and inanimate as the Earth is'.[151]

This was a theme developed at length by the most influential work on the plurality of worlds in the latter part of the seventeenth century, the Copernican and Cartesian Bernard Fontenelle's *Entretiens sur la pluralité des mondes,* translated into English by both Joseph Glanvill and Aphra Behn two years after its first publication in 1686. To Fontenelle, there were an infinite number of planets and an infinite number of inhabited worlds. For him, this was a consequence of the analogy between the nature of our earth and that of other worlds as a consequence of Copernicanism. But it was also the result of the fecundity of the divine being from whom all things proceed. It is this idea 'of the infinite Diversity that Nature ought to use in her Works' which governs his book, he declared, an idea which 'cannot be confuted by any philosopher'.[152]

All this raised the crucial issue of the salvific status of extraterrestrial beings. Stephen Dick puts the problem succinctly:

If there were indeed intelligent beings on the moon or planets, would they be 'men' and would they be tainted with Adam's sin? If so, had they been redeemed by Jesus Christ, or were they still in need of Redemption? If not, might they not need to be redeemed in the future, and by whom? Was Jesus Christ to be seen as a planet-hopping Saviour in the new cosmology?[153]

---

[149] John Dunton (ed.), *The Athenian Gazette,* vol. 1, q.1, no.7.
[150] Steven J. Dick, *Plurality of Worlds: The Extraterrestrial Life Debate from Democritus to Kant* (Cambridge, 1982), p. 156.
[151] John Ray, *The Wisdom of God Manifested in the Works of Creation* (London, 1691), p. 2. Quoted by Peter Harrison, *The Bible, Protestantism, and the Rise of Natural Science* (Cambridge, 1998), p. 180. See p. 179 n. 102 for a good collection of seventeenth-century citations as to the plurality of worlds.
[152] Bernard Fontenelle, *A Discovery of New Worlds,* trans. A. Behn (London, 1688), Author's Preface.

The simplest solution was to deny the existence of other worlds and of other intelligent beings. This was the answer offered by Melancthon. Christological objections held sway over divine plenitude. Melancthon's remained a geocentric and anthropocentric universe:

we know God is a citizen of this world with us, custodian and server of this world, ruling the motion of the heavens, guiding the constellations, making this earth fruitful, and indeed watching over us; we do not contrive to have him in another world, and to watch over other men also . . . The Son of God is One; our master Jesus Christ was born, died, and resurrected in this world. Nor does He manifest Himself elsewhere, nor elsewhere has He died or resurrected. Therefore it must not be imagined that there are many worlds, because it must not be imagined that Christ died and was resurrected more often, nor must it be thought that in any other world without the knowledge of the Son of God, that men would be restored to eternal life.[154]

As early as 1638, John Wilkins was wrestling with the theological implications of an inhabited Copernican universe. He was convinced that the existence of a plurality of worlds was not in conflict with reason or scripture. And granting the similarities between the earth and the moon, he was convinced that the moon was inhabited, 'for why else did Providence furnish that place with all such conveniences of habitation as have beene above declared?'[155] But he was less certain of the nature of their inhabitants, and he was reluctant to speculate on whether 'they are the seed of *Adam*, whether they are there in a blessed estate, or else what meanes there may be for their salvation.'[156]

For those committed to the existence of extraterrestrials, the safe option was to dodge the theological problems by denying their human status. This was the option which Wilkins preferred. It may be more probable, he suggested, that the inhabitants of the moon, rather than being infected with Adam's sin, or with some of their own, 'are not men as wee are, but some other kinde of creatures which beare some proportion and likenesse to our natures . . .'[157]

It was a solution which appealed also to Fontenelle, for it enabled him to get on with what he saw as the serious issues of the plurality of worlds without being sidetracked by theological subtleties. He admitted that should the moon be inhabited by men who were not descended from Adam, this would be 'a great perplexing point in Theology'. He only

[153] Steven J. Dick, *Plurality of Worlds*, p. 89.
[154] Philipp Melancthon, *Initia doctrinae physicae* (Wittenberg, 1550), fol. 43. Quoted *ibid.*, p. 89.
[155] John Wilkins, *The Discovery of a World in the Moone* (London, 1638), p. 190.
[156] *Ibid.*, p. 186.   [157] *Ibid.*, pp. 19[2]–3.

wished to argue for inhabitants, he declared, 'which, perhaps, are not Men'.[158] Similarly, Richard Bentley in 1692 in *A Confutation of Atheism* did not believe it improper to speculate on the existence of other inhabited worlds. Such speculations, he wrote, were not forbidden by the scriptures, which were only concerned with the origins of terrestrial animals. Neither was he to be sidetracked by what he called frivolous disputes about how such extraterrestrials might participate in Adam's sin or in the benefits of Christ's incarnation. He followed Fontenelle's solution:

God, therefore, may have joined immaterial souls, even of the same class and capacities in their separate state, to other kind of bodies, and in other laws of union; and from those different laws of union there will arise quite different affections, and natures, and species of the compound beings. So that we ought not upon any account to conclude, that if there be rational inhabitants in the moon or Mars, or any unknown planets of other systems, they must therefore have human nature, or be involved in the circumstances of our world.[159]

In the final analysis, neither antipodean androgynes nor pre-Adamitic Americans nor men in the moon could be allowed for too long to disrupt the necessity of focusing the theological imagination on the great human drama of redemption which began once, and only once, in the creation of Adam, the crown of creation, poised between the animals and the angels.

[158] Bernard Fontenelle, *A Discovery of New Worlds*, Author's Preface.
[159] Alexander Dyce (ed.), *The Works of Richard Bentley, D.D.* (London, 1838), iii.176.

CHAPTER 3

The quest for Paradise

A PARADISE WITHIN

And the Lord God planted a garden eastward in Eden; and there
he put the man whom he had formed.

Genesis 2.8 (Authorised Version)

Plantaverat autem Dominus Deus paradisum voluptatis a prin-
cipio; in quo posuit hominem quem formaverat.

Genesis 2.8 (Vulgate)

The translators of the King James version of the Bible read Genesis 2.8
as locating the first Paradise or Garden in an historical place and time.
In this, they firmly set themselves against those who had read the story of
Adam and the garden Paradise as having only an allegorical meaning.
And they were clearly indicating the primacy of the historical reading of
the story. In so doing, they put themselves at variance with the Latin
translation that Jerome had made in his Vulgate. For the Hebrew
rendered as 'a garden eastward in Eden' in the King James version had
there been rendered 'a paradise of pleasure from the beginning'.

The Hebrew itself is ambiguous with regard to the meaning of the
word '*eden*, and also with regard to 'Miqqedem', which can mean 'from
the East' or 'from the beginnings of the earth'. The Greek version of the
Old Testament, the Septuagint, reflected this ambiguity, rendering the
Hebrew as a 'paradise eastward in Eden' in Genesis 2.8, but as a
'paradise of pleasure' in Genesis 3.23 and 3.24. Where the Hebrew was
ambiguous and the Septuagint ambivalent, the King James version
consistently chose the historically particular, which rendered more
difficult an allegorical reading, over against the Vulgate's less particular
translation, which rendered more feasible an allegorical reading.[1]

---

[1] On the King James translation, see David Norton, *A History of the Bible as Literature* (Cambridge,
1993), i.139–61.

Walter Raleigh, citing the King James version and criticising the Vulgate translation, concluded, 'it is manifest, that in this place [i.e. Genesis 2.8] Eden is the proper name of a region'.[2]

Allegorical readings were, of course, common in the patristic and medieval periods. Philo had read the Paradise story allegorically and had been followed in this by, for example, Origen and Hugh of Saint Victor. Origen's Paradise had been regarded as a symbol of the celestial paradise. 'And who could be found so silly as to believe that God, after the manner of a farmer, planted trees in a Paradise eastward in Eden', declared Origen, for 'these statements are made by scripture in a figurative manner, in order that through them certain mystical truths may be indicated.'[3]

Not all were as keen on rejecting the historical meaning of Paradise as was Origen. Augustine, for example, in *The Literal Meaning of Genesis* stated that there were three options concerning the Paradise in which Adam and Eve had lived, the corporeal, the spiritual, and both. And it was the third of these that appealed to him.[4] To Moses bar Cephas in his ninth-century commentary on Paradise, it was both a physical and a spiritual place, the one to delight the body, the other the soul of Adam. In the mystical Paradise, the trees and plants were meditations, the rivers were the cardinal virtues, and 'the earth of the mystical paradise was the spirit and mind of Adam . . .'[5]

Such spiritual interpretations of the meaning of Paradise were to continue into the seventeenth century, and particularly the notion of the Paradise within. It was an image that appealed particularly to Platonists. Oliver Cromwell's chaplain, Peter Sterry, for example, believed that Paradise had been in the midst of man and had not so much been lost or ruined as hid beneath the besmirched image of God. It was to be found in the little world of man, more than in the large world. The knowledge of Paradise, he declared, is 'a *remembrance*, the Life of all good, an awakening by reason of the primitive image of pure Nature, raising itself by degrees, and sparkling through the *Rubbish*, the confusion of the present state'.[6] The Platonist Henry More read the story of Eden cabbalistically or mystically as reflecting events in the ethereal realm.[7] Sebastian Franck

[2] Walter Raleigh, *The History of the World*, in *The Works of Sir Walter Raleigh, Kt* (New York, 1829), ii.68.
[3] G. W. Butterworth (ed.), Origen, *On First Principles* (Gloucester, Massachusetts, 1973), 4.3.1.
[4] See J. H. Taylor (trans.), Augustine, *The Literal Meaning of Genesis* (New York, 1982), 2.32.
[5] *P.G.*, 111.583. See also Jean Delumeau, *History of Paradise: The Garden of Eden in Myth and Tradition* (New York, 1995).
[6] Peter Sterry, *Discourse of the Freedom of the Will* (London, 1675), p. 99. Quoted by Peter Harrison, *The Bible, Protestantism and the Rise of Science*, p. 210.

believed that 'God alone and his omnipotent Word is our Paradise, the *Tree* of Life, and the Temple wherein we inhabit, walk, serve, pray, &c.'[8]

The poet Henry Vaughan was influenced by the Augustinian notion of the interior illumination of the soul. For Vaughan, the retreat to the innocent days of the individual's childhood is at the same time a return to the days of human innocence and to the image of God retained in the memory: 'O how I long to travell back/ and tread again that ancient track!/ That I might once more reach that plaine,/ Where first I left my glorious traine . . .'[9]

For Thomas Traherne, as for Henry Vaughan, Paradise is to be regained through inner discipline, through the uncovering and developing of the Platonic forms of the good and the true within each individual. As Louis Martz writes, for Traherne 'the creative power bestowed on Adam still resides, though neglected within man, and . . . it is man's duty, through the powers of his soul, to realize the restoration of the Paradise within made possible by the sacrifice of Christ'.[10] Traherne rejected the Augustinian and Calvinist doctrine of original sin. Thus, the return to infancy is, for Traherne, a realisation of the Paradise within. To become like a little child was to become like Adam in Paradise before the Fall:

> *That Prospect* was the Gate of Hev'n; *that Day*
> The ancient Light of *Eden* did convey
> Into my Soul: I was an *Adam* there,
> A little *Adam* in a Sphere . . .
>
> Of Joys: O there my ravisht Sense
> Was entertain'd in Paradise;
> And Had a Sight of Innocence
> Which was to mee beyond all Price.[11]

The rejection of original sin, and the regaining of Paradise within were ideas which were also present among some of the radicals in the middle of the seventeenth century. Isaac Penington, while a Ranter, believed that Adam's vision of an unspoilt world could be regained in the here and now:

7 See Henry More, *Conjectura Cabbalistica*, in *A Collection of Philosophical Writings* (London, 1662).
8 Sebastian Franck, *The Forbidden Fruit* (London, 1640), p. 5. On Franck, see Rufus M. Jones, *Spiritual Reformers in the 16th and 17th Centuries* (Gloucester, Massachusetts, 1971).
9 Henry Vaughan, 'The Retreate'. Quoted by Louis L. Martz, *The Paradise Within: Studies in Vaughan, Traherne, and Milton* (New Haven, 1964), p. 29.
10 Quoted *ibid.*, p. 39.
11 Thomas Traherne, 'Innocence', in H. M. Margoliouth (ed.), Thomas Traherne, *Centuries, Poems, and Thanksgivings* (Oxford, 1958), ii.19.

To the creature, in the present state of the creature, under the present law of the creature, according to the judgment of the eye of the creature, everything is unlovely; and he that sees them not to be so, falls short of the perfection of the creaturely eye. But come deeper beyond this state, beneath this Law; look with a true eye, and then you shall find all this unloveliness pass away, and an excellency appear, that the creature could never so much imagine or dream of. And now come back with this eye into the present state of all things, and behold them through the true glass, and you shall see them all new here also, and as far differing from what you did or could take them to be in your creaturely apprehension.[12]

It is perhaps not a matter for surprise that, among the radicals, redemption, the return to Paradise, heaven, and hell should be realisable within and by the individual. For thereby the control of the salvific process was removed from ecclesiastical authority, and a radically new world was created in and by the experience of the individual. In the conversion experience of the Quaker George Fox, for example, he believed he had regained the position of Adam in Paradise:

Now was I come up in Spirit . . . into the *Paradise* of *God*. All things were New; and all the *Creation* gave another Smell unto me, than before, beyond what words can utter. I knew I knew nothing, but *Pureness*, and *Innocency*, and *Righteousness*, being renewed up into the *Image* of *God* by Christ Jesus; so that I say, I was come up to the *State* of *Adam*, which he was in, before he *fell*.[13]

For the Leveller Gerrard Winstanley, the whole story of Paradise was played out in the life of every individual. In his *Fire in the Bush*, around 1650, the allegorical relation between Eden and the life of each person was elaborately developed. Every living soul is Paradise, Adam, and the image of God. The selfish imagination is the source of weakness and disease, the tree of good and evil, and the serpent. Within us too is the tree of life, reason, and the second Adam: 'that which hath by Imagination, or *Judas* Ministry, been held forth to us, to be without us, as *Adam*, the Serpent, the Garden, the Tree of Knowledge, of Good and Evill; and the Tree of Life; and the fall of Man, and promise of redemption, all to be without; yet all these are within the heart of man clearly'.[14] The Paradise within can be cultivated by interior works, 'plaine heartedness without guile, quiet, patient, chast, loving, without envy . . . This is the Garden of *Eden* . . . this is the field of heaven . . .'[15]

[12] Isaac Penington, *Light or Darkness* (London, 1650), p. 3. Quoted by Christopher Hill, *The Collected Essays of Christopher Hill* (London, 1985–6), i.232.
[13] George Fox, *A Journal or Historical Account of the Life of . . . George Fox* (London, 1694), i.17–18.
[14] George H. Sabine (ed.), *The Works of Gerrard Winstanley*, p. 462.
[15] *Ibid.*, p. 481.

The symbolic understanding of Paradise in seventeenth-century England was, however, the last flowering of a tradition that was by then already waning. For the Renaissance had increasingly focused on an historical Paradise as the first stage in a drama of redemption which was increasingly seen in historical terms. Joseph Duncan writes, 'Faced with divisions within the Church, an increased rationalism in exegesis and in textual criticism, and expanding geographical exploration, both commentators and poets of the Renaissance sought the certainty of a natural paradise with a definite position in human history and a precise geographical location.'[16]

EASTWARD IN EDEN

There was therefore a strong sense that the historical meaning of the Paradise story was paramount. In 1601, for example, Nicholas Gibbens focused on the historicity of Adam as the foundation of all truth. Against the allegorising of Philo and Origen, he cited Epiphanius: 'If there was (saith he) no paradice but in an allegorie; if not trees, then no eating of the fruit; if no eating, then no *Adam*; if no *Adam*, then are there no men but all are allegories, and the truth it selfe is become a fable.'[17]

The historicity of the story of the Garden was important also because the sin of Adam and Eve, and thus the necessity of redemption, was continually constructed in the light of what was actually (and not merely symbolically) lost. The present human situation of pain, suffering, and death was particularly seen in relation to what our embodied existence might have been had our first parents not sinned. Allegory spoke only of the spirit, of the reason, of the passions and the emotions; history spoke of the body. Thus du Bartas:

> Nor think that *Moses* paints fantasticke-wise
> A mistike tale of fained Paradice:
> ('Twas a true Garden, happy plenties horne,
> And seat of graces) least thou make (forlorne)
> An ideall *Adams* food fantasticall,
> His sinne suppos'd, his paine poeticall:
> Such allegories serve for shelter fit
> To curious idiots of erronious wit,
> And chiefelie then when reading histories,
> Seeking the spirit, they do the body leese.[18]

---

[16] Joseph E. Duncan, *Milton's Earthly Paradise: A Historical Study of Eden* (Minneapolis, 1972), p. 89.
[17] Nicholas Gibbens, *Questions and Disputations concerning the Holy Scripture*, p. 62.
[18] Susan Snyder (ed.), *The Divine Weeks and Works*, i.321.

This wariness about metaphorical readings, and the emphasis on the literal or, more properly, the historical meaning of Paradise, was central to Protestant interpretation of the Bible. We must, declared Calvin, 'entirely reject the allegories of Origen, and of others like him, which Satan, with the deepest subtlety, has endeavoured to introduce into the Church, for the purpose of rendering the doctrine of Scripture ambiguous and destitute of all certainty and firmness'.[19] In his commentary on Genesis, Luther focused on the historical location of Eden and rejected the Vulgate translation.[20] For Luther, the literal sense was the highest and the best. And Origen was singled out for criticism, since, 'ignoring the grammatical sense, he turned trees and everything else . . . into allegories'.[21]

The relegation to obscurity of the allegorical meaning of Paradise, and the focus on its possible physical location, dominated the seventeenth century. John Salkeld, for example, although he accepted that Paradise might have a spiritual meaning, concentrated on the historical and the literal meaning, and in support he cited John Chrysostom: 'That Moses did therefore manifestly describe Paradise, the riuers, the trees, the fruites, and all other things thereto appertaining, that the simple and ignorant should not be deceiued, by the fabulous Allegories, and doting dreames, which some would pretend to diuulge for sole truth . . .'[22] Andrew Willet rejected both Jerome's translation and the allegorising of Philo and Origen.[23] Marmaduke Carver, rector of a Yorkshire parish, wrote *A Discourse of the Terrestrial Paradise* to defend the historical truth of the Genesis story against those who 'propound the History of *Paradise* to scorn and derision, as a mere *Utopia*, or Fiction of a place that never was'.[24]

During the Renaissance, Paradise had become a geographical reality. As Henri Baudet points out, the image of Paradise 'was removed from a distant past to a distant present. Where at first it had been characterized by the distance in time, it now became increasingly invested with a contemporary character. The distance became a matter of geography.'[25] And its location became in principle discoverable. That it was

[19] John King (trans.), *Commentaries on the First Book of Moses*, p. 114.
[20] Jaroslav Pelikan, *Luther's Works* (St Louis, 1958), i.87–8.
[21] Quoted by Peter Harrison, *The Bible, Protestantism, and the Rise of Natural Science*, p. 108. On Protestantism and the literal sense, see *ibid.*, pp. 107–20.
[22] John Salkeld, *A Treatise of Paradise*, p. 8.
[23] See Andrew Willet, *Hexapla in Genesin*, p. 27. See also George Walker, *God made visible*, p. 240.
[24] Marmaduke Carver, *A Discourse of the Terrestrial Paradise* (London, 1666), Epistle Dedicatory.
[25] Henri Baudet, *Paradise on Earth: Some Thoughts on European Images of Non-European Man* (New Haven, 1965), p. 15.

not discovered was accounted for theologically or historically: theologically, because, as the poet Thomas Peyton wrote, the lords of the earth have ventured forth, 'And none of them as yet haue euer found,/ Or came in sight of thy most heauenly ground:/ Which Farre in *Eden* in the orient lies,/ vnfit for man to see with sinfull eyes . . . ;'[26] or historically, because it disappeared at the time of the Flood.

This entailed that a number of medieval speculations on the place of Paradise were disposed of. That Paradise was near the moon or in the air under the moon was rejected by all. Andrew Willet described it as a ridiculous and childish fancy that needed no confutation.[27] Walter Raleigh, Thomas Peyton, Nicholas Gibbens, and George Walker agreed.[28]

Yet it was still a tradition sufficiently well diffused to make its appearance in fictional works. The moon depicted by Francis Godwin in *The Man in the Moone* in 1638 was clearly Edenic. There was no rain, wind, or change of season, and only a perpetual spring. The lunarians were giants who lived a thousand years or longer. Food grew everywhere without labour, or only the minimum of the most enjoyable kind. There was no illness and no crime: 'through an excellent disposition of that nature of people there, all, young and old doe hate all manner of vice, and doe live in such love, peace and amitie, as it seemeth to bee another Paradise'.[29] Most paradisal of all, wicked children were sent away to a 'certaine high hill in the North of *America*'.[30] There, he speculated, they were to become the natives of the New World.

A similar motif occurred in Cyrano de Bergerac's *Comical History of the States and Empires of the Worlds of the Moon and Sun*, first translated into English in 1687. There the hero who has ascended to the moon in a bubble of mist or dew is informed by a youth of majestic beauty that the moon was the place from which Adam and Eve left to go to earth 'betwixt *Mesopotamia* and *Arabia*'.[31] The ambience is Edenic:

There the whole Year is a Spring; there no poysonous Plant sprouts forth, but is soon destroyed; there the Brooks by an agreeable murmuring, relate their Travels to the Pebbles; there thousands of Quiristers make the woods, resound

---

[26] Thomas Peyton, *The glasse of time, in the two first ages diuinely handled* (London, 1620), p. 37.
[27] See Andrew Willet, *Hexapla in Genesin*, p. 27.
[28] See Thomas Peyton, *The glasse of time*, p. 45; Nicholas Gibbens, *Questions and Disputations concerning the Holy Scripture*, p. 61; Walter Raleigh, *The History of the World*, p. 39; and George Walker, *God made visible*, p. 239.
[29] Francis Godwin, *The Man in the Moone* (London, 1638), p. 104.   [30] *Ibid.*, p. 105.
[31] Cyrano de Bergerac, *The Comical History of the States and Empires of the Worlds of the Moon and Sun* (London, 1687), p. 26.

with their melodious Notes; and the quavering Clubs of these divine Musisians are so universal, that every Leaf of the Forest, seems to have borrowed the Tongue and shape of a Nightingale.[32]

That Paradise was to be found in the Antipodes or beneath the equator found some seventeenth-century support. This was a location proposed by Tertullian and Bonaventure, and tentatively supported by Thomas Aquinas, primarily because of its temperate climate.[33] It was the temperate climate which had also suggested to Christopher Columbus that Eden was to be found beneath the equator in South America.[34]

But it was the Dominican Luis de Urreta's speculation early in the seventeenth century that it was located in the equatorial region, not in the Americas but in Africa, that led to a renewed interest in this possibility. Urreta combined the traditional belief that the Christian kingdom of Prester John was in Africa and the view that this kingdom contained Paradise upon Mount Amara. It had characteristic Edenic features, an eternal and flowery spring, equal days and nights, and unique plants and trees.[35] Samuel Purchas followed Urreta's account of Mount Amara and noted that many had taken this place to be the Paradise of Adam and Eve.[36]

In spite of Foigny's antipodean Paradise and Tommaso Campanella's 'City of the Sun' below the line of the equator, Andrew Willet spoke for most when he rejected the equatorial region as the location of Paradise. The Tigris and Euphrates rivers, he wrote, 'which flowed out of Paradise, and the country Eden, where Paradise was, came not neare the equinoctiall: and they are knowne to bee in Asia, not in any remote and vnknowne countrey . . .'[37]

It was, of course, tempting to locate Eden at the source of the Nile, for this river had traditionally been identified with the biblical river Gihon of Genesis 2.13 which 'compasseth the whole land of Ethiopia'. Thus, for example, Thomas Peyton spoke of Amara as the home of the Queen of Sheba, Candace, and Homer's feasting Gods, 'whence a christall river downe to *Nilus* purled', but he rejected it as a possible location for Paradise, preferring Mesopotamia.[38] In 1625, the scholar and poet Sir

---

[32] *Ibid.*, p. 24.   [33] Thomas Aquinas, *Summa Theologiae*, 1a.102, 2, 4.

[34] See Jean Delumeau, *History of Paradise*, pp. 53–5.

[35] See Joseph E. Duncan, *Milton's Earthly Paradise*, pp. 196–7. I am indebted to Duncan for the sources on Amara.

[36] See *ibid.*, p. 196.

[37] Andrew Willet, *Hexapla in Genesin*, p. 27. See also George Walker, *God made visible*, p. 239; Walter Raleigh, *The History of the World*, p. 39.

[38] Thomas Peyton, *The glasse of time*, p. 42.

John Stradling, aware of Purchas' account, was unimpressed: 'The famous Hill *Amara*, to this clime,/ Is but a muddie moore of dirt and slime.'[39] Vincent Le Blanc in *The World Surveyed* was aware of the tradition of the height, extent, and beauty of Amara making it a veritable Paradise, though he believed such reports to be exaggerated.[40] Milton believed in an ideal realm deep within Africa, but did not believe it to be the site of Eden:

> Nor where Abassin Kings their issue Guard,
> Mount Amara, though this by some suppos'd
> True Paradise under the Ethiop Line
> By Nilus' Head, enclos'd with shining Rock,
> A whole day's journey high, but wide remote
> From this Assyrian Garden . . . [41]

Paradisal it might have been, but Milton's Garden was in Assyria.

To virtually all seventeenth-century Protestant commentators, Paradise was no longer extant, and the pious hope of its being located was just that – a pious hope. Walter Raleigh believed that 'if there be any place upon the earth of that nature, beauty, and delight, that Paradise had, the same must be found within . . . the tropics'.[42] For here, he went on, there are cooling breezes by day, the nights are cool and fresh, and he knew no part of the world to equal or better the tropics. In the main, there were good rivers, cedars and other stately trees, and 'so many sorts of delicate fruits, ever bearing, and at all times beautified with blossom and fruit, both green and ripe, as it may of all other parts be best compared to the paradise of Eden'.[43] However, having said all of which, the Protestant principle prevailed. For these were 'vicious countries', since 'nature being liberal to all without labour, necessity imposing no industry or travel, idleness bringeth forth no other fruits than vain thoughts and licentious pleasures'.[44] Du Bartas too was convinced it was lost forever:

> For as through sinne we lost that place; I feare
> Forgetfull, we have lost the knowledge where
> 'Twas situate: and of the sugred dainties
> Wherewith God fed us in those sacred plenties.[45]

For some, Paradise would never be found, its whereabouts forever hidden from us as a consequence of our sin. But for most, Paradise had

---

[39] John Stradling, *Divine Poemes. In seuen seuerall Classes* (London, 1625), p. 27.
[40] Vincent Le Blanc, *The World Surveyed* (London, 1660), p. 238.
[41] *Paradise Lost*, 4.280–5.   [42] Walter Raleigh, *The Works*, ii.88.   [43] *Ibid.*, ii.89.
[44] *Ibid.*, ii.89–90.   [45] Susan Snyder (ed.), *The Divine Weeks and Works*, i.322.

disappeared forever for historical reasons, namely the universal Flood of Noah. For Martin Luther, the issue of the location of Paradise was 'an idle question about something no longer in existence'. Moses was writing the history of the time before sin and the Deluge, he continued,

> but we are compelled to speak of conditions as they are after sin and after the Deluge . . . For time and the curse which sins deserve destroy everything. Thus when the world was obliterated by the Deluge, together with its people and cattle, this famous garden was also obliterated and became lost . . . Moreover, the text also states that it was guarded by an angel lest anyone enter it. Therefore even if that garden had not perished as a result of the ensuing curse, the way to it is absolutely closed to human beings; that is its location cannot be found. This is also a possible answer, although my first opinion, involving the Deluge, seems more probable to me.[46]

Bishop Joseph Hall agreed. For him, even the cherubim with the flaming swords 'did not defend it against those waters, wherewith the sins of men drowned the glory of that place'.[47] John Salkeld epitomized the English judgement: 'Paradise is not accessible, knowne, or seene as a Paradise, because it was destroyed with the Deluge, which passed all the highest places of the earth . . .'[48]

PARADISE LOST AND FOUND

> And a river went out of Eden to water the Garden; and from thence it was parted, and became into four heads.   Genesis 2.10

If Paradise had disappeared, it was only biblical exegesis and not geographical exploration that could solve the issue of where it might have been. During the seventeenth century, only two options remained: first, to try to identify the former site of the now destroyed Paradise; or second, to argue that Paradise was the whole earth.

The belief that Paradise was the whole earth went back to Philo, as part of his attempt to interpret the creation account in the terms of Greek philosophy. He was supported by Clement of Alexandria. Josephus was often interpreted as having so intended when he wrote in *Antiquities*, 'the garden was watered by one river, which ran about the whole earth, and was parted into four parts', an interpretation strengthened by his naming the four rivers as the Tigris, the Euphrates,

---

[46] Jaroslav Pelikan, *Luther's Works*, i.88.   [47] Joseph Hall, *The Works*, i.15.
[48] John Salkeld, *A Treatise of Paradise*, p. 35. See also Edward Leigh, *A Systeme or Bodie of Divinitie*, p. 366.

the Nile, and the Ganges.[49] And Hugh of Saint Victor was also read as accepting that Paradise covered the whole earth.[50]

During the Renaissance, this view was most fully developed by Goropius, a Fleming. In *Origines antwerpianae*, he wrote of Paradise as the whole earth, which offered a means of life with perpetual pleasure. The fountain that watered the garden had its source in the ocean which sent out rivers into the four corners of the world. After the Fall, the whole earth became a place of thorns, labour, and sweat.[51]

This was a view which received little support in seventeenth-century England. Indeed, until Thomas Burnet revisited this theory late in the century, I have found only one hint of it, namely in a poem by E. Philips prefatory to William Coles' history of flora in 1657: 'And Sacred Mysteries inform, that but for one Man's Sin,/ This now disorder'd Earth had all one florid Garden been.'[52]

The reformers had strongly rejected it. In *The Table Talk*, Luther had held that the name Paradise applied to the whole world, and that when Adam sinned, the whole earth lost its fertility.[53] But in his commentary on Genesis, he made it quite clear that Eden was a 'choice garden in comparison with the magnificence of the whole earth, which itself also was a Paradise compared with its present wretched state'.[54] And he went on to suggest that since it was designed for Adam and all his descendants, it would have been more than a narrow garden, and probably comprised Syria, Mesopotamia, Damascus, and Egypt. To those who thought of Paradise as the whole world, Calvin accused them of absurdly transferring 'what Moses said of a certain particular place to the whole world'.[55]

Walter Raleigh presented the most obvious objections, namely that if Paradise had been the whole world, Moses would not have spoken of a Garden eastward in Eden, and that it made no sense to speak of Adam's having been driven out of the Garden, if the Garden were the whole world.[56] The puritan Edward Leigh took a similar 'commonsense'

[49] William Whiston, *The Works of Flavius Josephus*, 1.1.3. (i.43). See also 'Concerning Noah's Work as a planter', 2.11.45, in *Philo*, trans. F. H. Colson and G. H. Whitaker, iii.235–7; and *Stromatum*, 5.11.74 (*P.G.*, 9.109).

[50] See *P.L.*, 175.39.

[51] See Joseph E. Duncan, 'Paradise as the Whole Earth', *Journal of the History of Ideas* 39 (1969), pp. 177–8.

[52] William Coles, *Adam in Eden*, prefatory poem.

[53] William Hazlitt (trans.), *The Table Talk or Familiar Discourse of Martin Luther* (London, 1848), p. 55.

[54] Jaroslav Pelikan, *Luther's Works*, i.89.

[55] John King (trans.), *Commentaries on the First Book of Moses*, p. 114.

[56] See Walter Raleigh, *The Works*, ii.83. See also Nicholas Gibbens, *Questions and Disputations concerning the Holy Scripture*, p. 61.

approach. It cannot be the whole world, he declared, 'for it is said, God took *Adam* and put him into it and likewise that he was cast out of it'.[57] Thomas Peyton saw it as a consequence of human vanity:

> Some men againe more farre than these are wide,
> Whose large conceits in *Eden* cannot bide:
> Fond, franticke men the sacred truth to reach,
> And Paradise ore all the world to streach.[58]

The most original contribution to this debate in seventeenth-century England was offered by Thomas Burnet in *The Sacred Theory of the Earth*, first published in Latin in 1681, and later in *Archaeologiae Philosophicae* in 1692. For Burnet, Paradise was lost forever, as were those three features which characterised it – the perpetual equinox, the longevity of animals, and the production of all things out of the fertile earth: ''Tis like seeking a perfect beauty in a mortal Body, there are so many things requir'd to it, as to complexion, Features, Proportions and Air, that they never meet altogether in one person; neither can all the properties of a Terrestrial *Paradise* ever meet together in one place, though never so well chosen, in this present Earth.'[59] He rejected those accounts which placed it in any particular place on earth. And he scorned 'the vain temerity of modern Authors; as if they could tell to an Acre of Land where *Paradise* stood, or could set their foot upon the Center of the Garden'.[60] For Burnet, the whole earth was, in some sense, paradisal.

The unique feature of Burnet's theory was, as Joseph Duncan puts it, 'While the earlier writers had speculated about God's purposes and *why* he had made a particular kind of Paradise, Burnet tried to demonstrate God's methods and show *how* He had created a paradisiac world.'[61] Geographical exploration and biblical exegesis now took second place to scientific explanation of the world as a whole.

Thus the perpetual spring and the earth's fruitfulness were the consequence of its direct posture to the sun, its smooth and uniform surface without mountains or seas, and its oval shape.[62] 'In this smooth Earth', he wrote, 'were the first scenes of the World, and the first Generations of Mankind; it had the Beauty of Youth and blooming Nature, fresh and fruitful, and not a wrinkle, scar, or fracture in all its body; no Rocks, nor Mountains, no hollow Caves, nor gaping Chanels, but even and uniform all over . . .'Twas suited to a golden Age, and to the first innocency

---

[57] Edward Leigh, *A Systeme or Bodie of Divinitie*, p. 366.   [58] Thomas Peyton, *The glasse of time*, p. 8.
[59] Thomas Burnet, *The Sacred Theory of the Earth* (1965), p. 181.   [60] *Ibid.*, p. 183.
[61] Joseph E. Duncan, 'Paradise as the Whole Earth', p. 183.
[62] See Thomas Burnet, *The Sacred Theory of the Earth*, p. 204.

of Nature.'[63] This was all to be destroyed in the Deluge, when the features of the earth as we know it took shape, the earth's diurnal rotation began, and the seasons came into being. For Burnet, the loss of Paradise was not so much a change of location as a change of state, and not so much the result of a divine curse as the consequence of natural causes consequent to the Deluge.

Erasmus Warren was one who saw the theological implications of Burnet's view that Paradise was not lost until the Deluge. And he saw Burnet as striking at the foundation of religion. It was an issue, he wrote, of 'whether some sacred and *revealed Truths*; or gay, but groundless *Philosophic Phancies*; shall be preferred'.[64] If the equinox had lasted until the Flood, he suggested, surely this would have been reported. And no sense can be made of the curse upon the earth at the time of the Fall: 'that rich and fat Earth would have been flourishing and fruitful, pleasant and *Paradisiacal* (as the *Theory* supposes it) a long time after *Adam* fell. So that where could be barrenness? Or how did the Curse of GOD take place?'[65] Like other critics of Burnet, he could not accept that the prediluvian world was so unlike its post-diluvian counterpart.

John Woodward, Professor of Physic in Gresham College, did not believe that Burnet's Paradise could have existed. A world without the sea, he suggested, would have been a mean dominion for Adam. And he pointed to fossil evidence in confirmation of its existence. In particular, he was troubled by the notion of Burnet's perpetual spring. Far from exalting the earth, such a situation would 'turn it to a general Desolation, and a meer barren Wilderness, to say no worse'.[66] For him, the earth's axis and rotation were then as they are now.

William Whiston, Isaac Newton's successor in the Lucasian Chair of Mathematics at the University of Cambridge, tried to demonstrate that the earth had been formed from the atmosphere of a comet. Unlike Burnet, he believed that the prediluvian world possessed mountains and seas, though the air then was more thin and homogeneous, the earth being watered by 'gentle mists and vapours' which ascended by day and descended by night.[67] The earth was then more fruitful, the weather more equable, the summers and winters more gentle (for the sun was not permanently and directly over against the earth), all of which conspired to generate long antediluvian lives.

---

[63] *Ibid.*, p. 64.   [64] Erasmus Warren, *Geologia*, Epistle to the Reader.   [65] *Ibid.*, p. 168.
[66] John Woodward, *An Essay Towards a Natural History of the Earth* (London, 1695), p. 271.
[67] William Whiston, *A New Theory of the Earth*, p. 183.

Uniquely, Whiston also argued that the earth had no diurnal rotation until after the Flood. The earth rotated only once every year, with the consequence that there were six months of light and six months of darkness, and a perpetual equality of day and night. Thus from the beginning of creation until the creation of Adam was just over five and one-half years (that is, in the second half of the 'sixth day'). And only after the Flood, according to Whiston, did the rotation of the earth lead to distinct seasons and distinct zones of temperature. Even so, the prediluvian world was not equally paradisal all over, the Garden of Eden, located in Mesopotamia, 'being a peculiarly fruitful and happy soil . . .'[68]

John Keill, Scottish mathematician and astronomer, agreed with neither Burnet nor Whiston and thought Erasmus Warren had spoken the least sense of all. Against Burnet, he argued that there must have been prediluvian rivers, for the development of human civilisation would depend upon them; and if rivers, then mountains. Moreover, he argued, the world would have been intolerable had the sun remained permanently over against the equator. In the torrid zone, there would have been 'an intolerable scorching heat . . .' and in the polar zones, 'the cold could not have been indured'.[69] And against Whiston's view that the earth had no diurnal rotation, he declared,

how cold and uncomfortable a darkness must that have been in which our first Parents passed the one half of their Paradisiacal life, when in the other half they must have been scorched and roasted with the immense heat of the Sun . . . This heat in my opinion, would have quite withered the Herbs and Plants which were then designed to be the food of Mankind; it w'd have forced our first Parents to seek for shelter in Dens and Caves, which w'd have been in such a state, more convenient than the Garden of Eden.[70]

This would have been more like hell than Paradise, he concluded.

For seventeenth-century interpreters, the crucial part of the solution to the location of Paradise was the identification of the river which watered the Garden and subsequently divided into four streams. Genesis had identified these as the Pison which encompassed the land of Havilah, the Gihon which covered Ethiopia, the Hiddekel which went toward the east of Assyria, and the Euphrates. But the question of the contemporary rivers to which these alluded was problematic. The

[68] *Ibid.*, p. 172. It is virtually impossible to construct a consistent and coherent account of Whiston's astronomical views.

[69] John Keill, *An Examination of Dr Burnet's Theory of the Earth* (Oxford, 1698), p. 66.

[70] *Ibid.*, p. 194.

Euphrates was clear enough. There was a general agreement that the Tigris and the Hiddekel were the same. But the medieval identification, following Josephus, of the Gihon as the Nile and the Pison as the Ganges had been all but abandoned by the end of the sixteenth century.

As late as 1590, the Elizabethan courtier and poet Lodowick Lloid located Paradise broadly in the East, and declared that the Ganges, Nile, Tigris, and Euphrates found their source within it.[71] But of all the discussions of Paradise examined by Arnold Williams, Lloid's was the only one which accepted the medieval identification. It did very occasionally occur in the seventeenth century. Thomas Milles identified the Pison with the Ganges, and the Gihon with the Nile.[72] Giovanno Loredano in *The Life of Adam* in 1659 declared the Nile, Ganges, Euphrates, and Tigris to be the four streams which flowed out of Eden, which he located in Mesopotamia. Like Luther's, however, it was an identification which he made only on the understanding that in the Flood, 'the waters overflowing all the earth, even rivers changed their Courses and Originalls'.[73] But the medieval tradition was rarely evident.

Nicholas Gibbens' conclusion in 1601 was more typical. The four rivers could not, he declared, be identified with the Nile, Ganges, Tigris, and Euphrates, 'which are so many thousand miles asunder, and can neuer bee deuided out of one streame, seeing in their nearest meeting, the greatest part of Asia is between them . . .'[74] It was a conclusion which Walter Raleigh, Andrew Willet, Alexander Ross, and George Hakewill endorsed.[75]

Apart from those few who, as we have seen, preferred Paradise to have covered the whole earth, all believed it to be a lost site somewhere in the Near or Middle East, not too far distant from the sites mentioned in other parts of the Old Testament or in the New. During the seventeenth century there were three main competing locations for the site of Paradise: Armenia, Babylonia, and the Holy Land.

The least popular of these three in seventeenth-century England was Palestine. It was a location promoted, for example, by Isaac La Peyrère in *A Theological Systeme* in 1655.[76] As the father of the Jews, it was proper,

---

[71] See Lodowick Lloid, *The Consent of Time* (London, 1590), p. 4.
[72] Thomas Milles, *The treasurie of auncient and moderne times*, i.12.
[73] Giovanno Loredano, *The Life of Adam*, p. 9. See Jaroslav Pelikan, *Luther's Works*, i.98.
[74] Nicholas Gibbens, *Qvestions and Dispvtations concerning the Holy Scriptvre*, p. 64.
[75] See Walter Raleigh, *The History of the World*, p. 39; Alexander Ross, *An Exposition on the Fovrteene first Chapters of Genesis*, p. 43; Andrew Willet, *Hexapla in Genesin*, p. 30; and George Hakewill, *An apologie*, p. 3. See also Pierre D. Huet, *A Treatise of the Situation of Paradise* (London, 1694), p. 12.
[76] See Isaac La Peyrère, *A Theological Systeme*, pp. 142–3.

he suggested, that Adam should have had the first natural possession of the Holy Land.

It was a solution particularly favoured too by those more inclined to a typological rather than a literal reading of Genesis, and disposed to read the history of the first Adam in the light of the events in the life of the second. The Jesuit Nicolas Abram was influential. In 1635, he published a commentary on Virgil's *Georgics* in which he committed himself to the Jordan as satisfying the requirements of the river which ran through Paradise, reviving the ancient idea that its waters disappeared under the earth only to surface again as the sources of the other rivers. Thus, Paradise comprised an area that included the Sea of Tiberias, Sodom, and the Dead Sea.[77]

In 1683, Henry Hare, Lord Coleraine, in *The Situation of Paradise found out* rejected both Mesopotamia and Burnet's whole-earth theory in favour of Palestine, and particularly Galilee. And it was to Nicolas Abram that he looked for his conclusion

that *where* the first *Adam* sinned, *there* it behoved the second *Adam* to *expiate* that sin; and that it was fit *where sin* entered the World, *there* it should be driven out . . . *here* he *lived* and *died*, acted his *Miracles*, crushed the *Serpent's* head, opened *Paradise where* the first had shut it, gave admission into a *Coelestial* and *Intellectual* Paradise, where the first was expelled a *Sensual* and an *Earthly one*; *here* stood his *Cross*, *here* it was planted by *evil* men, *where* stood the *Tree* of *Life* . . . [78]

Another possible location for Paradise was Armenia. The most elaborate seventeenth-century discussion of the Armenian option was offered by Marmaduke Carver in his *A Discourse of the Terrestrial Paradise*, published in 1666 but written twenty-six years earlier. To Carver, the source of the Tigris, the spring of the river of Paradise, was 'in *Armenia major*, in the Region of *Sophene*, on the South-side of the Mountain of *Taurus*'.[79] After passing through the earthly Paradise, where a noxious lake mentioned by Ptolemy still existed, it divided into four streams, giving rise to the Euphrates, the Gihon, and the Pison.

It was, however, Mesopotamia, or a part of it, which was by far the favourite location for Paradise. This was John Calvin's preferred option. Calvin was convinced that two of the four streams into which the river of Paradise divided itself were the Tigris and the Euphrates. The other two

---

[77] Nicolas Abram, *Diatriba de quatuor fluviis et loco paradisi* (Rouen, 1635), pp. 64–5. See Jean Delumeau, *History of Paradise*, p. 170.

[78] Henry Hare, *The Situation of Paradise found out* (London, 1683), pp. 21–2.

[79] Marmaduke Carver, *A Discourse of the Terrestrial Paradise*, p. 47. See also Matthew Poole, *Annotations upon the Holy Bible*, sig. B.2.v.

streams were the Tigris and Euphrates before they joined together to form one river which flowed through Eden. The map which accompanied Calvin's description of the location of Paradise, a version of which appeared in the first English translation of his commentaries on Genesis, showed a connection between the Tigris and the Euphrates above Seleucia, a complete joining of the two below Babylon, and a separation of the two above the Persian Gulf. Thus, the Gihon and the Pison were the lower Tigris and the lower Euphrates. As to the dwelling place of Adam, 'it makes no great difference', declared Calvin, 'whether Adam dwelt below the confluent stream towards Babylon and Seleucia, or in the higher part; it is enough that he occupied a well-watered country.'[80]

Calvin's location of the Garden in Mesopotamia was influential, not least because the map which appeared in both the original French and in the first English translation became more widely known by virtue of its inclusion in a dozen or so printings of the biblical text in the sixteenth century, including the Bishop's Bible in 1568. As a consequence, innumerable viewers and readers of the Bible saw the Genesis story through Mesopotamian eyes.

The dominance of the Mesopotamian solution was further reinforced by Walter Raleigh's adoption of it. Raleigh gave it a precise location in Mesopotamia, thirty-five degrees from the equator, and fifty-five from the North Pole. The region produced the most excellent wines, fruit, oil, and grain, he wrote, even in the present day. And while similar temperate conditions could be found in the East and West Indies, the latter had many disadvantages: 'laye down by those pleasures and benefits the fearefull and dangerous thunders and lightnings, the horrible and frequent Earthquakes, the dangerous diseases, the multitude of venimous beasts and wormes, with other inconueniences, and there will be found no comparison betweene the one and the other'.[81] And his accompanying map placed it near the confluence of the Tigris and the Euphrates, as did those in Gibbens' *Qvestions and Dispvtations* in 1601, in *Purchas his Pilgrimage* in 1626, and in Pierre Daniel Huet's *Treatise of the Situation of Paradise* in 1694.

The Mesopotamian solution became widespread during the seventeenth century. It made its appearance in works as vastly different as those of the proto-feminist William Austin and the theologians and commentators James Ussher, John White, George Walker, Richard

---

[80] John King (trans.), *Commentaries on the First Book of Moses*, p. 122.
[81] Walter Raleigh, *The History of the World*, p. 134.

Kidder, and Edward Leigh. It surfaced among the poets Thomas Peyton and Giovanno Loredano, the florist Ralph Austen, and the herbalist William Westmacott. And it found support with writers as different as the geographer Nathanael Carpenter, the philosopher Henry More, the popularist John Dunton, and the eclectic Alexander Ross.[82]

TIMES AND SEASONS

And God saw everything that he had made, and, behold, *it was* very good. And the evening and the morning were the sixth day. Thus the heavens and the earth were finished, and all the host of them.

Genesis 1.31–2.1

Once I had a debate in hall at dinner time with a doctor who began to criticize the study of mathematics. Since he was sitting next to me, I enquired if it was not necessary [to know] the divisions of the year. He replied that it was not all that necessary, since his peasants knew perfectly well when it was day, when it was night, when it was summer, and when it was noon without any knowledge of that sort. I said in reply: 'That answer is clearly unworthy of a doctor.' What a fine doctor he is, that uneducated fool; one should shit a turd into his doctor's hat and put it back on his head. What madness! It is one of God's great gifts that everyone can have the weekday letters on his wall.

Philipp Melancthon[83]

The matter of times and seasons was clearly a sensitive one for Philipp Melancthon. The ability to measure the days, the seasons, and the years was for him one of the divine gifts. For virtually all commentators on the Genesis tradition in the sixteenth and seventeenth centuries, time began with the creation of the world. And the six days of biblical creation were just that, literally six days. Aristotle's opinion on the eternity of the earth was firmly rejected. In *Specvlvm Mundi* in 1635, John Swan wrote that the first verse of scripture

---

[82] See William Austin, *Haec Homo*, p. 20; James Ussher, *A Body of Divinitie* (London, 1645), p. 126; John White, *A Commentary Upon the Three First Chapters of Genesis*, ii.38; George Walker, *God made visible*, p. 47; Richard Kidder, *A Commentary*, i.9; Edward Leigh, *A Systeme or Bodie of Divinitie*, pp. 365–6; Thomas Peyton, *The glasse of time*, p. 48; Giovanno Loredano, *The Life of Adam*, p. 9; Ralph Austen, *A Treatise of Fruit Trees* (Oxford, 1653), p. 13; William Westmacott, *Historia Vegetabilium Sacra* (London, 1695), p. 14; Nathanael Carpenter, *Geography Delineated*, ii.209; Henry More, *The Defense of the Threefold Cabbala* (London, 1662), p. 66; John Dunton (ed.), *The Athenian Gazette*, vol. 1, q. 1, no. 8; and Alexander Ross, *An Exposition on the Fovrteene first Chapters of Genesis*, p. 40.

[83] Quoted by Anthony T. Grafton, 'From *De Die Natali* to *De Emendatione Temporum*: The Origins and Setting of Scaliger's Chronology', *Journal of the Warburg and Courtauld Institutes* 48 (1985), p. 100.

makes it plain that the world began; and that Time (by which we measure dayes, weeks, moneths, and yeares) hath not been for ever. For, *in the beginning*, (saith Moses) *God created the heavens and the earth*: and why is it said *in the beginning he created*, but that it might be shown . . . that the world was not from everlasting.[84]

As it was important to locate the place of Paradise, so also its time. For the great drama of redemption – creation, fall, redemption, last things – was played out on a temporal stage. In 1597, in his computation of the time from creation to Christ, Thomas Pie spoke for many: 'How necessarie and requisite Chronologie is in the studie of all Historie, Diuine or Humane, it being the right eye thereof, as Geographie is the left . . .'[85] As C. A. Patrides reminds us, computations of chronology are among the most characteristic products of the Renaissance.[86]

The difficulty of the task can be measured by the variety of attempts. It was a difficulty recognised at the time. 'You will find it easier to make the wolf agree with the lamb', lamented Iacobus Curio in 1557, 'than to make all chronologers agree about the age of the world.'[87] A century later, in 1650, William Nisbet observed that 'There is great disagreement among Chronologues, in counting of the years from the Creation of the World to the death of our Saviour', a claim described by Patrides as one of the most spectacular understatements of the Renaissance.[88] The non-conformist divine Thomas Allen was moved to confess that there were 'very many (and some great) differences amongst *Chronologers* in the *Computation* of *Scripture-Chronologie*' before proceeding to establish his own reckoning.[89]

All were agreed, however, that the key was to be found in the correct interpretation of scripture. The rabbinical scholar Hugh Broughton, while admitting to the variations in the chronologists' accounts, was quite firm on the centrality of scripture. 'He that wyll deny the course of tyme', he wrote in 1594, 'to be in Scripture cleerely obserued, euen vnto the fulnes, the yeere of saluation, wherin our Lord dyed, may as wel deny the Sunne to haue brightnes.'[90] To John More, the 'apostle of

---

[84] John Swan, *Specvlvm Mundi*, pp. 3–4.
[85] Thomas Pie, *An Hourglasse Contayning a Computation from the Beginning of Time to Christ* (London, 1597), Epistle Dedicatory.
[86] See C. A. Patrides, 'Renaissance Estimates of the Year of Creation', *Huntington Library Quarterly* 26 (1963), p. 319.
[87] I. Curio, *Chronologicarum rerum, lib. II* (Basle, 1557), p. 8. Quoted by Anthony T. Grafton, 'Scaliger's Chronology', p. 102.
[88] William Nisbet, *A Golden Chaine of Time* (Edinburgh, 1650), p. 1. Quoted by C. A. Patrides, 'Renaissance Estimates of the Year of Creation', p. 315.
[89] Thomas Allen, *A Chain of Scripture Chronology* (London, 1659), p. 5.
[90] Hugh Broughton, *A Seder Olam, that is: Order of the worlde* (London, 1594), p. 1.

Norwich', the scriptures were to be the framework into which other chronologies needed to be fitted. We must bring the profane histories, he wrote, 'to that account which is set down in Scriptures, from the beginning of the worlde till the suffering of Christ, most exactly, and so labour to make the times of forreigne histories to agree with that account of the holy Scripture . . .'[91]

The initial problem to be overcome was the choice of the text – that of the Hebrew or of the Greek version of the Old Testament. Judaism, following the Hebrew text, had set the date of creation at 3760 BCE, or 1,676 years before the Flood. The Septuagint differed from the Hebrew by setting the year of creation as 2,242 years before the Flood. This was the result of the Septuagint's adding approximately one hundred years to the ages of each of the early patriarchs at the time of the birth of his first son, upon which ages the chronology of the period from the creation down to the exodus was based. During the sixteenth and seventeenth centuries, the Hebrew figures were almost universally followed.

The acceptance of the Hebrew dating was influenced too by the tradition of the earth's lasting for six thousand years, four thousand of which consisted of the period between creation and the coming of Christ. In the third century, for example, Julius Africanus combined the six days of creation with the biblical notion that a day for God is as a thousand years, to generate the six millennia of world history.[92] Lactantius, Augustine, Isidore of Seville, and Bede also divided history into six ages to last six thousand years, from Adam to Noah, to Abraham, to David, to the Babylonian captivity, to Christ, to the Last Judgement.[93]

It was a tradition which lasted into the sixteenth and seventeenth centuries. No doubt the tendency to settle on the year of creation as a century either side of 4000 BCE was a consequence of it. As Patrides puts it, 'to have accepted the Septuagint's chronology involved the inevitable conclusion that by the time of the Renaissance the world was, at the very least, 6500 years old – an obvious impossibility in view of the tradition that the world would end on or before its 6000th year'.[94] It was often

---

[91] John More, *A Table from the Beginning of the World to this Day* (Cambridge, 1593), Preface.

[92] The two biblical references are Psalm 90.4 – 'For a thousand years in thy sight *are but* as yesterday when it is past' – and 2 Peter 3.8 – 'be not ignorant of this one thing, that one day *is* with the Lord as a thousand years, and a thousand years as one day'.

[93] See Dennis Dean, 'The Age of the Earth Controversy: Beginnings to Hutton', *Annals of Science* 38 (1981), pp. 437–9. See also Francis C. Haber, *The Age of the World: Moses to Darwin* (Baltimore, 1959).

[94] C. A. Patrides, 'Renaissance Estimates of the Year of Creation', p. 320.

fused also with the rabbinic tradition, ascribed to the school of Elijah, of the world's lasting for three eras of two thousand years each.

John Swan's long discussion of both the six ages and the three eras in *Specvlvm Mundi* exemplifies how embedded these divisions were in considerations of chronology, both of when the world began and, perhaps more crucially, of when it would end. Even though Swan did not accept that the three eras or the six ages could be divided into equal parts, nor that the earth would last six thousand years, he did not deny 'that the world may stand six ages before it endeth; and so the ages, although not the yeares, may be compared to the six dayes of weekly labour: and that the seventh age shall begin at the resurrection . . .'[95]

In his discussion of Renaissance estimates of the year of creation, Patrides lists 107 sixteenth- and seventeenth-century writers who proposed forty-three different dates for the year of creation, ranging from 4103 BCE to 3928 BCE. That there was such variation is hardly surprising. For while it was feasible late in the history of Israel to identify biblical events with extra-biblical data, the Bible itself does not give us a chronology, and where it does so, it is anything but clear. As Hugh Trevor-Roper notes,

The period of the Kings of Israel, from Solomon to the last King Zedekiah, was of particular obscurity, with joint reigns, overlapping reigns, regencies, interregna, all imperfectly defined . . . But if the chronologer could thread his way through that Serbonian bog, the going gradually improved, and ultimately, as he waded ashore on the far side of Noah's Flood, he would be cheered by the beckoning figures of the long-lived pre-diluvian Patriarchs whose regularly recorded ages and generations provided accurate milestones back to the Creation.[96]

Of all the chronologies, the one most influential in seventeenth-century England was that proposed by Archbishop James Ussher in *Annales veteris testamenti* in 1650. It was a work described by William Winstanley ten years later as 'a Work acknowledged by the learnedst Men of this Age for the admirable Method and Worth of it, not to have hitherto been parallel'd by any preceding writers'.[97] Early in the next century, the orientalist Humphrey Prideaux was to describe the *Annals* as 'the exactest and most perfect work of chronology that has been published'.[98] The

---

95 John Swan, *Specvlvm Mundi*, p. 15.
96 Hugh Trevor-Roper, *Catholics, Anglicans and Puritans: Seventeenth Century Essays* (Chicago, 1988), p. 157.
97 William Winstanley, *England's Worthies* (London, 1660), pp. 476–7.
98 H. Prideaux, *The Old and New Testament connected* (London, 1714–18), i.xxv. Quoted by Hugh Trevor-Roper, *Catholics, Anglicans and Puritans: Seventeenth Century Essays*, p. 161.

success of its chronology was assured by its inclusion in the margins of Bishop William Lloyd's Bible in 1701.

Like his predecessor Joseph Scaliger, to whose chronology he was primarily indebted, James Ussher brought an array of linguistic, mathematical, scientific, astronomical, and exegetical skills to his task. The opening words of *The Annals of the World* are in effect the final outcome of his erudition: 'In the beginning God created Heaven and Earth, *Gen.1.v.1.* Which beginning of time, according to our Chronologie, fell upon the entrance of the night preceding the twenty third day of *Octob.* in the year of the Julian Calendar, 710.'[99] And his marginal annotation was 4004.[100] From that date – October 23, 4004 BCE – he proceeded comprehensively to synthesise all biblical and classical knowledge down to the fall of Jerusalem in 70 CE

In spite of all the skills which Ussher brought to the task, he was ideologically driven. For there can be little doubt that all his effort was determined by an acceptance of the six ages, and the desire to site the creation four thousand years before the birth of Christ. The four years remaining, as a result of which the year of creation was given as 4004 BCE, were the consequence of the work of Scaliger. He had shown that, if the story of the slaughter of the innocents were true, Christ could not have been born in the year traditionally assigned. For Herod the Great, who had ordered the slaughter, had died in 4 BCE, and thus Christ must have been born in that or the preceding year. Therefore, the date 4004 BCE was actually, on these calculations, four thousand years before the birth of Christ.

In the Epistle to the Reader in the *Annals*, Ussher made clear how he determined the actual day of creation. He believed that the creation took place in autumn, and he took it that the first day of creation was the first day of the week, namely Sunday. He consulted astronomical tables for the year 4004 BCE to determine which Sunday came closest to the autumnal equinox for that year. And, ignoring the occasions of the stopping of the sun in the time of Joshua and its going back in the time of Hezekiah, he found the Sunday to be October 23.

In choosing the equinoctial period for the time of creation, Ussher was in agreement with the long tradition which saw Paradise created

99 James Ussher, *The Annals of the World* (London, 1658), p. 1.
100 The 'Julian Period' was an innovation of Joseph Scaliger's intended to bring all ancient calendrical systems into one framework and thus into chronological relation with each other within it. See Anthony T. Grafton, 'Joseph Scaliger and Historical Chronology: The Rise and Fall of a Discipline', *History and Theory* 14 (1975), pp. 156–85. See also James Barr, 'Why the World Was Created in 4004 BC: Archbishop Ussher and Biblical Chronology', *Bulletin of the John Rylands University Library* 67 (1985), pp. 575–608.

spatially in a temperate zone, and temporally in a temperate season. Ideally, Paradise was to be found in that place where the days and nights were most even all year round, and to have been created at the time when the length of the light and darkness was most equal.

For some, as we have seen, the prediluvian world saw a perpetual equinox. But for many, the issue of whether the world was created around the vernal or autumnal equinox was a matter of moment. Both dates had a long history. Those who favoured the vernal equinox could point to the Chaldeans, Babylonians, Medes, Persians, Armenians, and Syrians, and cite Eusebius, Ambrose, Theodoret, Bede, Melancthon, and Scaliger (in the first edition). Those who preferred the autumnal period could look to the Jewish tradition and to Jerome, Josephus, and Scaliger (in the second edition).[101]

One simple solution was to speak of an autumnal spring or a vernal autumn. Giovanno Loredano, for example, wrote of Paradise as enriched with a perpetual autumnal spring, in which there was no summer heat or winter cold but only 'temperate gales and odoriferous aires'.[102] Unusually, he admitted to the presence of snow and hail, though they fell harmlessly 'without Frost'.[103] Henry Hare's Paradise had a perpetual autumnal fruitfulness, 'a place having always the Fertility of one Season of the Year, and yet the delightfulness and beauty of the other, ever blest with a rich autumnal Spring'.[104] In *Paradise Lost*, when Eve lays the table for Raphael there appeared upon it 'All Autumn pil'd, though Spring and Autumn here/ Danc'd hand in hand.'[105]

Most opted, in virtually even proportions, for one of the two alternatives. Thomas Milles juxtaposed the day of Adam's 'birth', and the day of Christ's death, deeming it necessary for the second Adam to have brought redemption on the same day of the same week and month as Adam was created.[106] The date of the Annunciation, March 25, was not popular in England, though George Walker opted for the vernal equinox, comparing the beginnings of man with both the Annunciation and the death of Christ in the same month.[107] Thomas Peyton looked to the month of May and an eternal spring.[108] To Samuel Pordage, in 1661, it was a golden age and a perpetual spring.[109]

[101] See John D. North, 'Chronology and the Age of the World', in Wolfgang Yourgrau and Allen D. Breck (eds.), *Cosmology, History, and Theology* (New York, 1977), p. 328.
[102] Giovanno Loredano, *The Life of Adam*, p. 7.   [103] *Ibid.*, p. 8.
[104] Henry Hare, *The Situation of Paradise found out*, p. 12.   [105] John Milton, *Paradise Lost*, 7.394–5.
[106] See Thomas Milles, *The treasurie of auncient and moderne times*, i.6.
[107] See George Walker, *God made visible*, p. 47.
[108] Thomas Peyton, *The glasse of time*, p. 6.
[109] Samuel Pordage, *Mundorum Explicatio*, p. 57.

John Swan provides a good example of the difficulties. It was clearly a matter for him of much uncertainty. In 1653 (according to Patrides), John Swan chose the spring of 4005 BCE as the season of creation in *Calamus Mensurans.*[110] His almanacs for 1657 and 1658 mentioned no season for creation, although he specified the number of years since creation, which gave its time as 4005 BCE. The 1659–61 editions included autumn as the season of creation in the first item of his chronology. But from the 1662 until the final (1684) edition, which was published some thirteen years after his death, spring was included in the title of his almanacs as the season of creation. Why he chose spring is not clear. But in *Specvlvm Mundi* in 1635, he declared himself for the autumnal option. There he had argued that things were created in their perfection rather than in their infancy, which suggested an autumnal creation. And he synchronised the creation with both the Fall of man and the falling leaves, and his restoration through Christ in the spring:

> surely me thinks it is farre more probable that there followed a sad winter for Adam to bewail his horrid fall in, rather then an acceptable and pleasant summer: for do but grant this that Adam fell presently after his creation, and then tell me what time of the yeare was fitter to expresse the time of his fall then autumne.[111]

Two main reasons were offered by those who argued for the season of autumn. The first was coincidence with the Jewish tradition. The second was the need for the flowers to be in full bloom, the fruits in full maturity. The perfect world was one in which food was readily available. Thus, for example, Hugh Broughton in 1612 felt certain that Adam was created at the time the fruits were ripe, which was, he said, at the time of the fall of the leaf. No doubt he was the source of Swan's autumnal argument. September was 'the fittest time', declared Broughton, 'seeing in the course of Nature ther was not fitter time to expresse the nature of Adams fall'.[112] And so, by contrast, Christ's death was in spring. And the same sentiments, in virtually the same words, were expressed by Thomas Hayne in 1640.[113]

Alexander Ross gave his support to autumn, since the Jews then began their year, 'and the fruits of the trees were ripe, and ready to be eaten'.[114] In 1643, the ejected royalist divine Arthur Jackson imagined that the trees were created with the fruit fully ripe upon them, strongly

---

[110] John Swan, *Calamus Mensurans* (London, 1653), i.35–6. Cited by C. A. Patrides, 'Renaissance Estimates of the Year of Creation', p. 319.   [111] John Swan, *Specvlvm Mundi*, p. 35.
[112] Hugh Broughton, *Observations Upon the first ten fathers*, p. 29.
[113] See Thomas Hayne, *The General View of the Holy Scriptures*, p. 24.
[114] Alexander Ross, *An Exposition on the Fovrteene first Chapters of Genesis*, p. 7.

suggesting to him autumnal beginnings.[115] The non-conformist Thomas Allen argued for September, since the fruits then are most perfect 'in their maturity and ripeness . . .'[116] Trees and plants were created in their perfection in autumn, suggested the Presbyterian Joseph Needler in 1655.[117] The noted Hebraist John Lightfoot declared for September 12, 3928 BCE, at nine o'clock in the morning.[118]

Sir Thomas Browne was having none of this. To him, such a question was not worthy of our leisure hours, much less our serious studies. For, he reasoned, if we are talking of the creation of the whole earth, then all four seasons were in existence at the time of creation, autumn above the equator, winter at the North Pole, spring below the equator, summer at the South Pole.[119] He was, of course, half right. And he did go on to admit that if Paradise were in Mesopotamia as is assumed, the question becomes a more reasonable one, yet its answer commensurably more difficult: 'for some contend that it began in the Spring . . . others are altogether for Autumne'.[120] That all the seasons were in place simultaneously was endorsed too by the orientalist John Gregory in 1650. As he put it, 'so soon as the Sun set forth in his Motion, the seasons immediately grew necessarie to several positions of the Sphear, so divided among the parts of the Earth, that all had everie one of these, and each one or other at the same time'.[121] Unlike Browne, however, he opted for a creation in spring in a paradisal Holy Land.

PLEASURES IN PARADISE

And out of the ground made the Lord God to grow every tree that is pleasant to the sight, and good for food.   Genesis 2.9

Cover'd with grasse, more soft then any silke,
The Trees dropt honey, & the Springs gusht milke:
The Flower-fleec't Meadow, & the gorgeous grove,
Which should smell sweetest in their bravery, strove;
No little shrub, but it some Gum let fall,
To make the cleere Ayre aromaticall:

Michael Drayton, *Noahs Floud*

---

[115] See Arthur Jackson, *A Help for the understanding of the Holy Scripture* (London, 1643), i.5.
[116] Thomas Allen, *A Chain of Scripture Chronology* (London, 1659), p. 36.
[117] See Benjamin Needler, *Expository Notes*, pp. 6–7.
[118] See John Lightfoot, *The Works of the Reverend and Learned John Lightfoot D.D.*, i.692.
[119] See Thomas Browne, *Pseudodoxia Epidemica*, 6.2.   [120] *Ibid.*
[121] John Gregory, *Gregorii Opuscula* (London, 1650), p. 147. See also John Dunton (ed.), *The Athenian Gazette*, vol. II, q. 7, no. 18.

Even to the casual reader of Genesis, it was clear that the garden which God had created was both aesthetic and functional. It was both to delight all the senses and to serve all its inhabitants' needs. It was both garden and orchard. To Samuel Pordage.

> No dainty Flower, which art now makes to flourish,
> But then the earth did naturally nourish.
> A constant verdure it retain'd, and then
> With thousand flowers spotted was the green:
> Each tree at one time bore both fruit, and flower;
> Each herb to heal, but not to hurt had power,
> No sharpnesse in the fruit, no naughty smell,
> The worst fruit then, our best now did excel.[122]

But if modern gardens lacked the perfection of the original, they were nevertheless imagined as paradisal. Thus, for example, William Lawson, author of Northern England's first gardening book in 1618, declared, 'When God made man after his own Image, in a perfect state, and would have him represent himselfe in authority, tranquility, and pleasure upon the earth, he placed him in *Paradise*. What was *Paradise*? but a Garden and Orchard of trees and hearbs, full of pleasure? and nothing there but delights.'[123] It was in a garden that our state before the Fall could most easily be recaptured. The Marchioness of Newcastle, Margaret Cavendish, put it simply. 'Where *Gardens* are', she wrote, 'them *Paradise* we call.'[124]

The pleasures of the garden were continually extolled. In his history of flora in 1657, William Coles explained to his readers that when God wanted Adam to partake of perfect happiness, 'he could find none greater under the Sun then to place him in a Garden'.[125] In the preface to *A Treatise of Fruit Trees* in 1653, Ralph Austen informs us that we should listen with our inner senses to the language of trees. We must 'be content', he wrote, 'to stoope to their way and manner of teaching, as the *Egyptians* and others in former times, who were instructed by *Characters* and *Hyeroglyphiques*, by something represented to the eye, *Notions* were conveyed to the understanding. *Dumbe Creatures* speake *virtually* and *convincingly, to the mynde, and Conscience*'.[126] He, for one, had listened carefully. For in his 1676 'Dialogue' between the husbandman and the

---

[122] Samuel Pordage, *Mundorum Explicatio*, p. 58.
[123] William Lawson, *A New Orchard and Garden*, pp. 52–3.
[124] Margaret Cavendish, *Poems and Fancies* (London, 1653), p. 152.
[125] William Coles, *Adam in Eden*, Epistle to the Reader.
[126] Ralph Austen, *A Treatise of Fruit Trees*, Preface.

fruit trees, we are informed by them that the gardens in which they dwell 'are the purest of humane Pleasures, the greatest refreshments of the spirits of man; without which Buildings, and Pallaces, are but grosse handiworkes'.[127] Similar sentiments were expressed by Abraham Cowley in a poem to John Evelyn, 'The Garden':

> When God did Man to his own likeness make,
> As much as Clay, though of the purest kind,
> By the great Potters Art refin'd,
> Could the Divine Impression take:
> He thought it fit to place him, where
> A kind of Heav'n too did appear,
> As far as Earth could such a likeness bear:
> That Man no happiness might want,
> Which Earth to her first Master could afford;
> He did a garden for him plant
> By the quick hand of his Omnipotent Word.
> As the chief Help and Joy of Humane Life,
> He gave him the first Gift, ev'n before a Wife.[128]

The Renaissance garden was intended to re-create in the present that which was now recognised as lost for ever, destroyed in the Deluge, to relocate in one place that which had been originally dispersed from the lost Garden. Some of the splendour of Eden, thought William Hughes, might be regained by 'that lovely, honest and delightful recreation of planting'.[129] In 1700, to Timothy Nourse husbandry was both recreation and re-creation. And he saw it as redeeming the earth from its post-lapsarian curse:

The same spot of Ground, which some Time since was nothing but Heath and Desart, and under the Original Curse of Thorns and Bryers, after a little Labour and Expence, seems restor'd to its Primitive Beauty in the State of Paradise. Curious Groves and Walks, fruitful Fields of Corn and Wine, with Flowry Meadows, and sweet Pastures, well stor'd with all sorts of Cattle for Food and Use, together with all the Advantages and Delights of Water-Currents and Rivolets; as also with infinite variety of Fruit-bearing Trees, of beautiful Flowers, of sweet and fragrant Herbs &. are the familiar and easie Productions of Industry and Ingenuity.[130]

---

[127] Ralph Austen, *A Dialogue* (Oxford, 1676), p. 21. See also Austen, *A Treatise of Fruit Trees*, p. 12.

[128] John Evelyn, *Silva, or a Discourse of Forest-Trees, and the Propagation of Timber* (London, 1706). See also Edward Leigh, *A Systeme or Bodie of Divinitie*, p. 321.

[129] Quoted by Keith Thomas, *Man and the Natural World*, p. 236.

[130] Timothy Nourse, *Campania Foelix, or a Discourse of the Benefits and Improvements of Husbandry* (London, 1700), p. 2.

In a very literal sense, the garden was a book of nature, the reading of which gave insight into the mind of its divine author and a restoration of Adamic wisdom. In the preface to Ralph Austen's *A Treatise of Fruit Trees*, we are informed, 'The *World* is a great *Library*, and *Fruit-trees* are some of the *Bookes* wherein we may read & see plainly the *Attributes of God*, his *Power, Wisdome, Goodnesse*, &c. and be Instructed and taught our duty towards him in many things even from Fruit-trees.'[131]

Thus, gardening could be seen as a religious activity. God himself was, for some, pre-eminently a gardener. The high expectations for gardening, according to Charlotte Otten, sprang from the vision of God 'as the prototype of all gardeners and his Paradise as the archetype for all gardens'.[132] Thus, for example, Walter Blith, at one time a captain in Cromwell's army, saw God as providing a pattern for man in tilling the earth and improving it. In making the world and all the plants, fruits, trees, herbs, and seed for the food of man and beast, 'God was the originall, and first Husbandman . . .'[133] In *The Mystery of Husbandry*, Leonard Meager praised gardening for its antiquity and its proximity to the origin of all things. For, he declared, 'all Excellency appears the most evidently the nearer . . . to the Great Majesty, the Almighty Husbandiser, God himself. . . God was the Original and Pattern of all Husbandry, and First Contriver of the Great Design, to bring that odd Mass, and Chaos of Confusion, unto so vast an improvement . . .'[134] To garden was divine, and therefore to garden was to re-create the divine image.

The religious nature of gardening was reinforced too by the resurrection of Jesus, having taken place in a garden, and by the image of Jesus as the gardener, for Mary Magdalene had so mistaken him on the morning of the Resurrection (John 20.15). The depiction of Christ as the gardener was one of the most common Renaissance images. Thus Charlotte Otten: 'He appears on altars, ivory book covers, in Biblical illustrations, in choirs, stalls, windows; in sculpture, paintings, illuminations, engravings, woodcuts, metalcuts. Sometimes he wears a gardener's cap or cowl, frequently a halo. He is always equipped with a gardener's tool – hoe, spade, shovel, dibble – and sometimes he has a watering can . . . No shame then in being a gardener. Only a reflected glory.'[135]

[131] Ralph Austen, *A Treatise of Fruit Trees*, Preface.
[132] Charlotte F. Otten, *Environ'd with Eternity: God, Poems, and Plants in Sixteenth and Seventeenth Century England* (Lawrence, Kansas, 1985), p. 5.
[133] Walter Blith, *The English improover improved* (London, 1653), p. 3.
[134] Leonard Meager, *The Mystery of husbandry* (London, 1697), pp. 1–2. Quoted in Charlotte Otten, *Environ'd with Eternity*, pp. xiii–xiv.   [135] Charlotte F. Otten, *Environ'd with Eternity*, p. 14.

The pleasures not only of gardens but of the activity of gardening were often extolled. Amongst all activites, claimed Lancelot Andrewes, 'the exercise of dressing and keeping a Garden or Orchard, is most pleasant and agreeable to our nature . . .'[136] John Evelyn believed it was the purest of human pleasures; and most innocent too. He quoted Abraham Cowley:

> Happy the Man, whom from Ambition freed,
> A little Garden, little Field does feed,
> The Field gives frugal Nature what's required;
> The Garden, what's luxuriously desir'd:
> The specious Evils of an anxious Life,
> He leaves to Fools to be their endless Strife.[137]

In a letter to Thomas Browne in 1658, he thought gardening might provide an ideal around which the defeated royalists could rally, 'whilst brutish and ambitious persons seeke themselues in the ruines of our miserable yet dearest country'.[138] A case, literally, of turning spears into pruning hooks.

Like the original garden, the Renaissance botanic garden was intended to be an encyclopedia. The Bible was read as suggesting the encyclopedic nature of Eden: every tree, every herb-bearing seed (Genesis 1.29) was present there. In Eden, Joseph Hall, Bishop of Exeter, explained, 'No herb, no flower, no tree was wanting there, that might be for ornament or use, or for sent, or for taste.'[139] To John Pettus, the Garden of Eden was '*a place* which contains all sorts of plants and Flowers from the Hysop to the Cedar, from the least to the greatest, as the Seminary and Nursery for all future Plantations'.[140] Sir Hugh Plat's encyclopedic description of all the English fruits and flowers was simply titled *The Garden of Eden*. John Parkinson's gardening encyclopedia was called *Paradisi in sole*. Its frontispiece shows an encyclopedic Eden, packed with trees, shrubs, and flowers of local and exotic varieties, and is captioned 'A Garden of all sorts of pleasant flowers which our English ayre will permit to be noursed vp: with A Kitchen garden of all manner of herbes, rootes, & fruites for meate or sauce . . . and An Orchard of all sorte of fruitbearing Trees and Shrubbes fit for our Land together'. In the *Kalendarium Hortense*, John Evelyn maintained

---

[136] Lancelot Andrewes, *Apospasmatia Sacra*, p. 179.
[137] John Evelyn, *A Discourse of Sallets* (London, 1706), p. 202.
[138] Quoted by Maren-Sofie Rostwig, *The Happy Man: Studies in the Metamorphoses of a Classical Ideal 1600–1700* (Oxford, 1954), p. 179.
[139] Joseph Hall, *The Works*, i.777.   [140] John Pettus, *Volatiles from the History of Adam and Eve*, p. 26.

that gardens should be made, as far as possible, to resemble the Garden of Eden.[141]

John Parkinson's Paradise was one which, although it included birds, excluded animals. And although there is no sense in the frontispiece to his *Paradisi in sole* that his Garden of Eden was an enclosed one, it is redolent of the tradition which saw the Garden of Eden as enclosed by walls, animals completely excluded. The walls of Thomas Peyton's garden of Eden 'were all of Iasper built . . . like a quadrangle seated on a hill', around which after the Fall Adam and Eve groped, 'Repenting sore, lamenting much their *Sin*,/ Longing but once to come againe within'.[142] An illustration in G. B. Andreini's *L'adamo, sacra representatione* in 1617 showed Adam naming the animals outside the entrance to an apparently enclosed garden.[143]

There is no sense in the Genesis text of the Garden as an enclosed one. The source of the image of the Garden of Eden as surrounded by walls must be sought elsewhere, notably in the medieval identifications of the Virgin Mary with Paradise on the one hand and on the other with the enclosed garden of the Song of Solomon: 'A garden inclosed *is* my sister, *my* spouse; a spring shut up, a fountain sealed' (Song of Solomon 4.12).

Such identifications were, not surprisingly, rare in a Protestant England. But they were occasionally suggested. The illustration to the title page of Ralph Austen's *Spiritual Use of an Orchard* in 1657 depicted a rectangular garden, divided into four quarters, enclosed by walls, and encircled by the text of Song of Solomon 4.12–13. And it was elaborated in the Jesuit Henry Hawkins' *Partheneia Sacra* in 1633. In this work, Mary the mother of Jesus is portrayed as a garden. His garden is clearly Edenic: 'by name of HORTVS CONCLUSUS; wherein are al things mysteriously and spiritually to be found, which euen beautifyes the fairest Gardens: being a place, no less delicious in winter, then in Summer, in Autumne, then in the Spring; and wherein is no season to be season, but a perpetual Spring; wher are al kinds of delights in great abundance . . .'[144]

The frontispiece to the work shows the garden divided geometrically into segments, enclosed by a circular wall, with a fountain in the middle, a palm tree, and a fruit tree. The palm tree, or more specifically the date palm, was a common feature of Paradise. It can be seen in the frontispiece of Parkinson's *Paradisi in sole*. And it appears in the right middle-

[141] John Evelyn, *Kalendarium Hortense: or, The Gardner's Almanac* (London, 1664), Introduction.
[142] Thomas Peyton, *The glasse of time*, pp. 8, 50.
[143] See John Prest, *The Garden of Eden*, p. 12.
[144] Henry Hawkins, *Partheneia Sacra, or the mysterious garden of the sacred Parthenes* (London, 1633), p. 11.

ground of 'the Creation of Adam and Eve' in du Bartas' *Les Oeuvres* in 1614.[145] In all of these, it represented the Tree of Life, since it was the only tree assumed to have a sex, a belief that went back to the days of Theophrastus, the keeper of Aristotle's garden.[146] The palm tree is also mentioned along with the apple tree in *Song of Solomon*, 7.8. As the belief that the Tree of the Knowledge of Good and Evil was an apple tree is related to its mention in this text, so it can be conjectured that the notion that the Tree of Life was a palm may be derived from this text. William Basse, for example, cited Pliny on male and female palms, 'the loue between whom is such, that if the female be farre disioyned from the masculine it becomes barren and without fruite: if the male haue his bowes broken by any accident, the female becomes desolate and droopes like a widdow'.[147] John Jonston in 1657 spoke of the desire of female for male palm trees, 'so about the Males, many females will grow enclining toward them and wagging their boughes'.[148] To Henry Hawkins, they were like the turtle-doves among trees, for they 'match and payre togeather as they, and are as loyal as they, and ful as chast as they.'[149] The male and female palms, he continued, 'are the hieroglyphicks of Nuptials' between husband and wife, Christ and his mother.[150] The Eden of du Bartas contained

> loving *Palmes*, whose lustie females (willing
> Their marrow-boyling loves to be fulfilling;
> And reach their husband trees on th'other banckes,)
> Bow their stiffe backes, and serve for passing planckes.[151]

But, except for the Palm, the Garden of Eden as an enclosed garden with the animals excluded was an asexual realm, an idea that appealed to those who believed that, had we not been expelled from the Garden, we, like the plants, would have reproduced ourselves in a non-sexual way. Jean-Baptiste van Helmont reflected the extreme view. God excluded animals from Paradise lest 'man should behold the bruitish copulation of the Sexes, whom he wished to live in the purity of innocency'.[152]

The image of the enclosed Paradise as an asexual one accounts too,

---

[145] See Arnold Williams, *The Common Expositor*, illustration pp. 146–7.

[146] See John Prest, *The Garden of Eden*, p. 81.   [147] [William Basse], *A Helpe to Discovrse*, p. 33.

[148] John Jonston, *An History of the Wonderful Things of Nature*, p. 150. See also William Westmacott, *Historia Vegetabilium Sacra*, pp. 140–1.

[149] Henry Hawkins, *Partheneia Sacra*, p. 154.   [150] See *ibid.*, p. 156.

[151] Susan Snyder (ed.), *The Divine Weeks and Works*, i.331.

[152] J.-B. van Helmont, *Van Helmont's Workes* (London, 1664), p. 161.

ironically perhaps for us, for the presence within it of the birds and the bees. The bee, it was supposed, lacked procreative ability. Virgil in the second half of his fourth *Georgic* put forward the idea that bees were spontaneously generated from the decaying carcases of oxen, as did Ovid, a view which Pliny repeated in *Natural History*.[153] It was a belief accepted by Thomas Browne.[154] Thus, Henry Hawkins allowed the 'busie BEE' to gather the dew as it fell from heaven. John Jonston praised bees for their chastity: 'they are so chaste, that they will sting those that smell of copulation, and they stall themselves in Virgins Sepulchres'.[155] For Thomas Peyton, honeycomb was part of the diet of the first couple.[156]

Birds too were acceptable in the ideal garden and orchard. For, as John Prest reminds us, that they had two legs like us and that they flew like the angels was interpreted in the Middle Ages to mean 'that birds had not participated in the original revolt against God, and that as a reward they had been permitted to live in the air, closer to the heavenly paradise than other animals and even than man himself'.[157] Henry Hawkins had hens and doves in his enclosed garden. The Edens of du Bartas and Milton were full of birds. John Evelyn expected an orchard to contain 'a constant aviary of sweet Singers'.[158] Parrots too made their appearance in illustrations of Eden. They are the only birds which appear in Parkinson's illustrated Eden. And although both birds and animals are present in Claude Paradin's Eden, the parrot is the only avian observer of the creation of man in his illustrations to the whole Bible. They symbolised its temperate clime. And their ability to mimic human speech was seen as the vestige of a time when all animals had the power of speech.

The Garden of Eden was encyclopedic in containing the flora which were subsequently dispersed to the four corners of the earth, often symbolised in the Renaissance garden by its division into four quarters. But it reflected too the Chain of Being, containing the range of plants from those that overlapped with the animal realm to those that overlapped with stones. In the seventeenth century, the former category was most likely to be represented by the so-called Scythian lamb. Its status was liminal, for it had the attributes of both animal and vegetable. Du

---

[153] See P. Ansell Robin, *Animal Lore in English Literature* (London, 1932), pp. 24–5.
[154] See Thomas Browne, *Pseudodoxia Epidemica*, 2.6.
[155] John Jonston, *An History of the Wonderful Things of Nature*, p. 245.
[156] See Thomas Peyton, *The glasse of time*, p. 32.   [157] John Prest, *The Garden of Eden*, p. 84.
[158] Quoted *ibid.*, p. 84.

Bartas imagined the lamb still existing in Scythia to have been present in Eden:

> Of slender seedes, and with greene fodder fed,
> Although their bodies, noses, mouthes, and eyes,
> Of New-yeand [*sic*] lambes have full the forme and guise,
> And should be verie lambes, save that for foote,
> Within the ground they fixe a living roote,
> Which at their navel growes, and dies that day
> That they have brouz'd the neighbour grasse away.
> O wondrous vertue of God onely Good!
> The beast hath roote, the plant hath flesh and bloud.[159]

It had a central position in the illustration to Parkinson's *Paradisi in sole*, and the description of it in John Jonston's *History of the Wonderful Things of Nature* in 1657[160] was probably derived from the long account which John Parkinson gave of it in *Theatrum Botanicum* in 1640.[161] Thomas Browne reported that a great fuss had been made of the strange vegetable lamb of Tartary, though he suspected it was no more than the appearance of the shape of a lamb in the plant or seed.[162] But it was to become a matter of scientific interest to the Royal Society. In 1666, Thomas Birch informs us, Sir Thomas de Vaux produced some papers read to the Society, one of which contained 'a relation of a furred robe, made of the skin of the Tartarian boramez, supposed to be a plant animal, which robe was said . . . to be kept in the library at Oxford, to which it was given by Sir Richard Lea, ambassador in Russia in the reign of Queen Elizabeth'.[163] Christopher Wren, Birch tells us, was one who, having heard of the robe, wished to view it upon his return to Oxford. In 1668, Sir Hans Sloane exhibited an object 'commonly, but falsely, in India, called '"the Tartarian Lamb"', which he clearly recognised to be only a vegetable.[164]

[159] Susan Snyder (ed.), *The Divine Weeks and Works*, i.332.
[160] See John Jonston, *An History of the Wonderful Things of Nature*, p. 131.
[161] See John Parkinson, *Theatrum Botanicum, The Theater of Plantes* (London, 1640), p. 1618.
[162] See Thomas Browne, *Pseudodoxia Epidemica*, 3.28.
[163] Thomas Birch, *The History of the Royal Society of London* (London, 1756), ii.110. The *OED* refers to the 'Barometz' as 'A spurious natural-history specimen, consisting of the creeping root-stock and frond stalks of a woolly fern (Cibotium barometz) turned upside down'.
[164] Quoted in Roy Vickery, *A Dictionary of Plant-Lore* (Oxford, 1995), p. 380. I am indebted to Roy Vickery for correspondence on the Mongolian lamb. The British Museum of Natural History still retains a Mongolian lamb which was shown some years ago in an exhibition entitled *Fake: The Art of Deception*. The existing lamb is not, according to Roy Vickery, related to those shown in the seventeenth century, but beyond this nothing is known of its origins. See also Peter Costello, *The Magic Zoo: The Natural History of Fabulous Animals* (London, 1979), pp. 148–58.

SUBDUING THE EARTH

And God blessed them, and said unto them, Be fruitful and
multiply, and replenish the earth, and subdue it.   Genesis 1.28

And the Lord God took the man, and put him into the garden of
Eden to dress it and to keep it.   Genesis 2.15

The most obvious features of sixteenth- and seventeenth-century gardens were their formality and regularity. Nature was to be tamed, the
earth to be subdued. Our British gardeners, declared Joseph Addison in
1712, 'instead of humouring Nature, love to deviate from it as much as
possible. Our Trees rise in Cones, Globes and Pyramids. We see the
Marks of the Scissars upon every Plant and Bush.'[165] The formal garden
was thus a symbol of the responsibility which, it was believed, the Book
of Genesis had laid upon us, to cultivate and to transform the wilderness,
both at home and abroad.

The imposition of human order on disordered nature was the conquest of nature by culture. Geometricality was seen as intrinsically more
beautiful than irregularity. Only those as stupid as the most base of
beasts, declared Henry More, would not agree that a cube, a tetrahed-
ron, or an icosahedron was more beautiful 'than any rude broken stone
lying in the field or highways'.[166]

But the ideal of a completely ordered world was a vision of the future
embedded in nostalgia for the past. 'The world had been a Wilderness',
declared Thomas Traherne, 'overgrown with Thorns, and Wild Beasts,
and Serpents: Which now by the Labour of many hands, is reduced to
the Beauty and Order of *Eden*.'[167] Thus, an ordered world was also a
return to the order which existed before the Fall. Culture triumphant
was nature redeemed and restored. And the geometric garden, in its
complex simplicity, manifested the image of God in man, his rationality.
The Garden of Eden was often imagined on the model of the
seventeenth-century geometric garden. Joseph Warton, for example,
tells us that the prints representing Paradise which accompanied
Giovanni Battista Andreini's *L'Adamo* in 1617 are 'full of clipt hedges,
square parterres, strait walks, trees uniformly lopt, regular knots and

---

[165] *Spectator*, no. 414 (June 25, 1712), p. 102.
[166] Henry More, *An Antidote against Atheism*, 2nd edn (London, 1655), p. 93. Quoted by Keith
Thomas, *Man and the Natural World*, p. 257.
[167] Thomas Traherne, *Christian Ethicks: or Divine Morality* (London, 1675), p. 103. Quoted by Peter
Harrison, *The Bible, Protestantism, and the Rise of Science*, p. 248.

carpets of flowers, groves nodding at groves, marble foundations, and water-works'.[168] The Eden of du Bartas was in the classic late-sixteenth-century fashion of love-knots, triangles, lozenges, intricate meanders, a maze.[169] Thomas Browne suggested that the trees had been planted in Eden in quincunx, that is in the form of a series of squares or rectangles, with a tree at the centre of each. George Herbert, in his poem *Paradise*, wrote,

> I Blesse thee, Lord, because I GROW?
> Among thy trees, which in a ROW
> To thee both fruit and order   ow. [170]

The Garden of Eden was never envisaged as a holiday resort. To be sure, there were some who in the seventeenth century envisaged the garden as primarily a place to develop the contemplative life.[171] But most saw it as involving the active life. For Adam was to work in the garden, 'to dress it and keep it'. On the basis of this text, John Donne preached for the active and against the contemplative life. Man, he declared, 'is not sent into this world to live out of it, but to live in it; Adam was not put into Paradise, only in that Paradise to contemplate the future Paradise, but to dress and keep the present'.[172] Though God planted a garden full of all necessary fruits for use and delight, wrote the puritan John White, 'yet he appointed man some labour about it, to keep and dresse it'.[173] While other creatures spent their day idly unemployed, man, declared Milton, 'hath his daily work of body or mind/ Appointed, which declares his Dignity,/ And the regard of Heav'n on all his ways.'[174]

Protestant moralists drew from the injunction to dress and keep the garden homilies on the dangers of idleness. It provided the biblical ground for the Protestant work ethic. On the basis of Genesis 2.15, John Calvin concluded, 'men were created to employ themselves in some work, and not to lie down in inactivity and idleness ... since, however, God ordained that man should be exercised in the culture of the ground, he condemned in his person, all indolent repose'.[175] In 1617, John Salkeld turned the text against the idle rich: 'euen in that place', he

---

[168] Joseph Warton, *An Essay on the Genius and Writings of Pope* (London, 1782), ii.184.
[169] See Susan Snyder (ed.), *The Divine Weeks and Works*, i.330.
[170] See John Prest, *The Garden of Eden*, p. 90.
[171] See Maren-Sofie Rostvig, *The Happy Man*, ch. 4.
[172] Henry Alford, *The Works* (1839), i.372. Quoted by Arnold Williams, *The Common Expositor*, p. 110.
[173] John White, *A Commentary Upon the Three First Chapters of Genesis*, i.114.
[174] *Paradise Lost*, 4.618–20.
[175] John King (trans.), *Commentaries on the First Book of Moses*, p. 125.

exclaimed, 'where there was no neede of labour God would not haue man idle: not an ill item for our lazie gallants, who think their gentilitie to consist in idlenes, and a point of honour to liue of other mens labour . . .'[176] To John Yates in 1622, idleness was the original sin: 'happinesse never consisted in doing nothing. Idlenesse neither gets, nor saues . . . Houres haue euer had wings, to flie vp to heaven, to the author of time, to carry newes of our vsage. *Eue* could not long keepe chat with the Serpent, but God had notice of it, and for such idlenesse turns her out of Paradise.'[177] George Walker hoped that the idea of Edenic labour might 'justly provoke and stirre us up to Loath and abhorre idlenesse, sloth, and laziness, as speciall marks and ignominious brands of naughty persons . . .'[178] If Adam had not been intended to live idly in Paradise, argued Andrew Willet, 'much lesse should we spend our daies now in doing of nothing'.[179]

Unlike work in a post-lapsarian world, labour in the Garden of Eden was pleasurable. Gervase Babington, for example, pointed out that labour then differed 'much from our labour nowe, for that was an iniunction inferring no greefe, and this is a paine deserued by sinne'.[180] It was more for delight than gain, explained du Bartas, 'a plesant exercise,/ A labour like't'.[181] Adam worked with pleasure, wrote Alexander Ross, 'to keepe himself from idlenesse',[182] an exercise rendered more easy, according to John White, by his greater physical and intellectual abilities.[183]

For many in the seventeenth century, as for many today, gardening was a joyful activity, one in which, as Andrew Willet remarked, 'many doe euen now take a delight, and hold it rather to be a recreation, then any wearines vnto them'.[184] But it also carried ideological weight. For to garden was to place oneself, metaphorically at least, in that state of grace which Adam enjoyed before the Fall. Thus, the vegetarian ascetic Roger Crab when digging in his garden 'saw into the Paradise of God from whence my father Adam was cast forth'.[185] William Coles aimed to bring his readers to see the world once again through the eyes of Adam:

---

[176] John Salkeld, *A Treatise of Paradise*, pp. 143–4.   [177] John Yates, *A Modell of Divinitie*, p. 159.
[178] George Walker, *God made visible*, p. 248.   [179] Andrew Willet, *Hexapla in Genesin*, p. 33.
[180] Gervase Babington, *Certaine Plaine, briefe, and comfortable Notes vpon euerie Chapter of Genesis*, sig. c.2.r.
[181] Susan Snyder (ed.), *The Divine Weeks and Works*, i.325.
[182] Alexander Ross, *An Exposition on the Fovrteene first Chapters of Genesis*, p. 45.
[183] See John White, *A Commentary Upon the Three First Chapters of Genesis*, ii.54–5.
[184] Andrew Willet, *Hexapla in Genesin*, p. 33.
[185] Quoted by Keith Thomas, *Man and the Natural World*, p. 237.

To make thee truly sensible of that happinesse which Mankind lost by the Fall of *Adam*, is to render thee an exact *Botanick*, by the knowledge of so incomparable a Science as the Art of *Simpling*, to re-instate thee into another *Eden*, or, *A Garden of Paradise*: For if we rightly consider the Addresses of this Divine Contemplation of Herbs and Plants . . . we cannot but even from these inferiour things arrive somewhat near unto a heavenly Contentment; a contentment indeed next to that Blessednesse of Fruition, which is onely in the other World . . . [186]

Adam was the archetypal gardener. Adam, wrote Moses Cooke,

> Was the first Gard'ner of the World, and ye
> Are the green shoots of Him th' Original Tree;
> Encourage then this innocent old Trade,
> Ye Noble Souls that were from Adam made;
> So shall the Gard'ners labour better bring
> To his Countrey Profit, Pleasure to his King.[187]

Adam was not the first chemist, as the alchemists vainly argue, declared William Westmacott. Rather he was the first botanist, and his work was 'the Art of Simpling in the Garden of Eden'.[188] Husbandry is the work of man, claimed George Hughes in 1672.[189] John Pettus saw Adam's task as creating a 'Diversity of Species by Transplantations, Ingraftings, Incoculatings, and other various Cultivations . . .'[190] The Adam of Pettus is best imagined with a pair of secateurs. The Adam of Milton, whose main task is to lop, prune, and clear the wild Edenic plateau, as Joseph Duncan reminds us, is best envisaged with a chainsaw.[191] But it is the image of Adam with a spade which dominates. As Charlotte Otten puts it,

From the woodcuts of the fifteenth century in the 'life of Christ', to the mosaics of San Marco in Venice; from the gilded sculpture of Ghiberti's doors of the Baptistery of Florence, to the spandrel carvings in the Chapter House of Salisbury Cathedral; from the four illustrated Bibles from Tours, to the Sienese triptych where Adam holds a mattock at the foot of the Cross . . . and hundreds of other instances – came the familiarity and the easy reference in terracultural books to 'our Grandsire *Adam*, who is commonly pictured with a spade in his hand'.[192]

---

[186] William Coles, *Adam in Eden*, Epistle to the Reader.
[187] Moses Cooke, *The Manner of raising, ordering, and improving forrest-trees* (London, 1678), p. 52. Quoted by Charlotte Otten, *Environ'd with Eternity*, p. 55. I am particularly indebted to Otten for this discussion.
[188] William Westmacott, *Historia Vegetabilium Sacra*, Preface.
[189] See George Hughes, *An Analytical Exposition of the Whole first Book of Moses, called Genesis*, p. 19.
[190] John Pettus, *Volatiles from the History of Adam and Eve*, p. 44.
[191] See Joseph E. Duncan, *Milton's Earthly Paradise*, p. 159.
[192] Charlotte F. Otten, *Environ'd with Eternity*, p. 56. The quotation included is from Leonard Meager, *The Compleat English Gardener* (London, 1710), p. 156.

KINGS, LEVELLERS, AND DIGGERS

When Adam delved and Eve span,
Who was then the gentleman?　　　　　John Ball

Ornitho-logie: or, The Speech of Birds was a pro-monarchist allegory written by the royalist preacher Thomas Fuller and published two years after the restoration of the monarchy and one year after his death. The birds, having dismissed the eagle, gather together to elect a new principal to command them. There were many against the election who believed in the equality of all and denied the right of any to rule over another: 'These held that all were free by nature; and that it was an assault on the Liberty of man, and a *rape* offered to his naturall freedom; that any should assume authority over another. These maintained (what certainly was not onely a paradox, but a flat falshood) that nature at the first Creation made all the world a flat levell and *Champion* . . . that all men were naturally equal; and it was the inundation and influx of humane *Tyranny* which made this disparity between them.'[193] But for the author, a society without hierarchy, and one with only fully autonomous individuals, was an impossibility. It was necessary that some one should rule. In spite of his size, the largest bird the ostrich was rejected; the parrot too, in spite of his capacity to imitate human speech, was not elected. The hawk was. Thus, even the birds located their discussion of the ideal society in the context of the original state of innocence.

John Ball was the leader of the unsuccessful English revolution of 1381. His ideas were summarised in the so-called Blackheath sermon, the text of which was the couplet above. It was a text much favoured by preachers in the ferment of the 1640s.[194] To those who asked it, the answer was clear: there were then no gentlemen, for all were of the same level. Others would have agreed with John Cleveland that it was a 'levelling lewd text'.[195]

The question it asked was actually unanswerable. But the asking of it points to the centrality of the Adamic myth in establishing the ideal structure of society. The text itself can give no indication of how society was structured before the Fall (for there were only Adam and Eve), or of how it was after the Fall. On this most important of issues, the silence of the text was deafening. The interpreters were not deterred. And readings therefore were even more discordant than usual.

---

[193] T. Fuller, *Ornitho-logie: or, The Speech of Birds* (London, 1662), pp. 6–7.
[194] So Christopher Hill, *The World Turned Upside Down*, p. 28.
[195] See Christopher Hill, *The Collected Essays of Christopher Hill*, ii.100.

For some, hierarchy in society was the natural order of things, but an order voluntarily accepted in a sinless world. In 1617, for example, John Salkeld cited Augustine to the effect that, in a world without sin, there would have been no subjection of men one to another. But he disagreed. Subjection and subordination were part of nature: 'Questionlesse there should haue beene a kinde of order, subiection and subordination, of children, inferiours, and subiects, to their parents, superiours, and politicall governours: not by way of an imperious command and absolute authoritie, but by a voluntary and sweet subiection, flowing from nature, and confirmed by grace.'[196] Even the angels had a hierarchy, he suggested. Similarly, for Alexander Ross in 1626, where there was no social and political hierarchy there could be no order. But the subjection of man to man would have been 'Voluntary, pleasant ciuill, not seruile, and by constraint'.[197] Such a world would, no doubt, have been paradisal to those who ruled, if not so obviously so for those who were ruled.

The more common Protestant position was the Augustinian one that in a world without sin government would, have been unnecessary and that therefore the ideal state of nature was one of equality between all. In a sinful world however, an hierarchical and coercive society was a necessity. Luther put it simply: 'And as to civil government (*politia*); before sin there was none; nor was it needed . . . There would then have been no ravisher, no murderer, no thief, no slanderer, no liar. And therefore, what need would there have been of civil government.'[198] And while the Presbyterian Benjamin Needler believed that the authoritative power of a man over his wife and children was natural, no man would have had power over another man had he not fallen.[199]

For the conservative, sin was here to stay, and so was civil government. Social inequality was its inevitable and necessary accompaniment; sin supported the status quo. In the words of Isaac Barrow, 'Inequality and private interest in things . . . were the by-blows of our Fall; sin introduced these degrees and distances, it devised the names of rich and poor; it begot these ingrossings and inclosures of things; it forged those two pestilent words, *meum* and *tuum*, which have engendered so much

---

[196] John Salkeld, *A Treatise of Paradise*, p. 127.
[197] Alexander Ross, *An Exposition on the Fovrteene first Chapters of Genesis*, p. 25. See also John Weemse, *The Portraiture of the Image of God in Man*, p. 278.
[198] Henry Cole (trans.), *The Creation: A Commentary by Martin Luther*, p. 142. See also Henry Parker, *Jus Populi* (London, 1644), p. 13.
[199] See Benjamin Needler, *Expository Notes*, p. 13.

strife among men.'[200] Sin even provided a justification for slavery. To the Calvinist William Perkins, slavery was 'indeed against the law of entire nature as it was before the Fall; but against the law of corrupted nature since the Fall, it is not'.[201]

One consequence of the belief that had sin not entered the world all men would have been equal was that all property would have been held in common. Private property was a consequence of sin, and the defence of it against wicked men a central task of government. 'If you take away the law', wrote John Pym in 1641, 'all things will fall into a confusion, every man will become a law unto himself, which in the depraved condition of human nature must needs produce many great enormities'.[202] Implicit in this was the assumption that political authority was derived from and imbedded in property ownership. It was an assumption against which John Locke argued in the first of his *Two Treatises of Government* in 1689. Locke read Genesis 1.28–9, as conferring proprietorial rights over all things not upon Adam and his heirs but upon all men: 'it is a confirmation of the original community of all things amongst the sons of men . . .'[203] And it entailed, as a natural right, the right of all men to subsistence. Man, he wrote, 'had a right to the use of the creatures, by the will and grant of God . . . And thus man's property in the creatures, was founded upon the right he had, to make use of those things, that were necessary or useful to his being.'[204] It was a right which survived the Fall, and it was, for Locke, the presupposition of any theory of the relation of property and politics.

In *Two Treatises*, Locke was directing his attack at Sir Robert Filmer's *Patriarcha: or, The Natural Right of Kings*, a work probably written around 1630, though first published in 1680. This work endorsed the view that God gave the world as private property to Adam and his descendants, notably the monarchs. It drew on the more general image of Adam as a king. Thomas Hayne, for example, described Adam as 'both King and Father of all the Earth . . .' and 'the statliest King that ever should be', a phraseology he had derived from Hugh Broughton.[205] Samuel

---

[200] Isaac Barrow, *The Duty and Reward of Bounty to the Poor* (London, 1671), pp. 120–2. Quoted by Christopher Hill, *The World Turned Upside Down*, pp. 283–4.

[201] William Perkins, *Works*, iii.698. Quoted by Christopher Hill, *The World Turned Upside Down*, p. 125.

[202] J. Rushworth, *Trial of Stafford* (1680), p. 662. Quoted by Christopher Hill, *The World Turned Upside Down*, p. 126.

[203] John Locke, *Two Treatises of Government* (London, 1993), I.4.40.   [204] *Ibid.*, I.9.86.

[205] Thomas Hayne, *The General View of Scripture*, pp. 15, 17. See also Hugh Broughton, *Observations Upon the first ten fathers*, p. 20.

Pordage in 1661 wrote of Adam as 'King, sole Prince, and Lord of all the Earth . . .'[206] As Adam was king, so was the king Adam. Thus, to Thomas Peyton in 1620, James I was 'A royall King deriued from the race,/ Of *Edens* Monarch in her greatest grace,/ Within whose face true Maiesty doth shine'.[207] If the blood of Charles I were spilt, the royalist Bishop of Worcester, John Gauden, exclaimed in *The Religious and Loyal Protestation* in 1648, it would cry out 'as the blood of *Adam* would have done if *Cain* had slaine him being his father, instead of *Abel* his brother'.[208] In his diary for May 1678, John Evelyn reported having heard a sermon which argued for the monarchical over all other systems of government, '& that from *Adam* (to whom God had given the *Empire* of all things & Persons) that it seemed to be not onely of divine, but most natural institution'.[209] And on January 30, 1694, the anniversary of the death of Charles I, he heard a young man preach on 'the Excellency of Kingly Government above all other, deriving it from Adam, The Patriarchs, God himselfe'.[210]

During the seventeenth century, the justification for political organisation was found in Adamic patriarchy. 'Humankind, and by consequence, all Societies and Families', wrote Richard Cumberland, friend of Samuel Pepys and latterly Bishop of Peterborough, 'sprang from the matrimonial Union of one *Man* with one *Woman*. And, consequently, all *Civil Government* is originally laid out in *a natural Parental Authority*.'[211] In 1606, the English bishops accepted John Overall's derivation of political and ecclesiastical power from Adam as head of his family. It is not to be doubted, he declared, 'but that, first Adam, for his time, and afterwards the heads of every family of the faithful, were not only civil governors over their kindred, but likewise had the power and execution of the priests office . . .'[212]

The issue became a matter of enormous moment in the 1640s. John Maxwell, chaplain to Charles I, in 1644 in *Sacro-Sancta Regum Majestas* argued against any suggestion that the king derived power from the people by their consent. Monarchy was fixed by God in the time before the Fall. 'Can we be so stupid', he asked, 'as to acknowledge the dominion

[206] Samuel Pordage, *Mundorum Explicatio*, p. 56.   [207] Thomas Peyton, *The glasse of time*, p. 60.
[208] John Gauden, *The Religious and Loyal Protestation of John Gauden* (London, 1648), p. 8.
[209] E. S. de Beer (ed.), *The Diary of John Evelyn* (London, 1959), p. 649.   [210] *Ibid.*, p. 976.
[211] Richard Cumberland, *De Legibus Naturae* (London, 1672), 6.4. Quoted by James Slotkin, *Readings in Early Anthropology*, p. 158.
[212] John Overall, *The Convocation Book of MDCVI. Commonly called Bishop Overall's Convocation Book* (Oxford, 1844). And see Joseph E. Duncan, *Milton's Earthly Paradise*, pp. 168–72.

over all creatures below, is given to man immediately by God, and to deny that the most noble and excellent Government, by which man hath Power and Empire over men is not from God ... but by the Compact and Contract, the Composition and Constitution of men?'[213] The royalist divine Henry Hammond, reputed by Charles I to be the worst orator he had ever heard, rose nonetheless to his defence. He believed it likely that, had Adam remained in an unfallen state, civil life would still have developed. But, in the fallen state, God designed and appointed government, refusing to all men that freedom 'which is the supposed foundation of that doctrine, which places *supreme power in the People*'.[214]

The most eloquent justification of monarchy on the grounds of Adamic patriarchy was that of Robert Filmer. According to him, Adam, and the patriarchs had by right of fatherhood royal authority over their children. And this authority was given to them by God. 'The first Father', wrote Filmer, 'had not only simply power, but power monarchical, as he was a Father immediately from God. For by the appointment of God, as soon as Adam was created he was monarch of the world, though he had no subjects.'[215] The lordship of Adam, he maintained, was 'as large and ample as the Absolutest Dominion of any Monarch which hath been since the Creation'.[216] On the analogy of fatherhood therefore, subjects had no more right to choose a ruler than sons to choose a father.

Opposed to the arguments for monarchy as an Adamic inheritance were those who saw political authority as the consequence of a social contract. Thomas Hobbes, for example, saw political power as the consequence of the willingness of the many to cede to one man or an assembly of men authority over them. In 1643, the political writer Philip Hunton argued, on the basis of God's command in Genesis 3.1, that Adam should rule over his wife and that government was divinely ordained, but that its nature was an open question. It was a matter, he argued, for men to choose, though he himself opted for a limited monarchy in which rule was shared by it, the aristocracy, and the people.[217]

[213] John Maxwell, *Sacro-Sancta Regum Majestas: or the Sacred and Royal Prerogative of Christian Kings* (London, 1680), p. 72.

[214] Henry Hammond, *To the Right Honourable, the Lord Fairfax ... The Humble Address* (London, 1649), p. 9.

[215] Peter Laslett (ed.), *Patriarcha and Other Political Works of Sir Robert Filmer* (Oxford, 1949), p. 289.

[216] Robert Filmer, *Patriarcha: or, The Natural Power of Kings* (London, 1680), p. 13.

[217] See Philip Hunton, *Treatise of Monarchy* (London 1680), pp. 2–3. The work was condemned by the University of Oxford in 1683 and publicly burnt. The Oxford decree was itself put to the torch in 1710 by order of the House of Lords.

Among the anti-royalists, John Selden used the idea of the social contract against the king. 'A King is a thing', he declared, 'men have made for their owne sakes for quietness sake.'[218] In 1647, John Lilburne, then imprisoned in the Tower of London by the Lords, appealed like many a Leveller to reason, the Magna Carta, and English history in defence of a social-contract theory of government.[219] Government, according to John Milton, unnecessary before the Fall, was the consequence of a contract made between fallen men. Robert Filmer had opened *Patriarcha* by declaring the natural freedom of mankind a plausible and dangerous opinion. Milton probably had him in his sights:

No man who knows aught, can be so stupid to deny that all men naturally were born free, being the image and resemblance of God himself, and were by privilege above all the creatures, born to command and not to obey: and that they liv'd so. Till from the root of *Adams* trangression, falling among themselves to doe wrong and violence . . . they agreed by common league to bind each other from mutual injury, and joyntly to defend themselves against any that gave disturbance or opposition to such agreement.[220]

To us, the weak point of the theory of the king as the descendant of Adam was in the nexus between fatherhood and monarchy. As Hans Aarsleff points out, Filmer's belief that royal power had descended by primogeniture in the line of Adam was a belief which 'by its very strangeness to us reveals the century's trust in the Adamic archetype'.[221] However that may be, this was the target at which the Presbyterian Samuel Rutherford aimed in his response to John Maxwell. He did not believe that because Adam was a father, and for no other reason, he should also be a universal king and monarch of the whole world. He wanted to separate paternal and political power. 'A father is a father by generation', he wrote, 'and is a natural head and root, without the free consent and suffrages of his children . . . but a prince is a prince by the free suffrages of a community.'[222] It was an argument reinforced by Locke in *Two Treatises*:

[218] F. Pollock (ed.), *Table Talk* (London, 1927), p. 61. Quoted by James Slotkin, *Readings in Early Anthropology*, p. 171.
[219] See John Lilburne, *Regal Tyrannie Discovered* (London, 1647), p. 7. See also Lilburne, *The Free-Mans Freedome Vindicated* (London, 1646), p. 11.
[220] John Milton, *The Tenure of Kings and Magistrates* (London, 1650). In Don M. Wolfe (ed.), *The Complete Prose Works of John Milton* (New Haven, 1980), iii.198–9.
[221] Hans Aarsleff, *From Locke to Saussure: Essays on the Study of Language and Intellectual History* (London, 1982), p. 257.
[222] Samuel Rutherford, *Lex, Rex, or the Law and the Prince* (London, 1644), in *The Presbyterian's Armoury* (Edinburgh, 1843), iii.63.

Fatherly power I easily grant our author [Filmer] if it will do him any good, can never be lost, because it will be as long in the world as. there are fathers: but none of them will have Adam's paternal power, or derive theirs from him, but everyone will have his own, by the same title Adam had his, *viz.* by begetting, but not by inheritance or succession . . . And thus we see as Adam had no such property, no such paternal power, as gave him sovereign jurisdiction over mankind; so likewise his sovereignty built upon either of these titles, if he had any such, could not have descended to his heir, but must have ended with him. Adam therefore, as has been proved, being neither monarch, nor his imaginary monarchy hereditable, the power which is now in the world, is not that which was Adam's . . . [223]

Neither conservative royalists nor anti-royalists wished to return to those prelapsarian days in which all men would have been equal and all things held in common. Those who did adjured those who did not to lay up treasures for themselves in heaven. As Christopher Hill suggests, this was precisely the message that the Levellers, the Diggers, and the Ranters challenged.[224] For they sought treasures on earth in the here and now by the restoration of the Adamic world. The sectaries saw the rich and powerful as descended from Cain, and the poor, oppressed, and ungodly from Abel.[225] Those whose kingdom was very much of this world saw the dangers. Thus Thomas Edwards on the errors of the sectaries: 'That seeing all men are by nature the sons of *Adam*, and from him have legitimately derived a naturall propriety, right, and freedom, Therefore . . . all particular persons in every Nation . . . ought to be alike free and estated in their naturall Liberties . . . For by naturall birth, all men are equally and alike born to like propriety, liberty and freedom.'[226]

Among the early Levellers, there was support for a universal franchise, on the ground that all men were descendants of Adam. 'Justice is my naturall right', declared Edward Selby, 'my heirdome, my inheritance, by lineall descent from the loins of Adam, and so to all the sons of men.'[227] The product of a group of extreme Levellers in 1648, *Light Shining in Buckingham-shire*, maintained the complete equality of all men: 'all men being a like priviledged by birth, so all men were to enjoy the creatures a like without proprietie one more than the other, all men by the grant of God are a like free . . . no man was to Lord or command over his owne kinde . . .'[228]

[223] John Locke, *Two Treatises*, I.9.103.
[224] See Christopher Hill, *The World Turned Upside Down*, p. 284.
[225] See A. L. Morton, *The World of the Ranters* (London, 1970), p. 139.
[226] Thomas Edwards, *Gangraena*, iii.17. See also i.153, iii.20, iii.9.
[227] Quoted by A. L. Morton, *The World of the Ranters*, p. 217.
[228] George H. Sabine (ed.), *The Works of Gerrard Winstanley*, p. 611. See also p. 627.

The Digger Gerrard Winstanley looked back to the halycon days of England prior to the Norman Conquest. As G. E. Aylmer suggests, it was almost as if 'he equated 1066 with the Fall of Man, and the free Anglo-Saxons with a pre-lapsarian state of grace in the Garden of Eden'.[229] But, as Aylmer points out, it was more than that. The reformation which Winstanley sought was 'according to the pure Law of righteousness before the Fall, which made all things, unto which all things are to be restored . . .'[230] For Winstanley, all things ought to be held in common by all. Thus, as long as there was private ownership of property, 'the common people shall never have their liberty'.[231] He dreamed of a return to how things ought to have been in the beginning and, since we are all still Adamic, ought to be now. Thus, for example, his *Declaration to the Powers of England, and to all the Powers of the World*, which gave his reasons for digging up George Hill in Surrey, began:

In the beginning of Time, the great Creator Reason, made the Earth to be a Common Treasury, to preserve Beasts, Birds, Fishes, and Man, the lord that was to govern this creation . . . but not one word was spoken in the beginning, That one branch of mankind should rule over another . . . But . . . selfish imagination taking possession of the Five Sences, and ruling as King in the room of Reason . . . did set up one man to teach and rule over another; and . . . man was brought into bondage, and became a greater Slave to such of his own kind, then the Beasts of the field were to him. And hereupon, The Earth . . . was hedged into In-closures by the teachers and rulers, and the others were made Servants and Slaves: And that Earth that is within this Creation, made a Common Store-House for all, is bought and sold, and kept in the hands of a few, whereby the great Creator is mightily dishonoured . . . From the beginning it was not so.[232]

Kings and Levellers and Diggers would never have agreed on how government would have been organised in a world untainted by sin. But they would all have agreed that the Paradise which once existed in some place and time provided the key to how social relations once ideally were and ought still to be.

[229] G. E. Aylmer, 'The Religion of Gerrard Winstanley', in J. F. McGregor and Barry Reay (eds.), *Radical Religion in the English Revolution* (Oxford, 1984), p. 104.

[230] George H. Sabine (ed.), *The Works of Gerrard Winstanley*, p. 292. Quoted in McGregor and Reay (eds.)., p. 104.

[231] George H. Sabine (ed.), *The Works of Gerrard Winstanley*, p. 159.   [232] *Ibid.*, pp. 251–2.

CHAPTER 4

Animalia

A ZOOLOGICAL GARDEN

And God made the beast of the earth after his kind, and cattle after
their kind, and everything that creepeth upon the earth after his
kind.   Genesis 1.25

In 1661, in a pamphlet entitled *Paradise Transplanted and Restored*, its
anonymous author reported to his readers on a model 'of that Beautifull
Prospect *Adam* had in Paradice' shown at Christopher Whitehead's at
the two wreathed posts in Shooe Lane in London.[1] It was so perfect that,
without indignation, one could not imagine the serpent putting the
deadly apple into Eve's hand. And it was a Paradise filled with animals,
'placed from the greatest to the least, from the Elephant to the Mouse,
from the Eagle to the Wren, from the Crocodile to the Glow-Worm;
with all sorts or kinds of Insects, and Creeping Things'.[2] In short, it
represented Paradise as a biological encyclopedia.

   In spite of the image of Paradise as an enclosed garden with animals
excluded, the zoological Eden predominated. In modern terms, it was
more of a safari park than a garden. Representations of an Eden full of
'wild life' (which it then wasn't) were common in Renaissance printed
Bibles. The frontispiece to Genesis in the Geneva Bible in 1583, for
example, was packed with animals – elephants, lions, leopards, wolves,
lambs, cattle, bears, camels, goats, deer, monkeys, rhinoceroses, and so
on, an image of nature reposing and benign.

   According to Diane McColley, the most familiar image of Adam and
Eve in the early seventeenth century was that in John Speed's *Genealogy*
in 1610, which was regularly bound into Authorised Bibles from 1610 to
1640, probably including the 1612 quarto which Milton owned.[3] Ani-

[1] H.I., *Paradise Transplanted and Restored* (London, 1661), p. 2.   [2] *Ibid.*
[3] See Diane Kelsey McColley, *A Gust for Paradise: Milton's Eden and the Visual Arts* (Urbana, Illinois,
    1993), p. 58; and see fig. 44.

mals were abundant, the lion and the elephant centrally featured. Similarly, the illustration of Adam and Eve in Joseph Fletcher's *The Historie of the Perfect-Cursed-Blessed Man* in 1628 has the familiar menagerie. The wolf, the lamb, the dog, and the rabbit lie together, the lion and the elephant are in repose, the crane stands by the river upon which the swan glides.

All of these reflect an idyllic Paradise in the past in the imagery of Isaiah's Paradise of the future when 'the wolf also shall dwell with the lamb, and the leopard shall lie down with the kid; and the calf and the young lion and the fatling together . . . and the cow and the bear shall feed; their young ones shall lie down together: and the lion shall eat straw like the ox' (Isaiah 11.6–7). The camel represented abundance, while the elephant, Adam's 'totemic animal', stood for temperance, benevolence, and piety.[4] In Milton's Eden, around Adam and Eve 'frisking play'd'

> All Beasts of th'Earth, since wild, and of all chase
> in Wood or Wilderness, Forest or Den;
> Sporting the Lion ramp'd, and in his paw
> Dandl'd the Kid; Bears, Tigers, Ounces, Pards
> Gamboll'd before them, th'unwieldy Elephant
> To make them mirth us'd all his might, and wreath'd
> His lithe Proboscis[5]

Neither for Adam, Eve, nor the animals was there any possibility of pain and suffering. Classical and medieval animal lore had no validity there. Thus, for example, Richard Franck:

the Creation was unacquainted with fear whiles our Ancestor stood in a state of innocency . . . The timerous *Hare* fled not then for fear, nor did the *Cunney* shelter her self in the burrough. The *Hind* calv'd naturally without corruscations; claps of thunder were then no help to disburden her. Nor did the *Bear* lick her Cubs into shape or form, for in the beginning was no deformity. The *Pellican* in those days I perswade myself pickt not those wounds in her tender breast infeebling her self to relieve her young ones. Nor did the *Ostridge* conceal her Eggs, dreading or fearing the crush of the *Elephant*. Nor can I hardly perswade myself in these halcion days that the *Swan* as now sang a lacrimy to her Funeral; nor the *Phenix* fire her Urn to generate her Species . . .

---

4 On the symbolism of the elephant and Adam, see Richard Barber (trans.), *Bestiary: Being an English Version of the Bodleian Library, Oxford M.S. Bodley 764* (Woodbridge, Suffolk, 1993), p. 41, and Michael J. Curley (trans.), *Physiologus* (Austin, Texas, 1979), p. 31. The elephant was often featured symbolising Adam on misericords. See Francis Bond, *Wood Carvings in English Churches*. Vol. 1, *Misericords* (London, 1910), p. 31.

5 *Paradise Lost*, iv.340–7.

Nor did the *Crocadile* dissemble her tears to moisten the Funerals of his fellow Creature.[6]

Unlike the botanic garden, the realisation of which was in principle possible, the restoration on this side of the Day of Judgement of a zoological Eden was practically impossible. The lion would not lie down with the lamb. Still, in the second half of the eighteenth century under the inspiration of Capability Brown, animals roaming and browsing freely were to become a central feature of the ideal landscape. By necessity, the animals chosen were those whose gentle natures had survived the Fall. Perhaps ironically, those whose natures had not so survived were to join the flowers and plants in enclosed spaces.

While most agreed that animals were in Eden, there was less accord on the issue of their final salvation. Paul's Epistle to the Romans provided the biblical grounds for those who sought the restoration of animals in a heavenly Paradise: 'the creature itself also shall be delivered from the bondage of corruption into the glorious liberty of the children of God' (Romans 8.21). In the sixteenth century, for example, that royal chaplain under Edward and fiery martyr under Mary, John Bradford, proclaimed the universal restoration of all things, and declared that plants, animals, and all living things would be restored to their original paradisal perfection.[7] In 1613, the divine Thomas Drax, preaching on Romans 8.22–3, argued for the salvation of animals (though he excluded fish, hybrids, and creatures born of putrefaction and corruption). In the heavenly Paradise, men would have eternal dominion over them. Thus, he said, 'The creatures vanity and bondage hath not beene alwaies, neither shall it so continue: For when mans sinne that caused and occasioned it, shall be (at the last day) wholly blotted out and abolished, then of necessity must the creatures bondage of *corruption and abuse* which is the effect of it, cease.'[8]

In 1675, John Hodges preached on the goodness of animals. In spite of the Fall, he maintained, animals continued to keep the law established for them by God. And they would be restored on the last day.[9] John Swan, though uncertain whether to embrace the idea, had no qualms about suggesting that animals 'shall be fellows with them [persons] in that glorious state, like as once they were in Paradise, before man had

---

[6] Richard Franck, *A Philosophical treatise of the original and production of things*, pp. 123–4.
[7] See George H. Williams, *Wilderness and Paradise in Christian Thought* (New York, 1962), pp. 83–4. For an excellent account of opinions on the final restoration of animals, see Alan Rudrum, 'Henry Vaughan, the Liberation of the Creatures, and Seventeenth-Century English Calvinism', *Seventeenth Century* 4 (1989), pp. 34–54.
[8] Thomas Drax, *The Earnest of our Inheritance* (London, 1613), p. 13.
[9] See Thomas Hodges, *The Creatures Goodness, As they came out of God's Hands* (London, 1675), pp. 6–18.

fallen'.[10] The mortalist Leveller Richard Overton believed that gnats and toads would rise on the Day of Resurrection. Fleas too, presumably on the ground that 'Adam, had 'em.'[11] According to Overton, since death came to all creatures through Adam, life must be restored to all through Christ. Thus, he claimed, 'all other *Creatures* as well as man shall be raised and delivered from Death at the Resurrection'.[12] Samuel Clarke thought it possible, Keith Thomas informs us, that the souls of animals would eventually be resurrected and lodged in Mars, Saturn, or some other planet.[13]

That animals might eventually be restored to Paradise was reinforced also, at least at the popular level, by the belief that they were religious beings. According to Psalm 148, 'Beasts and all cattle; creeping things, and flying fowl' praised the name of the Lord. Bishop Godfrey Goodman in *The Creatures Praysing God* envisaged the birds and animals worshipping in three-part harmony: 'in their Church-musick, here you haue a full, perfect, and compleate Quier; sufficient variety of voices; the little chirping birds, the Wren and the Robin, they sing a treble; the Gold-finch, the Nightingale, they ioyne in the meane; the black-bird, the Thrush, they beare the tenour, while the foure-footed beasts, with their bleating and bellowing, they sing a base . . .'[14] Margaret Cavendish thought it irreligious to confine sense and reason only to man and to say 'that no Creature adores and worships God, but Man'.[15]

The restoration of animals to Paradise was also a restoration of the dominion which man had over them in the original Eden. The original dominion of man over animals was a commonplace in the seventeenth century. The rule and dominion of man, wrote Andrew Willet in 1608, 'was absolute before his fall, for then both man should haue beene of more excellent gouernment, by reason of his excellent wisedome, to keepe the creatures in subiection, and the beasts also by Gods prouidence should haue had a naturall inclination to obedience'.[16] To John Salkeld, man was king of all the beasts: 'No Lion so terrible, no Elephant so mighty, no Tiger so fierce, no Fowle so rauening, no Whale so monstrous, no not any creature so indomite, but that it was subiect vnto

[10] John Swan, *Specvlvm Mundi*, p. 6.
[11] See Keith Thomas, *Man and the Natural World*, p. 139. The verse 'Adam, had 'em' was anonymously penned concerning the history of microbes; date unknown.
[12] Richard Overton, *Man wholly Mortal* (London, 1655), p. 111.
[13] See Keith Thomas, *Man and the Natural World*, p. 139.
[14] Godfrey Goodman, *The Creatures Praysing God: or, The Religion of Dumbe Creatures* (London, 1622), p. 24.
[15] Margaret Cavendish, *Philosophical Letters* (London, 1664), p. 519.
[16] Andrew Willet, *Hexapla in Genesin*, p. 16.

mans dominion, while man was subiect to his Lord and Maker.'[17] Man was God's deputy on earth, wrote John White in 1656.[18] The Anglican Edward Reynolds located man's dominion over the creatures in his ability to use, tame, and train them.[19] There was no enmity then between men and animals, nor between the beasts, wrote Samuel Pordage, for 'LOVE all conjoyn'd, in *Love* all still did feast./ *ADAM* is Lord, and King: each animal/ Comes at his beck, and doth obey his call.'[20]

THE LOST DOMINION

> And out of the ground the Lord God formed every beast of the field, and every fowl of the air; and brought *them* unto Adam to see what he would call them: and whatsoever Adam called every living creature, that *was* the name thereof.   Genesis 1.19

Man's dominion over the beasts was most manifest in God's parading them before Adam to be named. Most accepted that this happened soon after the creation of man, by the special intervention of God. God secretly moved and stirred them to present themselves, wrote Andrew Willet, just as he would do for Noah later.[21] God brought the animals to Adam, declared the commentator Matthew Poole, 'either by Winds, or Angels, or by their own secret instinct . . .'[22]

His ability to name the animals provided proof of his encyclopedic knowledge. The tradition of the rabbis, Augustine, and Chrysostom that this event demonstrated Adam's superior wisdom was accepted virtually by all.[23] To Lodowick Lloid, it proved 'the wisedome and perfection of *Adam* . . .'[24] That it did was not fortuitous. Adam knew the true natures of the animals, and their names – no merely arbitrary assigning – reflected these. There was a real relation between the sign and that

[17] John Salkeld, *A Treatise of Paradise*, p. 122.
[18] John White, *A Commentary Upon the Three First Chapters of Genesis*, i.103.
[19] Edward Reynolds, *A Treatise of the Passions and Faculties of the Soule of Man*, p. 433.
[20] Samuel Pordage, *Mundorum Explicatio*, p. 58. See also John Weemse, *The Portraiture of the Image of God in Man* (London, 1627), p. 274; Thomas Robinson, *The Anatomy of the Earth*, p. 5; John Bramhall, *Castigations of Mr Hobbes* (London, 1658), pp. 190–1; Keith Thomas, *Man and the Natural World*, p. 46; Susan Snyder (ed.), *The Divine Weeks and Works*, i.268; M. Archibald Simson, *Heptameron*, p. 80; and Michael Scott, *The Philosophers Banqvet*, p. 214.
[21] Andrew Willet, *Hexapla in Genesin*, p. 36.
[22] Matthew Poole, *Annotations upon the Holy Bible*, sig. B.3.r. But cf. Jean Le Clerc, *Twelve Dissertations out of Monsieur Le Clerk's Genesis* (London, 1696), p. 287, where he argues that the naming took place over a period of time as Adam and Eve encountered the animals.
[23] See J. M. Evans, *'Paradise Lost' and the Genesis Tradition*, p. 95.
[24] Lodowick Lloid, *The Consent of Time*, p. 4.

which was signified. 'All arts were engraven vpon the creatures', wrote the puritan John Yates, 'yet none but man could see them; for he receiued them both actiuely or passiuely; and therfore by logicke vnderstood their natures, and by grammar gaue them names.'[25] Joseph Hall surmised that Adam 'saw the inside of all the creatures at first; (his Posteritie sees but their skins euer since)' and was thus able to fit their names to their dispositions.[26] 'And thou their Natures know'st, and gav'st them Names', says Raphael to Adam.[27] John Webster, the Rosicrucian critic of higher education, demonstrates the breadth of the acceptance of this belief in seventeenth-century England. In *Academiarum Examen* in 1654, he wrote,

I cannot but conceive that Adam did understand both their [the animals'] internal and external signatures, and that the imposition of their names was adequately agreeing with their natures: otherwise it could not be univocally and truly be said to be their names, whereby he distinguished them.[28]

In post-modern style, for Franciscus Mercurius van Helmont language created reality. Just as when God spoke it came to be, so in the first human speech act of naming the animals, they came into being: 'to call things by their names', he wrote, 'is to give them their nature'.[29]

It was not a knowledge Adam gained from experience. The knowledge of the animals' natures was infused into him at his creation, wrote the Anglican Edward Reynolds, demonstrating that Adam was both a philosopher and their lord.[30] His knowledge had a divine cause, declared John Denham:

> And from their Natures *Adam* them did Name,
> Not from experience, (for the world was new)
> He only from their Cause their Natures knew.[31]

And it was a factor in their prelapsarian obedience. To Calvin, God's bringing the animals to Adam was to distinguish them by names

---

[25] John Yates, *A Modell of Divinitie*, pp. 159–60.   [26] Joseph Hall, *The Works*, i.776.

[27] John Milton, *Paradise Lost*, 7.493. See also Matthew Poole, *Annotations upon the Holy Bible*, sig. B.3.r; Giovanno Loredano, *The Life of Adam*, pp. 14–15; John White, *A Commentary Upon the Three First Chapters of Genesis*, ii.89; Samuel Pordage, *Mundorum Explicatio*, p. 59; Susan Snyder (ed.), *The Divine Weeks and Works*, i.289.

[28] John Webster, *Academiarum Examen, or the Examination of Academics* (London, 1654), p. 29.

[29] F. M. van Helmont, *Some Premeditate and Considerate Thoughts Upon Genesis* (London, 1701), p. 134. Quoted by Allison Coudert, 'Some Theories of a Natural Language from the Renaissance to the Seventeenth Century', *Studia Leibnitiana* 7 (1978), p. 59.

[30] Edward Reynolds, *A Treatise of the Passions and Faculties of the Soule of Man*, p. 438. See also p. 458.

[31] John Denham, 'The Progress of Learning', ii.4–6. Quoted by Arnold Williams, *The Common Expositor*, p. 81.

appropriate to their natures, but especially to endue them with the disposition to obedience.[32] Having been given its name, George Walker speculated, any creature being called by that name 'would come to *Adam* whensoever hee called upon it . . .'[33]

That Adam named the animals by virtue of his knowledge of their natures was a tradition that reached back via Tertullian to Philo.[34] But sceptical voices were to be heard during the seventeenth century. John Donne, for one, suggested that the relation between the names of the animals and their natures was an arbitrary one which emphasised Adam's authority more than his wisdom: 'Adam's first act was not an act of Pride, but an act of lawfull power and jurisdiction, in naming the Creatures; Adam was above them all, and he might have called them what he would; There had lyen no action, no appeale, if Adam had called a Lyon a Dog, or an Eagle an Owle.'[35]

As we shall see in more detail later, Adam was the first victim in the collapse of the belief that words could express the nature of things. For philosophical reasons, Locke was to be a crucial influence in its demise. But as early as 1674, Robert Boyle was expressing his doubts on philological grounds: 'I will not urge the received opinion of divines, that before the fall . . . *Adam*'s knowledge was such, that he was able at first sight of them, to give each of the beasts a name expressive of its nature; because that, in spight of some skill . . . in the holy tongue, I could never find, that the Hebrew names of animals, mentioned in the beginning of *Genesis*, argued a (much) clearer insight into their natures, than did the names of the same or some animals in Greek, or other languages . . .'[36]

That as a consequence of the Fall man had lost his dominion over the animals, all were agreed. But exactly how much was lost remained a matter of some debate. Some maintained that the dominion had been lessened but not abolished. Andrew Willet in 1605, for example, maintained that even after the Fall the more necessary and serviceable beasts remained in subjection, that they were subdued again for Noah, and that dominion was restored by Christ.[37] 'Sometimes', Jeremiah Burroughes affirmed, 'you may see a little child driving before him a

[32] John King (trans.), *Commentaries on the First Book of Moses*, i.132.
[33] George Walker, *God made visible*, p. 193. See also Richard Ames, *The Folly of Love; or, An Essay upon Satyr against Women* (London, 1691), p. 1.
[34] See e.g. F. H. Colson and G. H. Whitaker (trans.), *Philo*, i.111; and David L. Jeffrey (ed.), *A Dictionary of Biblical Tradition in English Literature*, p. 537.
[35] Quoted by David L. Jeffrey (ed.), *A Dictionary of Biblical Tradition in English Literature*, p. 537.
[36] Thomas Birch (ed.), Robert Boyle, *The Works* (London, 1772), iv.45–6. See also John Taylor, *The Scripture Doctrine of Original Sin* (London, 1740), pp. 169, 228.
[37] See Andrew Willet, *Hexapla in Genesin*, p. 16.

hundred oxen or kine this way or that way as he pleaseth; it showeth that God hath preserved somewhat of man's dominion over the creatures.'[38] Thomas Hodges maintained that in spite of the Fall men can still subdue and govern the wilder beasts.[39]

Generally, however, the loss of dominion over the animals was heightened to emphasise the enormity of human sin. Man was responsible for the creatures' turning against him. To Godfrey Goodman in *The Fall of Man*, the animals actively conspire against him:

since man hath forsaken his own ranke, cast off his maiesie, and feeding on the carcasses of creatures, cloathed with their skinnes, and their garments, doth together put on their qualities and beastly conditions, in so much that now in the time of darknesse, he walkes disguised in a strange habit; no marueile if hee bee set vpon and taken by the watch, euery one suspecting him for some fugitiue: and as in particular he abuseth them and himselfe in an immoderate vse of the creatures; so in generall, all of them conspire against him, and worke their own malice.[40]

Edward Topsell, author of several works on zoology, maintained that the animals, aware of our responsibility for their state, 'in reuenge of their miseries which for our sakes they endure . . . kill and spoile, and teare vs in peeces where euer they meete vs . . .'[41] The creatures were 'at deadly feud with men', wrote Robert Burton.[42] It seemed to John-Francis Senault as if the creatures held 'intelligence with the Devils to undo us; that they submit to our wils, onely to seduce us, and that as if they were incenst with anger and hatred against us, they seek out all occasions to ruin us'.[43]

As a consequence of human sin, the creatures were not only set against us, but were at odds with each other. 'The great birds are enimies to the small', declared Edward Topsell, 'the great fishes to the little, the great beastes to the inferiour . . . as man destroyed his owne nature, so God destroieth or altereth the nature of all other things . . .'[44] Although Aquinas believed that animals were carnivorous before the Fall, the mainstream view was that immediately after the Fall, or at the

[38] Jeremiah Burroughes, *An Exposition of the Prophesie of Hosea* (London, 1643), p. 576. Quoted by Keith Thomas, *Man and the Natural World*, p. 19.

[39] See Thomas Hodges, *The Creatures Goodness*, p. 24.

[40] Godfrey Goodman, *The Fall of Man*, pp. 104–5. See also p. 219.

[41] Edward Topsell, *Times Lamentation: An exposition on the prophet Ioel* (London, 1599), p. 194.

[42] Thomas C. Faulkner, Nicolas K. Kiessling, and Rhonda L. Blair (eds.), Robert Burton, *The Anatomy of Melancholy*, i.126.

[43] John-Francis Senault, *Man become Guilty*, p. 353. See also p. 11; and Joseph Fletcher, *The Historie of the Perfect-Cursed-Blessed Man* (London, 1628), p. 27.

[44] Edward Topsell, *Times Lamentation*, p. 235.

latest, after the Deluge, they began to eat each other.[45] After the Fall, Bishop John Richardson declared, 'beasts, and birds of prey, and fishes, eate and devour one another'.[46] Carnivorousness was the 'fruit of sin', wrote John White in 1656.[47] According to Lancelot Andrewes, 'The ravning and preying of savage beasts came by mans transgression.'[48] Similarly for Milton:

> Beast now with Beast 'gan war, and Fowl with Fowl,
> And Fish with Fish; to graze the Herb all leaving,
> Devour'd each other.[49]

MEAT OR VEGETABLES?

The question of when the creatures became carnivorous was matched by that of when we did. For a few, we ate meat from the day of creation. Benjamin Needler, for example, thought it likely that the flesh of beasts was eaten from the beginning, since it was the most obvious use of creatures.[50] The Genevan John Diodati believed that meat-eating was probably included within the notion of man's having dominion over the creatures, as did the chemist Jean-Baptiste van Helmont on the same textual ground (though he excluded fish), and Bishop Lancelot Andrewes (though he believed the animals were vegetarian until after the Flood).[51]

These were the exceptions. For most, humans were vegetarian until after the Fall if it was accepted that the wearing of skins by Adam and Eve represented the end of the vegetarian regime (Genesis 3.21); or until after the Flood, where, it could be argued, Noah's sacrifice of animals and birds signalled its demise. According to Samuel Pordage, Adam fed only upon the Tree of Life.[52] Andrew Willet argued for prelapsarian vegetarianism on the ground that death was absent from Paradise.[53]

---

[45] See Thomas Aquinas, *Summa Theologiae*, 1a.96.1. See also Richard Bradley, *A General Treatise of Husbandry and Gardening* (London, 1724), ii.242.

[46] John Richardson, *Choice Observations and Explanations upon the Old Testament* (London, 1655), sig. B.2.r.

[47] John White, *A Commentary Upon the Three First Chapters of Genesis*, i.127.

[48] Lancelot Andrewes, *Apospasmatia Sacra*, p. 109.

[49] *Paradise Lost*, 10.710–12. See also Samuel Pordage, *Mundorum Explicatio*, p. 75; Nicholas Gibbens, *Qvestions and Dispvtations concerning the Holy Scriptvre*, p. 41; [Samuel Gott], *The Divine History of the Genesis of the World* (London, 1670), p. 417; William Hinde, *A Faithfull Remonstrance of the Holy Life and Happy Death of John Bruen* (London, 1641), p. 31.

[50] See Benjamin Needler, *Expository Notes*, p. 17.

[51] See John Diodati, *Pivos Annotations Vpon the Holy Bible* (London, 1651), sig. D.1.r; and J.-B. van Helmont, *Van Helmont's Works*, p. 162; Lancelot Andrewes, *Apospasmatia Sacra*, pp. 104–9.

[52] See Samuel Pordage, *Mundorum Explicatio*, p. 59.

[53] See Andrew Willet, *Hexapla in Genesin*, p. 19.

Arthur Jackson pointed to the post-lapsarian wearing of skins as suggesting humans would also have eaten the flesh. More pragmatically, it was a matter too of population control: 'had they not made use of cattel for food in those sixteen hundred years and upwards before the Floud, the earth would have been overburdened because of their great increase . . .'[54] Alexander Ross, Nicholas Gibbens, John Richardson, and Thomas Hayne gave health reasons. All agreed that the fruit and vegetables were better before the Fall, and that Adam's simple and frugal diet would have been a healthier one, as the schoolmaster Hayne put it, 'without any such variety and curiosity, and uncouth and artificiall cookery, as is now in use . . .'[55] Samuel Gott and John Pettus believed that the eating of meat came only after the Flood, but both believed that, although it was a right exercised only after the Deluge, it was an original feature of the human dominion over animals.[56]

There was then a strong sense that humans were naturally vegetarians, and that eating meat was, even if necessary, a necessary evil. The puritan pamphleteer Phillip Stubbes, for example, warned his readers that the modern diet had made them subject to 'millions of discrasies and diseases'.[57] While he allowed meat to be eaten, a simple diet was to be recommended, for 'thei that giue them selues to daintie fare, and sweate meates, are neuer in health . . .'[58] Richard Baxter was forced late in life to give up meat for health reasons. It was a sacrifice which he didn't regret. Although he was convinced that it was lawful to eat meat, yet God has 'put into all good men that tender compassion to the bruites as will keep them from a senseless royoting in their blood . . . all my daies it hath gone, as against my nature with some regret; which hath made me the more contented that God hath made me long renounce it . . .'[59] James Bossuet was simply a little squeamish. Before the Flood, he wrote in 1686, the nourishment from the fruits and the ease of collecting them rendered meat superfluous. Afterwards, spilling of blood became a necessity, notwithstanding the horror of it: 'all the Delicacies we now use about our Tables, can scarcely

[54] Arthur Jackson, *A Help for the Understanding of the Holy Scripture*, p. 7.
[55] Thomas Hayne, *The General View of the Holy Scriptures*, p. 49. See also Alexander Ross, *An Exposition on the Fovrteene first Chapters of Genesis*, p. 26; John Richardson, *Choice Observations*, sig. B.2.r; and Nicholas Gibbens, *Qvestions and Dispvtations concerning the Holy Scriptvre*, p. 39.
[56] See John Pettus, *Volatiles from the History of Adam and Eve*, p. 85; and Samuel Gott, *The Divine History*, pp. 423–4. See also John Lightfoot, *The Works of the Reverend and Learned John Lightfoot D.D.*, i.9.
[57] Phillip Stubbes, *The Anatomie of Abuses*, sig. I.4.v.
[58] *Ibid.*, sig. I.8.r.
[59] Frederick J. Powicke (ed.), 'The Reverend Richard Baxter's Last Treatise', *Bulletin of the John Rylands Library* 10 (1926), p. 197.

conceal from us the nauseous Carcases which we are forced to eat to satisfy us'.[60]

To John Evelyn, humans were by nature vegetarian. And he cited John Ray's *Historia Plantarum*, a work which he possessed, to the effect that we had neither the teeth nor the hands appropriate to the carnivore, but useful only for the gathering and eating of fruit and vegetables. According to Evelyn, we were vegetarians until after the Flood; and so were the animals:

tis little probable that after their Transgression, and that they had forfeited their dominion over the Creature . . . the offended God should regale them with pampering *Flesh*, or so much as suffer them to slay a more innocent Animal: Or, that if at any time they had permission, it was for any thing save Skins to cloath them . . . Nor did the Brutes themselves subsist by Prey (tho' pleas'd perhaps with Hunting, without destroying their Fellow-Creatures) as may be presum'd from their long Seclusion of the most Carnivorous among them in the Ark.[61]

Evelyn himself was no vegetarian. His diary gives ample evidence of his fondness for flesh, fish, and fowl. And he provided one of the more spurious arguments in favour of carnivorousness. Since among the herbivores, he reasoned, their flesh is essentially the product of a diet of grass, we too (if we restrict our diet to the flesh of herbivores) are effectively not eating flesh at all but merely transformed grass. By extension, therefore, our flesh is but the transformation of transformed grass. Thus in eating the flesh of herbivores man, 'becoming an *Incarnate Herb*, and innocent *Canibal*, may truly be said to devour himself'.[62] We are all, after all, vegetarians – and vegetables.

Animals do not seem to have gained much from Adamic precedent. Most people appear to have accepted (and probably with relish) this aspect of our fallen natures. But for some, vegetarianism was a real choice, and one made for religious and ethical reasons. One motivation was ascetic, to demonstrate the triumph of spirit over flesh. Keith Thomas informs us of a Thomas Bushell who lived for three years in the 1620s on a diet of herbs, oil, mustard, and honey; and of a Mrs Traske who gave up meat and drank only water for seven years during the reign of Charles I.[63]

For some, the motivation was religious. This was clearly the case with Roger Crab, a hatter at Chesham in the middle of the seventeenth

---

[60] James Bossuet, *A Discourse on the History of the World* (London, 1686), p. 174. See also Howard Williams, *The Ethics of Diet* (London, 1896).
[61] John Evelyn, *A Discourse of Sallets*, p. 191.   [62] *Ibid.*, p. 195.
[63] See Keith Thomas, *Man and the Natural World*, pp. 289–90.

century and (according to Christopher Hill) he towards whom the expression 'mad as a hatter' was directed.[64] Around the age of twenty, seeking perfection, he gave all he had to the poor and began a vegetarian life, in which he persisted until his death in 1680 at the age of fifty-nine. His self-imposed poverty was the result of his following the advice of the second Adam to the rich young man. But his vegetarianism related to the first. For Crab, Adam's eating of meat was not the consequence of the Fall but its cause: 'if naturall *Adam* had kept to his single naturall fruits of Gods appointment, namely fruits and hearbs, we had not been corrupted. Thus we see that by eating and drinking we are swallowed up in corruption.'[65] The eating of beastly food, he declared, turns us into beasts. His diet was a simple one: 'Corne, Bread, and Bran, Hearbs, Roots, Dock-leaves, Mallowes, and grasse . . .'[66] He drank only water, and wore only a simple frock of sackcloth. He was a popular natural healer, advising his patients to avoid eating flesh and drinking strong beer. His only disciple, a Captain Norwood, died as a result of this meagre diet. Keith Thomas suggests that it might have been another follower of his who appeared in Yorkshire in 1674 'dressed in white and claiming to have drunk only water and eaten only roots for the past fourteen years'.[67]

Vegetarianism must have had some following among the sectarians. Thomas Edwards in *Gangraena* in 1646 listed the belief that it was unlawful to kill animals among his 'errors'. And he mentioned a Hackney bricklayer named Marshall who taught that it was 'unlawful to kill any creature that had life'.[68] John Robins, who shared many of his beliefs with the Ranters, claimed to be the reincarnation of Adam and Melchizedek. In preparation for travelling to the Holy Land, he imposed a diet of bread, fruit, and water, which some of his followers failed to survive.[69]

In 1693, in one of a miscellaneous collection of letters entitled *The Second Volume of The Post-Boy Robb'd of his Mail*, a Mr S. Rogers purportedly wrote to a Mr Lancelot of Broad Street, London. In this letter he described forty-five different kinds of religious opinion. And of these, the fortieth on the list was the sect of Tryonists:

[64] For a brief account of his life and teachings, see Christopher Hill, *Puritanism and Revolution* (London, 1965), ch. 11.

[65] Roger Crab, *The English Hermit, or Wonder of this Age* (London, 1655), Letter to the Impartial Reader.

[66] *Ibid.*, anonymous Epistle to the Reader.　　[67] Keith Thomas, *Man and the Natural World*, p. 291.

[68] Thomas Edwards, *Gangraena*, i.34, 80. Quoted by Keith Thomas, *Man and the Natural World*, pp. 290–1.

[69] See Richard L. Graves and Robert Zaller (eds.), *Biographical Dictionary of British Radicals in the Seventeenth Century* (Brighton, Sussex, 1982–), iii.101.

Tryonists, are such as forbid eating of Flesh, Fish, or anything that is kill'd, as contrary to Scripture . . . and the Command of God, and Example of Christ and his Apostles. That killing of Creatures, is from the fierce Wrath of God, hellish Nature in Man and a fruit of Hell; they being as it were our Brethren and Fellow-Creatures, and therefore 'tis Oppression in the fierce Wrath. *Adam* was to eat only of e'ry Herb of the Field, and of e'ry Fruit of the Trees; killing, entring the World after the Fall, and not permitted till after the Flood . . . That eating of Flesh, is the Doctrine of Devils, qualifies men to be sordid, surly; and Soldiers, Hunters, Pirates, Tories, and such as wou'd have the bestial nature fortify'd; that they might act like Lions, and Devils, over their own kind as well as over all other creatures.[70]

It is doubtful whether there was an organised group of followers of Thomas Tryon in the early 1690s. But their supposed leader was alive and well and living at Hackney in London, and was then aged fifty-nine. He had come to London in the early 1650s and been apprenticed to a hatter, and had become an Anabaptist. But it was in the mystical theosophy of Jacob Boehme that he found his precepts, and in vegetarianism, his practice. By the early 1660s he was fully committed to his vegetarian regime of 'herbs, fruits, grains, eggs, butter, and cheese, for food, and pure water for drink'. This diet, he argued, 'by thoroughly cleansing the outward court of the terrestrial nature . . . opens the window of the inward senses of the soul'.[71]

It was Tryon's conviction that, just as our forefathers lived to wonderful ages as a consequence of a vegetarian diet, so the adoption of such a diet in the present would lead to the restoration of Paradise. Vegetarianism, he argued, 'would not only lay a sure foundation for Health, both of Body and Mind, but Magneticall attract the benevolent Influxes of the Coelestial Bodies, and make even this *lower Life* a kind of *Paradise* both for *Innocency* and pure *unsullied pleasures*'.[72] And, as with Roger Crab, there is the suggestion that the craving after and eating of meat was the original sin. 'We fear all Inclinations after *Flesh* and *Blood*, they smell of the *Original Sin*, and of the awakened, fierce Wrath of God, which renders man fitter to live in a *Flesh Market* and *Butcher's*

---

[70] Anon., *The Second Volume of The Post-Boy Robb'd of his Mail* (London, 1693), p. 269. By 'Tories' was probably intended 'marauders, and not the members of a political group, although already by this time the word was beginning to have this meaning. See anon., 'A Pythagorean of the Seventeenth Century', *Proceedings of the Literary and Philosophical Society of Liverpool* 25 (1871), p. 278. I am indebted to this article for biographical information on Thomas Tryon.

[71] Anon., 'A Pythagorean', pp. 290–1. He was however later to warn against any overreliance on butter, eggs, milk, and cheese. See Thomas Tryon, *Tryon's Letters upon Several Occasions* (London, 1700), p. 86.

[72] Thomas Tryon, *The Way to Health, Long Life and Happiness* (London, 1697), p. 201.

Shambles, than in a *Garden*; there being no more affinity between *Slaugh-ter-houses, Shambles, Butcher's Shops*, and *Sheep*, than there is between a *pleasant Garden*, and the *Fruits* that grow therein, and *Dogs, Lions, Bears*, and the like *wild Beasts of Prey* . . .'[73]

To Tryon, animal life had an intrinsic worth. Animals 'bear the image of their Creator in a great measure as well as ourselves', he wrote.[74] And he broadened the Golden Rule to include the creatures.[75] Dominion over the animals, he argued, entailed a responsibility to protect and care for all creatures.[76]

But vegetarianism was also in our own best interests. According to Tryon, each kind of food exerts a particular kind of spiritual force. By eating the flesh of animals, we become beastly. In carnivorousness, he argued, lay the source of all violence between men. The lifestyle he recommended was that of a rejection of culture and a return to nature:

in open serene airs, as in fields, mountains, and by river sides and woods, there is no tumult, no stabbing of heaven with dreadful oaths, horrid curses, and frightful execrations; no banishing of temperance with drunken healths, and roaring huzzas; no fulsome fumes of tobacco, nor viler steams of detestable brothel-houses to infest the chaste air; no plays or vain games, no mistressing nor revelling to spend precious time . . . But, on the contrary, all is sedate and serene, still as the voice of good spirits, and quiet as the birth of flowers; no noise to be heard but the ravishing harmony of the wood-musicians, and the inno-cent lowings of cows and neighings of horses and bleating of the pretty lambs . . . everything praising the Creator according to the capacity and nature of each.[77]

Whether we would live longer in such an Arcadia is a matter of debate. Undoubtedly it would seem much longer.

While few, on the basis of Adamic precedent, were inclined to give up their carnivorous ways, the Genesis story was read by some as demand-ing the implementation of certain kinds of attitudes towards the crea-tures. Without doubt, they were minority voices. But, as Keith Thomas points out, between the fifteenth and the nineteenth century there was one coherent and constant attitude. This was to the effect that while animals could be domesticated and killed for food and clothing, man 'was not to tyrannize or to cause unnecessary suffering'.[78] Creatures

[73] *Ibid.*, pp. 313–14.   [74] Thomas Tryon, *Tryon's Letters upon Several Occasions*, p. 86.
[75] See *ibid.*, p. 63.
[76] See Thomas Tryon, *The Country-mans Companion* (London, n.d.), ch. 5, 'The Complaints of the Birds* and Fowls of Heaven to their Creator'.
[77] Thomas Tryon, *The Way to Health, Long Life and Happiness*, pp. 260–1.
[78] Keith Thomas, *Man and the Natural World*, p. 153.

were to be treated kindly and without cruelty. Genuine feelings of compassion are in evidence. The puritan Phillip Stubbes, for example, wondered 'what Christian harte can take pleasure to see one poore beaste to rent, teare, and kill another, and all for his foolish pleasure ...'[79] He endorsed hunting as a matter of necessity, but not for the sake of pleasure. There was a common saying among all men, he wrote, '*Loue me, loue my Dogge*: so loue God, loue his Creatures.'[80] Edward Topsell argued that kindness to domestic animals was in our interest: 'Mercie is a thing much loued of the Lord: and surely we are to vse it, not onely towards our beasts in their labour, that we tire them not too much; but also in their meate that we feed them sufficiently ...'[81] John Rawlinson, principal of St Edmund Hall, Oxford, in a sermon on Proverbs 12.10, preached mercy to domestic animals in feeding, in pardoning their infirmities, in guiding and ruling them, and in protecting and defending them, though he was not averse to lessening the numbers of wild beasts and venomous reptiles.[82] The puritan William Hinde thought it unlawful for any man to take pleasure 'in the paine and torture of any creature, or delight himself in the tyranny, which the creatures exercise one over another ...'[83] It was a short step, he maintained, from cruelty to animals to cruelty to human beings.

For some, hunting was a necessary evil. Montaigne found hunting generally indefensible.[84] The Anglican Edward Bury believed that it was lawful to kill beasts, 'but to sport ourselves in their death seems cruel and bloody'.[85] Thomas Drax supported hunting, as long as the same amount of effort were expended upon hunting 'the *Romish Gray Foxe*, and all his cubs, Iesuits, Seminaries, Priestes, Papists, Recusants . . .'[86] But he shared with many a dislike of the setting of animals one against another. Phillip Stubbes, for example rejected bear-baiting and cock-fighting, as did the puritan sympathiser William Perkins.[87] John Evelyn described cock-fighting and bull-, dog-, and bear-baiting as 'butcherly Sports, or rather barbarous cruelties'.[88] Samuel Pepys felt the same.[89]

---

[79] Phillip Stubbes, *The Anatomie of Abuses*, sig. Q.5.v.   [80] *Ibid.*, sig. Q.6.r.
[81] Edward Topsell, *Times Lamentation*, p. 196.
[82] See John Rawlinson, *Mercy to a Beast . . . A Sermon* (Oxford, 1612), p. 42.
[83] William Hinde, *A Faithfull Remonstrance*, pp. 31–2.
[84] See Michaell de Montaigne, *The Essayes* (London, 1603), p. 237.
[85] Edward Bury, *The Husbandman's Companion* (London, 1677), p. 222.
[86] Thomas Drax, *The Churches Securitie* (London, 1608), p. 17.
[87] See Phillip Stubbes, *The Anatomie of Abuses*, sig. Q.6.r – Q.8.v; and William Perkins, *The Workes of . . . Mr William Perkins* (London, 1616), ii.141.
[88] E. S. de Beer (ed.), John Evelyn, *The Diary* (Oxford, 1955), p. 540.
[89] See Keith Thomas, *Man and the Natural World*, pp. 159–60.

There may be a fragment of truth, as Keith Thomas suggests, in Macaulay's well-known remark that the puritans disliked bear-baiting because of the pleasure it gave to the spectators, not because of the pain it gave to the bears. But there were real sensitivities to the suffering of animals, even if they were a consequence of the continuing sense of man at the centre of all things. And such new sensitivities did generate fresh readings of the Genesis story. Thus, dominion over the animals could be read as entailing our responsibility for and stewardship of them. Philip Camerarius, for example, made it clear that our dominion over the beasts could not be a tyranny. Thus, he concluded, 'The rudeness . . . and crueltie of some lobs and lowts towards such beasts as are bred and accustomed to the seruice of man, and which these bruitish fellowes threaten, beat, hurt, torment . . . is not to be endured and borne withall.'[90] John White warned his readers not to tyrannise them, for God 'hath made us only stewards of that which he hath put into our hands, to preserve and cherish the Creatures, and to make use of it to our selves, when our necessities require it . . .'[91] In Thomas Tryon's *The Country-mans Companion* the birds inquired, 'does this Perfidiousness and Tyranny of thine towards us inferior-graduated, yet Innocent fellow Creatures, look like thy *first* Estate? Has not our Creator made and ordained thee his *Governour* and great *Vice-Gerent* over all the inhabitants of the lower Universe, to rule them with Meekness and Equity?'[92]

There was a strong sense too that, since their ferocity was the consequence of our sin, kindness towards them, or at the very least a refusal to take any pleasure in their suffering, was a moral obligation. According to Phillip Stubbes, the reason the creatures have become enemies to us was 'our disobedience to the LORD, which we are rather to sorrow for, than to hunt after their deaths by the sheading of their blood'.[93] If we had not sinned, wrote William Hinde, 'there should never have beene any variance or strife amongst the rest of the creatures'.[94] George Walker epitomises the Puritan position:

If any creature of God bee at enmity with us, and hurtfull and pernicious to us, it is for our owne sins, because so wee have broken the peace, and are at enmity with God . . . therefore the creatures made for our use, are become our enemies . . . though it is lawfull for man in his owne defence, and for his owne safety to destroy Serpents, hurtfull beasts and noysome creatures; yet to doe it with

[90] Philip Camerarius, *The Walking Librarie* (London, 1621), p. 69.
[91] John White, *A Commentary Upon the Three First Chapters of Genesis*, i.105.
[92] Thomas Tryon, *The Country-Mans Companion*, p. 142.
[93] Phillip Stubbes, *The Anatomie of Abuses*, sig.P.3.v.
[94] William Hinde, *A Faithfull Remonstrance*, p. 31.

cruelty, and with pleasure, delight, and rejoycing in their destruction, and without sense of our owne sins and remorse for them, is a kind of scorne and contempt of the workmanship of God our Creatour.[95]

THE LANGUAGE OF ADAM

In the spring of 1698, Edward Tyson, England's leading anatomist, received the body of the first recorded anthropoid ape to have arrived in England, a body which he classified generically as an orang-utan, though in fact it was a young chimpanzee.[96] By the middle of the following year, he published the results of his examinations under the title *Orang-Outang, sive Homo Sylvestris*. As H. W. Janson has pointed out, 'The publication of Tyson's book marks the formal entry of the anthropoid ape into the consciousness of Western civilisation.'[97]

During the seventeenth century, animal compendia almost always excluded a discussion of man. In contrast, the overall focus of Tyson's work was to compare the anatomy of his chimpanzee with human anatomy. And he was to list forty-eight similarities and thirty-four dissimilarities. Tyson's most important conclusion was that in the complex chain of being which, he believed, stretched from minerals to humans, the chimpanzee was the link between the animal and the human: 'The animal of which I have given the anatomy, coming nearest to Mankind; seems the Nexus of the Animal and Rational' and a sort of animal between the common ape and man.[98] On the basis of this similarity, and influenced by Thomas Browne's discussion of pygmies in *Pseudodoxia Epidemica*, he decided that the ancient mythology that there were several sorts of men was untrue. Those whom the ancients called Pygmies, Cynocephali, Satyrs, and Sphinges 'were only *Apes* and *Monkeys*'.[99]

Philosophically, Tyson seems to have been committed to the Cartesian view that animals were mere automata, and that between the animal and the human a qualitative gulf was fixed. And yet, in spite of this, there were

---

[95] George Walker, *God made visible*, p. 160. See also William Perkins, *The Workes*, ii.141; and *The Harleian Miscellaney* (London, 1744), vi.114.

[96] The name 'orang-outang' applied in Tyson's day to any of the anthropoid apes. The name 'chimpanzee' was introduced some forty years later. See M. F. Ashley Montagu, *Edward Tyson, M.D., F.R.S. 1650–1708 and the Rise of Human and Comparative Anatomy in England* (Philadelphia, 1943), p. 247.

[97] H. W. Janson, *Apes and Ape Lore in the Middle Ages and the Renaissance* (London, 1952), p. 336.

[98] Edward Tyson, *Orang-Outang, sive Homo Sylvestris* (London, 1699), Epistle Dedicatory. See also p. 91.

[99] *Ibid.*, Preface.

two particular features of the chimpanzee which suggested to Tyson that that gulf was much less broad. The first was its erect posture. Unlike other apes and monkeys, he suggested, it was natural for it to walk erect, although, 'Being weak, the better to support him, I have given him a Stick in his Right-Hand.'[100] The tradition of man as the only creature capable of standing erect may have influenced his suggestion that the chimpanzee was unable to stand erect independently and his depiction of its needing support to do so. Its posture was not fully human.

The second feature was its organs of speech, which Tyson recognised as essentially identical with ours, though, granting that apes could not speak, he was forced to the conclusion that they were functionally useless:

There is no reason to think, that Agents do perform such and such Actions, because they are found with Organs proper thereunto: for then our *Pygmie* might really be a *Man*. The *Organs* in *Animal* Bodies are only a regular *Compages* of Pipes and Vessels for the *Fluids* to pass through, and are passive . . . But those *nobler Faculties* in the *Mind* of *Man*, must certainly have a *higher Principle*; and *Matter organized* could never produce them . . . if all depended on the *Organ*, not only our *Pygmie*, but other *Brutes* likewise, would be too near akin to us.[101]

Thus, for Tyson, language itself (or that faculty of which it was a sign) kept the human and the animal qualitatively distinct. But in his anatomy of the chimpanzee, Tyson had inexorably moved the category of the animal far closer to the human.

As the animal moved closer to the human, so the human was perceived as approaching the bestial. Swift's Yahoos were the literary manifestations of this closing of the gap. For he perceived them as human, though in the most bestial form. And, like Tyson's chimpanzee, they were separated from Gulliver by an absence of speech and reason: 'When I thought of my Family, my Friends, and my Countrymen, or Human Race in general, I considered them as they really were, *Yahoos* in Shape and Disposition, only a little civilized, and qualified with the Gift of Speech, but making no other use of Reason, than to improve and multiply those Vices, whereof their Brethren in this Country had only the share that nature allotted them.'[102]

---

[100] *Ibid.*, p. 16. In so doing, he was following the tradition of showing a species of ape in an upright position holding a stick, popularised in Konrad Gessner's *Historiae animalium* of 1551, itself based on an earlier account of a nameless creature which appeared in Bernhard von Breydenbach's *Peregrinatio in terram sanctam* in 1486. See Robert Wokler, 'Tyson and Buffon on the Orang-utan', *Studies on Voltaire and the Eighteenth Century* 155 (1976), p. 2302.

[101] Tyson, *Orang-Outang*, p. 55.

[102] Jonathan Swift, *Gulliver's Travels* (London, 1926), pp. 394–5.

But Swift himself in his description of the Yahoos may well have been drawing upon seventeenth-century descriptions of man believed to be at his worst and to be found in the deserts of southern Africa or western Australia. The descriptions of the African Hottentots bear a striking resemblance to those of Swift's Yahoos. And the voyagers who described them loathed them as much as did Gulliver the Yahoos. They were perceived as humans who lacked reason. For John Ovington, they fell midway between men and the highly developed apes: 'if there's any medium between a Rational Animal and a Beast, the *Hotontot* lays the fairest claim to that Species'.[103] Sir Thomas Herbert described the Hottentots as 'an accursed progeny of *Cham*, who differ in nothing from bruit beasts save forme . . .'[104] In 1688, William Dampier thought the Australian aborigines worse than the Hottentots, and little short of brutes.[105]

But if the gap between the animal and the human was narrowing, in the spoken word remained the decisive difference between the human and animal realms. Language symbolised the dominion over nature which was still in part retained. And the desire for the dominion over nature once enjoyed by Adam motivated the quest to discover the language which would restore that dominion.

The loss of the Adamic tongue is not depicted in the Genesis text as the consequence of the Fall. Even in Genesis 3.20, after the Fall but before the expulsion from the Garden, Adam called his wife Eve 'because she was the mother of all living'. He retained his 'naming rights'. Even after the Flood, we are informed in Genesis 11.1 that 'the whole earth was of one language, and of one speech.' But, the story continues, the vanity of men led them into rivalry with God by their attempting to build a tower that reached to heaven. To punish them, and to stop their building the tower, God thought, 'Go to, let us go down, and there confound their language, that they may not understand one another's speech . . . Therefore is the name of it called Babel; because the Lord did there confound the language of all the earth: and from thence did the Lord scatter them abroad upon the face of all the earth, (Genesis 11.7, 9). This was the context in which all the attempts to

---

[103] John Ovington, *A Voyage to Suratt in the year 1689* (London, 1696), p. 489.
[104] Thomas Herbert, *Some Years Travels into Divers Parts of Asia and Afrique* (London, 1638), p. 16. Quoted by R. W. Frantz, 'Swift's Yahoos and the Voyagers', *Modern Philology* 29 (1931–2), p. 53. I am indebted to Frantz for the discussion of the Yahoos and the Hottentots.
[105] See *A Collection of Voyages* (London, 1729), p. 464.

determine the original Adamic language or to construct it anew were located.[106]

The early Greek fathers, Augustine, and Isidore of Seville believed that the language of Eden was Hebrew. This was the most commonly held opinion throughout the Middle Ages. As one thirteenth-century bestiary put it, 'Adam gave them names, not in Greek or Latin, nor in any of the languages of the barbarian peoples, but in that language which was common to all peoples before the Flood, and which is called Hebrew.'[107] The early Protestant reformers, emphasising Scripture over tradition, accepted that Hebrew was the language of Adam, and of God. Consequently, they saw the Hebrew text as that to which all questions had to be related. After the Council of Trent, Don Allen reports, 'the Protestant advocacy of the Hebrew Scriptures became more vigorous'.[108] Lancelot Andrewes was exaggerating, but he spoke nevertheless for most: it is agreed upon by all learned men, he wrote, 'that the Hebrew tongue is the original tongue and most ancient, by which *Adam* expressed his minde . . . and that which *Adam* here used in giving names to all the creatures'.[109] As the language of Adam and the language of God, Hebrew had a unique status in seventeenth-century England.

If Hebrew were the original language, this suggested that all other languages were derived from it. In 1606, for example, Estienne Guichard tried to show how Hebrew words transmuted into those of other languages, by demonstrating the harmony of Hebrew with Chaldean, Syriac, Greek, Latin, French, Italian, Spanish, German, Flemish, and English. Max Mueller has pointed out that Guichard went so far as to maintain that, since Hebrew was written from right to left, 'Greek words might be traced back to Hebrew by being simply read from right

[106] It should be noted that in Genesis 10.5 the text tells us that by the sons of Japheth 'were the isles of the Gentiles divided in their lands; every one after his tongue, after their families in their nations'; and similarly for the sons of Ham and the sons of Shem in vv. 20 and 31 respectively. Unlike in the Babel story, the suggestion is here that the division of languages was merely part of a natural process. It plays virtually no role in seventeenth-century discussions of language.

[107] Richard Barber (trans.), *Bestiary*, p. 19. On Augustine, see Henry Bettenson (trans.), *Augustine, Concerning the City of God against the Pagans* (Harmondsworth, 1972), pp. 667–8. On Isidore of Seville and e.g. Dante, see J. S. Slotkin, *Readings in Early Anthropology*, pp. 8, 10.

[108] Don C. Allen, *The Legend of Noah*, p. 47.

[109] Lancelot Andrewes, *Apospasmatia Sacra*, p. 209. See also John White, *A Commentary Upon the Three First Chapters of Genesis*, ii.89; and Giovanno Loredano, *The Life of Adam*, pp. 14–15. See also David S. Katz, 'The Language of Adam in 17th-Century England', in Hugh Lloyd Jones, Valerie Pearl, and Blair Worden (eds.), *History and Imagination: Essays in Honour of H. R. Trevor-Roper* (London, 1981), pp. 132–45.

to left'.[110] Sixty years later, Theophilus Gale presented this as if it were a commonplace: 'that all *languages* and *Letters* were derived originally from the *Hebrew* or *Jewish* Tongue, is an *Assertion* generally owned, and maintained by the most learned *Philologists* of this age'.[111] It was a belief which the nineteenth-century philologist Max Mueller was to decry as having prevented progress in philology.[112]

The belief that a restored Hebrew should once again become the universal language was also expressed. Around 1660, the missionary to the Indians of New England John Eliot, in correspondence with Richard Baxter, saw its universal adoption as paramount in his missionary endeavours. It was, he believed, the language spoken in heaven 'which by its "trigrammatical foundation" is "capable of a regular expatiation into millions of words, no language like it" '.[113]

For Franciscus Mercurius van Helmont, a natural Hebrew alphabet as the basis of a universal language would lead to religious peace and social harmony. His first work, in 1667, was entitled *A Most Compendious and truly Natural Draught of the Hebrew Alphabet*. It was a work intended to examine the possibilities of teaching the deaf to speak. He proceeded from the assumption that the original language was easy to speak and easy to learn, and could not but be Hebrew. He assumed too that it was a natural language, one in which there was a real relation between words and things. And he attempted to demonstrate that in making the sounds of Hebrew, the movements of the vocal organs reproduced the shapes of the letters. As Umberto Eco sums it up, 'not only did the Hebrew sounds reflect the inherent nature of things themselves, but the very mud from which the human vocal organs were formed had been especially sculpted to emit a perfect language that God pressed on Adam in not only its spoken but evidently its written form as well'.[114]

Implicit in van Helmont's discussion is the idea that Hebrew would be the language that, in a state of nature, would be spoken without having to be learned. Thus wild children opened up the possibility of rediscovering the original language. It was much to be desired, declared Thomas Browne, that children 'committed unto the school of Nature' should speak the primitive language 'not only for the easie attainment of

[110] Max Mueller, *Lectures on the Science of Language* (London, 1861), p. 124n.
[111] Theophilus Gale, *The Court of the Gentiles* (Oxford, 1669), i.61.
[112] Max Mueller, *Lectures on the Science of Language*, p. 123.
[113] John Stoughton, *Ecclesiastical History of England: The Church of the Restoration* (London, 1870), ii.249.
[114] See Umberto Eco, *The Search for the Perfect Language* (Oxford, 1995), p. 83. I am indebted to Eco for this brief account. See also Allison Coudert, 'Some Theories of a Natural Language from the Renaissance to the Seventeenth Century'.

that usefull tongue, but to determine the true and primitive Hebrew'.[115] That there was such a natural language (whether Hebrew or another) was an opinion already rejected by George Hakewill. He told of several occasions upon which children were isolated from language in the attempt to ascertain whether they had natural language. The results suggested to him that 'the speaking of any language is not in man by nature; the first man had it by divine *Infusion*, but all his posterity onely by *Imitation*'.[116] Similarly, for a more popular audience, John Dunton at the end of the century wrote: 'we suppose then . . . that such an Infant wou'd speak *no Language at all*, only express the conceptions of his mind by Natural Signs, or some *inarticulate noises*'.[117] This was one strike against the notion that Hebrew had been the primordial natural language.

Another was the fact that, to many, modern Hebrew did not appear particularly primordial. Those who argued for Hebrew as the original tongue of Adam were, implicitly at least, committed to the position that it had survived the dispersion at Babel. Generally it was held to have been preserved in the family of Heber the grandson of Noah (whence the word 'Hebrew') and thence to Abraham and the people of Israel.[118] But doubts were expressed about the relation of modern Hebrew to the primitive language. John Wilkins, for example, in 1668 suggested from the imperfections and defects of Hebrew that it was not the same language as that 'concreated with our first Parents, and spoken by *Adam* in *Paradise*'.[119] Jean le Clerc maintained there was no language in the world fuller of ambiguity and obscurity than Hebrew – a barren and unrefined language. Hebrew, he argued, along with Chaldean and Arabic, was the offspring of the language of Adam.[120] Richard Simon in 1682 followed Gregory of Nyssa in accepting that Hebrew was not as ancient as other languages.[121]

For a number of European scholars, the original language was to be found much closer to home. The sixteenth and seventeenth centuries witnessed the growth of linguistic patriotism. Thus, for example, in the

---

[115] Thomas Browne, *Pseudodoxia Epidemica*, 5.23. [116] George Hakewill, *An apologie*, p. 6.
[117] John Dunton (ed.), *The Athenian Gazette*, vol. ii, q. 6, no. 6.
[118] See Arnold Williams, *The Common Expositor*, pp. 228–9. See also Richard Simon, *A Critical History of the Old Testament* (London, 1682), i.97. It was held too by Athanasius Kircher and Claude Duret. On Kircher and Duret, see Umberto Eco, *The Search for the Perfect Language*, pp. 81–5; and Paul Cornelius, *Languages in Seventeenth- and Early Eighteenth-Century Imaginary Voyages* (Geneva, 1965), pp. 7ff. See also Brian Walton, *Biblia Sacra Polyglotta* (London, 1657), p. 18; George Offer (ed.), *The Whole Works of John Bunyan* (London, 1862), ii.500.
[119] John Wilkins, *An Essay Towards a Real Character and a Philosophical Language* (London, 1668).
[120] See Jean Le Clerc, *Twelve Dissertations*, pp. 1–41.
[121] See Patrick Simon, *A Critical History of the Old Testament*, p. 99.

mid sixteenth century, the Belgian scholar Goropius Becanus argued
that the original language of Eden was not Hebrew but Low German, a
belief which he supported by showing that the proper names of the Bible
would have had greater mystical meaning when understood as of Low
German origin.[122] Richard Rowlands gave an English version of Becanus' theory under the name of Richard Verstegen in a work entitled *A
Restitution of Decayed Intelligence in Antiquities*. Verstegen tells us of a conversation which he had with Ortelius:

> In conference one day with *Abraham Ortelius* (who had been acquainted with
> *Becanus*) I asked him if he thought that *Becanus* himself, being so learned as he
> was, did indeed believe this Language to be the first of all Languages of the
> World, to wit, that which was spoke by *Adam*: he told me, that he verily thought
> *Becanus* did so believe: and added further, that many learned men might
> peradventure laugh at that which he had written, but that none would be able
> to confute it: whereby I guessed that *Ortelius* did much incline unto *Becanus* his
> conceit.[123]

First published in 1605, the book had sufficient appeal to be reprinted a
further five times during the century. Although Verstegen himself ultimately decided in favour of the priority of Hebrew, the work's popularity suggests it struck a chord in England. That the Adamic language was
Dutch was parodied by Ben Jonson. His Epicure Mammon replies to
the question whether Adam spoke in High Dutch, 'He did. Which
proves it was the primitive tongue.'[124]

Other patriotic options were also available, though they verge on
the parodic. Adrianus Schriekius looked to the Celtic; Marcus Boxhor-
nius to the Scythian; the Danish linguist Ole Worm to runes; the
Swede Georg Stiernhielm to Swedish. In 1688, the Swede Andreas
Kempe wrote in *Die Sprachen des Paradises* a scene in which, while God
spoke to Adam in Swedish and Adam responded in Danish, the serpent was speaking to Eve in French.

Nevertheless, there remained the fervent hope that the lingua Ada-
mica had survived the Flood and was still extant somewhere in the
world. But all of the languages above, at least in their post-lapsarian
form, failed to evince the necessary criterion for the language of Adam
– that there should be a real relation between the sign and the thing
signified. In principle, this was impossible for an alphabetical language. As John Webb wrote, 'In vain do we search for the PRIMITIVE

---

[122] See Don C. Allen, 'Some Theories', p. 13.
[123] Richard Verstegen, *A Restitution of Decayed Intelligence in Antiquities* (London, 1673), p. 207.
[124] Alvin B. Kernan (ed.), Ben Jonson, *The Alchemist* (New Haven, 1974), p. 60.

Language to be remaining with those Nations whose Languages consist in Alphabets.'[125] But it was different for the characters of Egypt and China. They looked like the most likely candidates.

Egyptian hieroglyphics had been believed to have the features of a natural language at least since the time of Plotinus in the third century CE. The wise sages of Egypt, Plotinus wrote, 'left aside the writing-forms that take in the details of words and sentences . . . and drew pictures instead, engraving in the temple-inscriptions a separate image for every separate item . . .'[126] The primitive character of Egyptian hieroglyphics was reinforced by Renaissance dreams of the antiquity of the *Corpus Hermeticum*, imagined to be the writings of Hermes Trismegistus and to contain the fount of human wisdom. Thus, for example, Thomas Browne maintained that the Egyptians evaded the confusion that resulted from Babel and 'invented a language of things and spake unto each other by common notions in Nature'. And, he went on, 'This many conceive to have beene the primitive way of writing, and of greater Antiquity then letters; and this indeed might Adam well have spoken, who understanding the nature of things, had the advantage of naturall expressions.'[127] Henry Estienne, the sixteenth-century French scholar, traced the origin of hieroglyphs to Eden. John Wilkins in *Mercury: or, The Secret and Swift Messenger* in 1641 saw hieroglyphics as intending to express a real relationship between signs and the signified.[128]

It was an ultimately forlorn hope. In 1614, Isaac Casaubon showed that the hermetic writings fell well within the Christian era and were probably Christian forgeries.[129] Even if they were very early writings – and many continued so to believe for the remainder of the century – they were indecipherable. As such, they were a much less interesting choice as the original language. Chinese seemed a much better option.

It was a possibility opened up by Thomas Browne in his essay 'Of Languages'. Since the confusion of tongues, he wrote, fell only upon those who were involved in the building of the Tower of Babel, he wondered whether the primitive language might have been preserved among those who were absent from the land of Shinar. And he went on to suggest that 'The Chinoys, who live at the bounds of the Earth, who

---

[125] John Webb, *An Historical Essay, Endeavoring a Probability that the Language of the empire of China is the Primitive Language* (London, 1669).

[126] Stephen McKenna (trans.), Plotinus, *The Enneads* (London, 1956), 5.8.6.

[127] Thomas Browne, *Pseudodoxia Epidemica*, 5.20.

[128] See Thomas C. Singer, 'Hieroglyphs in the Seventeenth Century', *Journal of the History of Ideas* 50 (1989), pp. 49–70.

[129] See Frances A. Yates, *Giordano Bruno and the Hermetic Tradition* (Chicago, 1964), pp. 398–402.

have admitted little communication . . . may possibly give account of a very ancient language.'[130] It was a suggestion taken up by John Webb in 1669.

The likelihood that Chinese was a natural language had first been suggested by the Jesuit missionary Matthew Ricci. He was of the opinion that, though the inhabitants of China, Japan, Korea, Vietnam, and so on could not understand each other's spoken languages, they could all read written Chinese, 'because each written character in Chinese writing represents an individual thing'. If this were universally true, he continued, 'we would be able to transmit our ideas to people of other countries in writing, though we would not be able to speak to them'.[131] Ricci's claim was to influence Francis Bacon and influence the search for a universal language from that time on.[132]

Like Browne, John Webb suggested that the Chinese were absent from Babel and thus avoided the confusion of languages which arose there. Since Webb did not accept that Paradise had been located in China, he maintained that Noah carried the primitive language into the ark with him, that the ark landed in India, and that China was thence populated after the Flood either by Noah himself or by some of the sons of Shem. The Chinese characters were the invention of Adam: 'He that gave names to all things, knew best how to invent Characters for all things . . .' And it was his claim that the Adamic characters had there remained, pure and undiluted, until the present day.[133] For, he argued, the Chinese were never conquered, and they never engaged in commerce. Moreover, the Chinese too had a tradition of a flood at the time of the emperor Janus with many parallels to the Genesis story.

In 1676, two years before the second edition of Webb's *Historical Essay*, Sir Matthew Hale described Webb's theory as 'a novel conceit'.[134] In 1668, one year before its original publication, John Wilkins, the Bishop of Chester, aware of Ricci's comments and influenced by Bacon, flirted with the possibility of written Chinese as the original language before rejecting it.[135] But he himself had been influenced by this possibility in *Mercury: or, The Secret and Swift Messenger* in 1641, a work dealing with all

---

[130] Geoffrey Keynes (ed.), *The Works of Sir Thomas Browne*, iii.72. I am indebted to my colleague Peter Harrison for this reference.
[131] Quoted by Paul Cornelius, *Languages in Seventeenth- and Eighteenth-Century Imaginary Voyages*, p. 28.
[132] See Francis Bacon, *The Two Bookes of the Proficience and Advancement of Learning* (London, 1605), sig. P.p.3.r–4.v. See also John Wilkins, *Mercury: or, The Secret and Swift Messenger* (London, 1641), p. 107.
[133] See John Webb, *An Historical Essay*, p. 147.
[134] See Matthew Hale, *The Primitive Origination of Mankind*, pp. 162–5.
[135] See John Wilkins, *An Essay*, pp. 13, 450.

methods of transmitting messages in all sorts of circumstances. One of the chapters in this work explored the possibility of a universal musical language. He envisaged the possibility of a real relation between notes and things, thus leading to a tonal universal language accessible to all people: 'The utterance of these Musicall tunes', he wrote, 'may well serve for the universall *language*, and the writing of them for the universall *Character*. As all Nations do agree in the same conceit of things, so likewise in the same conceit of Harmonies.'[136]

Wilkins was influenced in considering the possibility of a musical universal language by Bishop Francis Godwin's *The Man in the Moone* in 1638. This was the story of the Spaniard Domingo Gonsales, who journeyed to the moon in a chariot drawn by teams of birds, partly like swans and partly like eagles. There Gonsales discovered a paradise. The lunar language was a musical one which consisted 'not so much of words and Letters, as of tunes and uncouth sounds'.[137] Thus, it was possible for the lunarians to say what they thought by means of tunes and not words: 'By occasion hereof, I discerne meanes of framing a Language (and that easie soon to be learned) as copious as any other in the world, consisting of tunes only.'[138] When Gonsales landed again on earth, it was in China. Like the lunarians, the Mandarins spoke a language that 'did consist much of tunes'.[139] The origins of Godwin's lunarian musical language and Wilkins' musical language (though the former was aware of it and the latter not) alike lay in the tonal nature of the language of the Mandarins.

Cyrano de Bergerac's imaginary Paradise, like Godwin's, was located on the moon. On Cyrano's moon, the whole year was like spring. It was the place whence Adam and Eve departed to go to earth. And, like Godwin's lunarians, its inhabitants could speak a musical language: 'they take either a Lute or some other Instrument, whereby they communicate their Thoughts, as well as by their Tongue: So that sometimes Fifteen or Twenty in a Company, will handle a point of Divinity, or discuss the difficulties of a Law-suit, in the most harmonious Consort, that ever tickled the ear'.[140]

Another non-verbal possibility for the language of Adam was that of gesture. Gesture was perceived as a somatic hieroglyph. In 1654, for

[136] John Wilkins, *Mercury, or the Secret and Swift Messenger*, p. 144.
[137] Francis Godwin, *The Man in the Moone*, p. 93.
[138] *Ibid.*, p. 95. And see H. Neville Davies, 'Bishop Godwin's "Lunatique Language"', *Journal of the Warburg and Courtauld Institutes* 30 (1967), pp. 296–316.
[139] Francis Goodwin, *The Man in the Moone*, p. 123.
[140] Cyrano de Bergerac, *The Comical History of the States and Empires of the worlds of the Moon and the Sun*, p. 43.

example, John Webster remarked that the language of gesture among the deaf and dumb was suggestive of a universal language.[141] Such a language had already been elaborated ten years previously by the physician John Bulwer in *Chirologia*. As one of the commendatory poems which preceded the text put it,

> The Hand & Meaning ever are ally'de
> All that are deafe & dumbe may here recrute
> Their language, & then blesse thee for the Mute
> Enlargements of thy Alphabets.

According to Bulwer, gesture was 'the only speech and generall language of Humane Nature'.[142] But it was more than this. It was the language of Adam and the language of nature. And, Bulwer believed, it was recoverable, for it had escaped the curse of Babel. Knowledge of the language of birds and beasts 'is a kinde of knowledge that *Adam* partly lost with his innocency, yet might be repaired in us, by a diligent observation and marking of the outward effects of the inward and secret motions of beasts'.[143]

UNDOING BABEL

If, for most, the original language of Adam had disappeared at Babel, there remained throughout the better part of the seventeenth century the hope of creating a new universal language, the words of which would actually and accurately mirror the nature of things. As Hans Aarsleff has remarked, such hopes for a natural language 'were sustained by an optimism for which nothing seemed unattainable, similar to other expectations that strike us as equally chimerical, for instance the perpetuum mobile and the squaring of the circle'.[144] Such a new language would provide a remedy for the curse of Babel. Against this curse, wrote John Wilkins, Latin and other learned languages provided some relief. But a universal character would be ideal: 'the confusion at *Babel* might this way have been remedied, if everyone could have expressed his own meaning by the same kinde of Character'.[145] Similarly, in March 1646, in

---

[141] See John Webster, *Academiarum Examen*, p. 25.
[142] John Bulwer, *Chirologia: or, The natural Language of the Hand* (London, 1644), p. 3.
[143] *Ibid.*, pp. 6–7. On the life and work of Bulwer, see H. J. Norman, 'John Bulwer (fl. 1654) The "Chirosopher"', *Proceedings of the Royal Society of Medicine* 36 (1943), pp. 589–602. See also Dilwyn Knox, 'Ideas on Gesture and Universal Languages, c.1550–1650', in John Henry and Sarah Hutton (eds.), *New Perspectives on Renaissance Thought* (London, 1990).
[144] Hans Aarsleff, *From Locke to Saussure*, p. 261.
[145] John Wilkins, *Mercury: or, The Secret and Swift Messenger*, p. 106.

a letter to Samuel Hartlib, who was engaged in developing a universal language, Robert Boyle wrote, 'If the design of *the Real Character* take effect, it will in good part make amends to mankind for what their pride lost them at the Tower of Babel.'[146] Nathaniel Smart saw Cave Beck's universal numerical language, translated into a language of gestures, as undoing Babel:

> Here Logarithmes, 'yond what *Napier* findes,
> That teach by Figures to Uncypher minds,
> And make our hands officious to help out,
> Of tongues confusion, made at Babels rout.[147]

Undoing the curse of Babel had Utopian possibilities. To the Pansophist John Comenius, if all people understand each other, 'they will become as it were one race, one people, one household, one School of God'.[148] For him, the failure to communicate was the cause of all problems. If linguistic strife is removed, 'there will be universal Peace over the whole world, hatred and the causes of hatred will be done away, and all dissension between men. For there will be no ground for dissenting, when all men have the same Truths clearly presented to their eyes.'[149]

Such linguistic Utopianism was common. William Petty, later a member of the Royal Society, Allison Coudert informs us, 'turned his attention to a dictionary of difficult words because he believed that the conflict between Catholics and Protestants rested largely on the misunderstanding of words like "God", "Devil", "Heaven", "Hell", "Catholic" and "Pope"'.[150] John Wilkins believed a natural language would be conducive to the spread of religion and the preaching of the gospel to all nations.[151] Seth Ward saw a universal language as a matter of great concern to the advancement of learning.[152] Charles II covered all the possibilities in his letter of recommendation to the Scottish schoolmaster George Dalgarno's *Ars Signorum* in 1661. He judged the plan for a universal language

---

[146] Quoted by Clark Emery, 'John Wilkins' Universal Language', *Isis* 38 (1947), p. 175. See also James Knowlson, *Universal Language Schemes in England and France, 1600–1800* (Toronto, 1975), pp. 9–10.

[147] Cave Beck, *The Universal Character* (London, 1657), introductory poem.

[148] John Amos Comenius, *The Way of Light* (Liverpool, 1938), p. 198.

[149] *Ibid.*, p. 202. Comenius' *The Way of Light* was circulating in manuscript form in England by 1641. On his influence on English universal language schemes, see B. De Mott, 'Comenius and the Real Character in England', *PMLA* 70 (1955), pp. 1068–81.

[150] See Allison Coudert, 'Some Theories of a Natural Language', p. 99. See also John Wilkins, *An Essay*, Epistle Dedicatory.

[151] See John Wilkins, *An Essay*, Epistle Dedicatory.

[152] See Seth Ward, *Vindiciae Academiarum* (Oxford, 1664), p. 22.

of singular use, for facilitating the matter of Communication and Intercourse between People of different Languages, and consequently a proper and effectual Means for advancing all the parts of Real and Useful Knowledge, Civilizing barbarous Nations, Propagating the Gospel, and encreasing Traffique and Commerce.[153]

The universal language systems of Wilkins, Ward, Beck, and Dalgarno were secular systems. They perceived themselves not so much as retrieving the original language of Adam as creating new languages. They themselves were Adams. The undoing of Babel was, for them, a metaphorical rather than a literal truth.

There were others for whom the undoing of Babel was part of a magico-mystical attempt to regain an Adamic language of nature. The Renaissance doctrine of signatures, according to which natural objects carried a signature which indicated their use, was part of this. Crucially, understanding the signatures of things enables the individual to give the right names to things. According to Paracelsus, this was the art which Adam knew: 'So it was that after the Creation he gave its own proper name to everything, to animals, trees, roots, stones, minerals, metals, waters, and the like, as well as to other fruits of the earth, of the water, of the air, and of the fire . . . Now these names were based upon a true and intimate foundation, not on mere opinion . . . Adam is the first signator.'[154] John Webster believed that Adam was able to name the animals according to their natures because he understood 'both their internal and external signatures'.[155] And Adam's naming of Eve, he declared, was 'nothing else but the pure language of nature which he then spake, and understood, and afterwards so miserably lost and defaced'.[156]

By their signatures, as the Paracelsian alchemist Oswald Croll put it, things 'Magically seem to speak to us' of their virtues and uses.[157] Signatures showed to which part of the body things were to be applied. Thus William Coles on Oswald Croll: 'Crollius in his book of Signatures saith that the woody scales, whereof the Pine Apple is composed . . . do very much resemble the formost teeth of Man; and therefore Pine leaves boiled in Vinegar make a good decoction to gargle the mouth for asswaging immoderate pains in the teeth and gums . . .'[158] Walnuts were

---

[153] George Dalgarno, *Ars Signorum, vulgo Character universalis et Lingua Philosophica* (London, 1661), letter of recommendation.
[154] Arthur E. Waite (ed.), *The Hermetic and Alchemical Writings of . . . Paracelsus the Great* (London, 1894), i.188. See also Oswald Croll, *Bazilica Chymica, & Praxis Chymiatricae* (London, 1670), sig. B.3.v.
[155] John Webster, *Academiarum Examen*, p. 29.   [156] *Ibid.*, p. 30.
[157] Oswald Croll, *Bazilica Chymica, & Praxis Chymiatricae*, sig.B.1.r.
[158] William Coles, *Adam in Eden*, p. 100.

prescribed for illnesses of the head. According to Coles, these 'Have the perfect Signature of the Head: the outer husk or green Covering represent the *Pericranium*, or outward skin of the skull . . . and therefore salt[s] made of those husks or barks, are exceeding good for wounds in the head . . . The *kernel* hath the very figure of the Brain, and therefore it is very profitable for the Brain . . .'[159] For baldness, suggested Coles, a 'decoction of the long Mosse that hangs upon Trees' was useful.[160]

The Paracelsian doctrine of signatures was taken up by Jacob Boehme. But here the doctrine of signatures is transmuted into a metaphor for the divine essence of all things, which could be mystically experienced. It was an experience which he had had. In the first Behmenist tract in England, Abraham von Franckenberg's *The Life of one Jacob Boehmen*, we read that in 1600 as a young man the Silesian cobbler was dazzled by sunlight glancing off a pewter dish. Immediately he 'was brought to the inward ground or *Centrum* of the hidden *Nature*. But he yet somewhat mistrusting, went out into an open field, and there beheld the *Wonder-workes* of the Creator in the Signatures of all created things, very clearly and manifestly laid open.'[161] So the language of nature, the language used by Adam to name all things, was a language which expressed the mystical vision of the essence of things:

When as all people spake in one Language then they *understood* one another; but when they would not use the *Naturall* Genuine tongue; then the true and right understanding was put *out* in them; for they brought the Spirits of the genuine tongue of Sence into an *externall grosse* forme . . . Now no people doe any more understand the Language of Sence, and yet the Birds in the aire, and the beasts in the fields understand it according *to their property*. Therefore *man* may well thinke and consider, what he is deprived of; and what he shall againe obtaine in the New-birth; although [perhaps] not *here* upon the Earth, yet in the Spiritual world.[162]

This was an experience similar to the conversion experience of the Quaker George Fox. In his journal, he reported that he was taken up in the Spirit into Paradise into the state of Adam before the Fall. The creation was opened to him, he wrote, 'And it was shewed me, how all things had their *Names* given them, according to their *Nature* and *Vertue*.'[163]

---

[159] *Ibid.*, p. 3. Quoted by John Prest, *The Garden of Eden*, p. 62.

[160] William Coles, *Adam in Eden*, p. 31. For other examples, see Peter Harrison, *The Bible, Protestantism, and the Rise of Natural Science*, p. 252.

[161] Abraham von Franckenberg, *The Life of one Jacob Boehmen* (London, 1644), sig. A.2.r.

[162] Jacob Boehme, *Mysterium Magnum: or, An Exposition of the First Book of Moses called Genesis* (London, 1654), pp. 229–30.

[163] George Fox, *A Journal: or, Historical Account of the Life . . . of George Fox*, i.18.

According to Boehme, the natural language had been lost at Babel, though it contained the seventy-two others that were to derive from it.[164] But the natural language was also a Pentecostal one, when '*Peter* from the opened Sensuall tongue spake *in one Language all Languages*; and this was also Adams Language . . .'[165] Thus, the Adamic language, that which expresses the mystical vision into the essences of things, would appear to be an inward version of that which expresses itself outwardly as Pentecostal glossolalia.

Jacob Boehme, via Rosicrucianism, influenced the English quest for the universal language by virtue of his influence on John Webster's plans for higher education. Webster continued the quest of Boehme, and of the Rosicrucians, for the pure language of nature. In the university as he envisaged it, the Rosicrucian linguist would toil in search of the Adamic language, still spoken and understood by every other creature, and spoken too originally by Adam: 'when I find *Adam* understand this heavenly *Dialect* . . . I cannot but believe that his was the language of nature infused into him in his Creation, and so innate and implantate in him, and not inventive and acquisitive'.[166] And he looked towards a 'Hieroglyphical, Emblematical, Symbolical, and Cryptographical learning' which would be comprehensible to all.[167]

It is difficult to tell the extent to which the secular language theorists like Ward and Wilkins were indebted to the magico-mystical attempts to discover the Adamic language. Arguably, they were indebted to the tradition for the premise that in the ideal language there ought to be a real relationship between words and things. Be that as it may, as Ormsby-Lennon has argued, the belief in Edenic signatures 'threatened that divorce of nature from a mystical reading of Scripture upon which Bacon (usually), Galileo (always), and their beneficiaries in the Royal Society (variously) believed that both scientific progress and a sound theology necessarily depended'.[168] And, he went on to say, nearly every Fellow of the Royal Society damned Rosicrucian linguistics as epistemologically dangerous and religiously intolerable.

---

[164] On the long tradition that after Babel there were seventy-two (or so) languages, see Herman J. Weigand, 'The Two and Seventy Languages of the World', *Germanic Review* 17 (1942), pp. 241–60.

[165] Jacob Boehme, *Mysterium Magnum*, p. 234.   [166] John Webster, *Academiarum Examen*, p. 29.

[167] *Ibid.*, p. 24.

[168] Hugh Ormsby-Lennon, 'Rosicrucian Linguistics: Twilight of a Rrenaissance Tradition', in Ingrid Merkel and Allen Debus (eds.), *Hermeticism and the Renaissance* (Washington, D.C., 1988), p. 315.

Such criticism is wonderfully illustrated in Seth Ward's merciless lampooning of magico-mystical renderings of the primitive language in *Vindiciae Academiarum*, his response to John Webster: :

The Paradisicall Protoplast, being Characteristically bound to the Ideal Matrix of Magicall contrition, by the Symphoniacall in-speaking of Aleph tenebrosum, and limited by Shem hamphorash to the central Ideas, inblowne by the ten numerations of Belimah, which are ten and not nine, ten and not eleven; and consequently being altogether absorpt in decyphering the signatures of Ensoph, beyond the sagacity of either a Peritrochiall, or an Isoperimentall expansion. The lynges of the faetiferous elocution, being disposed only to introversion, was destitute at that time of all Peristalticall effusion, which silenced the Otacousticall tone of the outflying word, and suppressed it in singultient irructations. But where the formes are thus enveloped in a reluctancey to Pamphoniacall Symbols, and the Phantasmaticall effluviums checked by the tergiversation of the Epiglottis, from its due subserviency to that concord and harmony which ought to have been betwixt lapsed man and his fellow strings, each diatesseron being failed of its diapente necessary to make up a Diapason no perfect tone could follow. And consequently this Language of nature must needs be impossible.[169]

The quests for the language of Adam and the attempts to create universal languages rested on the possibility that there could *in principle* be a language in which there was a real relationship between words and things. It was the collapse of this possibility that brought these quests to an end. As early as 1644, Sir Kenelm Digby expressed his doubts. 'It is true', he wrote, 'wordes serue to expresse thinges: but if you obserue the matter well; you will perceiue they doe so, onely according to the pictures we make of them in our owne thoughts, and not according as the thinges are in theire proper natures.'[170] Hobbes was drifting in this direction in *Leviathan*. For while he admitted that God was the first author of speech who had originally instructed Adam in the naming of the animals, he believed that from then on Adam was on his own. He invented the rest as the need arose.[171] Sir Thomas Urquhart satirised the search for the universal language in *Logopandecteision: or An Introduction to the Universal Language* in 1653. In his introduction, he enumerated sixty-six advantages of his new proposed language; for example, each noun had eleven cases, eleven genders, and four numbers, while verbs had ten tenses, seven moods, and four voices. After six further books of introduction, he neglected to set down the language.[172] Richard Simon, follow-

---

[169] Seth Ward, *Vindiciae Academiarum*, pp. 22–3. And see Allison Coudert, 'Some Theories of a Natural Language', p. 130.   [170] Kenelm Digby, *Two Treatises* (Paris, 1644), p. 2.

[171] Thomas Hobbes, *Leviathan* (London, 1973), p. 12.

[172] See Clark Emery, 'John Wilkins' Universal Language', p. 175.

ing Gregory of Nyssa, declared that God gave men understanding 'whereby to reason, which they have made use of to express their thoughts by the inventing of words'.[173]

It was John Locke who ended all hopes of a natural language. For it was he who maintained that the relationship between words and things was not a natural but an arbitrary one. Locke's discussion of language proceeded from this premise. Words, he wrote, 'came to be made use of by men as the signs of their Ideas; not by any natural connexion . . . but by a voluntary imposition, whereby such a word is made arbitrarily the Mark of such an idea'.[174] This was an argument against the central principle of the Adamic language. For it entailed that the names which Adam gave to the animals were arbitrary, and that consequently there was no essential difference between the language of Adam and the languages after Babel:

What liberty Adam had at first to make any complex ideas of *mixed modes*, by no other pattern, but by his own thoughts, the same have all men ever since had. And the same necessity of conforming his ideas of *substances* to things without him, as to archetypes made by nature, that Adam was under, if he would not wilfully impose upon himself, the same are all men ever since under too. The same liberty also, that Adam had of affixing any new name to any idea; the same has any one still . . . but only with this difference, that in places, where men in society have already established a language amongst them, the significa-tion of words are very warily and sparingly to be altered.[175]

Locke's principle of the arbitrary nature of the relation between words and things ruled out both magico-mystical interpretations of the Ada-mic language and secular attempts to construct a universal natural language. Undoing Babel was no longer a matter of practical difficulty but of theoretical impossibility.

[173] Richard Simon, *A Critical History of the Old Testament*, i.99.
[174] John Locke, *An Essay Concerning Human Understanding* (New York, 1959), 3.2.1.
[175] *Ibid.*, 3.6.51.

CHAPTER 5

Adam's rib

THE CREATION OF WOMAN

And the Lord God caused a deep sleep to fall upon Adam, and he
slept; and he took one of his ribs, and closed up the flesh instead
thereof; And the rib, which the Lord God had taken from man,
made he a woman, and brought her unto the man.

Genesis 2.21–2

> How ill did hee his *Grammar* skan
> that call'd a *Woman woe to* man?
> For (*contrary*) who doth not know,
> *Women* from *men* receive their *woe?*
> Yet love men too: but what's their *gaines?*
> Poore Soules! But *travaile* for their *paines*:
> Then let them all (in this) agree:
> 'Tis *woe* from *man*; if *woe* it bee.   William Austin[1]

In the story of Eden, in the second chapter of Genesis, there was a
recognition by God that it was desirable for man to have 'an help meet
for him' (v. 18). The creatures made by God for this purpose, and
named by Adam, were not suitable for this role. Thus, as his final
creative act, God created woman. Adam called her woman 'because
she was taken out of Man' (v. 23). And, after the Fall, he called her Eve
'because she was the mother of all living' (Genesis 3.20). This provided
the barrister William Austin in his essay on the excellence of women
with an opportunity for a homily on the duty of care owed to them by
men: 'The *first* [Woman] was the *last name* he gave to anything before
his *fall*: and the *last* [Eve] was the *first name*, he gave to anything *after his
fall*. So that in his *felicity* his *last case*, and in his *misery*, his *first care* was for
the *woman*.'[2]

---

[1] William Austin, *Haec Homo*, p. 164. See also John Wing, *The Crowne Coniugall or, the Spouse Royall*
(Middelburg, 1620), p. 11.
[2] *Ibid.*, pp. 152–3.

In order to create woman, God put Adam in a deep sleep. The commentators varied on the reasons for this. Calvin had suggested that the deep sleep was sent upon Adam not to hide from him the origin of his wife but to exempt him from pain.[3] Du Bartas pictured God as a surgeon who brings his patient into a senseless slumber the better to effect removal of the necessary parts, a metaphor also suggested by the Calvinist commentator David Pareus.[4] Thomas Browne regarded the removal of Adam's rib as the first surgical procedure. Somewhat obtusely, the puritan George Walker saw it not as a case of anaesthesia, but as a type of Christ's sleep of death before the Resurrection.[5] It could not have been to relieve pain, declared George Hughes sensibly, for Adam then was incapable of feeling any.[6]

It was also suggested that it was necessary for Adam to be unconscious during the event to emphasise the prerogative of God in creating. Eve owed everything to her creator, wrote Bishop Joseph Hall.[7] It was necessary for Adam to be asleep, declared Lancelot Andrewes, 'least any should fasly [*sic*] and foolishly suspect that Adam being present and awaked, should have been some help and means, and had somewhat to doe in the Creation of the Woman'.[8] As the major event preceding the first marriage the puritan divine Henry Smith saw it as a metaphor for unworldliness in the selection of a wife: 'As the man slept while his wife was making, so our flesh should sleepe while our wife is chusing, least as the loue of venison wan *Isaak* to blesse one for another, so the loue of gentrie, or riches, or beautie, make vs take one for another.'[9]

Yet for some the biblical text itself did not suggest the complete unconsciousness of Adam. For the text does imply that Adam, upon seeing her for the first time, knew her origin. 'This *is* now bone of my bones, and flesh of my flesh', said Adam (Genesis 2.23). The Greek translators of the Old Testament may well have recognised this, for in the Septuagint Adam falls not into a deep sleep but into an 'ecstasy' in which consciousness remained. Thus Andrew Willet at the end of the sixteenth century: 'we doe thinke', he wrote, 'that as this was a sound, heauy, or deepe sleepe of the bodie, so the soule of Adam was in an

---

3 See John King (trans.), *Commentaries on the First Book of Moses*, p. 135.
4 See Susan Snyder (ed.), *The Divine Weeks and Works*, i.290. See also Arnold Williams, *The Common Expositor*, p. 86.
5 See George Walker, *God made visible*, p. 197.
6 See George Hughes, *An Analytical Exposition of the Whole first Book of Moses called Genesis*, p. 23.
7 See Joseph Hall, *Workes*, i.776.
8 Lancelot Andrewes, *Apospasmatia Sacra*, p. 218. See also Thomas Adams, *The Works*, p. 1133.
9 Henry Smith, *The Sermons of Master Henry Smith* (London, 1601), p. 12.

ecstasis or trance, beeing illuminated of God, as it may appeare by this, that when he awaked, he knew that the woman was taken out of him'.[10] In *Paradise Lost*, God closed Adam's eyes, but he 'op'n left the Cell/ Of Fancy my internal sight, by which/ Abstract as in a trance methought I saw . . .'[11]

Considered as an anatomical possibility, the creation of Eve from a human rib (and/or the side) of Adam created many problems.[12] As Arnold Williams explains it, 'if it was a necessary rib, then Adam was mutilated when he lost it; if it was superfluous, then he was created monstrous'.[13] The majority of seventeenth-century commentators followed Luther in suggesting that Adam was born with one extra rib and that its loss did not entail his original monstrosity or his subsequent mutilation.[14] And in this they followed the rabbinic tradition.[15] Thus, for example, Andrew Willet thought it most likely that God created one above the usual number, 'not as a superfluous or monstrous part, but as necessarie for the creation of the woman which God intended'.[16] In 1617, John Salkeld argued that Adam was created with thirteen ribs on one side, making a total of twenty-five. This was part of the divine plan; and consequently there could be no suggestion of monstrousness: 'the name of *monster* is not so much in regard of superabundance or want, as in regard of the ends, and purposes intended by the author of nature . . .'[17] The Scottish divine John Weemse opted for Adam's having originally had an extra rib. But, he maintained, even if it were one of his ordinary ribs which was used, God would have replaced it, a position endorsed by a number of Renaissance commentators.[18] It was not one of the ribs necessary to make him a perfect man, declared George Walker in 1641, 'but a rib above the ordinary number, which God created in *Adam* of purpose . . .'[19]

(handwritten margin note: But then god would always have intended to create woman . . . ?)

---

[10] Andrew Willet, *Hexapla in Genesin*, p. 37.

[11] John Milton, *Paradise Lost*, 8.460–2. See also Giovanno Loredano, *The Life of Adam*, p. 16.

[12] The Hebrew is ambivalent, since the word for rib – *tzela'* – can denote rib or side. The Vulgate and the Septuagint clearly understand it to mean rib, as does the Authorised Version.

[13] Arnold Williams, *The Common Expositor*, p. 90.

[14] See Jaroslav Pelikan, *Luther's Works*, i.129–30.

[15] See for example John W. Etheridge, *The Targums of Onkelos and Jonathan ben Uzziel . . . from the Chaldee* (n.p., 1862), i.163.   [16] Andrew Willet, *Hexapla in Genesin*, p. 38.

[17] John Salkeld, *A Treatise of Paradise*, p. 176.

[18] See John Weemse, *The Portraiture of the Image of God in Man*, pp. 313–14. And see Arnold Williams, *The Common Expositor*, p. 90 n. 81.

[19] George Walker, *God made visible*, p. 197. See also [William Basse], *A Helpe to Discovrse*, p. 35; Joseph Hall, *The Works*, i.776; William Nicholls, *A Conference with a Theist*, p. 169; Matthew Poole, *Annotations upon the Holy Bible*, sig. B.3.r.

There was no support for the notion that men in general have fewer ribs than women. Luther rejected it outright on anatomical grounds.[20] It was one of the vulgar and common errors mentioned by Thomas Browne. The scientist in him preferred to understand Adam as having had one rib fewer than the normal twenty-four after the creation of Eve. For him, this could have no effect upon subsequent generations, 'for we observe that mutilations are not transmitted from father unto son'.[21] It was an argument popularised by John Dunton in *The Athenian Gazette* at the end of the century.[22]

Whether Eve was built from a rib taken from the left or the right side was another issue upon which Thomas Browne was not inclined to have an opinion.[23] Others were not so reluctant. Alexander Ross, for example, argued that Eve was formed from a rib taken from Adam's left side. It was the side of the heart, he maintained, and pointed to the hearty love desirable between a man and a woman. But it was also the weaker side, which was why woman was the weaker vessel; and, following Aristotle, the side on which woman was conceived.[24] In 1645, in *Medicus Medicatus*, he adds as a further reason for the weakness of the left side the presence of the liver – 'which is the fountain of blood' – on the right side.[25] Thomas Browne was uncertain 'which is the right side of a man, or whether there be any such distinction in nature'.[26] Ross wasn't. For him, the right side connoted the good side, and the left the inferior or evil. That Eve was born from his left side, Milton's Adam has no doubt. In book four, he says to Eve, 'Out of my side to thee, nearest my heart/ Substantial Life, to have thee by my side/ Henceforth an individual solace dear'.[27] After the Fall, the meaning of the left side has changed:

> but a rib
> Crooked by nature, bent, as now appears,
> More to the part sinister from me drawn.[28]

The creation of Eve from a rib, from whichever side, provided opportunities for mysogynists to criticise all women. Contemporary

---

[20] See Jaroslav Pelikan, *Luther's Works*, i.129.

[21] Thomas Browne, *Pseudodoxia Epidemica*, 7.2. See also John White, *A Commentary Upon the Three First Chapters of Genesis*, ii.96.

[22] See John Dunton (ed.), *The Athenian Gazette*, vol. iii, q. 8, no. 17. See also Alexander Ross, *An Exposition on the Fovrteene first Chapters of Genesis*, p. 56.

[23] See Thomas Browne, *Religio Medici*, 1.21.

[24] See Alexander Ross, *An Exposition on the Fovrteene first Chapters of Genesis*, p. 54.

[25] Alexander Ross, *Medicus Medicatus* (London, 1645), p. 36.

[26] Thomas Browne, *Religio Medici*, 1.21.   [27] *Paradise Lost*, 4.484–6.   [28] *Ibid.*, 10.884–6.

anatomists distinguished five perfect circular ribs from seven not so perfect. This raised the question from which came Eve.[29] To many, she was created from the imperfect, bent, or crooked ribs. And physical deformity entailed moral imperfection. Thus Edward Gosynhill in 1560:

> Crooked it was, stiff and sturdy,
> And that would bend no manner of way;
> Of nature like, I dare well say,
> Of that condition all women be,
> Evil to rule, both stiff and sturdy.[30]

In fact, Gosynhill went on to suggest, the story of the creation of Eve from the rib of Adam was incorrect. Rather a dog ran away with the rib and ate it, forcing God to create Eve from a rib of the dog. This was why the woman 'at her husband doth bark and bawl,/ as doth the cur, for nought at all'.[31] Over a century later, in a poem which proceeded on the assumption of Eve as both whore and temptress, Richard Ames endorsed the notion of women as crooked by nature:

> But while in pleasant Dreams intrans'd he lay,
> Some Spirit came and stole his Rib away,
> And of that *crooked shapeless* thing did frame
> The *World's great Plague*, and did it Woman name.[32]

Similar themes were developed by a man who became known as 'the woman hater' (not least because of his attack upon them in *The arraignment of lewde, idle, froward and unconstant women*), one Joseph Swetnam. Moses, he wrote, 'saith that they were made of the ribbe of a man, and that their froward nature sheweth; for a ribbe is a crooked thing good for nothing else, and women are crooked by nature...'[33] In her response to Swetnam, Esther Sowernam drew a logical (if somewhat laboured) conclusion:

Admit that this Author's doctrine be true, that woman receiveth her froward and crooked disposition from the rib; Woman may then conclude upon that Axiom in Philosophy, 'Quicquid efficit tale, illud est magis tale' ('that which giveth quality to a thing doth more abound in that quality'), as fire which

---

[29] See, for example, Helkiah Crooke, *Microcosmographia*, p. 983; and John Pettus, *Volatiles from the History of Adam and Eve*, p. 64.

[30] Edward Gosynill, *Here Begynneth the Scole house of women: wherein every man may reade a goodly prayse of the condicyons of women* (1560); see Katherine U. Henderson and Barbara F. McManus (eds.), *Half Humankind: Contexts and Texts of the Controversy about Women in England, 1540–1640* (Urbana, Illinois, 1985), p. 148.

[31] *Ibid.*, p. 149. [32] Richard Ames, *The Folly of Love*, p. 2.

[33] Joseph Swetnam, *The arraignment of lewde, idle, froward and unconstant women* (London, 1615), p. 1. It went through ten editions by 1667, and six more by 1880. See Linda Woodbridge, *Women and the English Renaissance* (Brighton, Sussex, 1984), for the controversy aroused by it. See also Lancelot Andrewes, *Apospasmatia Sacra*, p. 219.

heateth is itself more hot; the Sun which giveth light is itself more light. So if Woman received her crookedness from the rib and consequently from the Man, how doth man excel in crookedness, who hath more of those crooked ribs! See how this vain, furious, and idle Author furnisheth woman with an Argument against himself and others of his Sex.[34]

But if the anatomy of the rib was used on occasion as a symbol of female crookedness, more often it functioned as a sign of the intimacy and affection which ought to hold between lovers, and as an emblem of the love which ought to exist between man and wife. Thus, in a wedding sermon, Henry Smith reminded his listeners that the husband 'must set her at his heart, and therfore she which should lie in his bosome, was made in his bosome, and should be as close to him as his ribbe, of which she was fashioned'.[35] Eve was made out of a rib, declared John Swan, 'taken from his side and neare his heart, that thereby he might remember to nourish, love, and cherish her, and use her like bone of his bone, and flesh of his flesh'.[36]

· That the rib from which Eve was created was located in the centre of the body facilitated discussion of an equality between man and wife. Thus, for example, as Gervase Babington explained, woman was made 'Not of the head of Man, least shee should bee proude and looke for superioritie. Not of the foote of Man, least shee should be contemned and used as farre his inferiour, but of hys side, that shee might bee used as his fellowe, cleauing to hys side . . .'[37] These were common metaphors. The pseudonymous Mary Tattlewell and Joan Hit-him-home reminded their male readers that as women did not have 'their Original out of his head (thereby to command him), so it was not out of his foot to be trod upon, but in a *medium* out of his side to be his fellow feeler, his equal, and companion'.[38]

---

[34] See Katherine U. Henderson and Barbara F. McManus (eds.), *Half Humankind*, p. 222. The passage occurs on p. 3 of the 1617 original, *Esther hath hang'd Haman*.

[35] Henry Smith, *The Sermons of Master Henry Smith*, p. 12.

[36] John Swan, *Specvlvm Mundi*, p. 501. See also Gervase Babington, *Certaine Plaine, briefe, and comfortable Notes vpon euerie Chapter of Genesis*, sig. F.4.v; John Weemse, *The Portraiture of the Image of God in Man*, p. 310; Nicholas Gibbens, *Qvestions and Dispvtations concerning the Holy Scriptvre*, p. 97; John Salkeld, *A Treatise of Paradise*, p. 173; John Willet, *Hexapla in Genesin*, p. 37; William Secker, *A Wedding-Ring Fit for the Finger* (London, 1664), p. 17.

[37] Gervase Babington, *Certaine Plaine, briefe, and comfortable Notes vpon euerie Chapter of Genesis*, sig. C.4.r. See also Thomas Aquinas, *Summa Theologiae*, 1a.92.3, where the same metaphors are used.

[38] Mary Tattlewell and Joan Hit-him-home, *The womens sharpe revenge* (1640). see Katherine U. Henderson and Barbara F. McManus (eds.), *Half Humankind*, p. 317. See also Rachel Speght, *A Mouzell for Melastomus, The cynicall Bayter of, and foule mouthed Barker against Evahs Sex* (London, 1617), p. 10; Daniel Rogers, *Matrimoniall Honour* (London, 1592), p. 60; John Wing, *The Crowne Coniugall*, pp. 30–1; Alexander Ross, *An Exposition on the Fovrteene first Chapters of Genesis*, p. 54; George Walker, *God made visible*, p. 199; William Nicholls, *A Conference with a Theist*, pp. 167-8; John Diodati, *Piovs Annotations*, sig. D.I.v.

Equality it was, but it was often qualified. For the Genesis text was read through the Pauline understanding of the headship of men and the subordination of women: 'Wives', wrote Paul to the women of Ephesus, 'submit yourselves unto your own husbands, as unto the Lord. For the husband is head of the wife, even as Christ is the head of the Church . . . Therefore as the church is subject unto Christ, so *let* the wives *be* to their own husbands in everything' (Ephesians 5.22–4). John White's understanding of the wife as an 'help' is typically puritan:

> Let both married persons know their places, the woman contenting herself with that place, in which God hath set her, and for which He hath furnished her with abilities proportionable . . . And let the man so use his place of ruling and governing, that he may look on his wife as his helper . . . remembring that though she be an Helper, yet she is but an helper; so that he must undertake the greatest employment, in the government of the Family.[39]

Even Rachel Speght, in her lively response to Joseph Swetnam, accepted that the man was the head of the woman, though she denied his right to treat her as a slave.[40] As Linda Woodbridge remarks, her 'feminism is hobbled by her faith: she believes that although the bible does not promote misogyny, it does not allow for feminism either'.[41]

There was no dispute about the status of women after the Fall. The subordination of women was part of the divine punishment. About this, the text was unequivocal: 'thy desire shall be to thy husband, and he shall rule over thee' (Genesis 3.16). But the textual basis for the prelapsarian subordination of women was far less clear. Indeed, the text gives no grounds for any position on the status of women in innocence.

Even so, it was occasionally suggested that in the state of innocence there was total equality. Augustine and Aquinas were ambivalent. But Martin Luther accepted that Eve would have not been subject to Adam had they not fallen: 'Had Eve therefore stood in the truth, she would not only have been free from all subjection to the rule of the man, but she herself would have been an equal partaker of government, which now belongs to men alone.'[42] In the narrative poem *Salve Deus Rex Judaeorum*,

---

[39] John White, *A Commentary Upon the Three first Chapters of Genesis*, ii.87. see also William Secker, *A Wedding-Ring*, p. 17.

[40] Rachel Speght, *A Mouzell for Melastomus*, p. 16.

[41] Linda Woodbridge, *Women and the English Renaissance*, p. 90.

[42] Henry Cole (trans.), *The Creation: A Commentary by Martin Luther*, p. 271. See also p. 159. Luther too is ambivalent, for in spite of the words above, in comparing man and woman to the sun and the moon he concluded, 'For as the sun is more excellent than the moon . . . so the woman, although she was a most beautiful work of God, nevertheless was not the equal of the male in glory and prestige.' See Jaroslav Pelikan, *Luther's Works*, i.69. Gervase Babington used the same imagery; see *Certaine Plaine, briefe, and comfortable Notes vpon euerie Chapter of Genesis*, sig. c.4.r.

Shakespeare's Dark Lady, Emilia Lanier, pleaded, 'Then let us have our
Libertie again/ And challendge to yourselves no Sov'raigntie.'[43] The
Quaker Margaret Fell was persuaded that God 'makes no such distinc-
tions and differences as men do'.[44]

These were rare voices. The dominant one was that of the subordination of Eve, even in the state of innocence, and even among those who
read the metaphor of the rib as entailing her equality. As James Turner
perceptively notes, 'The ideological imperative, the passionate desire to
dominate the female, thus has the power to override the hermeneutic
process itself. The original non-subordination of Eve, and the original
immortality of man, are equally inferable from the text; and yet one is
almost universally accepted, the other almost universally denied.'[45]

The authority of Aristotle supported some in their belief that Eve was
naturally inferior. 'Wee all know', declared John Jonston in *An History of
the Wonderful Things of Nature*, 'there are two Sexes: the male the
superiour; and the female inferiour in all things. God gave the man the
Superiority, and comanded the woman to obey . . . They are easily
angry, and their choler kindled, soon will boyl over; and for want of
heat, they are not so ingenious.'[46] A hundred years earlier, John Knox
had blasted the monstrous regimen of women with, among other things,
the claim that the dominance of the male was universal: 'For nature
hath in all beastes printed a certein marke of dominion in the male, and
a certain subiection in the female, which they kepe inuiolate.'[47] Knox
would no doubt have been seriously irritated by the discovery that not
only the English but the bees also were ruled by a queen.

Several aspects of the creation of Eve were interpreted as entailing
her subjection. That Adam was created first and she last pointed to her
inferiority. Thus, for example, Pierre Charron in 1608: 'the woman
then the last in good and in generation, and by occasion the first in
euill and the occasion thereof, is iustly subiect vnto man, the first in
good, and last in euill'.[48] The puritan divine William Whately read

---

[43] A. L. Rowse (ed.), *The Poems of Shakespeare's Dark Lady: Salve Deus Rex Judaeorum*, pp. 43, 103–5.
Quoted by Peter Harrison, *The Bible, Protestantism, and the Rise of Natural Science*, p. 235.
[44] Quoted in James Grantham Turner, *One Flesh: Paradisal Marriage and Sexual Relations in the Age of
Milton* (Oxford, 1987), p. 108.
[45] James Grantham Turner, *One Flesh*, p. 119.
[46] John Jonston, *An History of the Wonderful Things of Nature*, p. 329.
[47] John Knox, *The First Blast of the Trumpet against the monstruous regimen of Women* (Geneva, 1558), sig.
D.6.r. In the latter part of the seventeenth century the Dutch entomologist Swammerdam proved
the large bee to have been female, though his findings were not published until the 1740s. See
Keith Thomas, *Man and the Natural World*, p. 62.
[48] Peter Charron, *Of Wisdome*, p. 180.

relations between Adam and Eve in Genesis through Pauline eyes. Man was made first and woman after him, he wrote, to show that man was by nature superior. Thus, 'You wives be content to be subject to your husbands, as it is sure *Evah* was before her fall at least, and probably after too, for we reade of no braules betwixt them.'[49] That Eve was created from man also suggested her natural subordination. To John Weemse, God did not make an original pair *ex nihilo*, as with the animals. Rather he made the one from the other to show 'the neere coniunction which is betwixt them' and so 'that he might be her head, and the fountaine of all mankinde . . .'[50] Lancelot Andrewes, like Henry Smith, saw Adam's superiority demonstrated in his having had the right to name her.[51]

After the Fall, Eve's subjection to Adam was seen to be much increased. To the Calvinist John Diodati, 'that sweet direction which he had over thee' became a domination 'wherein thou shalt be bound to yeeld to thy husbands will in humility and silence; or by force and violence, which peradventure he shall use, and shalt not be able to free thy self from the power he hath over thee'.[52] The voluntary subjection of the state of innocence was replaced by necessity. Andrew Willet spoke for many men: 'The woman should before haue been obedient to man, but of a louing societie to be made partaker of all his counsells, not of an vrging necessitie as now: whereby the woman in respect of her weaknes, both with her will dependeth of her husband, for her direction and prouision of things necessarie, and against her will shee often indureth the hard yoke of an vnequal comander.'[53]

In spite of this thinking, it was generally accepted that woman was made in the image of God. Genesis 1.27 was read in support of this. Thus, for example, John Swan interpreted 'male and female created he them' as showing 'that woman as well as man, was partaker of the same

---

49 William Whately, *The Primarie Precedent Presidents ovt of the Booke of Genesis* (London, 1640), p. 9. See also John Knox, *The First Blast of the Trumpet*, sig. B.5.r. See also sig. B.1.r.
50 John Weemse, *The Portraiture of the Image of God in Man*, p. 310. See also John Pettus, *Volatiles from the History of Adam*, p. 69.
51 See Lancelot Andrewes, *Apospasmatia Sacra*, p. 224; and Henry Smith, *The Sermons of Henry Smith*, p. 36.
52 John Diodati, *Piovs Annotations*, sig. D.2.r.
53 Andrew Willet, *Hexapla in Genesin*, p. 53. See also Alexander Ross, *An Exposition on the Fovrteene first Chapters of Genesis*, p. 26; John Salkeld, *A Treatise of Paradise*, p. 130; John White, *A Commentary Upon the Three First Chapters of Genesis*, iii.201; Benjamin Needler, *Expository Notes*, p. 106; John King (trans.), *Commentaries on the First Book of Moses*, p. 172; Gervase Babington, *Certaine Plaine, briefe, and comfortable Notes vpon euerie Chapter of Genesis*, sig. D.4.r.; Joseph Fletcher, *The Historie of the Perfect-Cursed-Blessed Man*, p. 26; Matthew Poole, *Annotations upon the Holy Bible*, sig. B.4.r.; John Knox, *The First Blast of the Trumpet*, sig. C.7.v; John Wing, *The Crowne Coniugall*, p. 47.

image'.[54] But Eve's image was for most only a reflected one. In modern terms, she merely bathed in reflected glory. In Pauline male-supremacist terms, man 'is the image and glory of God: but the woman is the glory of the man' (1 Corinthians 11.7). She was in the image of God, but less so.

Thus, with reference to 1 Corinthians 11.7, Nicholas Gibbens remarked that man bears more of the divine image, 'because hee is more honourable and beareth rule . . .'[55] Thomas Adams believed that as a human being woman bore the image of God, and as a woman the image of man until the Fall. But now, he declared, 'she beares the image of man indeed, but in a crosse and madde fashion; almost to the quite defacing of the image of God'.[56] The divine Elnathan Parr qualified his assertion that woman was made in the image of God by adding, 'though in regard of the subication of the woman to the man, it more excellently, in that, appeares in the man'.[57] Similarly, to George Walker in 1641, both men and women were made in the image of God. But man's glory, 'even the image of his *authority* appeares in the Womans *subjection* to him ever since the fall . . .'[58]

EVE'S PERFECTION

If the reading of Eve in the seventeenth century was dominated by male suprematism, there were nevertheless attempts to subvert this in terms of female perfectionism. In short, and for various reasons, Eve could be represented as the crown of creation. Thus, for example, in her response to Joseph Swetnam, the pseudonymous Constantia Munda exclaimed, 'A strange blasphemy . . . to call that imperfect, froward, crooked and peruerse to make an arraignment and Beare-baiting of that which the Pantocrator would in his omniscient wisedome haue to be the consummation of his blessed weekes worke, the end, crowne, and perfection of the neuer-sufficiently glorified creation.'[59] To William Austin in his essay on the excellence of women, Eve was the perfect conclusion of all

---

[54] John Swan, *Specvlvm Mundi*, p. 500. See also Andrew Willet, *Hexapla in Genesin*, p. 14; and William Austin, *Haec Homo*, p. 5.
[55] Nicholas Gibbens, *Qvestions and Dispvtations concerning the Holy Scriptvre*, pp. 38–9.
[56] Thomas Adams, *The Workes*, p. 500.
[57] Elnathan Parr, *The Grounds of Divinitie*, p. 120.
[58] George Walker, *God made visible*, p. 176. See also John King (trans.), *Commentaries on the First Book of Moses*, p. 129; Alexander Ross, *An Exposition on the Fovrteene first Chapters of Genesis*, p. 23; John Swan, *Specvlvm Mundi*, p. 500; John Knox, *The First Blast of the Trumpet*, sig. c.4.r; William Perkins, *An Exposition*, p. 113; John Milton, *Paradise Lost*, 8.540.
[59] Constantia Munda, *The Worming of a mad dogge, or a soppe for Cerberus* (London, 1617), p. 3.

God's works. She was created '*the last creature* in time as an *epitome*, conclusion, *period*, and full perfection *both of Heaven and Earth*'.[60] What seemed fair in all the world was 'in her summ'd up, in her contain'd', wrote Milton.[61] Of her beauty, there was no shortage of praise. To du Bartas, her beauty exceeded that of Adam:

> she had a more smiling Eye,
> A smoother Chinne, a Cheeke of purer Die,
> A fainter Voice, a more inticing Face,
> a deeper Tresse, a more delighting Grace,
> And in her bosome (More then Lilly-white)
> Two swelling Mounts of Ivorie panting light.[62]

Henry Cornelius Agrippa provided a number of arguments which were used in the seventeenth century in the cause of women. His *Treatise of the nobilitie and excellencye of womenkynde* was first translated into English in 1542 and was reissued in 1545 as *The Commendation of Matrimony*, in 1559 as *The Nobility of Women*, and as *The Glory of Women* in both prose and verse versions in 1652.

Agrippa's treatise, as part of the *querelle des femmes* tradition, was intended as much to show his literary and rhetorical skills in arguing a difficult topic as to promote an argument in favour of women. Be that as it may, for Agrippa she was his equal in many things: 'He hath giuen but one similitude and lykenes of the sowle, to bothe male and female, betwene whose soules there is no maner or dyfference of kynd. The woman hathe that same mynd that a man hath, that same reason and speche, she gothe to the same end of b[l]ysfulness, where there shall be noo exception of kynde.'[63] And his arguments on the the superiority of Eve from her name, from her order of creation, from the material from which she was made, and from the place of her creation, and so on, occurred regularly in seventeenth-century writings about the superiority of women.

In 1619, for example, Samuel Purchas argued for her 'preeminences aboue the Masculine in many things'.[64] She was made in a superior place, of superior matter, was superior in generation, of a better disposition and more capable of good, was ordained to a simpler life, and

---

[60] William Austin, *Haec Homo*, p. 13. [61] *Paradise Lost*, 8.473. See also 4.295-9, 440-3, 635-8.

[62] Susan Snyder (ed.), *The Divine Weeks and Works*, i.291. See also William Austin, *Haec Homo*, pp. 106-7; and Giovanno Loredano, *The Life of Adam*, p. 19.

[63] Henry Cornelius Agrippa, *A Treatise of the nobilitie and excellencye of womenkynde* (London, 1542), sig. A.2.r-v. For a critique of Agrippa, see Samuel Torshell, *The Womans Glorie* (London, 1650).

[64] Samuel Purchas, *Microcosmus*, p. 473. I am indebted to James Turner for this material. As he notes, Purchas went on immediately to condemn Eve on traditional grounds. See James Grantham Turner, *One Flesh*, p. 111.

brought about the redemption of men. Moreover, she was man's equal by virtue of her reasonable and immortal soul, and the equal supporter of the household.

That Eve was superior by virtue of her being a paradisal creature was a popular argument. Barnabe Rich, in his essay in defence of (and attack on) women, pointed to her origin in Paradise as evidence of her perfection.[65] For Esther Sowernam, woman could not degenerate from the 'naturall inclination of the place, in which she was first framed, she is a Paradician, that is, a delightfull creature, borne in so delightfull a country'.[66] Mary Tattlewell and Joan Hit-him-home concluded that 'as man was made of pollution, earth, and slime, and woman was formed out of that earth when it was first Refined, as man had his Original in the rude wide field and woman had her frame and composure in Paradise, so much is the womans Honour to be regarded and to be held in estimation amongst men'.[67] Eve's superiority was evidenced too by her having been God's final creative act. Eve was the 'last and therefore the perfectest handyworke of the Creator', wrote Barnabe Rich.[68]

For some, that Eve was created from Adam, and he from dust, was evidence of her superiority. To Jane Anger, in 1589, God 'making woman of man's flesh that she might be purer than he, doth evidently show how far we women are more excellent than men'.[69] The author of *Hic Mulier* in 1620 reminded female readers that 'God did not form you of slime and earth like man, but of a more pure and refined metal, a substance much more worthy . . .'[70] In *Much Ado About Nothing*, Shakespeare has Beatrice vow that she will never marry:

Not till God made men of some other metal than earth. Would it not grieve a woman to be overmaster'd with a piece of valiant dust? to make an account of

---

[65] Barnabe Rich, *The Excellency of Good Women* (London, 1613), p. 1. I say 'attack', for he soon lapsed from his defence of women. Thus, 'But as the sinne of *Adam beganne at Eve*, so the ruine the confusion the extortion the oppression yea and the sacriledge of many a man begins at the pride of his wife' (p. 13).

[66] Esther Sowernam, *Esther hath hang'd Haman* (London, 1617), p. 6.

[67] Mary Tattlewell and Joan Hit-him-home, *The womens sharpe revenge* (1640). Quoted by Katherine U. Henderson and Barbara F. McManus (eds.), *Half Humankind*, p. 319. Their conclusion was, on occasion, specifically rejected. Thomas Aquinas found no suggestion of female superiority in Eve's Edenic origins. Alexander Ross said she was born there only because Adam was there. See Thomas Aquinas, *Summa Theologiae*, 1a.102.4; and Alexander Ross, *An Exposition on the Fovrteene first Chapters of Genesis*, p. 45. Giovanno Loredano recognised the nobility of woman's place of birth, though he somewhat churlishly suggested that as a result women should stop complaining about their inferiority to men. See *The Life of Adam*, p. 17.

[68] Barnabe Rich, *The Excellency of Good Women*, p. 1. See also Esther Sowernam, *Esther hath hang'd Haman*, pp. 5–6.

[69] Jane Anger, *Her Protection for Women* (1589). Quoted by Katherine U. Henderson and Barbara F. McManus (eds.), *Half Humankind*, p. 181.   [70] Anon., *Hic Mulier* (1620). Quoted *ibid.*, p. 272.

her life to a clod of wayward marl? No, uncle, I'll none. Adam's sons are my brethren, and truly I hold it a sin to match in my kindred.[71]

LOVE AND MARRIAGE

And Adam said, This is now bone of my bones, and flesh of my flesh: she shall be called Woman, because she was taken out of Man. Therefore shall a man leave his father and his mother, and shall cleave unto his wife: and they shall be one flesh.

Genesis 2.23–4

The Genesis text could be read to justify the most extreme misogyny and the least assertive of feminisms. But it also provided the charter for the ideal of the companionate marriage, as a sexual and not a celibate relationship. And the passage above was interpreted as the first marriage ceremony. Thus, marriage was a paradisal institution. For the puritan Henry Smith 'it was the first ordinance that God instituted, euen the first thing which he did after man and woman were created, & that in the state of innocencie, before either had sinned, like ye finest flower, which will not thriue but in a cleane ground'.[72] To Daniel Rogers, it was the foundation of all other institutions: the 'Preservative of Chastity, the Seminary of the Commonwealth, seed-plot of the Church, pillar (under God) of the World, right hand of providence, supporter of lawes, states, orders, offices, gifts and services: the glory of peace, the sinewes of warre, the maintenance of policy, the life of the dead, the solace of the living, the ambition of virginity, the foundation of Countries, Cities, Universities, succession of Families, Crownes and Kingdomes . . .'[73] To be married was Paradise on earth. Marriage, wrote Rachel Speght, 'is a merri-age, and this worlds Paradise, where there is mutuall love'.[74] God was imagined as the first marriage celebrant, as Eve's father who gave away the bride, and by George Walker as 'the first *match-maker*'.[75]

[71] *Much Ado about Nothing* 2.1.50–5. Quoted by David L. Jeffrey (ed.), *A Dictionary of Biblical Tradition in English Literature*, p. 19. See also William Austin, *Haec Homo*, pp. 29ff; Esther Sowernam, *Esther hath hang'd Haman*, p. 6; John Wing, *The Crowne Coniugall*, p. 30; Mary Tattlewell and Joan Hit-him-home, *The womens sharpe revenge*, in Katherine U. Henderson and Barbara F. McManus (eds.), *Half Humankind*, p. 314; but cf. [Samuel Gott], *The Divine History*, p. 426.

[72] Henry Smith, *The Sermons of Master Henry Smith*, p. 10. See also William Secker, *A Wedding-Ring*, pp. 8–9.

[73] Daniel Rogers, *Matrimoniall Honour*, p. 7. Quoted by W. and M. Haller, 'The Puritan Art of Love', *Huntington Library Quarterly* 5 (1942), pp. 246–7.

[74] Rachel Speght, *A Mouzell for Melastomus*, p. 14.

[75] George Walker, *God made visible*, p. 202. See also George Hughes, *An Analytical Exposition of the Whole first Book of Moses, called Genesis*, p. 23; Matthew Poole, *Annotations upon the Holy Bible*, sig. B.3.r; and Thomas Peyton, *The glasse of time*, p. 29.

The Genesis text also provided a focus for the image of the companionate marriage. Diane McColley has pointed out that wedded love is a subject increasingly found in early-seventeenth-century visual representations of Genesis.[76] The same can be said of literary treatments. After God brought Eve to Adam, John Swan imagined 'a mutuall consent and gratulation followeth likewise between the parties, lest any one should tyrannically abuse his fatherly power, and force a marriage without love or liking'.[77] To Daniel Rogers, companionate marriage and romantic love intertwined:

Husbands and wives should be as two sweet friends, bred under one constellation, tempered by an influence from heaven, whereof neither can give any great reason, save that mercy and providence first made them so, and then made their match; Saying, see, God hath determined us, out of this vast world, each for other . . .[78]

As James Turner notes, the puritan art of love developed from Calvin's doctrine of the one flesh.[79] Thus, 'marital applications of Genesis do dwell upon the importance of love – not just the love that should endear the performance of duties, but also the sexual love specific to the marriage-bed'.[80] For Thomas Gataker, for example, husbands and wives re-enacted the original separation of Eve from Adam in reverse: 'There is in most *men* and *women* naturally an inclination and propension to the *nuptiall conjunction. The man seeketh his rib*, say the *Rabbines*; and the *woman the mans side*. The *man* misseth his *rib*, and seeketh to recover it againe, and the *woman* would bee in her old place againe, under the *mans arme or wing*, from whence at first shee was taken.'[81] To the puritan divine William Gouge, 'The first, highest, chiefest, and most absolutely necessary' feature of marriage was to be found in sexual union.[82]

---

[76] See Diane Kelsey McColley, *A Gust for Paradise: Milton's Eden and the Visual Arts*, p. 58.

[77] John Swan, *Specvlvm Mundi*, p. 502. See also Nicholas Gibbens, *Qvestions and Dispvtations concerning the Holy Scriptvre*, pp. 99–100.

[78] Daniel Rogers, *Matrimoniall Honour*, p. 245.

[79] See for example John King (trans.), *Commentaries on the First Book of Moses*, p. 128: 'Now the human race could not exist without the woman; and, therefore, in the conjunction of human beings, that sacred bond is especially conspicuous, by which the husband and the wife are combined in one body, and one soul . . .'

[80] James Grantham Turner, *One Flesh*, p. 73.

[81] Thomas Gataker, *A Good Wife Gods Gift, and A Wife in Deed* (1623), p. 37. Quoted *ibid.*, p. 73.

[82] See William Gouge, *Domesticall Duties* (1626), pp. 125–32. Quoted in Turner, *One Flesh*, pp. 74–5. The work is described by W. and M. Haller, in 'The Puritan Art of Love', p. 248, as 'The most systematic and detailed statement, from the Puritan pulpit, of this doctrine of the submission of woman . . .'

James Turner has rightly concluded that in the Protestant tradition it is 'in godly marriage, rather than in the extremes of asceticism and mystic rapture, that mankind comes nearest to regaining the glorious state of 'one flesh' that God originally intended for them'.[83] But several reservations should be entered. First, companionate marriage it was. But if the wife was a loving companion, she was nevertheless an inferior one. As one popular marriage manual put it, 'we would that the man when he loveth should remember his superiority'.[84]

Second, on occasion 'increase and multiply' rather than 'helpmeet' was seen as the central focus of marriage. There was a tendency to construe woman's role not in the spiritual terms of love, affection, and companionship, but in the physical terms of procreation. Thus John Salkeld not only believed that virginity was more laudable than marriage, but also that, had it not been necessary for generation, 'they might haue beene created males . . .'[85] And he went on to suggest, citing Aristotle, that in a paradisal world there would have been more men than women: 'nature then being in a full perfection, would for the most part haue produced the most perfect, which questionlesse is the male, for the most part I say, not alwaies, because the female also was necessary for the naturall propagation of mankinde'.[86] John White read the divine reflection on Adam's solitude (Genesis 2.18) as referring to procreation and enforcing the necessity to create another sex. Otherwise, he noted, 'man might have had as much assistance in his employment by the creating another Man, only he could have no Issue but by a woman'.[87] Thus, Eve's reason for being was re-creation rather than recreation. John Heydon endorsed the ideal of companionship in marriage, but only by interpreting it as equivalent to a friendship between men: '*a woman with a wise soul* is the fittest companion for man, otherwise God would have given him a friend rather than a Wife. A wise Wife comprehends both sexes; she is woman for her body, and she is man within, for her soul is like her Husbands.'[88]

The marriage service in the 1549 Anglican Book of Common Prayer

---

[83] James Grantham Turner, *One Flesh*, p. 77.
[84] J. Dod and R. Cleaver, *A Godly Forme of Householde Government* (London, 1614), sig. L.5.r–v. Quoted by Keith Thomas, 'Women and the Civil War Sects', *Past and Present*, no.13 (1958), p. 43.
[85] John Salkeld, *A Treatise of Paradise*, p. 181.
[86] *Ibid.*, p. 182. It was the position adopted by Aquinas in combining elements from Augustine and Aristotle. See Thomas Aquinas, *Summa Theologiae*, 1a.98.
[87] John White, *A Commentary Upon the Three First Chapters of Genesis*, ii.79. See also Henry Smith, *The Sermons of Master Henry Smith*, p. 13.
[88] John Heydon, *Advice to a Daughter* (1659). Quoted by James Grantham Turner, *One Flesh*, p. 116. I am indebted to Turner for the observation.

had defined marriage 'as an honourable estate, instituted of God in paradise, in the time of man's innocency, signifying unto us the mystical union which is betwixt Christ and his Church'. It went on to say that the purposes of matrimony were the procreation of children, the avoidance of lust, and 'the mutual society, help, and comfort, that the one ought to have of the other'. While some did read these as in descending order of importance, the majority saw the last as the main purpose of marriage.[89] And where mutual society was the major purpose for marriage, the failure of this provided for a few a justification for divorce. The canon laws of the Anglican Church expressly forbade divorce in 1604. And during the first half of the seventeenth century, no bishop or archbishop supported it. Still, in 1617, William Whately in *A Bride Bush* did suggest that, where matrimonial society had ceased, divorce could occur and the innocent party could remarry.[90] Importantly, Milton supported it. For Milton, where love had died, a marriage had already ended. Nothing remained 'but the empty husk of an outside matrimony; as unpleasing to God, as any other sort of hypocrisie'.[91] Thus, he concluded, 'it is a lesse breach of wedlock to part with wise and quiet consent betimes, then still to soile and profane that mystery of joy and union with a polluting sadnes and perpetual distemper; for it is not the outward continuing of mariage that keeps whole that cov'nant, but whosoever does most according to peace and love, whether in mariage, or in divorce, he it is that breaks mariage least'.[92]

Milton's four tracts on divorce between 1643 and 1645 were written during the period in which his wife had left him. He wrote no more on the subject after her return to him in 1645. His views had little influence on the theological mainstream. But they did have an impact on women among the radical sectarians. Thomas Edwards in *Gangraena* tells of a Mrs Attoway who after one of her sermons approached two gentlemen and 'spake to them of Master Milton's doctrine of divorce, and asked them what they thought of it, saying it was a point to be considered of; and that she for her part would look more into it, for she had an unsanctified husband, that did not walk in the way of Sion, nor speak the language of Canaan'.[93] She was soon after attached to a William Jenney

[89] See Derrick S. Bailey, *The Man–Woman Relation in Christian Thought* (London, 1959), p. 197.

[90] See William Whately, *A Bride Bush* (London, 1617). p. 25.

[91] John Milton, *The Works* (New York, 1931), iii.2.402.

[92] *Ibid.*, iii.2.403. See also John Halkett, *Milton and the Idea of Matrimony: A Study of the Divorce Tracts and 'Paradise Lost'* (New Haven, 1970).

[93] Thomas Edwards, *Gangraena*, 2nd edn (London, 1646), ii.10–11. Quoted by Keith Thomas, 'Women and the Civil War Sects', p. 50.

who also had divested himself of an unwanted partner. Jenney deduced 'from that Scripture in Genesis where God saith *I will make him an help meet for him*, that when a mans wife was not a meet help, he might put her away and take another; and when the woman was an unbeliever (that is, adds our informant, not a sectary of their church) she was not a meet help, and therefore Jenney left his wife, and went away with Mistress Attoway'.[94]

Serial monogamy was one thing, polygamy another. The patriarchs Abraham and Jacob had set a pattern. Milton endorsed it on the ground that, were it not lawful, the twelve tribes of Israel were all bastards. And Alan Rudrum has argued that lines 761–2 of the fourth book of *Paradise Lost* 'contain a veiled reference to Milton's belief that it was the Tyrant Custom, operating through the laws of the land, and not anything essential to Christianity, which prevented men of his own time from contracting polygamous marriages'.[95] But this was rare. Often the patriarchs were ignored. William Perkins, like Luther, tried to explain polygamy away. 'God did not approoue the polygamy of the fathers, or commend it', he wrote, 'but did onely tollerate it, as a lesser euill, for the preuenting of a greater.'[96] Others, like Calvin, disapproved. The polygamies of the patriarchs, declared John White, 'may be justly conceived to be recorded amongst their blemishes . . .'[97] The Protestant convert Bernardino Ochinus called them sinners, 'as being born of Adam'.[98]

The Genesis injunction to 'be fruitful and multiply' led the Anabaptists of Münster to make polygamy compulsory.[99] But in England the Edenic text was more often turned to the defence of monogamy. If God had wished to endorse polygamy, it was generally argued, he would have created more than one woman. Henry Smith was typical: 'God did create but one woman for the man, hee had power to create moe [*sic*], but to shew that he would haue him to stick to one, therefore he created of one ribbe, but one wife for one husband.'[100] William Secker pointed to God's having made only one man and one woman. And thus, 'Every Wife should be to her husband, as *Evah* was to *Adam*, a

---

94 Thomas Edwards, *Gangraena*, 2nd edn, iii.27. Quoted *ibid.*, p. 50.

95 Alan Rudrum, 'Polygamy in *Paradise Lost*', *Essays in Criticism* 20 (1970), pp. 22–3. And see also Don M. Wolfe (ed.), *The Complete Prose Works of John Milton*, vi.356.

96 William Perkins, *The Workes*, ii.296–7. See also William Hazlitt (trans.), *The Table Talk . . . of Martin Luther*, p. 304.

97 John White, *A Commentary Upon the Three First Chapters of Genesis*, ii.105. See also John King (trans.), *Commentaries on the First Book of Moses*, i.136.

98 Bernardus Ochinus, *A Dialogue of Polygamy* (London, 1657), p. 13.

99 See George Hunston Williams, *The Radical Reformation*, pp. 511–12.

100 Henry Smith, *The Sermons of Master Henry Smith*, pp. 13–14.

whole World of women; and every husband should be to his wife, as *Adam* was to *Evah*, a whole World of men.'[101] Phillip Stubbes imagined even the animals and the birds as dedicated monogamists.[102] The turtle-doves, renowned for their fidelity, sang the praises of monogamy.[103] The image of 'one flesh' was also interpreted to suggest it. The couple's becoming one flesh, declared Lancelot Andrewes, 'is the cut-throat of polygamie and adultery . . .'[104]

The Protestant understanding of marriage as a paradisal institution was an important part of anti-Catholic rhetoric. The Protestant confessions endorsed the appropriateness of marriage, as had Luther, Zwingli, and Calvin. And while some seventeenth-century Protestant writers continued to endorse the celibate state,[105] most saw marriage as a state equal to if not superior to celibacy. Thus, for example, Nicholas Gibbens and John Weemse made cases for the equal virtue of marriage and celibacy.[106] More harshly, Henry Smith called Catholic celibacy 'the doctrine of diuels . . .'[107] The Papists' position, declared John Wing, 'robs *heaven* of saints, *earth of* men; *men, of a sanctifyed and powerfull* meanes *to prevent sin*'.[108] According to George Walker, vows of virginity and celibacy were 'cursed and corrupt inventions of men'.[109] To Lancelot Andrewes, marriage was becoming to sanctity: 'There were never such Saints in the world, as were Saint *Adam* and Saint *Eve* in the estate of their innocencie and integrity, and yet they were married.'[110]

---

[101] William Secker, *A Wedding-Ring*, pp. 31–2. See also Andrew Willet, *Hexapla in Genesin*, p. 43; Giovanno Loredano, *The Life of Adam*, p. 18, who suggested that polygamy would only increase a man's miseries; Lancelot Andrewes, *Apospasmatia Sacra*, p. 99; George H. Sabine (ed.), *The Works of Gerrard Winstanley*, p. 185; John Dunton (ed.), *The Athenian Gazette*, vol. 1, q. 3, no. 4; George Walker, *God made visible*, p. 203. On an early rejection of polygamy by Pope Innocent III, see Thomas J. Motherway, 'The Creation of Eve', *Theological Studies* 1 (1940), pp. 97–116.

[102] Phillip Stubbes, *The Anatomie of Abuses*, sig. H.I.r.

[103] See Thomas Fuller, *Ornitho-logie: or The Speech of Birds*, pp. 28–9.

[104] Lancelot Andrewes, *Apospasmatia Sacra*, p. 227. See also John King (trans.), *Commentaries on the First Book of Moses*, i.136.

[105] See for example John Salkeld, *A Treatise of Paradise*, p. 164, who saw virginity as more laudable than marriage. See also Derrick S. Bailey, *The Man–Woman Relation in Christian Thought*, p. 194.

[106] See Nicholas Gibbens, *Questions and Disputations concerning the Holy Scripture*, p. 94; and John Weemse, *The Portraiture of the Image of God in Man*, p. 331.

[107] Henry Smith, *The Sermons of Master Henry Smith*, p. 16.

[108] John Wing, *The Crowne Coniugall*, p. 65.   [109] George Walker, *God made visible*, p. 219.

[110] Lancelot Andrewes, *Apospasmatia Sacra*, p. 229. See also Andrew Willet, *Hexapla in Genesin*, pp. 21, 41; Thomas Cooper, *A Briefe Exposition*, sig. N.I.r–v; William Secker, *A Wedding-Ring*, pp. 10ff; [Allen Apsley], *Order and Disorder* (London, 1679), p. 37.

SEX IN PARADISE

And Adam knew Eve his wife.   Genesis 4.1

The Genesis text made it clear that Adam and Eve had sexual relations after their expulsion from the Garden of Eden. But the text was silent on whether they had a sexual relationship in the Garden, or would have done had they not fallen and been expelled. That Adam and Eve were 'married' suggested to many that sexual relations were, in principle, possible. That they had been encouraged to 'be fruitful and multiply' implied the same, especially among those for whom Eve was created primarily for procreative purposes. God could have provided for human generation by divine fiat, wrote John Salkeld. Yet 'it was more agreeable to the nature of things, and for the sweeter disposition of the course of nature, that mankinde should rather be multiplied by naturall course of generation, then by supernaturall power and immediate creation'.[111] In this Adam and Eve were no different from other creatures.[112] That sexual, as well as social, relations between men and women were paradisal provided a further argument against virginity and celibacy as the ideal. In contrast to the corrupt inventions of culture – virginity and celibacy – declared George Walker, 'the affection and desire of procreation is most natural . . .'[113] A letter to a Madam Love at her lodging near Covent Garden saw the origins of the kiss in Paradise: 'Nature taught our first Parents in the very Garden of Bliss, to make their Approaches to Happiness by the lips.'[114]

There was, however, one crucial difference between pre- and post-lapsarian sexuality. In contrast to the fallen state, sexuality in Paradise was firmly under the control of the will. This was Augustine's position, supported by Aquinas and endorsed by Luther.[115] Thus, for example, to Luther, 'whenever they wished to devote themselves to the procreation of children, they would have come together, not maddened with that lust which now reigns in our leprous flesh; but with an admiration of the

---

[111] John Salkeld, *A Treatise of Paradise*, p. 162.
[112] See Susan Snyder (ed.), *The Divine Weeks and Works*, i.292.
[113] George Walker, *God made visible*, p. 222.
[114] Anon., *The Second Volume of the Post-Boy Robb'd of his Mail*, ii.240.
[115] See Henry Bettenson (ed.), Augustine, *Concerning the City of God against the Pagans*, pp. 578, 583, 585–9; Thomas Aquinas, *Summa Theologiae*, 1a.98–9. Aquinas was to reject Augustine's suggestion in *Against the Manichees* that 'increase and multiply' should be understood spiritually before the Fall and carnally only after it. See Ronald J. Teske (trans.), *Saint Augustine on Genesis*, pp. 77–8.

ordinance of God'.[116] The children of such a Paradisal union would
have been less dependent. The children of Adam and Eve, when born,
'would not long have needed the breast of their mother; but in all
probability would have started on their feet, as we now see chickens do,
by nature, and would have sought their own food from the fruits of the
earth, without helplessness or weakness . . .'[117] According to William
Whiston, in Paradise reason controlled the emotions: 'Those inclinations which provide for the Propogation of Mankind were, it seems, so
regular, and so intirely under the command of Reason, that not so much
as an Apron was esteem'd necessary to hide those Parts . . .'[118] After the
Fall, Adam and Eve knew they were naked, declared Matthew Poole,
because of 'that sinful Concupiscence which they now found working in
them'.[119] To the puritan Francis Rous, lust and sexuality were insepar-
able. And lust was the 'chiefe Lord both of body and soule . . .'[120] The
way back to Paradise was to be found through the rejection of sexuality.
'To bee without lust is a true Paradise; for man had not this lust when
hee was first placed in Paradise, neither could Paradise endure man,
when this lust was placed in him.'[121]

There were many, however, for whom the carnality of post-lapsarian sexuality ruled out its paradisal origin. Sexuality was distasteful, to
say the best; depraved, to say the worst. Innocence could only be
envisaged as sexless. This was inherited from the Gnostics and some of
the early fathers, notably Gregory of Nyssa.[122] Thus, for example,
Samuel Purchas in *Microcosmus* regretted the fact that, in contrast to
Adam who was made by God's own hand, all further generation took
place through lust. And he found the location of the foetus abominable,
enclosed as it was 'betweene the sinkes and passages of the Parents
ordure on the one side, and *Urine* on the other'.[123] To John-Francis
Senault, sex was by definition shameful: 'Man hides himselfe to re-
produce himself; marriage which is holy in it's [*sic*] Institution, and

[116] Henry Cole (trans.), *The Creation: A Commentary by Martin Luther*, p. 225. See also pp. 90, 100, 143.
[117] *Ibid.*, p. 140. Luther was following an Augustinian tradition here. For Augustine, paradisal infants would have attained adulthood almost immediately. Aquinas differed with Augustine on this. See *P.L.* 44.149–56; and Thomas Aquinas, *Summa Theologiae*, 1a.99.
[118] William Whiston, *A New Theory of the Earth*, p. 169. See also p. 270.
[119] Matthew Poole, *Annotations upon the Holy Bible*, sig. B.3.v.
[120] Francis Rous, *The Mystical Marriage* (London, 1635), p. 25.
[121] *Ibid.*, p. 38. Rous was influenced by Jacob Boehme. There are strong hints in Rous that, as for Boehme, the Fall was caused by sexuality.
[122] See Gary Anderson, 'Celibacy or Consummation in the Garden? Reflections on Early Jewish and Christian Interpretations of the Garden of Eden', *Harvard Theological Review* 82 (1989), pp. 121–48.
[123] Samuel Purchas, *Microcosmus*, p. 159.

sacred in it's type, is shameful in it's use; nor hath the necessity which doth authorize it, been able to take away the shame which doth accompany it.'[124]

The bachelor Thomas Browne viewed the whole business with distaste:

> I could be content that we might procreate like trees, without conjunction, or that there were any way to perpetuate the world without this triviall and vulgar way of coition; it is the foolishest act a wise man commits in all his life, nor is there any thing that will more deject his coold imagination, when hee shall consider what an odde and unworthy piece of folly hee hath committed.[125]

Against Browne, Alexander Ross waxed satirical: 'as great folly as you think coition to be', he wrote, 'without it you could not have been; and surely, there had been no other way in Paradise to propogate man, but this *foolish way*'.[126] And *The Athenian Gazette*, asked about the pain of childbirth, thought women had much more reason to desire propagation like trees than men, though 'one of *our own Sex* first *started that odd Whimsie*'.[127] But Thomas Browne did have his supporters. Luther endorsed paradisal marriage, as we have seen. But he remained seriously troubled by its post-lapsarian physical expression.[128] And he admitted in *The Table Talk* that had God consulted him, he 'should have advised him to continue the generation of the species by fashioning them of clay, in the way Adam was fashioned'.[129] Foigny's aboriginal Australians also reproduced non-sexually. 'Children grew within them like Fruits upon the Trees', James Sadeur was informed.[130] In contrast to them, Europeans were the brutal and malicious product of the rape of a woman by a giant serpent. The Utopia of Richard Ames was an island inhabited only by men, a misogynist's heaven:

\

---

[124] John-Francis Senault, *Man become Guilty*, p. 299.

[125] Thomas Browne, *Religio Medici*, 2.9. The 1686 edition of *Religio Medici* located this idea in Aulus Gellius, Paracelsus, Campanella, and Montaigne. See K. Svendsen, *Milton and Science* (Cambridge, Massachusetts, 1956), p. 281 n. 11.

[126] Alexander Ross, *Medicus Medicatus*, p. 77.

[127] John Dunton (ed.), *The Athenian Gazette*, vol. 1, q. 6, no. 13. See also William Nicholls, *A Conference with a Theist*, p. 168.

[128] See James Turner, *One Flesh*, pp. 60–1.

[129] William Hazlitt (trans.), *The Table Talk . . . of Martin Luther*, p. 307.

[130] Gabriel de Foigny, *A New Discovery of Terra Australis*, p. 85.

> There with a Score of *Choice Selected Friends*,
> Who know no private Interests nor Ends,
> We'd Live, and could we Procreate like Trees,
> And without *Womans Aid*
> Promote and Propogate our *Species* . . .
> Blest with *Strong-Health*, and a most quiet mind,
> Each day our *Thoughts* should new Diversion find,
> But *never, never*, think on *Woman-kind*.[131]

The Muggletonians' ideal heaven was one which consisted only of men. In the words of one of their songs, we shall be 'all males, not made to generate,/ But live in divine happy state'.[132]

Pierre Bayle was familiar with both Browne's desires and Foigny's fantasies. He saw them as similar to those of the seventeenth-century visionary Antoinette Bourignon. It was her belief that Adam had the principles of both sexes within him and was thus able to generate independently, 'as Trees and Plants do'.[133] She was the recipient of an ecstatic vision of Adam, in the genital region of whose body

was situated the Structure and Resemblance of a Face; which was a Source of admirable odours and perfumes: From thence likewise Men were to spring, whose principles he had all within himself: for there was a Vessel in his Belly, which bred small Eggs, and another Vessel full of Liquor, which impregnated the Eggs. And when Man grew enflamed with the Love of his God, the Desire he had that there should be other Creatures, beside himself, to praise, love, and adore the divine Majesty, made that Liquor, by the Fire of God's Love to spread itself on one or more of these Eggs with unconceivable Delight; which, being impregnated, came out sometime after from the Man, by the forementioned Canal, in the form of an Egg, and a little after hatch'd a perfect Man.[134]

Like Mme. Bourignon Edward Taylor was influenced by the theosophy of Jacob Boehme and its denial of carnality. Non-sexual propagation by Adam alone was his preferred option. The necessities of postlapsarian generation had resulted in physical changes: 'The hanging on him the Bestial Genitals is, that wherof Nature itself . . . is Ashamed and Blusheth at: The Soul hideth it self all it can from this Monstrous filthy Brutish Deformity . . .'[135] Also influenced by Boehme, Francis Mercurius van Helmont held that, as Adam created the animals by speech, so he would have similarly reproduced himself. The Behmenist Samuel Pordage held to paradisal magical procreation, a power which was lost after the Fall:

---

[131] Richard Ames, *The Folly of Love*, pp. 26–7.
[132] Quoted by Christopher Hill, *The World Turned Upside Down*, p. 252.
[133] Pierre Bayle, *Mr Bayle's Historical and Critical Dictionary*, i.102.   [134] *Ibid.*, i.103. See also v.6.
[135] Edward Taylor, *Jacob Behmen's Theosophick Philosophy Unfolded* (London, 1691), p. 23.

(Such members as we have now he had none
To propogate) he magically, as
The Sun's bright beames the waters surface passe
Doth without pain, so should he have brought forth
in *Paradise*. By a Caelestial birth,
He should in God's Bless'd *Image* more have got,
Aeternal all, none subject to *Fate's* Lot.
He should both Father be, and Mother then,
For *Male* and *Female* God created *Man*:
Both *Man*, and *Woman*, *Wife*, and *Virgin* he
Together was, in State of purity.[136]

Virtually without exception, all were agreed that Adam and Eve did not have a sexual relationship in Paradise. For those who adopted the Gnostic solution, it was of course ruled out in principle. But even those who accepted that physical sexuality was, in principle, possible for the first couple denied that it occurred. The most notable exception was John Milton. To Milton's Adam, Eve 'Yielded with coy submission, modest pride,/ And sweet reluctant amorous delay'.[137]

The issue of the first couple's sexual relationship in Eden was rhetorically minimised by narrowing the time between their creation and their expulsion from the Garden. Virtually all were agreed that life in Paradise lasted but a short time. 'Long in the place it's like he did not abide', declared John Stradling in 1625.[138] For some, Adam and Eve, created on the sixth day, fell on the seventh or eighth day of creation. Thus, for example, John White: 'we might probably guesse, that the Creation being ended the sixth day, the Law was given on the seventh, in which also the woman . . . surveighing the fruits of the Garden was seduced by Satan and fell: and her husband the eighth day when . . . [Christ's] Conquest over Satan . . . was perfected by his Resurrection from the dead which was upon the eighth day'.[139]

---

[136] Samuel Pordage, *Mundorum Explicatio*, p. 62. See also Richard Brathwait, *A Muster Roll of the evill Angels* (London, 1655), p. 74. Granting the textual base, it is not surprising that Christian exegetical opinion on the issue of sexuality in Paradise is as confused now as then. What is surprising is the amount of exegetical ink still spilt upon what is essentially hermeneutically insoluble. For an extensive bibliography of modern views, see David P. Wright, 'Holiness, Sex, and Death in the Garden of Eden,' *Biblica* 77 (1996), pp. 306–29.

[137] *Paradise Lost*, 4.310–11. See also 4.741ff. Richard Ames has Eve conceiving in Eden. But since his idyll consisted of an all-male paradisal island, this has no relevance to the desirability of paradisal sex. See Richard Ames, *The Folly of Love*, p. 3.

[138] John Stradling, *Divine Poems*, p. 3.

[139] John White, *A Commentary Upon the Three First Chapters of Genesis*, iii.113. See also Alexander Ross, *An Exposition on the Fovrteene first Chapters of Genesis*, p. 71; Susan Snyder (ed.), *The Divine Weeks and Works*, i.316, but cf. p. 334; John Salkeld, *A Treatise of Paradise*, p. 224; George Hughes, *An Analytical Exposition of the Whole first Book of Moses, called Genesis*, p. 26; Henry Cole (trans.), *The Creation: A Commentary by Martin Luther*, p. 113, but cf. William Hazlitt (trans.), *The Table Talk . . . of Martin Luther*, p. 248.

For the vast majority, Adam and Eve fell on the same day on which they were created. Thomas Burnet was sceptical: 'In the Morning God said all things were good; and in the Evening of the same Day all things are accursed. Alas! how fleeting and unconstant is the Glory of Things created! A work that was six days e'er it could be elaborate and brought to perfection, and that by an Omnipotent Architect to be thus in as few Hours ruined by so vile a Beast?'[140] Burnet's doubt was one of many he held about the details of the story of Eden. But on this he, along with John Milton, was very much alone. John Swan, Thomas Peyton, William Pynchon, Edward Vaughan, John Richardson, Mathias Prideaux, and William Perkins all followed the Augustinian tradition of a Fall on the day of creation.[141]

There was much discussion of just how long Adam and Eve spent in Paradise on the first and only day there. The rabbinic tradition, for example, had Adam and Eve expelled twelve hours after God first assembled the dust to create Adam.[142] In *The Table Talk*, Luther imagined the creation of Adam at midday and the expulsion two hours later. To John Calvin, Adam sinned at noon and was called to account at sunset.[143] Andrew Willet had Adam and Eve defending themselves early in the evening, around eight or nine hours after Adam's creation.[144] Giovanno Loredano allowed Adam only three hours of happiness, a reminder to us all of the fleetingness of pleasure: 'About three of clock he was brought into the Garden; at six a clock, he sinned; and in the Evening, was expulsed. In a word, Humane felicities are no other than moments. They for the most part find their Coffin in their Cradle, and their death in their birth.'[145]

The endorsement of a six-hour sojourn in the Garden was common. John Lightfoot imagined creation at nine o'clock in the morning, a Fall at midday after an early lunch, and the judgement of God at three in the afternoon.[146] Some followed the example of the early fathers in drawing

[140] Charles Blount, *The Oracles of Reason*, p. 48. See also William Nicholls, *A Conference with a Theist*, pp. 180ff; and George Hakewill, *An apologie*, p. 2.
[141] See John Swan, *Specvlvm Mundi*, p. 36; Thomas Peyton, *The glasse of time*, p. 63; William Pynchon, *A Treatise of the Sabbath* (London, 1654), p. 21; Edward Vaughan, *Ten Introductions: How to Read, and in Reading How to Understand the Holie Bible* (London, 1594), sig. E.3.r; John Richardson, *Choice Observations*, sig. B.3.r; Mathias Prideaux, *An Easy and Compendious Introduction for Reading All Sorts of Histories* (London, 1648), p. 2; William Perkins, *An Exposition*, p. 152.
[142] See *Encyclopaedia Judaica*, ii.236–7.
[143] See John King (trans.), *Commentaries on the First Book of Moses*, p. 160.
[144] See Andrew Willet, *Hexapla in Genesin*, p. 56.
[145] Giovanno Loredano, *The Life of Adam*, p. 54.
[146] See John Lightfoot, *The Works*, i.2, 692. See also Lodowick Lloid, *The Consent of Time*, p. 59.

the analogy with the Passion of Christ. Thus, for example, according to Thomas Hayne, as Christ was crucified in the sixth hour of the sixth day, as the earth was in darkness from the sixth to the ninth hour, and as Christ gave up the ghost in the ninth hour, so Adam was created in the sixth hour of the sixth day, so his soul was in darkness from the sixth to the ninth hour, and so he was called to account in the ninth hour.[147] 'The sixt day in which Christ was crucified, and about the euening-tide', declared Edward Vaughan, 'pointed plainly to the day, and to the verie time in the which *Adam* fel . . .'[148]

There were other reasons suggested for an immediate Fall. That there was no evidence of their having eaten anything before the fruit of the Tree of the Knowledge of Good and Evil suggested that this was their first meal. The Fall was on the day of creation, wrote William Pynchon in his treatise on the Sabbath, because Adam fell 'the very first time that ever he eat anything . . .'[149] The Fall was early, surmised Andrew Willet, because the carnivorous animals, unable to eat fruit, and not allowed to eat each other, could not long have survived.[150] Adam could not have remained in Paradise on the Sabbath, mused Hugh Broughton, since, had he done so, he would have performed perfectly some part of the law 'and thereby bene partaker with Christ in the worke of our redemption'.[151] It was implicit in the absence of any narrative gap between creation and Fall, suggested William Perkins.[152] That Satan moved swiftly was another popular explanation of the brief sojourn in Paradise of the first couple.[153]

The most pressing, and theologically the most cogent, reason given for the immediacy of the Fall related to the sexual relationship between Adam and Eve. Had Adam and Eve made perfect love in the garden, conception would have been the inevitable result, a race free from original sin the unavoidable outcome, and the universality of the redemption effected by the second Adam placed in doubt. Paradoxically,

---

[147] See Thomas Hayne, *The General View of the Holy Scriptures*, pp. 25ff. See also Hugh Broughton, *Observations Upon the first ten fathers*, p. 33.

[148] Edward Vaughan, *Ten Introductions*, sig. E.4.r. See also John Swan, *Specvlvm Mundi*, p. 36.

[149] William Pynchon, *A Treatise of the Sabbath*, p. 5. See also William Perkins, *An Exposition*, p. 152; Hugh Broughton, *Observations Upon the first ten fathers*, p. 30; and John Richardson, *Choice Observations*, sig. B.3.r.

[150] Andrew Willet, *Hexapla in Genesin*, p. 56.

[151] Hugh Broughton, *Observations Upon the first ten fathers*, p. 31. See also Thomas Hayne, *The General View of the Holy Scriptures*, p. 25.

[152] William Perkins, *An Exposition*, p. 152. See also William Pynchon, *A Treatise of the Sabbath*, p. 1; and Hugh Broughton, *Observations Upon the first ten fathers*, p. 30.

[153] See John Swan, *Specvlvm Mundi*, p. 36; John Richardson, *Choice Observations*, sig. B.3.r; William Perkins, *An Exposition*, p. 152; William Pynchon, *A Treatise of the Sabbath*, p. 6.

to ensure the sinfulness of all humanity, Adam and Eve needed to fall before they had an opportunity to become one flesh. This was not moral timidity but theological necessity. To the puritan George Walker, for example, since the affection and desire of procreation is most natural, paradisal sex would have been morally unproblematic. But 'if man in the state of innocency had *knowne* his Wife, shee had without faile conceived *a seed pure without sin,* and had brought forth children *in Gods image* perfect and upright; wherefore they did without doubt fall in the end of the sixth day . . .'[154] Similarly, the puritan divine George Hughes: 'If Adam and his wife had continued in innocency the night before the seventh, it is probable, seeing there was no cause to hinder it, they might have the blessing of an innocent seed; but they had not; therefore they were fallen, before we read, Adam knew his wife.'[155]

A radical reading of the Genesis text could lead not only to the denial of sexuality but to libertine endorsement of it. The return to Paradise, through the redemption from sin, was a restoration of the sexual freedom promised to Adam and Eve, if unrealised by them. Redemption found its obvious expression in the return to the prelapsarian state in which good and evil were abolished, especially among those who looked to Paul's Epistle to Titus: 'Unto the pure all things are pure' (1.15).

Theologies which saw redemption as a return to the paradisal state in which good and evil were as yet to be distinguished were seen as covertly libertine. Protestant radicals were certainly believed to be sexually liberated by those for whom the distinction between the excesses of religious enthusiasm and sexual expression was a fine one. Thus, for example, Henry More believed that all enthusiasm was sexual in origin.[156] Alexander Ross demonstrated his belief that the Edenic myth had always been turned upside down:

The *Adamians,* or *Adamites,* so called either from the one *Adam* their author, or from *Adam* the first man, whose nakedness they imitate, sprung up shortly after the *Gnosticks* . . . Of this Sect there be many extant at this day. They held it unlawful for men and women to wear cloathes in their Congregations and assemblies, seeing their meetings were the onely Paradise on Earth, where they

---

[154] George Walker, *God made visible,* p. 222.
[155] George Hughes, *An Analytical Exposition of the Whole first Book of Moses, called Genesis,* p. 26. See also John Swan, *Specvlvm Mundi,* p. 36; Andrew Willet, *Hexapla in Genesin,* p. 56; Edward Vaughan, *Ten Introductions,* sig. E.3.v – E.4.r; John Richardson, *Choice Observations,* sig. B.3.r; Thomas Hayne, *The General View of the Holy Scriptures,* p. 25; and William Pynchon, *A Treatise of the Sabbath,* p. 21.
[156] See Henry More, *An Explanation of the Grand Mystery of Godliness* (London, 1660), pp. 158–9, 254, 365, 510. See also James Grantham Turner, *One Flesh,* p. 90.

were to have life Eternall, and not in Heaven, as *Adam* then in his Paradise, so *Christians* in theirs should be naked . . . They rejected marriages as diabolical; therefore they used promiscuous Copulation in the dark.[157]

Ross was drawing upon the description of the Adamiani which Augustine had given in *Liber de Haeresibus* (31), and Epiphanius in *Panarion* (4.52). These set the pattern for all later accounts. Ross himself spoke of a group who styled themselves Anabaptists in Amsterdam 'where the men and women did pray in their meetings, and perform other divine services naked. This posture they called the state of innocency, and their meetings, Paradise.'[158] Edward Leigh gave a similarly stylised description: 'They say they are as good a state as *Adam* was before his fall . . . Whensoever they met together at Prayers, or on any other publick occasion, they were naked, and called the place of their meeting Paradise.'[159] Richard Brathwait followed the account of Epiphanius. If any Adamite sinned, he wrote, he was expelled, 'for they said, that he was *Adam*, who had eaten of the forbidden fruit; and therefore deserved to bee thrust out of Paradise, *i.e.* to be put out of their Church; for they thought their Church to be Paradise, and themselves to bee *Adam*, and *Eve*'.[160]

Whether Ross's Amsterdam Adamites really were Anabaptists cannot be determined. But Anabaptists were generally thought to embody most heretical deviations, nakedly or otherwise. Liturgical nakedness was a feature often commented on. Late in the sixteenth century, for example, Gervase Babington reminded his readers that Adam and Eve's lack of shame at their nakedness

fauoreth nothing any fantasticall *Anabaptists*, that will go naked, but declared the innocency that then was in them is now lost by sinne, yet regayned in measure by Christ, and shall perfitly be inioyed in the life to come, when nakedness shall shame vs no more then it did at first.[161]

Andrew Willet maintained that the nakedness of Adam and Eve did not make them 'impudent and vnshamefast persons: such as the Adamites are, pretending this example, companying together like bruit beastes'.[162] The puritan divine Robert Abbott sounded like the old of every generation:

[157] Alexander Ross, *Pansebeia: or, A View of all Religions in the World* (London, 1653), pp. 186–7.
[158] *Ibid.*, p. 405. [159] Edward Leigh, *A Systeme or Bodie of Divinitie*, p. 495.
[160] Richard Brathwait, *A Muster Roll of the evill Angels*, pp. 78–9.
[161] Gervase Babington, *Certaine Plaine, briefe, and comfortable Notes vpon euerie Chapter of Genesis*, sig. c.5.v. See also Thomas Drant, *Two Sermons*, sig. k.4.v.
[162] Andrew Willet, *Hexapla in Genesin*, p. 39.

look upon the present world as upon a *Monster* of many young men and women, so *disorderly* in their courses, and so *disguised* in their attires, that all ages read of before us, cannot give the like precedents. How do *young women* rejoyce in baring their *Nakednesse?* *Ranters* have brought it in upon this deceitful account, that they have attained to that perfection in Christ already which they lost in *Adam*, and so that they may go naked as he did, and live above sin and shame . . .'[163]

Liturgical nakedness was one thing, sexual libertinism quite another. The Family of Love, founded by Heinrich Niclaes, a German mercer, in the Low Countries around 1540, was routinely accused of libertinism, so much so that the term Familist was synonymous with it. In 1596, for example, George Gifford called them 'filthy monsters'. John Norden warned his congregation to be watchful for 'Papists, Brownists, Anabaptists, the Family of lust and lewdness termed the Family of Love'.[164] That the Familists believed that they were able to attain the state of Adam in his innocence is beyond doubt. That they engaged in Adamic sexual libertinism is much less likely. Early in the eighteenth century, John Strype suggested that they might have been more sinned against than sinning, and offered an explanation: 'Whether this sect of the service of love were of such profligate principles and practices may be doubted; but that Anabaptists and Libertines (of whom those crimes were too true) shrouded themselves under those of this denomination, may be justly suspected.'[165]

Whether any of these groups, or any of the individuals loosely called Familists, Anabaptists, enthusiasts, libertines, and so on, did actually engage in Adamic sexual libertinism cannot be easily determined. That radical sectarians were believed to behave promiscuously cannot be doubted. Richard Carter, for example, imagined among those women at a sectarian gathering in 1641 Agnes Anabaptist, Kate Catabaptist, Franck Footbaptist, Penelope Punck, Merald Makebate, Ruth Rak-Hell, Tabitha Tattle, Pru Prattle, 'and that poore, silly, simple, senceless, sinlesse, shamelesse naked wretch, *Alice the Adamite*. As bare as ones naile/ She shames not her taile.'[166] The anonymous *Religions Lotterie* in 1642 numbered the Adamites among the sixteen sorts of religion liable

---

[163] Robert Abbott, *The Young Mans Warning-Piece* (London, 1657), sig. A.3.r–v.

[164] George Gifford, *Sermons upon the Whole Booke of the Revelation* (London, 1596), p. 47; and John Norden, *A Progress of Piety* (Parker Society, vol. XXXI, Cambridge, 1847), p. 114. Both quoted by Jean Dietz Moss, 'The Family of Love and English Critics', *Sixteenth Century Journal* 6 (1975), p. 44.

[165] John Strype, *Annals of the Reformation* (Oxford, 1824), 2.i.559. Quoted by Moss, 'The Family at Love', p. 48.

[166] Richard Carter, *The Schismatick Stigmatized* (London, 1641), p. 15.

to destroy both church and kingdom, not least because of their reading of Genesis 1.28: 'they would be mere Libertines and live as they list, following that place of Scripture, *Increase and multiply*, and in their society they are so overcome with the flesh that they cannot pray'.[167] Gerrard Winstanley was sufficiently concerned about such accusations specifically to deny them:

. . . they report, that we Diggers hold women to be common, and live in that bestialnesse: For my part, I declare against it; I owne this to be a truth, That the earth ought to be a common treasury to all; but as for women, *Let every man have his owne wife, and every woman her own husband*; and I know none of the Diggers that act in such an unrationall excesse of female communitie . . .[168]

That sexual promiscuity was central to Ranter theology was a commonplace. John Holland pointed to their understanding of Genesis 3.16 as applicable only to a post-lapsarian order: 'They say that for one man to be tyed to one woman, or one woman to be tyed to one man, is a fruit of the curse; but they say, we are freed from the curse; therefore it is our liberty to make use of whom we please . . . this opinion they infer from those words of the Lord to *Eve, Thy desire shall be to thy husband.*'[169] In the late 1640s, John Reeve became a disciple of the Ranter John Robins. He informs us that Robins thought he was God the Father, and he himself claimed to be Adam risen from the dead to deliver his people. He called his new wife Eve and prophesied that she would deliver another Messiah. He commanded his disciples to abstain from meat, and fed them on paradisal food – apples and water.[170]

The Routing of the Ranters reported that at a meeting in Shoemakers Alley their time was spent 'in drunkenness, uncleanness, blasphemous words, filthy songs, and mixt dances of men and women stark naked'. A female Ranter who claimed to be pregnant by the Holy Spirit allegedly learned from Genesis that 'Woman was made to be a helper for man, and . . . it was no sin to lie with any man, whether Batchelor, Widdower, or married, but a thing lawful, and adjured thereunto by Nature.'[171]

Sexual promiscuity was certainly consistent with the theology of the Ranter Lawrence Clarkson. Having been redeemed, he claimed to have the 'Single Eye' of unfallen Adamic vision by means of which he had transcended both good and evil: 'Sin hath its conception only in the

---

[167] Anon., *Religions Lotterie, or the Churches Amazement* (London, 1642), sig. A.2.v.
[168] George H. Sabine (ed.), *The Works of Gerrard Winstanley*, pp. 366–7.
[169] John Holland, *The Smoke of the Bottomlesse Pit*, p. 4.
[170] See John Reeve and Lodowick Muggleton, *A Transcendent Spiritual Treatise*, pp. 8–10.
[171] Quoted by James Grantham Turner, *One Flesh*, pp. 84–5.

imagination; therefore so long as the act was in God, or nakedly produced by God, it was as holy as God: but after there was an appearance in thee, or apprehension to thee, that this act is good, and that act is evil, thou hast with *Adam* eat of the fruit of the forbidden Tree, of the Tree of knowledge of good and evil . . . it was he who made all things good: yea that which by you is imagined evil, he made good.'[172] The Ranter Abiezer Coppe may also have adopted Adamitic ways. Anthony Wood in *Athenae Oxoniensis* wrote that it was 'usual with him to preach stark naked many blasphemies and unheard-of Villainies in the Daytime, and in the night to drink and lye with a Wench, that had also been his hearer, stark naked'.[173] Humphrey Ellis in *Pseudochristus* in 1650 reported on the Ranters William Franklin and Mary Gadbury. Convinced that Franklin had destroyed his former body by which he had been attached in the flesh to his former wife, she slept with him 'spiritually'. When asked why she was not ashamed, she replied that 'Adam and Eve in innocency were naked, and were not ashamed; but sin brought shame into the world: but when they come to be in Christ, it is again taken away!'[174]

Thus, for many among the radicals, the story of Adam and Eve reflected a time of sexual freedom, and the expression of sexuality in the present a re-entry into a prelapsarian Paradise. But for others, sexuality, far from being a reflection of paradisal life, was the ultimate cause of our expulsion from it.

[172] Lawrence Clarkson, *A Single Eye* (London, 1650), p. 8. Quoted by A. L. Morton, *The World of the Ranters*, p. 71.
[173] Quoted by Norman Cohn, *The Pursuit of the Millennium* (London, 1957), p. 354.
[174] Humphrey Ellis, *Pseudochristus* (London, 1650), p. 48. See also Norman Cohn, *The Pursuit of the Millennium*, pp. 330–1.

CHAPTER 6

The Fall

METAPHORS OF THE FALL

And the woman said, The Serpent beguiled me, and I did eat.

Genesis 3.13

The story of the Fall in the book of Genesis is bordered on the one hand by unclothed shamelessness (Genesis 2.25) and on the other by clothed shame (Genesis 3.21). So it is not surprising that a sexual act was often seen as the cause of the transition, and the expulsion from Paradise its consequence. The sexual Fall was present in the Jewish tradition from the time of Philo's allegorical interpretation, and in the Christian tradition from Origen's.[1] And there were rabbinic precedents for the view that the Fall occurred as the result of the seduction of Eve by the serpent.[2] Around the first century, *The Book of the Secrets of Enoch* had Eve sexually seduced by a fallen angel.[3]

These traditions of a serpentine and an angelic sexual assault on Eve come together in Jacob Boehme. The serpent, which to Boehme signified sexuality, appeared to Eve as 'an exceeding well-favoured, comely handsome, neat fine, brave pretty beast, accurately drest, and set forth, according to the pride of the Devill . . .'[4] The essence of the serpent entered into her as a result of her desire to be a goddess, and her heavenly essence died. The serpent, 'being it was the most suttle Beast among all the Beasts . . . slew *Eve* her virgin-like chastity, that she lusted after the beastiall copulation; thereupon we understand in the Serpents property, the *desire* of [carnal] brutall copulation, and all *unchastity*, wanton uncleannesse, and Beastiall Whoredome of man'.[5]

Influenced by Boehme, a number of the sectarians saw the serpent's attack on Eve as resulting in conception, in the birth of Cain and in his

---

[1] See J. M. Evans, *'Paradise Lost' and the Genesis Tradition*, pp. 71–4.   [2] See *ibid.*, p. 47.
[3] See *ibid.*, p. 33.   [4] Jacob Boehme, *Mysterium Magnum*, ch. 20.19.   [5] *Ibid.*, ch. 23.24.

reprobate progeny – the seed of Cain. To John Reeve and Lodowick Muggleton, for example, ever since the birth of Cain, there have been two distinct worlds, 'A redeemed world of elect lost Israelites, and an unredeemed world of unlost Cananitish reprobates . . .'[6] To them, the serpent was an angelical demon cast down from heaven who appeared to Eve in the form of a man 'more amiable or glorious . . . to the outward appearance of *Eves* eyes, then the Person of the man *Adam* was'.[7] The serpent overpowered Eve, entered into her womb, and there 'was changed from his spirituality, and immediately he quickned in her pure undefiled seed; wherefore she being now naked from her former pure created Virginity, presently she is full of lust after her innocent Husband, that had no desire to a woman at all'.[8] Their sexual act brought about the Fall of Adam. The eating of the fruit of the Tree of the Knowledge of Good and Evil was an alternative account of the same events. The tree symbolised 'the outcast unclean person of that Serpent Dragon Devil'.[9] Thus, the first-born Cain 'was the very seed or spirit of that reprobate Serpent Angel in the body of *Eve*, and the first born child or son of the Devil . . .'[10] Cain, declared Muggleton elsewhere, was 'the first and right Devil . . . and of the same stature and bigness as the Serpent Angel was who beguiled *Eva*, who was *Cains* Father'.[11]

The demonisation of the other, and especially of the rich and powerful, is to be expected among those groups who see themselves as among the poor and the oppressed minority. As John Bunyan put it, 'It is the lot of Cain's brood to be lords and rulers first, while Abel and his generation have their necks under oppression.'[12] To Laurence Clarkson, the wealthy were the seed of Cain:

what by art in their wisdom can be invented, shall not in the least be wanting, if it can be had for gold or silver; and whatever Science, Pastime, or Pleasure their soul can desire, as Hawking, Hunting, Bowling, Shooting, Gaming, at Dice, Cards, or Tables, or any other delight of Musick, Dancing, Courting of Ladies, with the satisfaction of ther greatest lust, and that with the greatest pomp and state this their heaven can afford; and then in the last place for carriage and

---

[6] John Reeve and Lodowick Muggleton, *A Divine Looking-Glass*, p. 155.
[7] John Reeve and Lodowick Muggleton, *A Transcendent Spiritual Treatise*, p. 20. See also their *A Divine Looking-Glass*, p. 135.
[8] John Reeve and Lodowick Muggleton, *A Transcendent Spiritual Treatise*, p. 20.
[9] John Reeve and Lodowick Muggleton, *A Divine Looking-Glass*, p. 139.
[10] John Reeve and Lodowick Muggleton, *A Transcendent Spiritual Treatise*, p. 21.
[11] Lodowick Muggleton, *A Looking-Glass for George Fox the Quaker* (n.p., 1668), p. 44.
[12] Quoted by A. L. Morton, *The World of the Ranters*, p. 139.

behaviour none in this world like unto them, as observe how proud, and *Lucifer-like*, their Father, they carry themselves . . .[13]

The doctrine of the two seeds was traditional among the radicals. It occurred in the writings of John Saltmarsh, Gerrard Winstanley, Abiezer Coppe, George Fox, and elsewhere.[14] To Lodowick Muggleton, all those who failed to accept him as one of the Lord's last two witnesses and prophets were the progeny of the devil. As A. L. Morton remarks, 'The power to damn, which Reeve and Muggleton claimed and exercised freely, was really no more than the power to recognise at sight the seed of Cain and to pronounce upon it the sentence of a damnation already existing.'[15] The Quakers are 'the children of Cain', declared Lodowick Muggleton, and they have the 'influence of John Robins his spiritual witchcraft-power upon them'.[16]

The seduction of Eve by the serpentine angel played a central part in the thought of Laurence Clarkson after he had converted to Muggletonianism early in 1657. And his 1659 work *Look About You, for the Devil that you fear is in you* was the first Muggletonian work devoted to the doctrine of the two seeds. As with Reeve and Muggleton, the serpent was a fallen angel. The serpent of the Genesis story, he declared,

was no horned beast or creeping Serpent, as the Priests vainly teach; neither was it any Pippin or Pearmain, or any other sort of Apple that was so pleasant in *Eves* eye, or delightful to her taste: No, no it was that reprobate glorious Angel, that was far more pleasant and sweeter to *Eves* taste then the sweetest fruit whatsoever . . .[17]

Thus Eve, seduced by Satan, allowed him to enter her body and conceived a serpent-dragon devil who was to be born as the man Cain. Awakened to the delights of sex, she enticed Adam into their first sexual act and defiled him: 'as the Pox or Gangraena doth eat throughout the whole man, so *Eves* soul and body being defiled, did putrifie the seed of Adam'.[18] Of the seed of Cain, there are millions of legions.

In the patristic and medieval traditions, the meaning of the biblical text was indeterminate and therefore capable of a multilayered reading. Beneath the literal or historical meaning of the text were other symbolic

---

[13] Laurence Clarkson, *Look About You, for the Devil that you fear is in you* (London, 1651), p. 86. The wealthy were not exclusively of the seed of Cain. Many of the poor and uneducated were also his progeny. And Clarkson included libertines, the hypocritical, the pious, and his former friends the Ranters among them.
[14] See Christopher Hill, Barry Reay, and William Lamont, *The World of the Muggletonians*, p. 85.
[15] A. L. Morton, *The World of the Ranters*, p. 140.
[16] Lodowick Muggleton, *The Neck of the Quakers Broken* (Amsterdam, 1663), pp. 14, 16.
[17] Laurence Clarkson, *Look About You*, p. 1.   [18] *Ibid.*, p. 3.

meanings – most commonly, the allegorical, the anagogical, and the tropological, with specific sets of interpretative rules.[19] Jacob Boehme and his supporters were influenced by this tradition, but with significant variations. Their understanding of Genesis was not a multilayered one. On the contrary, their understanding of the text was a literal one upon which they imposed a metaphorical reading. Thus, in the cases of Reeve, Muggleton, and Clarkson, the temptation of Eve by the serpent was read metaphorically as her sexual seduction by a fallen angel, the temptation of Adam by Eve as her seduction of Adam. The text was read literally as suggesting a double Fall, and read metaphorically as a double sexual seduction.

Boehme's complex account of a multiple Fall was most elaborately developed in *Mysterium Magnum*, originally written in 1623 and translated by John Sparrow into English in 1654. Fortunately, for his readers, Boehme was magically present at the creation and fall of Adam.

Following the neoplatonic understanding of the vehicles of the soul, Boehme saw man as originally an angelic being consisting of a heavenly spiritual body united with an outward body extracted from the good part of the earth. In this transparent unified body, without organs of procreation or excretion, Adam should have walked upon the earth, eating and drinking in a magical way. The original Adam was equally male and female, 'with both divine *heavenly* Tinctures . . .' But the centre of the original Adam was Eve: 'she is the *Matrix* in which the Love desire stood in *Adam*, viz. the Magicall Impregnation and birth; she was *Adams* Paradisicall Rose-Garden in peculiar Love, wherein he loved him-selfe . . .'[20] Procreation should have occurred through the joyful and delightful union of male and female tinctures, which stirred up desire and led to the creation of substantial images.

Adam's musings on the beasts led to his downfall – the development of a gross physical body. He 'introduced himselfe into Beastiall *lust*, to eat and generate according as the beasts doe: and so likewise the *Fiat* tooke in the same lust, and formed him in his *sleep* even as the lust was; and every member was formed in its place to the Conjunction of the beast-like copulation'.[21] At the same time, God turned him into a male and a female 'and hung upon him the wormes-*Carkasse* with the bestiall members for propagation'.[22] As James Turner succinctly puts it, 'Eve is virtually created by Adam's revolting Genital

---

[19] For the common fourfold system, see John Cassian, *Colationes*, 14.8 (*P.L.* 49.962–5). See Peter Harrison, *The Bible, Protestantism, and the Rise of Natural Science*, p. 27.
[20] Jacob Boehme, *Mysterium Magnum*, ch. 19.8.   [21] *Ibid.*, ch. 19.25.   [22] *Ibid.*, ch. 18.6.

longings.'[23] As we have already noted, Eve was then seduced by the serpent, and Adam by Eve. The naming of the animals, the sleep of Adam and the creation of Eve, the temptation of Eve, and her temptation of Adam were, for Boehme, all metaphors for sexuality.[24]

Multiple Falls also occur in the writings of the Behmenist poet Samuel Pordage. The original Adam, created to procreate magically, fell downwards from the orb of love to this dark world, where he was changed bodily. In his first sleep, God clad his former power in flesh in the form of Eve. Only half what he once was, Adam lived with Eve in Paradise. Satan, having entered the serpent, tempted Eve, and she Adam, to taste of the forbidden fruit:

> His [Satan's] poison doth diffuse immediately
> Thorow their Bodies: now they 'ave fading breath,
> Bodies to sicknesse Subject and to Death:
> Now they *Sol's* heat do feel, now *Hyems* cold;
> Which do keep off themselves in leaves they 'nfould.[25]

In the writings of Boehme and of those he influenced, the separately embodied Eve was an unintended and undesirable outcome of the early history of creation. She was the result of an already fallen Adam. Traditional allegorical readings of the Genesis text like those of Philo, Origen, Ambrose, Augustine in *Against the Manichees*, Isidore of Seville, and John Scotus Erigena, and metaphorical readings like those of Boehme, Reeve, Muggleton, Clarkson, and Pordage, are almost invariably misogynistic.

The neoplatonist Henry More's threefold literal, moral, and philosophical reading of the creation story was the most elaborate traditional interpretation of the seventeenth century.[26] In his *Conjectura Cabbalistica*, that Eve existed at all was seen as problematic. Read philosophically, Adam was originally an ethereal being, placed in an ideal spiritual condition, his soul watered by the four virtues of prudence, justice, fortitude, and temperance. The warning to avoid the fruit of the Tree of

---

[23] James Turner, *One Flesh*, p. 145.
[24] There is an echo of Boehme in John Pettus' suggestion that woman was created to avoid two equally unnatural modes of life – celibacy on the one hand and sexual relations with animals on the other. See John Pettus, *Volatiles from the History of Adam and Eve*, p. 54. On the history of bestiality, see Vern L. Burrough and Bonnie Bullough, *Sin, Sickness and Sanity: A History of Sexual Attitudes* (New York, 1977), ch. 3. Boehme may also have been influenced by a Talmudic tradition that Adam copulated with the animals as he named them. See John A. Phillips, *Eve: The History of an Idea* (San Francisco, 1984), p. 32.
[25] Samuel Pordage, *Mundorum Explicatio*, p. 71.
[26] On More as a Neoplatonist, see Philip C. Almond, *Heaven and Hell in Enlightenment England*, ch. 1.

the Knowledge of Good and Evil was a caution against the illicit use of personal will. Nevertheless, the feminine passions within Adam were attacked by the devil with the promise that the exercise of the will would lead to wisdom. As a result,

the *Feminine* part in *Adam* was so tickled with this Doctrine of the *old Deceiver*, that the *Concupiscible* began to be so immoderate as to resolve to doe any thing that may promote pleasure and experience in things, and snatch'd away with it *Adam*'s Will and Reason . . .[27]

Adam was thence sent to earth. Clothed in a terrestrial body, he was free without pain and sorrow to indulge in the pleasures of the body, with his feminine passions 'under the chastisement and correction of his Reason'.[28] Morally read, the serpent which is 'the inordinate desire of Pleasure' entered into the feminine part of Adam. His lust for pleasure became so strong it overcame his rationality. The skin of beasts in which God dressed Adam and Eve was a metaphor for their bestiality. And, wrote More, God 'deservedly reproached them saying, Now get you gone for a couple of Brutes'.[29]

There were however several metaphorical readings of the Genesis story which saw the Fall as the result of sexuality, with Adam the aggressor and Eve the victim of rape. Jean-Baptiste van Helmont's *Oriatrike* was one. He was renowned in England as an experimental scientist and as a religious leader in the style of Jacob Boehme.[30] Unlike More, he rejected the multilayered understanding of the text for a metaphorical reading of its literal truth.

For van Helmont, to be a paradisal being was to live in a non-sexual world. Thus Adam was placed in a Paradise without animals: 'Yea neither would the Almighty, that man should behold the bruitish copulation of the Sexes, whom he wished to live in the purity of innocency.'[31]

[27] Henry More, *Conjectura Cabbalistica*, in *A Collection of Philosophical Writings*, p. 26. The title should not be read as implying that More was committed to cabbala in the strict Jewish sense. For him, a cabbalistic reading meant no more than a mystical allegorical reading.

[28] *Ibid.*, p. 27.

[29] *Ibid.*, p. 39. More's philosophical reading of the story makes sense only if Adam is construed as aethereally (at least) hermaphroditic. But More clearly rejected Plato's *Symposium* view that men were originally and literally so. See *The Defence of the Threefold Cabbala*, in *ibid.*, p. 64. Similarly, the serpent literally spoke, but allegorically it was the devil. As we have seen, for the Muggletonians, God had literally a human shape. So also for More: God has a human shape literally. Unlike the Muggletonians' God, More's also has an allegorical 'shape': 'God's walking in the Garden, his calling after *Adam*, his pronouncing the doom upon him, his wife, and the Serpent, and sundry passages before, do again and again inculcate the opinion of the *Anthropomorphites*, that God has an human shape; which I already acknowledged to be the meaning of the *Literal Cabbala*.'

[30] See Charles Webster, *The Great Instauration*, p. 277.

[31] Jean-Baptiste van Helmont, *Oriatrike* (London, 1662), p. 161. It was originally published in Amsterdam in 1648 as *Ortus Medicinus*.

And as a consequence, God brought only one of each kind of animal to be named. Similarly, Eve was created in Paradise and on the eighth day, lest she 'whom he had made and appointed to remaine a Virgin, should behold the copulation of Bruit-beasts in the Earth'.[32] Van Helmont was following the suggestion of Augustine that the male seed could have been dispatched into the womb with no loss of virginity, the seed following the same path but in the opposite direction as the menses.[33] Thus, Eve would have reproduced virginally. But unlike Augustine's, in van Helmont's vision Adam was altogether redundant. Eve, having been made from Adam, meant for van Helmont that any sexual relationship between them would have been an incestuous one. Thus, Eve would have produced not only virginally but non-sexually. There was 'a perpetual Virginity appointed in propogating: To wit, that she had conceived and brought forth, her Womb being shut'.[34]

Be that as it may, the serpent, disguised as a man, tempted Eve into eating the apple, and she likewise Adam. Sex and death were the *natural* outcomes of eating the apple:

Death proceeded not from the Will, or from sin; but from the Apple: neither indeed, because Death itself was in the Apple, as in a mortal Poyson, but there was in the Apple the Concupiscence of the Flesh, an incentive of Lust, a be-drunkening of Luxury for a Beast-like Generation in the Flesh of Sin, which Flesh caused with it the natural Causes of Defects and necessities of Death.[35]

After eating the apple, Adam began to lust after Eve. The apple acted more slowly upon Eve than Adam, she being more chaste. Struggling against his advances, she was 'deflowred by *Adam* by force . . .' His body forever was to bear the signatures of his beastliness:

Wherefore that the first Infringer of Modesty, and deflowrer of a Virgin might be made known; God would that Hairs should grow on the Chin, Cheeks, and Lips of *Adam*, that he might be a Compeere, Companion, and like unto many four-footed Beasts, might bear before him the Signature of the same.[36]

Edward Taylor too constructed variations on Behmenist and Helmontian themes. Adam ought to have reproduced magically the child Eve. But his lust after the world led God to separate her from an unwilling Adam by holy violence. Upon awakening, he raped her. Eve also succumbs to the serpent's tempting. They are cast out of Paradise, metaphorically 'dying a Nescience or Oblivion of Divine Tranquillity

[32] *Ibid.*, p. 665.
[33] See Henry Bettenson (trans.), Augustine, *Concerning the City of God against the Pagans*, 14.26.
[34] Jean-Baptiste van Helmont, *Oriatrike*, p. 654.   [35] *Ibid.*, p. 657.   [36] *Ibid.*, p. 666.

and peaceable Fruition of Eternity, and an awakening to the Turmoils, Impotence, Discords, Pain, Care, Sorrow, Enmity, and anguish of Mortality and Confines of time in the third Principle or Outbirth'.[37]

ERECT SERPENTS AND FALLEN ANGELS

> Now the serpent was more subtil than any beast of the field which the Lord God had made.   Genesis 3.1

For metaphorical readings of the story of Adam and Eve, the literal or historical sense was ignored or rejected in favour of the true sense of the text – its inner and spiritual meaning. To Gerrard Winstanley, for example, the story had only a metaphorical meaning. Adam symbolised the covetousness in every man, as did Eve the imagination which arose from it. The public preachers, he declared, 'have cheated the whole world, by telling us of a single man, called Adam, that kiled us al by eating a single fruit, called an Apple'.[38] And therefore 'that which hath by Imagination, or *Judas* Ministry, been held forth to us, to be without us, as *Adam*; the Serpent, the Garden, the Tree of Knowledge, of Good and Evill; and the Tree of Life; and the fall of Man, and promise of redemption, all to be without; yet all these are within the heart of man clearly'.[39]

The dominant seventeenth-century reading of the Garden of Eden was an historical one, and the serpent was seen as a real serpent. Reflecting the demonological tradition according to which Satan could assume any desired shape, the biblical scholar Joseph Mede was inclined to believe the devil had taken a serpentine form, supposing it 'to be *the law of Spirits*, when they have intercourse and commerce with men, to take some visible shape upon them'.[40] But this was rare. Similarly aware of the demonological tradition, du Bartas wondered whether it was merely the appearance of a serpent which Eve saw, but concluded otherwise:

> I thinke 'twas no conceipt,
> No fained Idoll, nor no jugling sleight
> Nor body borrowed for this uses sake,
> But the selfe serpent which the Lord did make
> In the beginning: for his hatefull breed
> Beares yet the pain of this pernicious deed.[41]

---

[37] Edward Taylor, *Jacob Behmen's Theosophick Philosophy*, p. 107. 'In the third Principle or Outbirth' here simply means 'in a corporeal physical form'.

[38] George H. Sabine (ed.), *The Works of Gerrard Winstanley*, p. 203.   [39] *Ibid.*, p. 462.

[40] Joseph Mede, *The Works of the Pious and Profoundly-Learned Joseph Mede* (London, 1677), p. 223. See also Jean Le Clerc, *Twelve Dissertations*, p. 144.

As John Salkeld suggested, it was a true and natural serpent, 'by which the deuill tempted and overcame *Eue*, speaking with her in the shape and substance of a serpent . . .'[42]

The belief that Satan had entered into the serpent can be found in the Jewish tradition for the first time around the first century in *The Book of the Secrets of Enoch*.[43] Thence it became part of the rabbinic tradition.[44] And by the time of Augustine, the belief that Satan had insinuated himself into the serpent was a central feature of Christian doctrine.[45] That the serpent was said to be naturally subtle or crafty contributed to its demonisation. According to Andrew Willet, 'whereas the serpent is a most subtill beast, it was not by chance, that Sathan vsed him as his instrument, beeing by his naturall subtiltie apt thereunto'.[46] Edward Topsell in *The Historie of Serpents* in 1608 disapproved of those who thought that the devil could have entered any animal: 'that old Serpent knewe very well . . . that he could not haue so fit a subiect in all the World, as the shape, wit, and cunning of a Serpent'.[47] To John Salkeld, no creature was so 'naturally bent by a malicious craftinesse to hurt man, as the serpent is . . .'[48]

Josephus and some of the rabbis believed that the serpentine language was lost as a consequence of God's punishment of the serpent.[49] Calvin had declared that the serpent's voice was not natural. Rather 'when Satan, by divine permission, procured it as a fit instrument for his use, he uttered words also by its tongue, which God himself permitted'.[50] The mainstream seventeenth-century opinion followed Calvin. Thus, for example, according to Nicholas Gibbens, Eve heard the serpent speaking Hebrew, not through any power of its own 'but of the

---

[41] Susan Snyder (ed.), *The Divine Weeks and Works*, i.343. Arnold Williams' common expositors agreed that the serpent was a real one.

[42] John Salkeld, *A Treatise of Paradise*, p. 211.

[43] See J. M. Evans, *'Paradise Lost' and the Genesis Tradition*, p. 34.

[44] See Henry Ansgar Kelly, 'The Metamorphoses of the Eden Serpent during the Middle Ages and Renaissance', *Viator* 2 (1971), p. 302.

[45] See J. M. Evans, *'Paradise Lost' and the Genesis Tradition*, p. 95.

[46] Andrew Willet, *Hexapla in Genesin*, p. 45.

[47] Edward Topsell, *The Historie of Serpents* (London, 1608), p. 18. The allusion is to Revelation 20.2: 'And he laid hold on the dragon, that old serpent, which is the Devil, and Satan, and bound him a thousand years.'

[48] John Salkeld, *A Treatise of Paradise*, p. 215. See also James Ussher, *A Body of Divinitie*, p. 129; John White, *A Commentary Upon the Three First Chapters of Moses*, iii.162; Gervase Babington, *Certaine Plaine, briefe, and comfortable Notes vpon euerie Chapter of Genesis*, sig. c.7.v; and John Milton, *Paradise Lost*, 4.347–50.

[49] See for example William Whiston (trans.), *The Works of Flavius Josephus*, i.44; and J. M. Evans, *'Paradise Lost' and the Genesis Tradition*, p. 47.

[50] John King (trans.), *Commentaries on the First Book of Moses*, p. 145.

Diuell, who because he is a Spirit, was able to enter into him, and . . . guide his tongue . . .'[51] Similarly, Henry Ainsworth wrote, 'Wheras *beasts are knowen* in nature to be speechless . . . because they want reason or understanding . . . Moses under the name of the *Serpent speaking*, closely meaneth *Satan*, who opened the serpents mouth, and caused it to speak with mans voice.'[52] According to the royalist divine Arthur Jackson, 'The serpent, speechlesse in himself, had his mouth opened by Satan, who caused him to speak, or spake in and by him.'[53]

Since the serpent was a natural one, it was tempting to try to identify its species. Thomas Browne reported on a number of suggestions made by the commentators: 'Bonaventure and Comestor affirme it was a Dragon, Eugubinus a Basiliske, Delrio a viper, and others a common snake.'[54] Browne himself favoured the viper, for he included the Fall in his discussion of its 'natural history'.[55] The basilisk was a common suggestion. Imagined as having the body of a cock and the tail of a snake, it was identified with the devil in the medieval tradition.[56] Like the original serpent of Eden, it stood upright. Unlike the original serpent, it was believed still to do so. On this ground, Joseph Mede rejected it as the Edenic serpent. Having lost its upright status, it could not have been a basilisk, he concluded, 'because the *Basilisk* goes with his breast and fore-part of his body advanced . . .'[57] The Catholic exegete Pererius opted for the scytala, a snake renowned for its beauty. Topsell described it as 'very full of markes or spots vppon the back so variable and delectable that it possesseth the beholders with admiration'.[58] Before giving up the task, John Pettus considered the basilisk and the scytala as possible candidates, since they enticed many to destruction 'by their beauty, splendour, and subtilty . . .';[59] and the 'Lyzard' was considered as a possibility because of its affectionate nature.

If the species of the serpent remained indeterminate, there was much clearer agreement on its stature before the curse. That it crawled as a punishment after the Fall suggested it stood upright before it. Josephus

---

[51] Nicholas Gibbens, *Qvestions and Dispvtations concerning the Holy Scriptvre*, p. 105.
[52] Henry Ainsworth, *Annotations Upon the first book of Moses*, sig. c.3.r.
[53] Arthur Jackson, *A Help for the understanding of the Holy Scripture*, i.10. See also Alexander Ross, *An Exposition on the Fovrteene first Chapters of Genesis*, p. 59; Susan Snyder (ed.), *The Divine Weeks and Works*, i.344; Henry Holland, *The Historie of Adam, or the foure-fold state of Man* (London, 1606), p. 7.
[54] Thomas Browne, *Pseudodoxia Epidemica* 7.1.   [55] See *ibid.*, 3.16.
[56] See for example Richard Barber (trans.), *Bestiary*, p. 185.   [57] Joseph Mede, *The Works*, p. 231.
[58] Edward Topsell, *The Historie of Serpents*, p. 232. John Dryden implied the scytala in his description of the Edenic serpent as 'spotted'. See *The State of Innocence, and Fall of Man: An Opera* (London, 1677), p. 31.
[59] John Pettus, *Volatiles from the History of Adam and Eve*, p. 93.

and the rabbinic tradition imagined an upright serpent with legs and feet.[60] That the serpent had feet was established early in the Eastern tradition of Christianity, and that it had feet and/or stood erect on the tip of its tail was common in the Western medieval tradition.[61] Calvin argued there was no change to the serpent after the Fall, as did Alexander Ross.[62] Thomas Browne believed that the serpent, 'from his proper form and figure, made his motion on his belly before the curse'.[63] But they were in the minority.

Luther, for one, accepted that it both had feet and stood erect.[64] To Matthew Poole, it seemed more probable that the Edenic serpent 'before the fall either had Feet, or rather did go with erected Breast, and didst feed upon the fruits of Trees and other Plants . . .'[65] Milton's serpent stood erect upon its coils. He

> Address'd his way, not with indented wave,
> Prone on the ground, as since, but on his rear,
> Circular base of rising folds, that towr'd
> Fold above fold a surging Maze, his Head
> Crested aloft, and Carbuncle his Eyes;
> With burnisht Neck of verdant gold, erect
> Amidst his circling Spires . . . [66]

The biblical story proceeded upon the assumption that Eve, when confronted by the serpent, was neither surprised nor afraid. This demanded explanation. There was general agreement that the serpent was

---

[60] See John W. Etheridge, *The Targums of Onkelos and Jonathan ben Uzziel . . . from the Chaldee*, i.166; and H. Freedman and M. Simon (eds.), *Midrash Rabbah*, i.149; and William Whiston (trans.), *The Works of Flavius Josephus*, i.44.

[61] See Henry Ansgar Kelly, 'The Metamorphoses of the Eden Serpent', pp. 303–6.

[62] See John King (trans.), *Commentaries on the First Book of Moses*, p. 167; and Alexander Ross, *An Exposition on the Fovrteene first Chapters of Genesis*, p. 66.

[63] Thomas Browne, *Religio Medici*, 1.9.

[64] See Henry Cole (trans.), *The Creation: A Commentary by Martin Luther*, p. 249; and William Hazlitt (trans.), *The Table Talk . . . of Martin Luther*, p. 58.

[65] Matthew Poole, *Annotations upon the Holy Bible*, sig. B.4.r.

[66] *Paradise Lost*, 9.496–502. J. B. Medina's illustration to the 1688 edition of *Paradise Lost* depicts the coiled serpent balancing precariously upon the tip of its tail. See Ernest W. Sullivan II, 'Illustration as Interpretation: *Paradise Lost* from 1688 to 1807', in Albert C. Labriola and Edward Sichi, Jr (eds.), *Milton's Legacy in the Arts* (University Park, Pennsylvania, 1988), p. 69. Milton's coiled serpent may reflect the devil's laying the coils of sin in front of those on their way to heaven. See Richard Barber (trans.), *Bestiary*, pp. 183–4. For other references to the erect serpent, see Nicholas Gibbens, *Qvestions and Dispvtations concerning the Holy Scripture*, p. 142; John Salkeld, *A Treatise of Paradise*, pp. 216, 224; Thomas Milles, *The treasurie of auncient and moderne times*, i.26; Arthur Jackson, *A Help for the understanding of the Holy Scripture*, i.11; George Hughes, *An Analytical Exposition of the Whole first Book of Moses, called Genesis*, p. 37; John White, *A Commentary Upon the Three First Chapters of Genesis*, iii.161–2; Richard Kidder, *A Commentary*, i.15; and Joseph Mede, *The Works*, p. 233.

beautiful. It 'was the most beautiful of creatures', declared Martin Luther.[67] It was a very proper creature for the devil to make use of, wrote William Nicholls, for

> It is most probable something like that flying fiery sort, which are bred in *Arabia* and *Aegypt*, that are of a shining yellowish Colour, like that of Brass; which by the motion of their wings and the vibration of their Tails reverberating the Sun Beams, do afford a most glorious appearance.[68]

The tradition that the serpent had a human face – generally female, all the better to ensnare Eve – survived into the seventeenth century. It was attributed to Bede by Peter Comestor in the twelfth century, though no source in Bede is known. Lucifer 'also chose a certain kind of serpent, as Bede says', wrote Comester, 'which had the countenance of a virgin, because like follows like'.[69] Comestor's invention was highly influential throughout the medieval period in both the literary and visual arts, as Nona Flores has shown.[70] And it reached its pictorial high point in Michelangelo's virgin-headed serpent in the Sistine Chapel.

With the increasing dominance of the literal sense of the Genesis story (and thus of a natural serpent) in the seventeenth century, this image was disappearing. That Satan appeared with a virgin's head so that 'thereby he might become more acceptable, and his temptation find the easier entertainment', wrote Thomas Browne, 'is a conceit not to be admitted, and the plain and received figure, is with better reason embraced'.[71] Still, vestiges of the tradition remained. John Salkeld, for example, pictured the serpent speaking with a female voice 'most accommodate for to deceiue the woman', and he discussed the tradition of Eve's not being afraid 'because the deuill had chosen such a serpent, as which (in face at leastway) represented a woman, yea and one most beautifull like vnto herselfe'.[72] Thomas Milles cited Comestor to the effect that 'The Deuill chose a Serpent, that had a face like to a Womans . . . that like might be pleasing to like.'[73] At the end of the century, John Dunton hazarded, if only half-heartedly, a natural explanation for the tradition:

[67] William Hazlitt (trans.), *The Table Talk . . . of Martin Luther*, p. 58. See also Henry Cole (trans.), *The Creation: A Commentary by Martin Luther*, p. 203.
[68] William Nicholls, *A Conference with a Theist*, p. 201.
[69] Peter Comestor, *Historia scholastica*, i.21 (*P.L.* 198.1072). Quoted by Henry Ansgar Kelly, 'The Metamorphoses of the Eden Serpent', p. 307.
[70] See Nona Cecilia Flores, '"Virgineum Vultum Habens": The Woman-Headed Serpent in Art and Literature from 1300 to 1700', Ph.D. dissertation, University of Illinois, 1981. See also John K. Bonnell, 'The Serpent with a Human Head in Art and Mystery Play', *American Journal of Archaeology* 21 (1917), pp. 255–91.
[71] Thomas Browne, *Pseudodoxia Epidemica*, 5.4.   [72] John Salkeld, *A Treatise of Paradise*, p. 216.
[73] Thomas Milles, *The treasurie of auncient and moderne times*, i.27.

'The Naturalists tell us of Serpents, and other Creatures that have humane faces, and we are not without instances of this in *Madagascar*, where some of our Ships trade: But whether it was such a Serpent as this, is not material; but we are really perswaded it was a true Serpent which some envious *Angel* did actuate.'[74]

Why, it was asked, was Eve unafraid when the serpent spoke to her? The twelfth-century Andrew of Saint Victor had seen her lack of amazement at the serpent's speaking to her as a sign of her great simplicity.[75] A related seventeenth-century explanation was that she was unaware that serpents didn't speak. Thus, for example, Thomas Browne, following Pererius: 'some conceive she might not yet be certain that only man was priviledged with speech; and being in the novity of the Creation, and inexperience of all things, might not be affrighted to hear a Serpent speak'.[76] Similarly, in 1655, Benjamin Needler suggested Eve was unaware that serpents had no language. It was probable, he conjectured, that '*Eve* had lesse knowledge then *Adam*, and yet had as much as was required to the perfection of a woman . . .'[77]

The most obvious and simplest explanation for Eve's lack of fear was that there was nothing to be afraid of. Andrew Willet canvassed a number of options before deciding on this one. It was not a virgin-headed serpent, or a basilisk or scytala, it was quite simply that it, like all the animals, was tame.[78] Thomas Cooper in 1573 suggested that Eve and the serpent were friends.[79] Similarly, almost ninety years later, Samuel Pordage:

> There was a Serpent whose fine speckled hide,
> And pretty features with rare colours dy'd,
> Had gain'd EVE's Love, and who it may be had
> Entwin'd about her naked neck, and play'd
> With her white hands; or favour'd in her lap.[80]

---

[74] John Dunton (ed.), *The Athenian Gazette*, vol. 1, q. 5, no.15. See also Giovanno Loredano, *The Life of Adam*, p. 26. John White used the feminine pronoun for the serpent. See John White, *A Commentary Upon the Three First Chapters of Genesis*, iii.162.

[75] See Henry Ansgar Kelly, 'The Metamorphoses of the Christian Serpent', p. 303.

[76] Thomas Browne, *Pseudodoxia Epidemica*, 5.4.

[77] Benjamin Needler, *Expository Notes*, p. 61. See also Gervase Babington, *Certaine Plaine, briefe, and comfortable Notes vpon euerie Chapter of Genesis*, sig. c.8.r.

[78] Andrew Willet, *Hexapla in Genesin*, p. 47. See also Alexander Ross, *An Exposition on the Fovrteene first Chapters of Genesis*, pp. 59–60; John Salkeld, *A Treatise of Paradise*, p. 216; Henry Holland, *The Historie of Adam*, p. 7; Giovanno Loredano, *The Life of Adam*, pp. 26–7; George Hughes, *An Analytical Exposition of the Whole first Book of Moses, called Genesis*, p. 27; Henry Cole (trans.), *The Creation: A Commentary by Martin Luther*, p. 249.

[79] Thomas Cooper, *A Briefe Exposition*, sig. N.I.V.

[80] Samual Pordage, *Mundorum Explicatio*, p. 66.

Sexuality lurks not far beneath the surface of the seductively entrancing Satan of serpentine beauty winding himself around the body of Eve. 'And lovely, never since of Serpent kind/ Lovelier', declared Milton.[81] Philip Camerarius reminded his readers that serpents have been noted to desire the company of women; all the more reason for Satan to have used such a creature. 'All the Rabbins are of this mind', he continued, 'that the deuils (through Gods sufferance) haue great power ouer ones concupiscence and privie members . . . *Philo* and the Hebrewes say, That the Serpent signifieth allegorically, Lecherie'.[82]

It was an intimacy that was not to survive the Fall. The hatred between serpents and women was greater even than that between them and men. If there is one woman in a great assembly of people, wrote Camerarius, 'the serpent will assay to hurt her first'.[83] Serpents hate women more, declared William Basse, by virtue of the perpetual enmity that God put between the seed of the serpent and that of the woman.[84] Edward Topsell developed the opinion of the Roman poet Lucretius that the saliva of men and serpents was mutually dangerous: 'as by the tongue of a serpent, was wrought mans confusion, so by the spettle of a mans tongue, is wrought a serpents astonishment'.[85] The heavens placed a mutual enmity between them and us, wrote John-Francis Senault, so that 'if their venom be fatall to us, our spittle is mortall to them . . .'[86] Between the snake and man, there was a 'most deadly enmity', declared Joseph Mede. Their humours were poison to each other. And he embellished the tradition of the medieval *Physiologus* and the bestiaries that serpents were afraid of naked men and only attacked those who were clothed.[87] A serpent is scared of men, he believed, and especially if they are naked, 'As though his instinct even remembred the time of his malediction'.[88] And serpents were said to be even more afraid of women: 'if but the naked foot of a *Woman* doth never so little press the *head of a Serpent* before he can sting her, both the body and head presently dieth'.[89]

That the serpent was cursed to eat dust was a sign of his vile and

[81] *Paradise Lost*, 9.504–5.
[82] Philip Camerarius, *The Walking Librarie*, p. 249. But cf. Andrew Willet, *Hexapla in Genesin*, p. 48: 'The Hebrewes here are not to be approoued, that say the serpent coueted to have companie with the woman: for that is against the nature of beasts.'
[83] Philip Camerarius, *The Walking Librarie*, p. 251. He was following the Renaissance historian Jean Bodin.   [84] See [William Basse], *A Helpe to Discourse*, pp. 41–2.
[85] Edward Topsell, *The Historie of Serpents*, p. 21.
[86] John-Francis Senault, *Man become Guilty*, p. 381.
[87] See Michael J. Curley (trans.), *Physiologus*, p. 19; and Richard Barber (trans.), *Bestiary*, p. 196. This was occasionally given as the reason for the serpent's attack on Eve.
[88] Joseph Mede, *The Works*, p. 234.   [89] *Ibid.*

sordid nature, declared John Calvin.[90] Whereas the serpent once ate the same food as man, explained Luther, now 'he eats the crude earth only'.[91] After the curse, the serpent was forced to graze upon the ground, wrote John White, and as a result 'must necessarily take her food out of the dust, and so lick in some dust withal'.[92] The serpent fell from the second most exalted position to the least of all, maintained Benjamin Needler. He had therefore to take dust into his mouth, 'whether he will or not'.[93]

IT WAS ALL HER FAULT!

And the man said, The woman whom thou gavest to be with me,
she gave me of the tree and I did eat.   Genesis 3.12

There is no indication in the Genesis text why the serpent should have desired the downfall of Adam and Eve. But with the entrance of Satan into the reading of the Fall, his motives cried out for explanation. During the seventeenth century, envy was seen as his primary motivation. Having fallen himself, he envied 'the happy estate and the great felicitie of *Adam*', declared Lodowick Lloid in 1590.[94] He tempted Eve 'out of a cruell enuy of Mans happinesse, and an insatiable desire of doing hurt', suggested Elnathan Parr.[95] A further reason for Satan's envy was his discontent that Christ intended to become incarnate in human form, thus demeaning the status of angelic nature. It was proposed by Thomas Heywood in *The Hierarchie of the blessed Angells*:

> With Pride and enuy *Lucifer* now swelling
> Against Mankinde, whom from his heav'nly Dwelling,
> He seemes in supernaturall Gifts t'outshine,
> (Man being but Terrene and himselfe Diuine)
> Ambitiously his Hate encreasing still,
> Dares to oppose the great Creators Will:
> As holding it against his Iustice done
> That th'Almighties sole begotten Sonne,
> Mans nature to assume purpos'd and meant,
> And not the Angels, much more excellent.[96]

[90] See John King (trans.), *Commentaries on the First Book of Moses*, p. 167.
[91] Henry Cole (trans.), *The Creation: A Commentary by Martin Luther*, p. 250.
[92] John White, *A Commentary Upon the Three First Chapters of Genesis*, iii.163.
[93] Benjamin Needler, *Expository Notes*, p. 89.   [94] Lodowick Lloid, *The Consent of Time*, p. 5.
[95] Elnathan Parr, *The Grounds of Divinitie*, p. 154. See also Godfrey Goodman, *The Fall of Man*, p. 428; Thomas Peyton, *The glasse of time*, p. 29; Thomas Hayne, *The General View of the Holy Scriptures*, p. 16; James Ussher, *A Body of Divinitie*, p. 128, and *The Annals of the World*, p. 2.
[96] Thomas Heywood, *The Hierarchie of the blessed Angells*, vi.339.

It was a solution which Luther rejected and Calvin dismissed as a frivolous speculation.[97] Andrew Willet followed Calvin in suggesting that Satan was motivated by a desire to bring man to damnation.[98] It was his envy of Adam's being created in God's image which moved him to tempt Eve, wrote the Scottish poet William Alexander in 1614: 'It neuer ended yet which then beganne,/ His Hate towards God, his Enuy vnto Man.'[99]

All were agreed that Eve had separated from Adam when Satan, waiting his chance, approached her. Thus, for example, according to Thomas Peyton, Lucifer bided his time,

> And watching *Time*, when *Adam* stept aside,
> Euen but a little from his louely Bride,
> To pluck perhaps a Nut vpon the Trees,
> Or get a combe amongst the hony Bees.[100]

Eve's solitude was an advantage, declared Matthew Poole, 'which the crafty Serpent quickly espieth, and greedily embraceth . . .'[101] Luther took the opportunity to deliver a homily about solitude's enhancing the propensity to sin.[102] Giovanno Loredano restricted the dangers of solitude to women: 'the more distant she is from her Husband, the more adjacent she is to Sin; and whilst alone, is in perill of destroying herself'.[103] But it was John Milton who was alone in crediting to Eve the virtue of separating from her husband in order to increase their productivity, an expression of her liberty and responsibility.[104]

Whatever the reasons for Eve's being alone, the most commonly adduced reason for Satan to approach her rather than Adam was her status as 'the weaker vessel' (1 Peter 3.7). Henry Holland spoke for most: 'Sathan begins his battery where the wall is weakest, he knew that euen then the woman was the weaker vessel.'[105] Thomas Browne made the

[97] See John King (trans.), *Commentaries on the First Book of Moses*, p. 146.
[98] See Andrew Willet, *Hexapla in Genesin*, p. 47.
[99] William Alexander, *Doomes-Day; or, The Great Day of the Lords Ivdgment* (Edinburgh, 1614), sig. B.4.v.
[100] Thomas Peyton, *The glasse of time*, p. 32.
[101] Matthew Poole, *Annotations upon the Holy Bible*, sig. B.3.v. See also James Ussher, *A Body of Divinitie*, p. 129.
[102] See William Hazlitt, *The Table Talk . . . of Martin Luther*, p. 279.
[103] Giovanno Loredano, *The Life of Adam*, p. 23.
[104] See *Paradise Lost*, 9.204–25. And see Diane K. McColley, *Miltons Eve* (Urbana, Illinois, 1983), ch. 5.
[105] Henry Holland, *The Historie of Adam*, p. 7. See also Gervase Babington, *Certaine Plaine, briefe, and comfortable Notes vpon euerie Chapter of Genesis*, sig. C.8.v; Susan Snyder (ed.), *The Divine Weeks and Works*, i.346; Nicholas Gibbens, *Qvestions and Dispvtations concerning the Holy Scripture*, p. 114; John White, *A Commentary Upon the Three First Chapters of Genesis*, iii.34–5; Joseph Needler, *Expository Notes*, p. 63.

same point: 'the Serpent was cunning enough', he wrote, 'to begin the deceit in the weaker; and the weaker of strength, sufficient to consummate the fraud in the stronger'.[106] That women were more prone to the temptations of Satan made them more liable to be witches. John Stearne, for example, in 1648 explained witchcraft as a female phenomenon, since women were more easily displeased and revengeful of men owing to Satan's 'prevailing with Eve'.[107] That there was in women a greater facility to fall, explained Alexander Roberts in *A Treatise of Witchcraft*, led to their being one hundred times more likely than men to be witches.[108]

Still, that they were seen to be the weaker vessels could be offered as mitigating Eve's actions. Bishop Thomas Ken, for example, in a funeral sermon for a Lady Mainard informed his listeners that

women are made of a temper more soft and frail, are more endangered by snares and temptations, less able to control their passions, and more inclinable to extremes of good or bad than men, and generally speaking, goodness is a tenderer thing, more hazardous and brittle in the former than in the latter, and consequently a firm and steady virtue is more to be valued in the weaker sex than in the stronger.[109]

It was an image used by women themselves to excuse their grandmother Eve. In her response to Joseph Swetnam, Esther Sowernam had asked men to cease charging women with faults 'which come from the contagion of Masculine Serpents'.[110] But her colleague Rachel Speght took a softer approach: 'she being the weaker vessell was with more facility to be seduced . . .'[111] And Elizabeth Warren was willing to admit that 'we of the weaker sex, have hereditary evil from our grandmother Eve.'[112] Such self-deprecation, as Antonia Fraser suggests, 'might be expected to win the sympathy of a masculine audience, or at very least avoid arousing its hostility'.[113]

If the fault of Eve was mitigated by her natural weakness, it was aggravated by her involving Adam in her sin. The misogynistic Richard Ames pictured a malicious and demonic Eve determined not to be

[106] Thomas Browne, *Pseudodoxia Epidemica*, 1.1.
[107] John Stearne, *The Discoverie of Witchcraft* (London, 1648), p. 15. Quoted by Antonia Fraser, *The Weaker Vessel: Woman's Lot in Seventeenth-Century England* (London, 1984), p. 105.
[108] See Alexander Roberts, *A Treatise of Witchcraft* (London, 1616), p. 43.
[109] W. Peacock (ed.), *English Prose in Five Volumes* (Oxford, 1921), ii.214.
[110] Esther Sowernam, *Esther hath hang'd Haman*, p. 48.
[111] Rachel Speght, *A Mouzell for Melastomus*, p. 4.
[112] Elizabeth Warren, *Spiritual Thrift* (London, 1648), p. 81. Quoted by Antonia Fraser, *The Weaker Vessel*, p. 249.
[113] Antonia Fraser, *The Weaker Vessel*, p. 247.

cursed alone: 'And therefore with insinuating smiles/ Her *too believing* Husband soon beguiles.'[114] And Adam's guilt was mitigated by his love for Eve. Adam's firm faith melted 'before that soft seducer, love', wrote John Dryden.[115] Thus was Adam's reason overcome by passion. He was a warning to all men. If both Adam and Solomon disobeyed God, wrote Sir Walter Raleigh, 'by the perswasion and for the loue they bare to a woman, it is not so wonderfull as lamentable, that other men in succeeding ages haue beene allured to so many inconuenient and wicked practises by the perswasions of their wives, or other beloued Darlings, who couer ouer and shadow many malicious purposes with a counterfait passion of dissimulate sorrow and vnquietnesse'.[116] Adam's loss of a rib exposed his heart, explained John Pettus, 'so that all its Loves and desires had no sence against her'.[117] Milton's Adam worshipped her, and it was his undoing: 'Against his better knowledge, not deceiv'd/ But fondly overcome with Female charm'.[118]

APPLES, TREES, AND FIG LEAVES

> And out of the ground made the Lord God to grow every tree that is pleasant to the sight and good for food; the tree of life also in the midst of the garden, and the tree of knowledge of good and evil . . . But of the tree of the knowledge of good and evil, thou shalt not eat of it.
> Genesis 2.9, 17

Generally, seventeenth-century commentators believed that, had Adam not sinned, he would have been immortal. This had been a central feature of Christian doctrine since the Council of Carthage in 417 CE declared anathema those who believed that Adam was created mortal.[119] But about the relationship of the immortality of Adam and Eve to the Tree of Life, there was much uncertainty whether its effects were natural or symbolic. For Calvin, for example, the Tree of Life had only a symbolic (or sacramental) value.[120] God intended, he wrote, 'that man, as often as he tasted the fruit of that tree, should remember

---

[114] Richard Ames, *The Folly of Love*, p. 3.   [115] John Dryden, *The State of Innocence*, p. 33.
[116] Walter Raleigh, *The History of the World*, p. 142. On Eve as temptress, see also Susan Snyder (ed.), *The Divine Weeks and Works*, i.348.
[117] John Pettus, *Volatiles from the History of Adam and Eve*, p. 66.
[118] *Paradise Lost*, 9.998–9. See also 8.471–8 for Adam's love of her at first sight. For a discussion of Milton and feminism, see Diane K. McColley, 'Milton and the Sexes', in Dennis Danielson (ed.), *The Cambridge Companion to Milton* (Cambridge, 1989), pp. 147–66. See also Susan Snyder (ed.), *The Divine Weeks and Works*, i.291; Thomas Peyton, *The glasse of time*, pp. 27–8; and Joseph Mede, *The Works*, p. 227.
[119] See Henry Bettenson (ed.), *Documents of the Christian Church* (London, 1967), p. 83.
[120] Arnold Williams is undoubtedly correct in pointing out that there was no real difference between descriptions of the tree as a symbol or as a sacrament. See *The Common Expositor*, p. 103.

whence he received his life, in order that he might acknowledge that he lives not by his own power, but by the kindness of God alone . . .'[121] To Milton, it was a pledge of immortality.[122] The Tree of Life was so called, declared Benjamin Needler, 'because it was a sacramental signe annexed to the Covenant of works assuring life, and immortality, upon condition of perfect obedience'.[123] As a sign of life, it also symbolised Christ, from whom eternal life was to be gained. As Thomas Peyton put it, it signified 'that deare Lambe out of whose bleeding heart/ Our soules were held much to his paine and smart'.[124] It was a 'symbole of Christ who is our true life', declared Andrew Willet.[125]

Arthur Jackson, George Hughes, and John White believed that the Tree of Life had not only a symbolic value but a natural or supernatural capacity to prolong life.[126] This was the majority viewpoint. Like Luther, Nicholas Gibbens believed that the fruit of the Tree of Life had a natural ability to preserve life, at least until such time as Adam, like Enoch and Elijah, was translated into heaven. And it would have preserved us not only from death but from sorrow, sickness, and aging.[127] John Salkeld was convinced that the fruit 'was of such qualities and excellent properties, that being eaten, it did renew our *humidum radicale*, our natural humidity and moisture', so that we should never have died.[128] The chemist J. B. van Helmont held to the natural ability of the fruit to continually act as a restorative. It was created, he maintained, 'for the powers and necessities of Renovation, renewing of Youth, yea and prevention of Old Age'.[129] To deny him access to it, Adam was banished, he remarked elsewhere.[130] Similarly, Matthew Poole was convinced that it had a singular virtue 'for the support of Nature, prolongation of Life, and the prevention of all Diseases, Infirmities, and decays through age'.[131]

[121] John King (trans.), *Commentaries on the First Book of Moses*, p. 117.

[122] See *Paradise Lost*, 4.200–1.

[123] Benjamin Needler, *Expository Notes*, p. 34. See also Henry Ainsworth, *Annotations Upon the first book of Moses called Genesis*, sig. B.4.v; and George Walker, *God made visible*, p. 244.

[124] Thomas Peyton, *The glasse of time*, p. 62.

[125] Andrew Willet, *Hexapla in Genesin*, p. 28. See also John King (trans.), *Commentaries on the First Book of Moses*, p. 117; and Edward Leigh, *A Systeme or Bodie of Divinitie*, p. 367.

[126] See Arthur Jackson, *A Help for the understanding of the Holy Scripture*, p. 9; George Hughes, *An Analytical Explanation of the Whole first book of Moses, called Genesis*, p. 18; and John White, *A Commentary Upon the Three First Chapters of Genesis*, ii.38.

[127] See Nicholas Gibbens, *Questions and Disputations concerning the Holy Scripture*, p. 70. See also Henry Cole (trans.), *The Creation: A Commentary by Martin Luther*, pp. 83, 127; and Walter Raleigh, *The History of the World*, p. 135.

[128] John Salkeld, *A Treatise of Paradise*, p. 49.   [129] J.-B. van Helmont, *Van Helmont's Works*, p. 745.

[130] See J.-B. van Helmont, *Oriatrike*, p. 649.

[131] Matthew Poole, *Annotations upon the Holy Bible*, sig. B.2.v. See also Giovanno Loredano, *The Life of Adam*, p. 8; William Austin, *Haec Homo*, p. 19; and William Whiston, *A New Theory of the Earth*, p. 169.

To John Pettus, the Tree of the Knowledge of Good and Evil also had a natural poisonous quality which infected Adam and Eve with all their infirmities.[132] But in this he was alone. Whereas the majority of interpreters saw the effects of the Tree of Life as natural, virtually all viewed the eating of the fruit of the Tree of the Knowledge of Good and Evil as having a symbolic value only.

That the eating of the fruit had only a symbolic meaning avoided the theological dilemma of how something evil could have been created in a world which was wholly good. But also, since the effect of the fruit was not natural, and since no specific tree was specified in the Genesis text, it provoked speculation on what kind of tree it might have been. After reviewing a number of options, Thomas Browne had wittily concluded that 'after this fruit, curiosity fruitlessely enquireth'.[133] Others were more hopeful. One of the possibilities which he rejected was the fig tree, and more specifically the Indian fig tree, a suggestion originally made by Moses Barcephas and revived by Goropius Becanus. Since it was the leaves of the fig tree with which Adam and Eve were to clothe themselves, and since the leaves of the Indian fig were reputed to be of sufficient size to cover their sexual organs, it was an obvious candidate for the Tree of the Knowledge of Good and Evil. Along with wheat and grapes, the rabbinic tradition had seen the fig as a possible candidate for the fruit of the Fall. It had no support among seventeenth-century commentators. Thomas Browne put it aptly: 'Surely, were it not requisite to have been concealed, it had not passed unspecified, nor the tree revealed which concealed their nakednesse, and that concealed which revealed it.'[134] There was no support for the medieval suggestion that the fruit of the Fall was the mandrake, even among those who, committed to the idea of a sexual Fall, might have been tempted by its reputed aphrodisiacal qualities.[135]

The most common identification remained the apple. That Adam was thought to have been tempted by an apple is no doubt due to the connection of the apple with love and lovesickness in the Song of Solomon (2.5, 7.8). It may also be related to the rendering of the Hebrew term *tappuach* (apple) in these verses as *malum* in the Vulgate and the association

---

[132] See John Pettus, *Volatiles from the History of Adam and Eve*, p. 122.
[133] Thomas Browne, *Pseudodoxia Epidemica*, 7.1. See also [William Basse], *A Helpe to Discovrse*, p. 34.
[134] Thomas Browne, *Pseudodoxia Epidemica*, 7.1. For other rejections of the fig, see Walter Raleigh, *The History of the World*, pp. 136–7; Benjamin Needler, *Expository Notes*, p. 76; John White, *A Commentary Upon the Three First Chapters of Genesis*, iii.101. Thomas Peyton mentions the speculations of the 'Cabalists and Rabbies' that it was the grape; the Saracens and Turks, that it was an ear of Indian wheat and the olive-like fruit of the Indian fig. See Peyton, *The glasse of time*, pp. 35–6. On the rabbinic tradition, see H. Freedman and M. Simon (eds.), *Midrash Rabbah*, i.114.
[135] See Richard Barber (trans.), *Bestiary*, p. 41; and Michael J. Curley (trans.), *Physiologus*, p. 31.

of this term with evil. Milton's fruit of the Tree of the Knowledge of Good and Evil was an apple (though only Satan called it so).[136] The frontispiece to John Parkinson's *Paradisi in sole* depicted the fruit as apple-like. Thomas Peyton blamed Adam for eating the apple 'painted like a gay:/ Fit for a woman, or some lickerish foole,/ a silly child, or one that goes to schoole'.[137] John Pettus suggested that 'if one Cut an Apple cross the Core, that is, beteen [*sic*] the stalk and the top, the Beds of the Seeds are just ten in number, representing the ten commandments; all which *Eve* did at once break by eating the Apple . . .'[138] *The Athenian Gazette* didn't doubt that it was an apple but did rather oddly suggest that the tree from which it came was the Tree of Life.[139]

There was virtual unanimity in the belief that the prohibition on eating the fruit of the Tree of the Knowledge of Good and Evil was to test the obedience of Adam and Eve. Luther and Calvin followed Augustine and Chrysostom on this.[140] Nicholas Gibbens maintained that its fruit was as wholesome as that of any other tree but that 'What made it euill to eate thereof [was] nothing els but disobedience vnto the commaundement.'[141] The tree was a 'kind of pledge or memorial of obedience,' declared Milton.[142] The divine prohibition, wrote Thomas Goodwin in 1642, 'was to *Adam, Praeceptum Symbolicum*, (as Divines call it) given . . . to be a *Tryall*, a *signe* or *symbole* of his obedience'.[143]

That the fruit itself had no ill effects did, of course, lead to the question why the tree was so called. By far the most common explanation focused, following Augustine, on the results of its being eaten. The knowledge gained was of good lost and evil got, as Milton put it.[144] John

---

[136] *Paradise Lost*, 9.585. [137] Thomas Peyton, *The glasse of time*, p. 7.

[138] John Pettus, *Volatiles from the History of Adam and Eve*, p. 104. James Ussher also suggested that in eating the apple Adam and Eve broke all of the ten commandments. See Ussher, *A Body of Divinitie*, p. 132. In modern neopaganism, the apple sliced similarly is seen as a pentagram within a circle. See Lynne Hume, *Witchcraft and Paganism in Australia* (Melbourne, 1997), p. 140.

[139] John Dunton (ed.), *The Athenian Gazette*, vol. 1, q. 6, no. 15.

[140] See Henry Cole (trans.), *The Creation: A Commentary by Martin Luther*, p. 133; John King (trans.), *Commentaries on the First Book of Moses*, p. 118. On Augustine and Chrysostom, see J. M. Evans, *'Paradise Lost' and the Genesis Tradition*, pp. 89, 96. See also [William Basse], *A Helpe to Discovrse*, p. 32, who cites Augustine.

[141] Nicholas Gibbens, *Qvestions and Dispvtations concerning the Holy Scriptvre*, p. 72.

[142] Don M. Wolfe (ed.), *The Complete Prose Works of John Milton*, vi.352.

[143] Thomas Goodwin, *The Heart of Christ in Heaven* (London, 1642), p. 51. See also Giovanno Loredano, *The Life of Adam*, p. 9; Arthur Jackson, *A Help for the understanding of the Holy Scripture*, i.10; George Hughes, *An Analytical Exposition of the Whole first Book of Moses, called Genesis*, p. 18; John White, *A Commentary Upon the Three First Chapters of Genesis*, ii.38; John Salkeld, *A Treatise of Paradise*, p. 149; Andrew Willet, *Hexapla in Genesin*, p. 33; and George Walker, *God made visible*, p. 246.

[144] On Augustine, see J. M. Evans, *'Paradise Lost' and the Genesis Tradition*, p. 96. See also John Milton, *Paradise Lost*, 9.1072.

Salkeld spoke for most: 'this tree was called the tree of the knowledge of good and evil, ab eventu, from the event, for that which presently followed in the eating thereof: which was that Adam then knew by woefull experience the difference betweene good and euill'.[145] More poetically, Edward Cooke:

> did not *Adam* know both *Good and Evill*,
> Before he was foretold it of the *Divell?*
> Yes, he new ill, by rule of opposition,
> And good, as we distinguish by possession:
> After his *fall*, he likewise understood,
> The *Guilt* of *Evill* by the *losse* of *Good.*[146]

There is no suggestion in the Genesis text that in the eating of the fruit any particular sin was being committed. But the narrative gap was filled in with an enormous variety of suggestions. The staging of sins under the three headings of 1 John 2.16 was common. Thomas Browne followed Pererius: 'Eve before the fall, was by the same path and beaten way of allurements inveigled, whereby her posterity hath been deluded ever since; that is those three delivered by St. John, the lust of the flesh, the lust of the eye, and the pride of life, wherein indeed they seemed as weakly to faile as their debilitated posterity ever after.'[147] Long lists of sins of which Eve and/or Adam was guilty were compiled. Pride (Ross, Calvin, Milton, du Bartas, Goodman, Burton, Parr), disobedience (Burton, Milton, Willet, Holland, Goodman, Leigh, Mede), and curiosity (Willet, Holland, Burton, du Bartas, Parr, Leigh) were most often cited. Gluttony (Willet, Goodman, du Bartas, Ross, Milton), infidelity (Parr, Milton, Leigh, Ross), lack of belief (Burton, Willet, Holland, Mede), and murder of themselves and future generations (Willet, Milton, Parr, Leigh) were common. Ambition (Calvin, Burton, Mede) and presumption and blasphemy (Milton, Willet, Holland, Leigh) had limited support. Lying (Babington), vanity and desire for knowledge (Raleigh), doubt (Parr), negligence (Milton), lust (Willet, Babington), theft (Milton, du Bartas), intemperance (Burton), robbery

---

[145] John Salkeld, *A Treatise of Paradise*, p. 83.
[146] Edward Cooke, *Bartas Junior. Or the Worlds Epitome; Man* (London, 1631), p. 8. See also Alexander Ross, *An Exposition on the Fourteene first Chapters of Genesis*, p. 42; Andrew Willet, *Hexapla in Genesin*, pp. 28–9; Walter Raleigh, *The History of the World*, p. 141; Thomas Wilson, *Theological Rules* (London, 1615), ii.30; William Alexander, *Doomes-day*, i.65; Nicholas Gibbens, *Questions and Disputations concerning the Holy Scripture*, p. 102; Antony Stafford, *Meditations* (London, 1612), p. 1.
[147] Thomas Browne, *Pseudodoxia Epidemica*, 1.1. See also Thomas Heywood, *The Hierarchie of the blessed Angells*, vi.344; and Henry Stebbing (ed.), *The Entire Works of John Bunyan* (London, 1860), iii.383.

(Milton), idolatry (Parr, Leigh), discontent (Leigh), sacrilege (Milton), apostasy (Leigh), arrogance (Milton), contempt of God (Parr, Leigh), treason (du Bartas), and envy (Mede, du Bartas) received occasional mention.[148]

There is no doubt that there was a consensus that Adam and Eve were each culpable. But, granting that they both sinned, the question of whose sin was greater was much debated. And on this there was no consensus. Eve, along with most other women, was roundly condemned by John Donne:

> Man all at once was there by woman slaine,
> And one by one we're here slaine o'er againe
> By them. The mother poison'd the well-head,
> The daughters here corrupt us . . .
> Shee sinn'd, we beare; part of our paine is, thus
> To love them, whose fault to this painfull love yoak'd us.[149]

To the divine Christopher Newstead, woman 'was the siren that allured man vnto euill'.[150] Edward Gosynhill was his usual misogynistic self in apportioning more blame to her than to Adam.[151] But such outright condemnations were rare. More commonly, even where Eve was held to be ultimately responsible, her guilt was lessened by her weakness, and Adam's consequently increased. Thus, for example, Thomas Browne: 'although the condition of sex and posteriority of creation might somewhat extenuate the error of the woman: Yet it was very strange and inexcusable in the man, especially if as some affirme, he was the wisest of all men since, or if as others have conceived, he was not ignorant of the fall of the Angels, and had thereby example and punishment to deterre him'.[152] Eve was tempted, suggested John Pettus, not only by the serpent's subtlety but by his beauty. Thus, he maintained, Eve could be excused more than Adam, 'for here was a Lovely Serpent, a delicate Fruit pleasing to the Eye, delightful to the taste, and of a promising

---

[148] See John King (trans.), *Commentaries on the First Book of Moses*, p. 152; Don M. Wolfe (ed.), *The Complete Prose Works of John Milton*, vi.383; Susan Snyder (ed.), *The Divine Weeks and Works*, i.353; Andrew Willet, *Hexapla in Genesin*, p. 58; Henry Holland, *The Historie of Adam*, p. 10; Geoffrey Goodman, *The Fall of Man*, p. 434; Thomas C. Faulkner et al. (eds.), Robert Burton, *The Anatomy of Melancholy*, i.122–3; Elnathan Parr, *The Grounds of Divinitie*, p. 157; Edward Leigh, *A Systeme or Bodie of Divinitie*, p. 382; William Perkins, *The Workes*, p. 152; Alexander Ross, *An Exposition on the Fovrteene first Chapters of Genesis*, p. 61; Gervase Babington, *Certaine Plaine, briefe, and comfortable Notes vpon euerie Chapter of Genesis*, sig. c.6.v, c.7.r; Walter Raleigh, *The Historie of the World*, p. 142.
[149] John Donne, *The Complete English Poems* (London, 1991), p. 409.
[150] Christopher Newstead, *An Apology for Women* (London, 1620), p. 3.
[151] See Katherine U. Henderson and Barbara F. McManus (eds.), *Half Humankind*, p. 153.
[152] Thomas Browne, *Pseudodoxia Epidemica*, I.I.

virtue; what Woman could well resist those Temptations?'[153] John Wing was almost glad it was Eve, on the ground that had it been Adam who initiated the Fall, men would never have heard the end of it.[154]

In *A Gust for Paradise*, Diane McColley points out that English Bible illustrations put the blame squarely on Adam, or else they represent an entirely mutual Fall.[155] And the same can be said for the majority of seventeenth-century literary readings of the Fall. In particular, this was theologically driven. Since the infection of the whole human race was the result of the sin of Adam, his role could not be minimised. John Salkeld explained, 'it seemeth more probable, that the whole cause of originall sinne in vs ought to bee reduced vnto *Adam*, so that by *Adams* consent onely, and not by *Eues* we were to be borne in original inius-tice.'[156]

More generally however, this focus on the Adamic inheritance may itself be read as part of the dominance of androcentric readings of the text. Such readings were offered not only by male but also by female writers. Thus, for example, for Emilia Lanier there was no comparable mitigation for Adam's or Eve's weakness:

> But surely Adam cannot be excused,
> Her fault though great, yet he was most to blame;
> What weakness offered, strength might have refused,
> Being lord of all, the greater was his shame.[157]

He was stronger, claimed Rachel Speght, and ought to have resisted more.[158] Similarly, to Andrew Willet, since Adam was woman's head, he sinned more.[159] The puritan John Yates believed that Adam stood by all the time of the temptation of Eve, and therefore his failure to rebuke the serpent increased his culpability.[160]

Granting the centrality of the doctrine of original sin to Augustinian Christianity, and the important role it is believed to have played in the Protestant tradition, it is remarkable how little discussion it received

---

[153] John Pettus, *Volatiles from the History of Adam and Eve*, p. 129.
[154] See John Wing, *The Crowne Coniugall*, pp. 54–5.
[155] See Diane K. McColley, *A Gust for Paradise*, pp. 56–7.
[156] John Salkeld, *A Treatise of Paradise*, p. 304.
[157] Quoted by Antonia Fraser, *The Weaker Vessel*, p. 2.
[158] See Rachel Speght, *A Mouzell for Melastomus*, p. 5.
[159] See Andrew Willet, *Hexapla in Genesis*, p. 48.
[160] See John Yates, *A Modell of Divinitie*, p. 175. See also Nicholas Gibbens, *Questions and Disputations concerning the Holy Scripture*, p. 123; George Hughes, *An Analytical Exposition of the Whoe first Book of Moses, called Genesis*, p. 31; Benjamin Needler, *Expository Notes*, pp. 71–2; and Alexander Ross, *An Exposition on the Fovrteene first Chapters of Genesis*, p. 63.

among seventeenth-century commentators. Still, it represented a deeply felt conviction that humans were inherently and hereditarily sinful. 'The man without a navell yet lives in me', complained Thomas Browne.[161] Theological and medical discourse intertwined. As disease was often the consequence of sin, so original sin was an infectious and sexually transmitted disease. Adam's actual sin, explained Samuel Purchas, 'is originally ours, the guilt made ours by imputation, the corruption conueyed with nature it selfe in the Conduits of generation: that first person voluntarily infecting Nature, and this infected nature naturally infecting our persons'.[162] To Godfrey Goodman, as the Black Death most affected those related to each other, so original sin affected the human family. 'Doth not one man sicke of the plague infect the whole Citie', he asked, 'and is not the same infection alwaies aptest to taint the same blood: why should it seeme strange, that the first man corrupted with sinne, should taint his whole seed?'[163] Sin, death, and disease were all of a piece to Archbisop Ussher: 'as by the act of generation in leprous parents, the parents Leprosie made the childrens, and the slavish and villanous estate of the parents is communicated unto all the offspring', so also sin is transmitted.[164] The natural man is dead in sin, he continued, like 'a loathsome carrion, or as a dead corps, and lieth rotting and stinking in the grave having in him the seed of all sins . . .'[165]

Still, the doctrine of the inherited depravity of human nature was occasionally mitigated by the doctrine of the 'fortunate fall'. It was a notion that went back to Irenaeus, according to whom, had Adam not sinned, man himself would have not had the chance morally to perfect himself.[166] When the Fall was seen as fortunate in the seventeenth-century England, it was because without it there would have been no redemption in Christ. A redeemed world was seen as preferable to an innocent one. By virtue of the first Fall, explained John Salkeld, 'we obtained that fruit of life to be prepared for vs vpon the tree of the crosse, yea and thence communicated vnto vs in the sacred communion, and bread of life, which doubtless wee should not have obtained, at least after that manner and measure, if wee had not transgressed . . . O happy fall, and happy vnhappinesse, which was occasion of so great happinesse.'[167] Milton believed that had Adam and Eve not fallen their

---

[161] Thomas Browne, *Religio Medici*, 2.10.   [162] Samuel Purchas, *Microcosmus*, p. 151.
[163] Godfrey Goodman, *The Fall of Man*, p. 443.   [164] James Ussher, *A Body of Divinitie*, pp. 142–3.
[165] *Ibid.*, p. 143.   [166] See N. P. Williams, *The Ideas of the Fall and Original Sin* (London, 1927), p. 195.
[167] John Salkeld, *A Treatise of Paradise*, p. 51.

lives in Paradise would have continued happily. But he did nonetheless look forward to the day when Christ would re-establish Paradise on earth, 'far happier place/ Then this of Eden, and far happier days'.[168] In *The Saints Everlasting Rest*, the puritan Richard Baxter wrote,

If Man had kept his first Rest in Paradise, God had not had opportunity to manifest that far greater Love to the World in the giving of his Son. If Man had not fallen into the depth of misery, Christ had not come down from the height of Glory, nor died, nor risen, nor been believed on in the World.[169]

Fortunate or otherwise, the most immediate and apparent result of the Fall was the first couple's awareness of nakedness and the subsequent covering of themselves with fig leaves. The Genesis text gives no hint of which parts of their bodies they covered nor of why they should have become aware of their nakedness. But commentators had a firm conviction that they covered their sexual organs, and that they did so as a result of shame at their nakedness.

To be sure, Samuel Purchas believed that they were awakened above all to their symbolic nakedness – of divine and angelic protection, of the creatures' subservience, of happiness and hope.[170] But for most androcentric readers, the genitals needed to be covered, since (in men) they presented the most obvious and visible site of lust. Moreover, it was through the male organs of generation that the original sin was transmitted. Thus, according to Alexander Ross, the sexual organs were covered because 'inordinate lust began most to appear here: secondly, these are the instruments of generation, which then became sinfull; therefore all people are ashamed to see those parts, because sinne comes by generation'.[171] The generative organs were the most shameful, declared Henry Ainsworth, 'because syn is become naturall, and derived by generation'.[172]

The intimate link between sexuality and the Fall was seldom far beneath the surface. Quoting Bernard of Clairvaux, John Donne called the genitals 'the sewer of all sin; not only because all sin is devolved upon us, by generation and so implied, and involved in original sin; but

[168] *Paradise Lost*, 12.464–5.
[169] Richard Baxter, *The Practical Works . . . of Richard Baxter* (London, 1707), p. 109. Quoted by George H. Williams, *Wilderness and Paradise*, p. 74. See also Godfrey Goodman, *The Fall of Man*, p. 435; and James Ussher, *A Body of Divinitie*, p. 128.
[170] See Samuel Purchas, *Microcosmus*, p. 152. See also William Nicholls, *A Conference with a Theist*, p. 240.
[171] Alexander Ross, *An Exposition on the Fovrteene first Chapters of Genesis*, p. 64.
[172] Henry Ainsworth, *Annotations Upon the first book of Moses called Genesis*, sig. c.4.v.

because almost all other sins have relation to this'.[173] For him, male circumcision was the visible manifestation of sexuality as the root of all sin. To Andrew Willet, Adam and Eve became aware of their loss of control over their sexuality. They felt 'the rebellion and disobedience of their members in their disordered and vnruly motions, which maketh for them to couer them; which use of vailing and couering the secret parts, euen nature hath taught the barbarous nations . . .'[174] Clothing 'was ordained as a covering for lust', Lancelot Andrewes decided.[175] The imagery of the Fall as a rite of puberty was occasionally hinted at. 'When they come to the knowledge of good and evill', wrote Giovanno Loredano, 'they blush at nakednesse. That which befalls children in regard of age, happened to them in regard of original righteousnesse.'[176]

After God had cursed Adam and Eve, God made garments of skins for them. For many, as we have seen, this was read as the end of the regimen of vegetarianism for both humans and animals. God empowered humans to kill beasts, Lancelot Andrewes informed his readers.[177] Clothing served too as a reminder of their guilt and shame. Wearing coats of skins, explained Gervase Babington, was the contemporary equivalent of wearing a halter every day in remembrance of one's fault.[178] Adam's shame was never so great, declared John-Francis Senault, 'as when he was forced to cloth himself, the skins he wore were the apparrell of a penitent; before that vanity had found out means to imbellish them, they drew tears from his eyes, and sighs from his mouth'.[179] They also symbolised the beastliness to which Adam and Eve had descended. God demonstrated their monstrous form 'by the Beastiall clothing which he put on them', wrote Jacob Boehme.[180] And, following Augustine and Luther, the coats of skins were imagined as reminders of the immortality forfeited and the mortality gained.[181] The

---

[173] John Donne, *Works*, 5.331. Quoted by Arnold Williams, *The Common Expositor*, p. 126.
[174] Andrew Willet, *Hexapla in Genesin*, p. 50. See also Susan Snyder (ed.), *The Divine Weeks and Works*, i.348; John White, *A Commentary Upon the Three First Chapters of Genesis*, iii.101; William Perkins, *The Workes*, ii.137.
[175] Lancelot Andrewes, *Apospasmatia Sacra*, p. 331.
[176] Giovanno Loredano, *The Life of Adam*, p. 36.
[177] Lancelot Andrewes, *Apospasmatia Sacra*, p. 331. See also Andrew Willet, *Hexapla in Genesin*, p. 54.
[178] See Gervase Babington, *Certaine Plaine, briefe, and comfortable Notes vpon euerie Chapter of Genesis*, sig. D.5.r.
[179] John-Francis Senault, *Man become Guilty*, p. 293.
[180] Jacob Boehme, *The Second Booke. Concerning the Three Principles* (London, 1648), p. 257. See also Arthur Jackson, *A Help for the understanding of the Holy Scripture*, p. 13; Thomas Hayne, *The General View of the Holy Scriptures*, p. 19; and Richard Kidder, *A Commentary*, i.17.
[181] See Ronald J. Teske (trans.), *Saint Augustine on Genesis*, p. 127; and Henry Cole (trans.), *The Creation: A Commentary by Martin Luther*, p. 295.

clothes of skins, declared Giovanno Loredano, 'are emblematicall tokens of their mortality, which being of slaughtered beasts should daily remind them of death . . .'[182]

The clothing of Adam and Eve in animal skins provided for many puritanical homilies on frugality in dress and ornament and against the elaborate dress codes of the wealthy. The puritan pamphleteer Phillip Stubbes railed against men's pampering of themselves: 'we haue brought ourselues into suche pusillanimitie, and effeminacie of condition, as we maie seeme rather nice dames, and wanton girles, then puissant agentes, or manly men, as our forefathers haue been'.[183] The poet William Vaughan reminded his readers that the clothes of Adam and Eve were only to protect them from the cold and to cover their shame. When men and women first wore clothes, he exclaimed,

They had no beuer hats sharpe on the top, like vnto the spine of a steeple, nor flatte crownde hats, resembling rose-cakes. They wore no embrodered shirts, nor garments of cloth of Gold. They knew not what meant our Italianated, Frenchified, nor Duch and Babilonian breeches. They bought no silken stockins, nor gaudies pantoffles. Their women could not tel how to frizle and lay out their haire on borders. They daubed not their faces with deceitfull drugs, wherewith, hiding the handi-work of God, they might seem to haue more beautie, then hee hath vouchsafed to giue them.[184]

Whereas clothing was intended to cover shame, wrote Godfrey Goodman, it now served to proclaim pride. And for him men were worse than women: 'you shall finde *viros molles & effoeminatos*, as likewise woemenviragines like Amazons; men in their pouders, perfumes, false haires and paintings, exceeding the wantonnesse of woeman'.[185] There were no good reasons to be proud of one's clothes, declared Edward Bury in 1677, since they were usually only the excrement of beasts or insects.[186]

[182] Giovanno Loredano, *The Life of Adam*, p. 52. See also Gervase Babington, *Certaine Plaine, briefe, and comfortable Notes vpon euerie Chapter of Genesis*, sig. D.5.r; Arthur Jackson, *A Help for the Understanding of the Holy Scripture*, p. 13; Richard Kidder, *A Commentary*, i.17.
[183] Phillip Stubbes, *The Anatomie of Abuses*, sig. E.2.v.
[184] William Vaughan, *The Golden-groue, moralized in Three Bookes* (London, 1600), sig. B.2.v. See C. Willett and Phillis Cunnington, *Handbook on English Costume in the Seventeenth Century* (London, 1966).
[185] Godfrey Goodman, *The Fall of Man*, p. 237.
[186] See Edward Bury, *The Husbandman's Companion*, pp. 273–4. On Genesis 3.21 and frugality in dress, see also John King (trans.), *Commentaries on the First Book of Moses*, p. 182; Andrew Willet, *Hexapla in Genesin*, p. 55; William Whately, *The Primarie Precedent*, p. 8; Giovanno Loredano, *The Life of Adam*, p. 52; John White, *A Commentary Upon the Three First Chapters of Genesis*, iii.107; Lancelot Andrewes, *Apospasmatia Sacra*, p. 331; Henry Cole (trans.), *The Creation: A Commentary by Martin Luther*, p. 295; Benjamin Needler, *Expository Notes*, p. 117; Arthur Jackson, *A Help for the understanding of the Holy Scripture*, p. 13; Richard Kidder, *A Commentary*, i.17.

That both women and men were originally minimally clothed also provided ammunition for the more misogynistically inclined. And women were generally held to be more prone to the sin of vanity. Peter Charron, for example, saw excesses in apparel as a vice more familiar to women: 'a true testimonie of their weaknesse, being glad to winne credit and commendations by these small and slender accidents, because they know themselues to be too weak and vnable to purchase credit and reputation by better meanes . . .'[187] The most beautiful women were the most proper for the designs of Satan, John-Francis Senault informed his readers. There are women, he went on, 'who would rather have their souls sullied, then their cloths; who would rather have the state be out of order, then their head attire; and who would be lesse troubled to see their honour steined, then their gown. To disabuse these weak women, they must be made to know, that luxury in apparell deserves to be despised by men, and to be punished by God.'[188] The pamphleteer John Hall argued for female nudity on the grounds that women would then be sexually less provocative.[189] John Bunyan agreed. Women would be better naked than overdressed. The reason for decking themselves out 'with their bull's foretops, with their naked shoulders, and paps hanging out like a cow's bag' was 'to please their lusts, to satisfy their wild and extravagant fantasies . . . to stir up lust in others . . .'[190] William Herbert encouraged his female readers, to pray at the birth of a daughter, 'let her in her attire love what's decent, seek what's needful, and reject that which is superfluous, never being so childish or senseles as to glorie in apparel.'[191]

The Genesis text itself would appear to be congenial not only to an argument for simplicity in dress (which it was) but also for a similarity in male and female attire (which it wasn't). Aprons of fig leaves and coats of skins did not, after all, suggest difference. Thus, the conviction that there was an essential difference between male and female attire was therefore something that was read against the text. This appeared clearly in the so-called transvestite controversy which began in the 1570s when women began to wear male attire, and peaked in the five years after 1615.[192] Thus, for example, the author of *Haec Vir* in 1620 argued that since men had gone soft and begun to disport themselves like women,

[187] Peter Charron, *Of Wisdome*, p. 542.   [188] John-Francis Senault, *Man become Guilty*, p. 290.
[189] See John Hall, *Paradoxes* (London, 1650), pp. 64–7.
[190] George Offer (ed.), *The Whole Works of John Bunyan*, iii.645. 'Bull's foretops' were part of a fashionable cap. See also Henry Stebbing (ed.), *The Entire Works of John Bunyan*, iii.381.
[191] William Herbert, *Herbert's child-bearing woman* (London, 1648), p. 47.
[192] See Linda Woodbridge, *Women and the English Renaissance*.

women needed to take up men's garments to preserve 'those manly things which you haue forsaken . . .'[193] It was only through custom and not nature, it was suggested, that women and men dressed differently, and '*Custome* is an *Idiot* . . .'[194] This argument was a direct response to the author of *Hic Mulier* in the same year. There it was argued that sexual variation in clothing was an outcome of the divine plan. Genesis 3.21 was appropriately so (mis)read: 'Remember how your Maker made for our first Parent coates, not one coat, but a coat for the man, and a coat for the woman; coates of seuerall fashions, seuerall formes, and for seuerall vses: the mans coat fit for his labour, the womans fit for her modestie.'[195] Thus, the Genesis text had not only clothed the world but was read as having done so in a gender-specific way.

CURSED AND EXPELLED

Therefore the Lord God sent him forth from the garden of Eden.

Genesis 3.23

The need to cover their nakedness was only one of many consequences of the Fall of Adam and Eve. Sexuality was out of control. The image of God was defaced if not effaced. Adam's knowledge and wisdom was much reduced. Government was to be introduced, with the involuntary subjection of the ruled to the ruler. The length of life was shortened. Immortality had been lost and death introduced. In the words of Andrew Willet, following Jerome, 'Adam began in that day to die, not actually, but because then he became mortall and subiect to death . . . and beside that, then actually Adam entred into miserie and sorrow, labour, hunger, thirst, which are the forerunners of death'.[196] Nicholas Gibbens believed that death began the day of the Fall. Life itself, he declared, with all its miseries, seemed 'to be not life but a prolonged death'.[197] Diseases arose to vex the body.[198]

Work in Paradise was intended to be a pleasure for Adam. It was no longer so for him or his descendants. To the Genevan John Diodati, 'the pleasant and easie manuring, which was before sin, is changed into a

[193] Anon., *Haec-Vir: or, The Womanish-Man*, sig. C.2.v.   [194] *Ibid.*
[195] Anon., *Hic Mulier: or, The Man-Woman* (n.p., 1620), sig. B.2.v – B.3.r.
[196] Andrew Willet, *Hexapla in Genesin*, p. 35.
[197] Nicholas Gibbens, *Qvestions and Dispvtations concerning the Holy Scriptvre*, p. 80. See also Susan Snyder (ed.), *The Divine Weeks and Works*, i.336–7; Robert Bostocke, *Auncient Phisicke*, Author's Obtestation; John Locke, *The Reasonableness of Christianity, As delivered in the Scriptures*, pp. 3–4.
[198] See Godfrey Goodman, *The Fall of Man*, p. 23.

toilsome labour, as well through the growing weak of mans body, as through the malignancy of the earth, and the disorder of nature'.[199] Adam toiled in view of the Paradise from which he had been expelled, suggested John White. The expulsion, he wrote, brought about a 'great change in his employment from keeping and dressing (which was rather a recreation then any painful labour) to Tilling, a tiresome toile, especially to him who wanted tooles, beasts, servants and all helps for that work'.[200] Labour now is 'a paine deserued by sinne', declared Gervase Babington.[201]

Eve's subjection to Adam was much increased after the Fall. And if it was voluntary before the Fall, no choice was possible after. But it was woman's procreative activity that was the focus of God's punishment. Three features of the Genesis text were much elaborated: an increase in conceptions; the multiplication of suffering during pregnancy; and the sorrows of childbirth. Alexander Ross summed up:

The conceptions of the woman are a punishment, because sometimes their conceptions are imperfect and deformed: secondly, many children being conceiued, doe perish before they come to maturitie: Thirdly, many children are wicked and rebellious . . . fourthly . . . many infirmities doe accompany a woman that is with childe, as swimmings in the head, tooth-aches, perturbations in the minde, vitiosities in the stomacke; as to refuse good and wholesome meates, to desire to eate those things which Nature . . . abhorreth.[202]

William Herbert's *Child-Bearing Woman* provided not only prayers and songs but also meditations on various aspects of pregnancy. On pregnant longings, the following meditation was offered to his readers: 'We are in longing *Eves* daughters, yea worse then she; for she longed for that, which was both good for food & pleasant to the eyes, yea desirable to make one wise: wheras sometimes we long for that, which should neither delight the eye, nor relish in the mouth, nor digest well in the stomach.'[203] Godfrey Goodman saw all female diseases as attributable directly to the sin of Eve, among which he included hysteria and what we would recognise as breast cancer and syphilis.[204]

[199] John Diodati, *Pious Annotations*, sig. D.2.r–v.
[200] John White, *A Commentary Upon the Three First Chapters of Genesis*, iii.238–9.
[201] Gervase Babington, *Certaine Plaine, briefe, and comfortable Notes vpon euerie Chapter of Genesis*, sig. C.2.r.
[202] Alexander Ross, *An Exposition on the Fovrteene first Chapters of Genesis*, p. 68. See also Matthew Poole, *Annotations upon the Holy Bible*, sig. B.4.r.
[203] William Herbert, *Herbert's child-bearing woman*, p. 25. See also Nicholas Gibbens, *Qvestions and Dispvtations concerning the Holy Scriptvre*, pp. 153–5; and Godfrey Goodman, *the Fall of Man*, p. 325.
[204] See Godfrey Goodman, *The Fall of Man*, pp 321–2.

But it was upon the pains of childbirth that Goodman and many others particularly focused. The pains of childbirth, it was believed, were unique to the female of the human species. In contrast to women, Goodman held, animals 'crie for no helpe of midwiues, they want no keepers or nurses; they are deliuered without paine, or sorrow, they haue forthwith strength to make their owne prouision, for themselues, for their brood'.[205] As they approached labour, Herbert's mothers-to-be were encouraged to reflect that 'The time is come, in which I must pay the old debt, *Eve* contracted for me. I feele the forerunners of sorrow and anguish. Alas! what shall I doe, to escape the danger, into which I am brought, by my first mothers sin?'[206] The puritan Samuel Hieron provided a similar prayer for the reflective woman in labour: 'O Lord, I now find by experience the truth and certaintie of thy word, and the smart of ye punishment which thou laidst upon me beeing in the loynes of my Grandmother *Eue* for my disobedience towardes thee.'[207]

As a result of the Fall, not only were humans corrupted, but all of nature had gone awry. Theologically, this expressed the enormity of the sin, as well as providing a moral explanation of the difficulties inherent in human life. Philosophically, the world could not but be affected by the sin of Adam. As in the microcosm – man – so in the macrocosm – the world. Thus, the animals turned not only against man, but against each other. The extremes of four seasons replaced the temperate climes of Paradise. The briars, thorns, and so on which were harmless before the Fall now became harmful. 'It is rightlie supposed', declared Nicholas Gibbens, 'there were thorns before, and thistles, and venemous herbes, and Serpents; but they were not noisome, nor had the power to hurt . . . But when the curse was powred forth for sinne, thornes and thistles and such like fruits of barrennes increased euerie where . . .'[208]

---

[205] *Ibid.*, p. 313. See also Benjamin Needler, *Expository Notes*, pp. 105–6.
[206] William Herbert, *Herbert's child-bearing woman*, p. 26. See also p. 14.
[207] Samuel Hieron, *All the Sermons of Samuel Hieron* (London, 1614), p. 283. See also Alice Sutcliffe, *Meditations of Mans Mortalitie* (London, 1634), pp. 145–6.
[208] Nicholas Gibbens, *Qvestions and Dispvtations concerning the Holy Scripture*, pp. 162–3. In keeping with the Genesis text stating that God finished his creative activity on day six, the belief that thorns, thistles, and so on existed but were harmless until the Fall was the dominant one by far. See also Alexander Ross, *An Exposition on the Fovrteene first Chapters of Genesis*, pp. 6–7, 33; Lambertus Daneau, *The Wonderful Workmanship of God* (London, 1578), sig. y.3.r; George Hakewill, *An apologie*, p. 153; Thomas Adams, *The Workes*, p. 1055; Arthur Jackson, *A Help for the understanding of the Holy Scripture*, i.5; George Hughes, *An Analytical Exposition of the Whole first Book of Moses, called Genesis*, p. 40; George Walker, *The history of the Creation* (London, 1631), p. 234; Susan Snyder (ed.), *The Divine Weeks and Works*, i.292–3; and Andrew Willet, *Hexapla in Genesin*, p. 13. They are clearly apparent in the frontispiece to John Parkinson's *Paradisi in sole*. For counterclaims, see Godfrey Goodman, *The Fall of Man*, p. 224; and probably Alice Sutcliffe, *Meditations of Mans Mortalitie*, pp. 143–4.

For the destruction of nature, man was responsible. 'Let the groanes of beasts slain for us', wrote George Walker,

> and their bloud shed and poured out with strugling, and with cryes and sighes: Let the sourenesse of wilde grapes, the loathsome smell and bitternesse of some herbes, and fruits, and the poison of some plants, all and every one smite us with the sight of our naturall corruption, and make us loath our sinnes, and sigh and groane under the burden of them.[209]

Nature was corrupted, for 'euerything containeth in itselfe the inbred seedes of corruption', wrote Godfrey Goodman.[210] God cursed the ground, declared Joseph Fletcher, 'with *sterility,/* or else with hurtfull weeds *fertility*'.[211] The earth was cursed because of man, and the earth cursed him for it. As John-Francis Senault put it,

> The earth which had served us for a nurse, became barren to make us perish by famine; she grew hard under our feet to weary us: forgoing her flowers wherewith she adorned herselfe to appear more pleasing to us, she loaded herself with thornes to prick us; she opened her bowels to bury us; and she who was grounded upon her own proper weight, was always immoveable, quaked under our feet to work our astonishment. The Sea which judged aright, that our ambition & avarice would not be contented with the Empire of the earth, hid rocks underneath her waves, troubled her calmnesse with storms, called in winds to her aid to undo us, and advancing her waters into the fields, came to set upon us . . .[212]

That the earth had been affected, and seriously so, as a result of the Fall was a commonplace. But that since the time of the Fall the earth had been in a progressive state of decay was more debatable. There were hints to this effect in the exilic and post-exilic Old Testament literature. And it was strongly supported in apocryphal and intertestamental works. Although not part of the received Christian doctrine, it occurred periodically throughout the patristic and medieval periods, especially where expectations of the Apocalypse and the idea of the universe winding down to an end came into play.[213]

---

[209] George Walker, *God made visible*, p. 235.   [210] Godfrey Goodman, *The Fall of Man*, p. 24.

[211] Joseph Fletcher, *The Historie of the Perfect-Cursed-Blessed Man*, p. 27.

[212] John-Francis Senault, *Man become Guilty*, p. 5; and see pp. 11, 291. See also John King (trans.), *Commentaries on the First Book of Moses*, pp. 173, 177; Godfrey Goodman, *The Fall of Man*. pp. 17, 104, 219; Richard Barckley, *A Discourse of the Felicitie of Man* (London, 1598), pp. 5–6; David Person, *Varieties: or, A Surveigh of Rare and Excellent Matters* (London, 1635), p. 87; Thomas C. Faulkner et al. (eds.), Robert Burton, *The Anatomy of Melancholy*, i.125–6; John-Francis Senault, *Man become Guilty*, p. 334; C. A. Patrides, 'The Experience of Otherness', p. 176; Walter Raleigh, *The History of the World*, p. 33; Nicholas Gibbens, *Questions and Disputations concerning the Holy Scripture*, p. 158; and Lancelot Andrewes, *Apospasmatia Sacra*, p. 318.

[213] See David Brooks, 'The Idea of the Decay of the World in the Old Testament, the Apocrypha, and the Pseudepigrapha', in J. D. North and J. J. Roche (eds.), *The Light of Nature* (Dordrecht, 1985), pp. 383–404.

In England, it played a significant role from the 1570s until the 1630s, a period of increased social, political, and religious uncertainty. As Victor Harris writes in *All Coherence Gone*, 'in the 1570's and 1580's there grew up a more explicit concern over the progressive or cumulative corruption, over the decay that did not stop with the original supernatural curse'.[214] In 1614, for example, Barnabe Rich, in the ironically entitled *Honestie of this Age*, believed he lived in a world in which all impiety had now become honourable, not least because of the existence of at least seven thousand tobacco shops: 'I cannot see but that those that doe take it fastest, are as much (or more) subiect to all these infirmities, (yea and to the poxe itself) as those that haue nothing at all to do with it . . .'[215] And moral degeneration was matched by cosmic decay. The world might have run smoothly, he complained, 'but I say now, it goes on *Crouches*, for it is waxen old, blind, decrepit and lame, a lymping world God knowes . . .'[216] In 1628, Samuel Rowlands saw the heavens as in decline, and thus too the inferior bodies: 'the materiall heauens by continuance of yeares decrease in beauty and vertue. The neerer the Sunne drawes to the end of his daily course, the lesse is his strength; in the euening we feele the Sunne to decay in his heat, and he waxeth alway the weaker. Now if those superiour bodies, then much more things inferiour and sublunary, are included within the compasse of vanity.'[217] Three years earlier, John Donne had vividly expressed this sense of the organic decay of a world 'all in pieces, all cohaerence gone'.[218] In a sermon preached at Saint Paul's on Whitsunday, 1625, he proclaimed,

As the world is the whole frame of the world, God hath put into it a reproofe, a rebuke, lest it should seeme eternall, which is, a sensible decay and age in the whole frame of the world, and every piece thereof. The seasons of the yeare irregular and distempered; the Sun fainter, and languishing; men lesse in stature, and shorter-lived. No addition, but only every yeare, new sorts, new species of wormes, and flies, and sicknesses, which argue more and more putrefaction of which they are engendred.[219]

[214] Victor Harris, *All Coherence Gone*, pp. 3–4. For an excellent history of the debate, see ch.4.
[215] Barnabe Rich, *The Honestie of this Age* (London, 1614), p. 25.
[216] *Ibid.*, p. 18. For reasons that are not obviously clear, Rich saw tailors as the most wicked of men, 'that like *Moles* doe lye and wrot in sinne . . .' (p. 23).
[217] Samuel Rowlands, *Heavens Glory seeke it* (London, 1628), pp. 97–8.
[218] John Donne, *The First Anniversary*, l.213. Quoted in C. A. Patrides (ed.), John Donne, *The Complete English Poems* (London, 1994), p. 255.
[219] John Hayward (ed.), *Complete Poetry and Selected Prose* (London, 1930), p. 619. Quoted by George Williamson, 'Mutability, Decay, and Seventeenth-Century Melancholy', *ELH: A Journal of English Literary History* 2 (1935), p. 141.

The image of the microcosm and the macrocosm also played a role. For the world mirrored the decay present in the life of every individual. In a sermon entitled 'The sinners Passing Bell', Thomas Adams declared that 'the world waxeth old, and old age is weake and sickly . . . As the *little world* thus decaies in the great, so the *great* decaise in itselfe.'[220] Godfrey Goodman's *The Fall of Man*, first published in 1616, was the most elaborate work in the seventeenth century to be devoted to the decline of man and the progressive decay of the universe. To Goodman, the link between individual and cosmic decline was made by appeal to the image of the great and little worlds. For the most part of this work, Goodman detailed the corruption of man. Only in the last quarter of the third and final part was the link to the great world made:

me thinks I haue subdued the little world, and brought man as a captiue or slaue, through much misery and sorrow, at length to the place of his execution; and hauing now possest myself of the fairest fortresse, or tower in nature (man that is a little world), I cannot here content my selfe, but I begin to enquire, whether there are as yet more worlds to be conquered? and behold in the second place, I will fall vpon the great world, and I will attempt with Archimedes, to shake her foundations, to threaten her ruine, in this generall corruption and dissolution of man: for this punishment (*morte morieris*) though it principally concerns man, yet the whole world cannot be exempted from it, being directed and ordained only for mans vse, containing in it selfe the very same seedes, and causes of death and destruction; and as it is most fit and agreeable to our present condition, that being corruptible in our selues, we should like wise dwell in houses of corruption.[221]

It was a melancholy time. To Thomas Milles, for example, 'in these our instant daies, the delicate and sweet floures of contentment doe fall from our heartes, as leaues doe from the Trees in Autumne, and, in stead of clear and free thoughts; obscure, troubled, melancholy, and sad conceits get entrance, accompanied with a thousand calamities'.[222] According to George Williamson, seventeenth-century melancholy plunged to new depths in the idea of the decay of the world.[223] Thus Walter Raleigh in a sentence described by Williamson as 'full of the sombre elegance and reason which the decay theme provoked in a Jacobean mind':

And as all things under the sun have one time of strength and another of weakness, a youth and beauty, and then age and deformity; so time itself (under

---

[220] Thomas Adams, *The Workes*, p. 246.   [221] Godfrey Goodman, *The Fall of Man*, pp. 348–9.
[222] Thomas Milles, *The treasurie of auncient and moderne times*, i.366.
[223] See George Williamson, 'Mutability, Decay, and Seventeenth-Century Melancholy', p. 138.

the dreadful shade of whose wings all things decay and wither) hath wasted and worn out that lively virtue in man, and beasts, and plants, yea the heavens themselves, being of a most pure and cleansed matter, shall *wax old as a garment*; and then much more the power generative in inferior creatures, who by the ordinance of God receive operative virtue from the superior.[224]

If for many the belief in the decay of the universe provoked melancholy, for George Hakewill it was melancholy which produced the belief. Only in our imagination, and that of every generation, do things really appear to be worse. Much was the consequence of old men's envy:

men for the most part, being most affected with the present, more sensible of punishment then of blessings, and growing in worldly cares, and consequently in discontent, as they growe in yeares & experience; they are thereby more apt to apprehend crosses then comforts, to repine and murmure for the one, then to returne thanks for the other. Whence it comes to passe that unseasonable weather, and the like crosse accidents are printed in our memories, as it were with red letters in an Almanacke; but for seasonable and faire, there stands nothing but a blanke: the one is graven in brasse, the other written in water.[225]

George Hakewill's *Apologie*, first published in 1627, was the most substantial critique of Goodman and of the idea of decay in general. And he attacked it at its most vital and its weakest point – the microcosm–macrocosm relationship: 'the sinne of man could not alter the worke of God, or marre that sweet harmony which hee had set in it'.[226] This work signalled the death knell of the idea of the progressive decay of nature. By the middle of the seventeenth century, it had all but disappeared. Whereas Samuel Purchas had spoken in 1619 of 'the olde and decrepit age of the world',[227] Milton could write a poem in 1645 to show 'That Nature Submits Not to the Decay of Old Age'. By 1694, William Wotton declared that the world, far 'from decaying, has gone on, from Age to Age, Improving . . .'[228]

Victor Harris has shown how the decline of the belief in the decay of nature correlated with the rise of the scientific attitude among the 'new philosophers'. As Joseph Glanvill put it in 1661 in *The Vanity of Dogmatising*, the 'sole instances of those illustrious Heroes *Cartes, Gassendus, Galilaeo, Tych, Harvey, More, Digby*; will strike dead the opinion of the

[224] Walter Raleigh, *Works* (Oxford, 1829), ii.149–50. Quoted *ibid.*, p. 139.
[225] George Hakewill, *An apologie*, pp. 126–7.   [226] See *ibid.*, p. 143.
[227] Samuel Purchas, *Microcosmus*, p. 41. See also James Slotkin, *Readings in Early Anthropology*, pp. 141–3.
[228] William Wotton, *Reflections upon Ancient and Modern Learning* (London, 1705), p. 5. Quoted by James Slotkin, *Readings in Early Anthropology*, p. 143.

worlds decay, and conclude it, in its *prime*'.[229] Science bespoke a more optimistic view of the world. It saw nature as evidencing the wisdom and benevolence of God. In *The Wisdom of God Manifested in the Works of the Creation*, John Ray wrote of 'The vast multitude of Creatures, and those not only small but immensely great . . . The admirable Contrivance of all and each of them, the adapting all the parts of Animals to their several uses: The Provision that is made for their Sustenance . . .'[230] A world of decay was replaced by a world of design. That which was formerly seen as part of the divine curse was now seen as part of the divine plan. John Ray saw the virtues of thorns and prickles in allowing plants to protect themselves from grazing animals.[231] The natural historian Thomas Robinson wondered if it were 'with poisonous Weeds and Plants as it is vulgarly fansied to *Toads* and *Serpents*, that they lick up the Venom of the Earth; so poysonous *Plants* may reasonably be supposed to draw to their Visible Bodies that malignant *Juice*, which if diffused through the other *Plants*, would make them less wholsome and fit for Nourishment'.[232]

By the end of the seventeenth century, the world had freed itself from a system in which man was the centre and the end. The nature of the part was no longer relevant to a grasp of the whole, and the world could now be understood outside of the economy of human behaviour depicted in the Genesis story of the Fall.

[229] Joseph Glanvill, *The Vanity of Dogmatising*, p. 240.
[230] John Ray, *The Wisdom of God Manifested in the Works of the Creation* (London, 1691), Preface.
[231] See *Ibid.*, i.102.   [232] Thomas Robinson, *A Vindication*, p. 58.

Epilogue

> [Sir Hudibras] knew the seat of Paradise,
> Could tell in what degree it lies;
> And, as he was disposed, could prove it,
> Below the moon, or else above it:
> What Adam dreamt of when his bride
> Came from her closet in his side:
> Whether the devil tempted her
> By a High-Dutch interpreter;
> If either of them had a navel;
> Who first made music malleable;
> Whether the serpent, at the fall,
> Had cloven feet, or none at all.
>
> Samuel Butler, *Hudibras*, 1.173–84

The publication of John Milton's *Paradise Lost* in 1667 marked the culmination of the elaboration of the story of Adam and Eve in the Garden of Eden. Written to 'justifie the ways of God to men', it represents the high point in the seventeenth century of the literary development of the Edenic myth. As James Turner correctly observes, after *Paradise Lost* no major literary work, or any significant work of history or psychology, began with the story of the creation and fall of Adam and Eve.[1]

The power of the story of the Garden was beginning to wane. Some four years before *Paradise Lost*, Samuel Butler in *Hudibras* was already satirising many of those issues which, as we have seen, were so often the focus of attention – the location of Paradise, the nature of Adam's sleep, the language of the serpent and its stature. Thomas Browne was willing to argue whether Adam and Eve had navels, but there were many other curiosities about the text which he hinted either were not serious or were incapable of resolution. In his words, 'There are a bundle of curiosities,

[1] See James Turner, *One Flesh*, p. 4 n. 3.

not onely in philosophy, but in Divinity, proposed and discussed by men of most supposed abilities, which indeed are not worthy [of] our vacant houres, much lesse our [more] serious studies . . .'[2] John Hall, a contemporary of Browne's, mocked the quest for literal answers: 'Whether ye reinforce old times, and con/ What kind of stuff Adam's first suit was on;/ Whether Ev's toes had cornes; or whether he/ Did cut his beard spadwise or like a T'.[3] Christopher Hill has also pointed to a tradition of plebeian scepticism about the Bible. Thus, for example, in 1615 Richard Rogers attacked those who mocked Adam's sin: 'he did but eat an apple (a matter of nothing)'. And in 1630, Essex parishioners asked where Adam and Eve obtained thread to sew their fig-leaves.[4]

But the ballad that John Robins forwarded to Sir William Trumbull suggests that doubts were growing among the middling and upper classes;

> That all the books of Moses
> Were nothing but supposes;
> That he deserv'd rebuke, sir,
> Who wrote the Pentateuch, Sir,
> 'Twas nothing but a sham,
> 'Twas nothing but a sham.

> That as for father Adam,
> With Mrs. Eve his madam,
> And what the serpent spoke, Sir,
> 'Twas nothing but a joke, Sir,
> And well-invented flam,
> And well-invented flam.[5]

The first verse of this ballad suggests the way in which many would have read Thomas Burnet's *The Sacred Theory of the Earth*. As Scott Mandelbrote indicates, it clearly referred to one of the central tenets of Burnet's biblical interpretation, namely 'that the creation accounts found in Genesis . . . were stories told in a language which might be understood by the ill-educated audiences who had originally heard them, rather than being divinely-inspired descriptions of the events, which had happened in the manner in which they were described, intended for intelligent and discerning modern readers'.[6]

---

[2] Thomas Browne, *Religio Medici*, 1.21. [3] John Hall, *Poems* (Cambridge, 1646), p. 5.
[4] See Christopher Hill, *The English Bible and the Seventeenth-Century Revolution*, pp. 227–86, 226.
[5] Quoted by Scott Mandelbrote, 'Biblical Criticism and the Crisis of Late Seventeenth-Century England', in James E. Force and Richard Popkin (eds.), *The Books of Nature and Scripture* (Dordrecht, 1994), p. 154.
[6] *Ibid.*

But, as he goes on to point out, the second verse is redolent of Burnet's own defence of his interpretation in *Archaeologiae Philosophicae* in 1692. For there Burnet had given in Latin a deeply ironic reading of the story of the Garden, one which (no doubt to his horror) was included one year later in an English translation of Charles Blount's *The Oracles of Reason*. Blount's defence of Burnet did serious damage to Burnet's reputation. As John Redwood notes, Blount pointed 'Burnet's message in just the way all feared it was tending; towards flippancy and ridicule of the Bible'.[7]

Blount also selectively cited passages in *Religio Medici* and *Pseudodoxia Epidemica* where Browne had expressed some reservations. He had read La Peyrère's account of the pre-Adamites, and along with him expressed doubts about Old Testament miracles. And he denied original sin. But it was the translation of Burnet that undoubtedly had the largest impact.

The key to Burnet's apology was his acceptance of the twofold philosophy. According to this, humanity was divided into two groups – the credulous, superstitious majority and a small intellectual elite. It had been present in the Christian tradition since the time of Origen and Basil the Great, and it provided the possibility of reconciling philosophical truth with revealed truth.[8]

This twofold philosophy was Burnet's defence of his scientific reconstruction of the biblical account of the creation of the world. Thus, he wrote, 'among the Orientals, there were two different ways of delivering their Divinity & Philosophy . . . a Popular and a hidden one: of which dubious sort of style the Holy Scripture seems to make use in the explaining natural things; sometimes accommodating itself to the capacities of the People, and sometimes to the real but more clouded truth'.[9] And the six parts of the story of the Garden which he listed – the creation of humankind, the description of the Garden, the history of the two trees, the serpent's conference with Eve, the wrath of God and his curse, and the expulsion from Eden – were 'Hypotheses adapted to the Vulgar'.[10]

Burnet had doubts about many of the elements which are central to the story of the Garden and, more important, crucial to its mythological function. He presented many of the traditional problems, but he had no

---

[7] John Redwood, *Reason, Ridicule and Religion* (London, 1976), p. 123.
[8] See Peter Harrison, *'Religion' and the Religions in the English Enlightenment* (Cambridge, 1990), pp. 85–92.
[9] Charles Blount, *The Oracles of Reason*, pp. 22–3.   [10] *Ibid.*, p. 32.

inclination to provide any solutions. He had serious problems with the creation of Eve from one of Adam's ribs. In keeping with his belief in Paradise as covering the whole earth, he rehearsed the arguments against the traditional identification of the four rivers as the Nile, the Ganges, the Tigris, and the Euphrates. He suggested that the idea of a talking serpent was ludicrous, and that the belief in Satan's entering the serpent had no textual support. That the snake either formerly walked erect, or was punished by having to do after the Fall what it formerly did naturally, he found inexplicable or ridiculous. He was sceptical of any literal understanding of the effects of the trees of Life and the Knowledge of Good and Evil. He found it difficult to accept that the mere eating of a fruit could bring about shame in nakedness; and he intimated that he found Augustine's account of how Eve could have conceived virginally unintelligible. Like others, he wondered (perhaps not all that seriously) whence Adam and Eve would have obtained the needles and thread to sew their aprons, and he was troubled by the extinction of a species necessitated by their clothing themselves in skins. And of the whole story taking place in one day? 'In the Morning God said all things were good; and in the Evening of the same Day, all things are accursed. Alas! how fleeting and unconstant is the Glory of Things created! A work that was six days e're it could be elaborate and brought to perfection, and that by an Omnipotent Architect to be thus in as few Hours ruined by so vile a Beast'.[11]

The seventeenth century was the century par excellence of the literal reading of the biblical text. John Donne declared that 'the word of God is not the word of God in any sense other than literall'.[12] One of Thomas Wilson's 'Theologicall Rules' in 1615 was that

Histories in scripture, as that of creation, of paradise, of mans fall, of *Adams* progenie, *Abraham* his leauing his country, and many such are vttered in plaine wordes, and proper without allegories, or other figures. Because that would make the scriptures to bee laughed at, and breede infinite absurdities, if one should attempt to make all tropicall [i.e. figurative], and turne every thing into Allegoricall senses, as some wanton unsanctified wittes too much do endeauor it.[13]

Wilson was undoubtedly right in recognising that a belief in the multi-layered meaning of the text would lead to multiple and, more

[11] *Ibid.*, p. 48.
[12] John Donne, *Essays in Divinity*, ed. E. M. Simpson (Oxford, 1952), p. 39. Quoted by C. A. Patrides, 'The Experience of Otherness', p. 181.
[13] Quoted by C. A. Patrides, 'The Experience of Otherness', p. 181.

troublingly (for him), heterodox readings of the text. But he was quite wrong if he believed that a literal and historical approach to the Genesis text would rescue the scriptures from becoming a laughingstock.

On the face of it, Burnet was arguing for a return to a multilayered understanding of the text. As he put it, 'in the first Ages of the Christian Church . . . as also among the *Jews* before Christ's Birth, the more candid Interpreters deviated from the literal reading of *Moses*'s History'.[14] But it was Burnet who, focusing on the literal sense, emphasised the incoherencies of the literal readings. In defence of his own theory of the earth, Burnet was driving his readers towards an acceptance of a scientific reading of the Garden of Eden by trying to convince them that the literal and historical sense sank under the cumulative weight of its own inherent absurdities. Thus, far from recommending a multilayered understanding of the text, he was in effect rejecting the literal in favour of the scientific.

As we have seen, there was nothing fresh or original about the problems which Burnet raised about the story of the Garden. The seventeenth century abounded with discussions of these issues and many more. The Edenic myth was central. And because of its centrality, as both history and myth, the text was an incentive to inquiry, discussion, and debate, and readings of it were indispensable parts of the religious, social, and political life of the time.

But Burnet's treatment of it does symbolise something fresh and original. For it symbolised a turning point in the history of the interpretation of the story of Adam and Eve. It represented that point at which the difficulties inherent in the text are no longer being seen as catalysts for inquiry but as grounds for scepticism. And it signalled the beginnings of the progessive marginalisation of the story in English intellectual life, as a consequence of the developing secularisation of our forms of description. For the better part of the seventeenth century, the story of Adam and Eve was a handbook for science, a document of history, and a source for literary themes. With the decline of its scientific, historical, and literary functions towards the end of the century, it began to lose its mythological role. No longer the definitive key to the understanding of how things were and came to be, it could no longer provide the dominant insight into why things are as they are. Thus, with the defining myth of Western culture in decline, the modern West began.

[14] Charles Blount, *The Oracles of Reason*, p. 49.

Bibliography

PRIMARY SOURCES

Abbott, Robert, *The Young Mans Warning-Piece* (London, 1657).

Adams, Thomas, *Heaven and Earth Reconcil'd* (London, 1613).

The Workes (London, 1629).

Agrippa, Henry Cornelius, *A Treatise of the nobilitie and excellencye of womenkynde* (London, 1542).

Ainsworth, Henry, *Annotations Upon the first book of Moses called Genesis* (London, 1616).

Alexander, William, *Doomes-Day; or, The Great Day of the Lords Ivdgment* (Edinburgh, 1614).

Allen, Thomas, *A Chain of Scripture Chronology* (London, 1659).

Ames, Richard, *The Folly of Love; or, An Essay upon Satyr against Women* (London, 1691).

Andrewes, Lancelot, *Apospasmatia Sacra* (London, 1657).

Anon., *A Discourse of the Terrestrial Paradise* (London, 1666).

Anon., *Haec-Vir: or, The Womanish-Man* (London, 1620).

Anon., *Hic Mulier: or, The Man-Woman* (n.p., 1620).

Anon. (trans.), *Ovid's Metamorphoses* (London, 1717).

Anon., *Religions Lotterie, or the Churches Amazement* (London, 1642).

Anon., *The Second Volume of The Post-Boy Robb'd of his Mail* (London, 1693).

Apsley, Allen (attrib.), *Order and Disorder* (London, 1679).

Aquinas, Thomas, *Summa Theologiae* (London, 1964–76).

Augustine, *Against the Manichees*, in Ronald J. Teske (trans.), *Saint Augustine on Genesis* (Washington, D.C., 1991).

Austen, Ralph, *A Dialogue* (London, 1676).

A Treatise of Fruit Trees (Oxford, 1653).

Austin, William, *Haec Homo wherein the Excellency of the Creation of Woman is described, By way of an Essaie* (London, 1637).

Babington, Gervase, *Certaine Plaine, briefe, and comfortable Notes vpon euerie Chapter of Genesis* (London, 1592).

Bacon, Francis, *The Two Bookes of the Proficience and Advancement of Learning* (London, 1605).

Barber, Richard (trans.), *Bestiary: Being an English Version of the Bodleian Library, Oxford M.S. Bodley 764* (Woodbridge, Suffolk, 1993).

Barckley, Richard, *A Discovrse of the Felicitie of Man* (London, 1598).

Barrough, Philip, *The Method of Phisicke* (London, 1583).

Basse, William (attrib.), *A Helpe to Discovrse. Or a Miscelany of Merriment* (London, 1619).

Bayle, Pierre, *Mr Bayle's Historical and Critical Dictionary* (London, 1734–8).

Beck, Cave, *The Universal Character* (London, 1657).

Bettenson, Henry (ed.), Augustine, *Concerning the City of God against the Pagans* (Harmondsworth, 1972).

Documents of the Christian Church (London, 1967).

Beveridge, Henry (trans.), John Calvin, *Institutes of the Christian Religion* (London, 1953).

Birch, Thomas, *The History of the Royal Society of London* (London, 1756).

Birch, Thomas (ed.), *Robert Boyle: The Works* (London, 1772).

Blith, Walter, *The English improover improved* (London, 1653).

Blount, Charles, *The Miscellaneous Works of Charles Blount, Esq.* (London, 1695).

The Oracles of Reason (London, 1693).

Boehme, Jacob, *Mysterium Magnum: or, An Exposition of the First Book of Moses called Genesis* (London, 1654).

The Second Booke. Concerning the Three Principles (London, 1648).

The Signature of All Things (London, 1912).

Bossuet, James, *A Discourse on the History of the World* (London, 1686).

Bostocke, Robert, *Auncient Phisicke* (London, 1585).

Bourke, Vernon J. (trans.), Saint Augustine, *Confessions* (Washington, D.C., 1953).

Bradley, Richard, *A General Treatise of Husbandry and Gardening* (London, 1724).

Bramhall, John, *Castigations of Mr Hobbes* (London, 1658).

Brathwait, Richard, *A Muster Roll of the evill Angels* (London, 1655).

Broughton, Hugh, *Observations Upon the first ten fathers* (London, 1612).

A Seder Olam, that is: Order of the worlde (London, 1594).

Browne, Thomas, *Of Languages*, in Geoffrey Keynes (ed.), *The Works of Sir Thomas Browne* (London, 1964).

Pseudodoxia Epidemica, ed. Robin Robbins (Oxford, 1991).

Religio Medici, in Geoffrey Keynes (ed.), *The Works of Sir Thomas Browne* (London, 1964).

Bullinger, Heinrich, *Looke from Adam* (London, 1624).

The olde fayth (London, 1641).

Bulwer, John, *Anthropometamorphosis: Man transformd; or the Artificial Changeling* (London, 1650).

Chirologia: or, The natural Language of the Hand (London, 1644).

Burnet, Thomas, *The Sacred Theory of the Earth*, 2 vols. (London, 1722).

The Sacred Theory of the Earth (London, 1965).

Bury, Edward, *The Husbandman's Companion* (London, 1677).

Butterworth, G. W. (ed.), Origen, *On First Principles* (Gloucester, Massachusetts, 1973).

Camerarius, Philip, *The Walking Librarie* (London, 1621).

Carpenter, Nathanael, *Geography Delineated Forth in Two Books* (Oxford, 1625).
Carter, Richard, *The Schismatick Stigmatized* (London, 1641).
Carver, Marmaduke, *A Discourse of the Terrestrial Paradise* (London, 1666).
Cavendish, Margaret, *Philosophical Letters* (London, 1664).
  Poems and Fancies (London, 1653).
Charleton, Walter, *The Darkness of Atheism* (London, 1652).
Charron, Peter, *Of Wisdome* (London, 1608).
Clarkson, Laurence, *Look About You, for the Devil that you fear is in you* (London, 1659).
  The Lost Sheep found (London, 1660).
  A Single Eye (London, 1650).
Cole, Henry (trans.), *The Creation: A Commentary by Martin Luther* (Edinburgh, 1858).
Coles, William, *Adam in Eden* (London, 1657).
Colson, F. H., and Whitaker, G. H. (trans.), *Philo* (London, 1929).
Comenius, John Amos, *The Way of Light* (Liverpool, 1938).
Cooke, Edward, *Bartas Junior. Or the Worlds Epitome; Man* (London, 1631).
Cooper, Thomas, *A Briefe Exposition of such Chapters of the olde Testament as usually are redde in the Church on the Sondayes* (London, 1573).
Crab, Roger, *The English Hermit, or Wonder of this Age* (London, 1655).
Croll, Oswald, *Bazilica Chymica, & Praxis Chymiatricae* (London, 1670).
  Philosophy Reformed and Improved (London, 1657).
Crooke, Helkiah, *Microcosmographia* (London, 1615).
Cuffe, Henrie, *The Differences of the Ages of Mans Life* (London, 1607).
Curley, Michael J. (trans.), *Physiologus* (Austin, Texas, 1979).
Cyrano de Bergerac, *The Comical History of the States and Empires of the Worlds of the Moon and Sun* (London, 1687).
  Other Worlds: The Comical History of the States and Empires of the worlds of the Moon and the Sun (London, 1965).
Dalgarno, George, *Ars Signorum, vulgo Character universalis et Lingua Philosophica* (London, 1661).
Daneau, Lambertus, *The Wonderful Workmanship of God* (London, 1578).
de Beer, E. S. (ed.), *The Diary of John Evelyn* (London, 1959).
  The Diary of John Evelyn (Oxford, 1955).
Digby, Kenelm, *Two Treatises* (Paris, 1644).
Diodati, John, *Pious Annotations Vpon the Holy Bible* (London, 1651).
Donne, John, *The Complete English Poems* (London, 1991).
Drant, Thomas, *Two Sermons* (London, 1569).
Drax, Thomas, *The Churches Securitie* (London, 1608).
  The Earnest of our Inheritance (London, 1613).
Drayton, Michael, *The Muses Elizium lately discovered* (London, 1630).
Dryden, John, *The State of Innocence, and Fall of Man: An Opera* (London, 1677).
Dunton, John (ed.), *The Athenian Gazette* (London, 1691–7).
Durye, John, *Israels Call to March Out of Babylon* (London, 1646).
Dyce, Alexander (ed.), *The Works of Richard Bentley, D.D.* (London, 1838).

Edwards, Thomas, *Gangraena* (London, 1646).
Ellis, Humphrey, *Pseudochristus* (London, 1650).
Etheridge, John W., *The Targums of Onkelos and Jonathan ben Uzziel . . . from the Chaldee* (n.p., 1862).
Evelyn, John, *Acetaria: A Discourse of Sallets* (London, 1699).
　A Discourse of Sallets (London, 1706).
　Kalendarium Hortense: or, The Gardner's Almanac (London, 1664).
　Silva, or a Discourse of Forest-Trees, and the Propogation of Timber (London, 1706).
Faulkner, Thomas C., Kiessling, Nicolas K., and Blair, Rhonda L. (eds.), Robert Burton, *The Anatomy of Melancholy*, vol. 1 (Oxford, 1989).
Filmer, Robert, *Patriarcha: or the Natural Power of Kings* (London, 1680).
Fletcher, Joseph, *The Historie of the Perfect-Cursed-Blessed Man* (London, 1628).
Foigny, Gabriel de, *A New Discovery of Terra Incognita Australis* (London, 1693).
Fontenelle, Bernard, *A Discovery of New Worlds*, trans. A. Behn (London, 1688).
Fox, George, *A Journal: or Historical Account of the Life . . . of George Fox* (London, 1694).
Franck, Richard, *A Philosophical treatise of the original and production of things* (London, 1687).
Franck, Sebastian, *The Forbidden Fruit* (London, 1640).
Franckenberg, Abraham von, *The Life of one Jacob Boehmen* (London, 1644).
Freart, Roland, *An Idea of the Perfection of Painting* (London, 1668).
Freedman, H., and Simon, M. (eds.), *Midrash Rabbah* (London, 1939).
Fuller, T., *Ornitho-logie: or, The Speech of Birds* (London, 1662).
Gale, Theophilus, *The Court of the Gentiles* (Oxford, 1669).
Gauden, John, *The Religious and Loyal Protestation of John Gauden* (London, 1648).
Gibbens, Nicholas, *Qvestions and Dispvtations concerning the Holy Scriptvre* (London, 1601).
Glanvill, Joseph, 'The Usefulness of Real Philosophy to Religion', *Essays on Several Important Subjects in Philosophy and Religion* (London, 1676).
　The Vanity of Dogmatising (London, 1661).
Godwin, Francis, *The Man in the Moone* (London, 1638).
Goodman, Godfrey, *The Creatures Praysing God: or, The Religion of Dumbe Creatures* (London, 1622).
　The Fall of Man. Proved by Reason (London, 1618).
Goodwin, Thomas, *The Heart of Christ in Heaven* (London, 1642).
Gott, Samuel (attrib.), *The Divine History of the Genesis of the World* (London, 1670).
Gouge, William, *Of Domesticall Duties, Eight Treatises* (London, 1634).
Gregory, John, *Gregorii Opuscula* (London, 1650).
Hakewill, George, *An apologie or Declaration of the Power and Providence of God in the Government of the World* (Oxford, 1635).
Hale, Matthew, *The Primitive Origination of Mankind* (London, 1676).
Hall, John, *Paradoxes* (London, 1650).
　Poems (Cambridge, 1646).
Hall, Joseph, *The Works of Joseph Hall* (London, 1634).

Hall, Thomas, *Comarum akosmia: The Loathsomeness of Long Haire* (London, 1653).
Hammond, Henry, *To the Right Honourable, the Lord Fairfax . . . The Humble Addresse* (London, 1649).
Hare, Henry, *The Situation of Paradise found out* (London, 1683).
Hawkins, Henry, *Partheneia Sacra, or the mysterious garden of the sacred Parthenes* (London, 1633).
Hayne, Thomas, *The General View of the Holy Scriptures* (London, 1640).
Hazlitt, William, (trans.), *The Table Talk or Familiar Discourse of Martin Luther* (London, 1848).
Helmont, J.-B. van, *Oriatrike* (London, 1662).
Van Helmont's Works (London, 1664).
Henderson, Katherine U., and McManus, Barbara F. (eds.), *Half Humankind: Contexts and Texts of the Controversy about Women in England, 1540–1640* (Urbana, Illinois, 1985).
Herbert, William, *Herbert's child-bearing woman* (London, 1648).
Heydon, Christopher, *A Defence of Judiciall Astrologie* (Cambridge, 1603).
Heylyn, Peter, *Cosmographie in foure Bookes* (London, 1666).
Microcosmus: a little description of the great world (London, 1621).
Heywood, Thomas, *The Hierarchie of the blessed Angells* (London, 1635).
Hieron, Samuel, *All the Sermons of Samuel Hieron* (London, 1614).
Hinde, William, *A Faithfull Remonstrance of the Holy Life and Happy Death of John Bruen* (London, 1641).
Hobbes, Thomas, *Leviathan* (London, 1973).
Hodges, Thomas, *The Creatures Goodness, As they came out of God's Hands* (London, 1675).
Holland, Henry, *The Historie of Adam, or the foure-fold state of Man* (London, 1606).
Holland, John, *The Smoke of the Bottomlesse Pit* (London, 1651).
Hooke, Robert, *Micrographia* (London, 1665).
Huet, Pierre D., *A Treatise of the Situation of Paradise* (London, 1694).
Hughes, George, *An Analytical Exposition of the Whole first Book of Moses, called Genesis* (London, 1672).
Hunton, Philip, *Treatise of Monarchy* (London, 1680).
Huygens, Christian, *The Celestial Worlds Discover'd* (London, 1698).
I.H., *Paradise Transplanted and Restored* (London, 1661).
Imerti, Arthur D. (ed. and trans.), Giordano Bruno, *The Expulsion of the Triumphant Beast* (New Brunswick, New Jersey, 1964).
Jackson, Arthur, *A Help for the understanding of the Holy Scripture* (London, 1643).
Jonston, John, *An History of the Wonderful Things of Nature* (London, 1657).
Keill, John, *An Examination of Dr Burnet's Theory of the Earth* (Oxford, 1698).
Kernan, Alvin B. (ed.), Ben Jonson, *The Alchemist* (New Haven, 1974).
Keynes, Geoffrey (ed.), *The Works of Sir Thomas Browne* (London, 1964),
Kidder, Richard, *A Commentary on the Five Books of Moses* (London, 1694).
Kiessling, Nicholas, Faulkner, Thomas C., and Blair, Rhonda L. (eds.), Robert Burton, *The Anatomy of Melancholy*, vol. II (Oxford, 1990).
King, John (trans.), *Commentaries on the First Book of Moses called Genesis by John*

Calvin (Grand Rapids, Michigan, 1984).

Knox, John, *The First Blast of the Trumpet against the monstruous regimen of Women* (Geneva, 1558).

L.P., *Two Essays sent in a Letter from Oxford to a Nobleman in London* (London, 1695).

La Peyrère, Isaac, *Men before Adam* (London, 1656).

A Theological Systeme upon that Presupposition that Men were before Adam (London, 1655).

Laslett, Peter (ed.), *Patriarcha and Other Political Works of Sir Robert Filmer* (Oxford, 1949).

Lawson, William, *A New Orchard and Garden* (London, 1653).

Le Blanc, Vincent, *The World Surveyed* (London, 1660).

Le Clerc, Jean, *Twelve Dissertations out of Monsieur Le Clerk's Genesis* (London, 1696).

Leigh, Edward, *A Systeme or Bodie of Divinitie* (London, 1662).

Lightfoot, John, *A few, and new observations upon the Booke of Genesis* (London, 1642).

The Works of the Reverend and Learned John Lightfoot D.D. (London, 1684).

Regal Tyrannie Discovered (London, 1647).

Lilburne, John, *The Free-Mans Freedome Vindicated* (London, 1646).

Lloid, Lodowick, *The Consent of Time* (London, 1590).

Locke, John, *An Essay Concerning Human Understanding* (New York, 1959).

The Reasonableness of Christianity, As delivered in the Scriptures (London, 1695).

Two Treatises of Government (London, 1993).

Loredano, Giovanno, *The Life of Adam* (London, 1659).

Manley, Frank (ed.), John Donne, *The Anniversaries* (Baltimore, 1963).

Marano, G. P., *The Eighth and Last Volume of Letters Writ by a Turkish Spy* (London, 1694).

Margoliouth, H. M. (ed.), Thomas Traherne, *Centuries, Poems, and Thanksgivings* (Oxford, 1958).

Maxwell, John, *Sacro-Sancta Regum Majestas: or the Sacred and Royal Prerogative of Christian Kings* (London, 1680).

McKenna, Stephen (trans.), Plotinus, *The Enneads* (London, 1956).

McKerrow, Ronald B. (ed.), *The Works of Thomas Nashe* (Oxford, 1968).

Mede, Joseph, *The Works of the Pious and Profoundly-Learned Joseph Mede* (London, 1677).

Melancthon, Philipp, *The iustification of man by faith only* (London, 1548).

Milles, Thomas, *The treasurie of auncient and moderne times* (London, 1613–19).

Milton, John, *Paradise Lost* (Harmondsworth, 1989).

The Tenure of Kings and Magistrates (London, 1650), in Don M. Wolfe (ed.), *The Complete Prose Works of John Milton* (New Haven, 1980).

The Works (New York, 1931).

Montaigne, Michaell de, *The Essayes* (London, 1603).

More, Henry, *An Antidote against Atheism* (London, 1655).

Conjectura Cabbalistica, in *A Collection of Philosophical Writings* (London, 1662).

Democritus Platonissans, or, an Essay upon the Infinity of Worlds out of Platonick Principles (Cambridge, 1646).

The Defense of the Threefold Cabbala (London, 1662).

An Explanation of the Grand Mystery of Godliness (London, 1660).

More, John, *A Table from the Beginning of the World to this Day* (Cambridge, 1593).

Morgan, Morris Hicky (trans.), Vitruvius, *The Ten Books on Architecture* (New York, 1960).

Morris, Brian, and Withington, Eleanor (eds.), *The Poems of John Cleveland* (Oxford, 1967).

Muggleton, Lodowick, *A Looking-Glass for George Fox the Quaker* (n.p., 1668).

The Neck of the Quakers Broken (Amsterdam, 1663).

A True Interpretation of the Eleventh Chapter of the Revelation of St John (London, 1662).

Munda, Constantia, *The Worming of a mad dogge, or a soppe for Cerberus* (London, 1617).

Munday, Anthony, *A Briefe Chronicle* (London, 1611).

Nabbes, Thomas, *Microcosmus* (London, 1637).

Needler, Benjamin, *Expository Notes* (London, 1655).

Newstead, Christopher, *An Apology for Women* (London, 1620).

Nicholls, William, *A Conference with a Theist* (London, 1696).

Nisbet, William, *A Golden Chaine of Time* (Edinburgh, 1650).

Nourse, Timothy, *Campania Foelix, or a Discourse of the Benefits and Improvements of Husbandry* (London, 1700).

Ochinus, Bernardus, *A Dialogue of Polygamy* (London, 1657).

Offer, George (ed.), *The Whole Works of John Bunyan* (London, 1862).

Overall, John, *The Convocation Book of MDCVI. Commonly called Bishop Overall's Convocation Book* (Oxford, 1844).

Overton, Richard, *Man wholly Mortal* (London, 1655).

Ovington, John, *A Voyage to Suratt in the year 1689* (London, 1696).

Pagitt, Ephraim, *Heresiography* (London, 1645).

Pallister, Janis L. (trans.), Ambroise Paré, *On Monsters and Marvels* (Chicago, 1982).

Paradin, Claude, *The true and lyvely historyke purtreatures of the woll bible* (Lyons, 1553).

Parker, Henry, *Jus Populi* (London, 1644).

Parkinson, John, *Paradisi in sole* (London, 1629).

Theatrum Botanicum, The Theater of Plantes (London, 1640).

Parr, Elnathan, *The Grounds of Divinitie* (London, 1615).

Patrides, C. A. (ed.), John Donne, *The Complete English Poems* (London, 1994).

Peacock, W. (ed.), *English Prose in Five Volumes* (Oxford, 1921).

Pelikan, Jaroslav, *Luther's Works* (St Louis, 1958).

Perkins, William, *An Exposition of the Symbole or creede of the Apostles* (Cambridge, 1597).

The Workes of . . . Mr William Perkins (London, 1616).

Person, David, *Varieties: or, A Svrveigh of Rare and Excellent Matters* (London, 1635).

Pettus, John, *Volatiles from the History of Adam and Eve* (London, 1674).

Peyton, Thomas, *The glasse of time, in the two first ages diuinely handled* (London, 1620).

Philalethes, Eugenius, *A Treatise of the Plague* (London, 1721).

Pie, Thomas, *An Hourglasse Contayning a Computation from the Beginning of Time to Christ* (London, 1597).

Poole, Matthew, *Annotations upon the Holy Bible* (London, 1696).

Pordage, Samuel, *Mundorum Explicatio* (London, 1661).

Powicke, Frederick J. (ed.), 'The Reverend Richard Baxter's Last Treatise', *Bulletin of the John Rylands Library* 10 (1926), pp. 163–218.

Prideaux, Mathias, *An Easy and Compendious Introduction for Reading All Sorts of Histories* (London, 1648).

Purchas, Samuel, *Microcosmus: or the historie of man* (London, 1619).

Purchas his Pilgrimage (London, 1626).

Pynchon, William, *A Treatise of the Sabbath* (London, 1654).

Raleigh, Walter, *The History of the World* (London, 1614).

The Works of Sir Walter Raleigh (New York, 1829).

Rawlinson, John, *Mercy to a Beast . . . A Sermon* (Oxford, 1612).

Ray, John, *The Wisdom of God Manifested in the Works of the Creation* (London, 1691).

Reeve, John, and Muggleton, Lodowick, *A Divine Looking-Glass* (London, 1661).

A Transcendent Spiritual Treatise (London, 1652).

Works (London, 1832).

Reynolds, Edward, *A Treatise of the Passions and Faculties of the Soule of Man* (London, 1640).

Rich, Barnabe, *The Excellency of Good Women* (London, 1613).

The Honestie of this Age (London, 1614).

Richardson, John, *Choice Observations and Explanations upon the Old Testament* (London, 1655).

Roberts, Alexander, *A Treatise of Witchcraft* (London, 1616).

Robinson, Thomas, *The Anatomy of the Earth* (London, 1694).

A Vindication (London, 1709).

Rogers, Daniel, *Matrimoniall Honour* (London, 1592).

Rogers, John, *The displaying of an horrible secte . . . naming themselves the Familie of Love* (London, 1578).

Ross, Alexander, *An Exposition on the Fovrteene first Chapters of Genesis* (London, 1626).

Medicus Medicatus (London, 1645).

Pansebeia: or, A View of all Religions in the World (London, 1653).

Rous, Francis, *The Mystical Marriage* (London, 1635).

Rowlands, Samuel, *Heavens Glory seeke it* (London, 1628).

Rutherford, Samuel, *Lex, Rex, or the Law and the Prince* (London, 1644), in *The Presbyterian's Armoury* (Edinburgh, 1843).

Sabine, George H. (ed.), *The Works of Gerrard Winstanley* (Ithaca, New York, 1914).

Salkeld, John, *A Treatise of Paradise* (London, 1617).

Scott, Michael, *The Philosophers Banqvet* (London, 1633).

Secker, William, *A Wedding-Ring Fit for the Finger* (London, 1664).
Senault, John-Francis, *Man become Guilty, or the Corruption of Nature by Sinne* (London, 1650).
Simon, Richard, *A Critical History of the Old Testament* (London, 1682).
Simson, M. Archibald, *Heptameron* (St Andrews, 1621).
Smith, Henry, *The Sermons of Master Henry Smith* (London, 1601).
Snyder, Susan (ed.), *The Divine Weeks and Works of Guillaume de Saluste Sieur du Bartas* (Oxford, 1979).
South, Robert, *Sermons preached Upon Severall Occasions* (Oxford, 1679).
Sowernam, Esther, *Esther hath hangd Haman* (London, 1617).
Speght, Rachel, *A Mouzell for Melastomus, The cynicall Bayter of, and foule mouthed Barker against Evahs Sex* (London, 1617).
Sprat, Thomas, *The History of the Royal Society of London* (London, 1667).
Stafford, Antony, *Meditations* (London, 1612).
Stebbing, Henry (ed.), *The Entire Works of John Bunyan* (London, 1860).
Stillingfleet, Edward, *Origines Sacrae: or, A Rational Account of the Grounds of Natural and Revealed Religion*, 7th edn (Cambridge, 1702).
Stradling, John, *Divine Poemes. In seuen seuerall Classes* (London, 1625).
Stubbes, Phillip, *The Anatomie of Abuses* (London, 1583).
Sutcliffe, Alice, *Meditations of Mans Mortalitie* (London, 1634).
Swan, John, *Specvlvm Mundi or A Glasse Representing the Face of the World* (Cambridge, 1635).
Swetnam, Joseph, *The arraignment of lewde, idle, froward and unconstant women* (London, 1615).
Swift, Jonathan, *Gulliver's Travels* (London, 1926).
Taylor, Edward, *Jacob Behmens Theosophick Philosophy Unfolded* (London, 1691).
Taylor, J. H. (trans.), Augustine, *The Literal Meaning of Genesis* (New York, 1982).
Taylor, John, *The Scripture Doctrine of Original Sin* (London, 1740).
Teske, Ronald J. (trans.), *Saint Augustine on Genesis* (Washington, D.C., 1991).
Topsell, Edward, *The Historie of Serpents* (London, 1608).
Times Lamentation: An exposition on the prophet Ioel (London, 1599).
Torshell, Samuel, *The Womans Glorie* (London, 1650).
Tryon, Thomas, *The Country-mans Companion* (London, n.d.).
The good House-wife made a Doctor (London, 1692).
Tryon's Letters upon Several Occasions (London, 1700).
The Way to Health, Long Life and Happiness (London, 1683).
The Way to Health, Long Life and Happiness (London, 1697).
Tyson, Edward, *Orang-Outang, sive Homo Sylvestris* (London, 1699).
Ussher, James, *The Annals of the World* (London, 1658).
A Body of Divinitie (London, 1645).
Vane, Henry, *The Retired Mans Meditations* (London, 1655).
Vaughan, Edward, *Ten Introductions: How to Read, and in Reading How to Understand the Holie Bible* (London, 1594).
Vaughan, William, *The Golden Groue, moralized in Three Bookes* (London, 1600).

Verstegen, Richard, *A Restitution of Decayed Intelligence in Antiquities* (London, 1673).
Waite, Arthur E. (ed.), *The Hermetic and Alchemical Writings of . . . Paracelsus the Great* (London, 1894).
Walker, George, *God made visible in His Workes* (London, 1641).
The history of the Creation (London, 1631).
Walton, Brian, *Biblia Sacra Polyglotta* (London, 1657).
Ward, Seth, *Vindiciae Academiarum* (Oxford, 1664).
Warren, Erasmus, *Geologia: or, A Discourse concerning the Earth before the Deluge* (London, 1690).
Warton, Joseph, *An Essay on the Genius and Writings of Pope* (London, 1782).
Webb, John, *An Historical Essay, Endeavoring a Probability that the Language of the empire of China is the Primitive Language* (London, 1669).
Webster, John, *Academiarum Examen, or the Examination of Academics* (London, 1654).
Weemse, John, *The Portraiture of the Image of God in Man* (London, 1627).
Westfall, Richard S. (ed.), *The Posthumous Works of Robert Hooke* (New York, 1969).
Westmacott, William, *Historia Vegetabilium Sacra* (London, 1695).
Whately, William, *A Bride Bush* (London, 1617).
The Primarie Precedent Presidents ovt of the Booke of Genesis (London, 1640).
Whiston, William, *A New Theory of the Earth* (London, 1696).
Whiston, William (trans.), *The Works of Flavius Josephus* (London, 1825).
The Works of Josephus (Peabody, Massachusetts, 1987).
White, John, *A Commentary Upon the Three First Chapters of The First Book of Moses called Genesis* (London, 1656).
Wilkins, John, *The Discovery of a World in the Moone* (London, 1638).
An Essay Towards a Real Character and a Philosophical Language (London, 1668).
Mercury: or, The Secret and Swift Messenger (London, 1641).
Willet, Andrew, *Hexapla in Genesin* (London, 1608).
Wilson, Thomas, *Theologicall Rules* (London, 1615).
Wing, John, *The Crowne Coniugall or, the Spouse Royall* (Middelburg, 1620).
Winstanley, William, *England's Worthies* (London, 1660).
Wolfe, Don M. (ed.), *The Complete Prose Works of John Milton* (New Haven, 1973).
Wolseley, Charles, *The Unreasonableness of Atheism* (London, 1669).
Woodward, John, *An Essay Towards a Natural History of the Earth* (London, 1695).
Yates, John, *A Modell of Divinitie* (London, 1622).

SECONDARY SOURCES

Aarsleff, Hans, *From Locke to Saussure: Essays on the Study of Language and Intellectual History* (London, 1982).
Allen, Don Cameron, *The Legend of Noah* (Urbana, Illinois, 1949).
Allers, Rudolf, 'Microcosmus from Anaximandros to Paracelsus', *Traditio* 2 (1944), pp. 319–407.

Almond, Philip C., *Heaven and Hell in Enlightenment England* (Cambridge, 1994).

Anderson, Gary, 'Celibacy or Consummation in the Garden? Reflections on Early Jewish and Christian Interpretations of the Garden of Eden', *Harvard Theological Review* 82 (1989), pp. 121–48.

Anon., 'A Pythagorean of the Seventeenth Century', *Proceedings of the Literary and Philosophical Society of Liverpool* 25 (1871), pp. 277–321.

Aylmer, G. E., 'The Religion of Gerrard Winstanley', in J. F. McGregor and Barry Reay (eds.), *Radical Religion in the English Revolution* (Oxford, 1984).

Bailey, Derrick S., *The Man–Woman Relation in Christian Thought* (London, 1959).

Ballantyne, J. W., *Teratogenesis: An Inquiry into the Causes of Monstrosities* (Edinburgh, 1897).

Barr, James, 'Why the World Was Created in 4004 BC: Archbishop Ussher and Biblical Chronology', *Bulletin of the John Rylands University Library* 67 (1985), pp. 575–608.

Baudet, Henri, *Paradise on Earth: Some Thoughts on European Images of Non-European Man* (New Haven, 1965).

Bendysche, Thomas, 'The History of Anthropology', *Memoirs Read before the Anthropological Society of London* 1 (1863–4), pp. 335–458.

Bond, Francis, *Wood Carvings in English Churches*. Vol. 1, *Misericords* (London, 1910).

Bonnell, John K., 'The Serpent with a Human Head in Art and Mystery Play', *American Journal of Archaeology* 21 (1917), pp. 255–91.

Brooks, David, 'The Idea of the Decay of the World in the Old Testament, the Apocrypha, and the Pseudepigrapha', in J. D. North and J. J. Roche (eds.), *The Light of Nature* (Dordrecht, 1985), pp. 383–404.

Bullough, Vern L., and Bullough, Bonnie, *Sin, Sickness and Sanity: A History of Sexual Attitudes* (New York, 1977).

Clancy, Robert, *The Mapping of Terra Australis* (Macquarie Park, New South Wales, 1995).

Cohen, Jeremy, *'Be Fertile and Increase, Fill the Earth and Master It'* (Ithaca, New York, 1989).

Cohn, Norman, *The Pursuit of the Millennium* (London, 1957).

Cornelius, Paul, *Languages in Seventeenth- and Early Eighteenth-Century Imaginary Voyages* (Geneva, 1965).

Costello, Peter, *The Magic Zoo: The Natural History of Fabulous Animals* (London, 1979).

Coudert, Allison, 'Some Theories of a Natural Language from the Renaissance to the Seventeenth Century', *Studia Leibnitiana* 7 (1978), pp. 56–114.

Crawford, Patricia, *Women and Religion in England, 1500–1720* (London, 1993).

Darnton, Robert, *The Great Cat Massacre and Other Episodes in French Cultural History* (London, 1985).

Davies, H. Neville, 'Bishop Godwin's "Lunatique Language"', *Journal of the Warburg and Courtauld Institutes* 30 (1967), pp. 296–316.

Dean, Dennis, 'The Age of the Earth Controversy: Beginnings to Hutton',

Annals of Science 38 (1981), pp. 435–56.

Debus, Allen G., *The English Paracelsians* (London, 1965).

Delumeau, Jean, *History of Paradise: The Garden of Eden in Myth and Tradition* (New York, 1995).

De Mott, B., 'Comenius and the Real Character in England', *PMLA* 70 (1955), pp. 1068–81.

Dick, Steven J., *Plurality of Worlds: The Extraterrestrial Life Debate from Democritus to Kant* (Cambridge, 1982).

Duncan, Joseph E., *Milton's Earthly Paradise: A Historical Study of Eden* (Minneapolis, 1972).

'Paradise as the Whole Earth', *Journal of the History of Ideas* 39 (1969), pp. 171–86.

Eco, Umberto, *The Search for the Perfect Language* (Oxford, 1995).

Egerton, Frank N., 'The Longevity of the Patriarchs', *Journal of the History of Ideas* 27 (1966), pp. 575–84.

Emery, Clark, 'John Wilkins' Universal Language', *Isis* 38 (1947), pp. 174–85.

Encyclopaedia Judaica (Jerusalem, 1971–2).

Engel, Mary Potter, *John Calvin's Perspectival Theology* (Atlanta, Georgia, 1988).

Evans, J. M., *'Paradise Lost' and the Genesis Tradition* (Oxford, 1968).

Flores, Nona Cecelia, '"Virgineum Vultum Habens": The Woman-Headed Serpent in Art and Literature from 1300 to 1700', Ph.D. dissertation, University of Illinois, 1981.

Frantz, R. W., 'Swift's Yahoos and the Voyagers', *Modern Philology* 29 (1931–2), pp. 49–57.

Fraser, Antonia, *The Weaker Vessel: Woman's Lot in Seventeenth-Century England* (London, 1984).

Glacken, Clarence J., *Traces on the Rhodian Shore* (Berkeley, California, 1973).

Goldscheider, Ludwig, *Leonardo: Paintings and Drawings* (London, 1959).

Grafton, Anthony T., 'From *De Die Natali* to *De Emendatione Temporum*: The Origins and Setting of Scaliger's Chronology', *Journal of the Warburg and Courtauld Institutes* 48 (1985), pp. 100–43.

'Joseph Scaliger and Historical Chronology: The Rise and Fall of a Discipline', *History and Theory* 14 (1975), pp. 156–85.

Graves, Richard L., and Zaller, Robert (eds.), *Biographical Dictionary of British Radicals in the Seventeenth Century* (Brighton, Sussex, 1982–).

Graves, Robert, and Patai, Raphael, *Hebrew Myths: The Book of Genesis* (London, 1963).

Guerrini, Anita, 'Animal Experimentation in Seventeenth Century England', *Journal of the History of Ideas* 50 (1989), pp. 391–407.

Haber, Francis C., *The Age of the World: Moses to Darwin* (Baltimore, 1959).

Halkett, John, *Milton and the Idea of Matrimony: A Study of the Divorce Tracts and 'Paradise Lost'* (New Haven, 1970).

Haller, W., and Haller, M., 'The Puritan Art of Love', *Huntington Library Quarterly* 5 (1942), pp. 235–72.

Harris, Victor, *All Coherence Gone* (London, 1966).

Harrison, Peter, *The Bible, Protestantism, and the Rise of Natural Science* (Cambridge, 1998).
'Religion' and the Religions in the English Enlightenment (Cambridge, 1990).
Hill, Christopher, *The Collected Essays of Christopher Hill* (London, 1985–6).
The English Bible and the Seventeenth-Century Revolution (London, 1994).
The Experience of Defeat (London, 1984).
Puritanism and Revolution (London, 1965).
The World Turned Upside Down (London, 1972).
Hill, Christopher, Reay, Barry, and Lamont, William, *The World of the Muggletonians* (London, 1983).
Hodgen, Margaret T., *Early Anthropology in the Sixteenth and Seventeenth Centuries* (Philadelphia, 1964).
Hughes, Robert, *The Fatal Shore* (London, 1987).
Hume, Lynne, *Witchcraft and Paganism in Australia* (Melbourne, 1997).
Janson, H. W., *Apes and Ape Lore in the Middle Ages and the Renaissance* (London, 1952).
Jeffrey, David L., *A Dictionary of Biblical Tradition in English Literature* (Grand Rapids, Michigan, 1992).
Jones, Rufus M., *Spiritual Reformers in the 16th and 17th Centuries* (Gloucester, Massachusetts, 1971).
Katz, David S., 'The Language of Adam in 17th-Century England', in Hugh Lloyd Jones, Valerie Pearl, and Blair Worden (eds.), *History and Imagination: Essays in Honour of H. R. Trevor-Roper* (London, 1981), pp. 132–45.
Kelly, Henry Ansgar, 'The Metamorphoses of the Eden Serpent during the Middle Ages and Renaissance', *Viator* 2 (1971), pp. 301–28.
Knowlson, James, *Universal Language Schemes in England and France, 1600–1800* (Toronto, 1975).
Knox, Dilwyn, 'Ideas on Gesture and Universal Languages, c.1550–1650', in John Henry and Sarah Hutton (eds.), *New Perspectives on Renaissance Thought* (London, 1990).
Kocher, Paul H., *Christopher Marlowe* (New York, 1962).
Laqueur, Thomas, *Making Sex: Body and Gender from the Greeks to Freud* (Cambridge, Massachusetts, 1992).
Lovejoy, Arthur O., *The Great Chain of Being* (New York, 1960).
Maclean, Ian, *The Renaissance Notion of Woman* (Cambridge, 1980).
Mandelbrote, Scott, 'Biblical Criticism and the Crisis of Late Seventeenth-Century England', in James E. Force and Richard Popkin (eds.), *The Books of Nature and Scripture* (Dordrecht, 1994).
Martz, Louis L., *The Paradise Within: Studies in Vaughan, Traherne, and Milton* (New Haven, 1964).
McColley, Diane K., *A Gust for Paradise: Milton's Eden and the Visual Arts* (Urbana, Illinois, 1993).
'Milton and the Sexes', in Dennis Danielson (ed.), *The Cambridge Companion to Milton* (Cambridge, 1989), pp. 147–66.
Milton's Eve (Urbana, Illinois, 1983).

McGregor, J. F., and Reay, B. (eds.), *Radical Religion in the English Revolution* (Oxford, 1984).

Montagu, M. F. Ashley, *Edward Tyson, M.D., F.R.S. 1650–1708 and the Rise of Human and Comparative Anatomy in England* (Philadelphia, 1943).

Morris, Paul, and Sawyer, Deborah, *A Walk in the Garden: Biblical, Iconographical and Literary Images of Eden* (Sheffield, 1992).

Morton, A. L., *The World of the Ranters* (London, 1970).

Moss, Jean Dietz, 'The Family of Love and English Critics', *Sixteenth Century Journal* 6 (1975), pp. 35–52.

Motherway, Thomas J., 'The Creation of Eve', *Theological Studies* 1 (1940), pp. 97–116.

Mueller, Max, *Lectures on the Science of Language* (London, 1861).

Norman, H. J., 'John Bulwer (fl. 1654) the "Chirosopher"', *Proceedings of the Royal Society of Medicine* 36 (1943), pp. 589–602.

North, John D., 'Chronology and the Age of the World', in Wolfgang Yourgrau and Allen D. Breck (eds.), *Cosmology, History, and Theology* (New York, 1977), pp. 307–33.

Norton, David, *A History of the Bible as Literature* (Cambridge, 1993).

Ormsby-Lennon, Hugh, 'Rosicrucian Linguistics: Twilight of a Renaissance Tradition', in Ingrid Merkel and Allen Debus (eds.), *Hermeticism and the Renaissance* (Washington, D.C., 1988).

Otten, Charlotte F., *Environ'd with Eternity: God, Poems, and Plants in Sixteenth and Seventeenth Century England* (Lawrence, Kansas, 1985).

Pagels, Elaine, *Adam, Eve, and the Serpent* (New York, 1988).

Park, Katharine, 'The Rediscovery of the Clitoris', in D. Hillman and Carla Mazzio (eds.), *The Body in Parts: Fantasies of Corporeality in Early Modern Europe* (New York, 1997), pp. 171–93.

Park, Katherine, and Nye, Robert M., 'Destiny Is Anatomy', *New Republic*, January 31, 1991, pp. 53–7.

Passmore, John, *Man's Responsibility for Nature* (London, 1974).

Patrick, J. Max, 'A Consideration of *La Terre australe connue* by Gabriel de Foigny', *PMLA* 61 (1946), pp. 739–51.

Patrides, C. A., 'The Experience of Otherness: Theology as a Means of Life', in C. A. Patrides and Raymond B. Waddington (eds.), *The Age of Milton: Backgrounds to Seventeenth-Century Literature* (Manchester, 1980).

'The Microcosm of Man: Some References to a Commonplace', *Notes and Queries* 7 (1960), pp. 54–6.

Milton and the Christian Tradition (Oxford, 1966).

'Renaissance Estimates of the Year of Creation', *Huntington Library Quarterly* 26 (1963), pp. 315–22.

'Renaissance Ideas on Man's Upright Form', *Journal of the History of Ideas* 19 (1958), pp. 256–8.

Phillips, John A., *Eve: The History of an Idea* (San Francisco, 1984).

Phillips, Roderick, *Untying the Knot: A Short History of Divorce* (Cambridge, 1991).

Popkin, Richard, *Isaac La Peyrère (1596–1676): His Life, Work, and Influence* (Leiden, 1987).

Redwood, John, *Reason, Ridicule and Religion* (London, 1976).

Robbins, Frank Egleston, *The Hexaemeral Literature: A Study of the Greek and Latin Commentaries on Genesis* (Chicago, 1912).

Robin, P. Ansell, *Animal Lore in English Literature* (London, 1932).

Rostwig, Maren-Sofie, *The Happy Man: Studies in the Metamorphoses of a Classical Ideal 1600–1700* (Oxford, 1954).

Rudrum, Alan, 'Henry Vaughan, the Liberation of the Creatures and Seventeenth-Century English Calvinism', *Seventeenth Century* 4 (1989), pp. 32–54.

'Polygamy in *Paradise Lost*', *Essays in Criticism* 20 (1970), pp. 18–23.

Singer, Thomas C., 'Hieroglyphs in the Seventeenth Century', *Journal of the History of Ideas* 50 (1989), pp. 49–70.

Slotkin, James S., *Readings in Early Anthropology* (London, 1965).

Stoughton, John, *Ecclesiastical History of England: The Church of the Restoration* (London, 1870).

Sullivan, Ernest W. II, 'Illustration as Interpretation: *Paradise Lost* from 1688 to 1807', in Albert C. Labriola and Edward Sichi, Jr (eds.), *Milton's Legacy in the Arts* (University Park, Pennsylvania, 1988).

Svendsen, K., *Milton and Science* (Cambridge, Massachusetts, 1956).

Thomas, Keith, *Man and the Natural World* (Harmondsworth, 1984).

'Women and the Civil War Sects', *Past and Present*, no. 13 (1958), pp. 42–62.

Torrance, T. F., *Calvin's Doctrine of Man* (London, 1952).

Trevor-Roper, Hugh, *Catholics, Anglicans and Puritans: Seventeenth Century Essays* (Chicago, 1988).

Trible, Phyllis, *God and the Rhetoric of Sexuality* (Philadelphia, 1978).

Turner, James Grantham, *One Flesh: Paradisal Marriage and Sexual Relations in the Age of Milton* (Oxford, 1987).

Vickery, Roy, *A Dictionary of Plant-Lore* (Oxford, 1995).

Webster, Charles, *The Great Instauration: Science, Medicine and Reform 1626–1660* (London, 1975).

Weigand, Herman J., 'The Two and Seventy Languages of the World', *Germanic Review* 17 (1942), pp. 241–60.

White, Lynn, Jr, 'The Historical Roots of Our Ecologic Crisis', *Science* (New York) 155 (1967), pp. 1203–7.

Willett, C., and Cunnington, Phillis, *Handbook on English Costume in the Seventeenth Century* (London, 1966).

Williams, Arnold, *The Common Expositor* (Chapel Hill, North Carolina, 1948).

Williams, George H., *The Radical Reformation* (London, 1962).

Wilderness and Paradise in Christian Thought (New York, 1962).

Williams, Howard, *The Ethics of Diet* (London, 1896).

Williams, N. P., *The Ideas of the Fall and Original Sin* (London, 1927).

Williamson, George, 'Mutability, Decay, and Seventeenth-Century Melancholy', *ELH: A Journal of English Literary History* 2 (1935), pp. 121–50.

Wind, Edgar, *Pagan Mysteries in the Renaissance* (London, 1968).

'The Revival of Origen', in Dorothy Milner (ed.), *Studies in Art and Literature for Belle da Costa Greene* (Princeton, 1954).

Wokler, R., 'Tyson and Buffon on the Orang-utan', *Studies on Voltaire and the Eighteenth Century* 155 (1976), pp. 2301–19.

Woodbridge, Linda, *Women and the English Renaissance* (Brighton, Sussex, 1984).

Wright, David P., 'Holiness, Sex, and Death in the Garden of Eden', *Biblica* 77 (1996), pp. 306–29.

Yates, Frances A., *Giordano Bruno and the Hermetic Tradition* (Chicago, 1964).

The Rosicrucian Enlightenment (London, 1972).

Index

Jonston, John, 40–1, 95, 96, 97, 150
Josephus, 17, 19, 21, 23, 74, 79, 87, 181, 182–3

Keill, John, 78
Kempe, Andreas, 132
Ken, Thomas, 189
Kidder, Richard, 58, 81–2
King, Henri, 31–2
Knox, John, 150

La Peyrère, Isaac, 52–8, 60, 79–80, 212
Laetius, Johannes, 59
lamb, Scythian, 96–7
language
    as able to express the nature of things,
        114–16, 136, 140
    Adamic, 128–36
    and animals, 96, 126–8
    Celtic, 132
    Chinese, 133
    Danish, 132
    and doctrine of signatures, 138–9
    Dutch, 132
    Egyptian hieroglyphs, 133
    French, 132
    Hebrew, 129–32
    Low German, 132
    music, 134–5
    and Pentecostal glossolalia, 140
    and pre-Adamites, 50
    quest to create new universal, 136–42
    runes, 132
    Scythian, 132
    sign, 135–6
    Swedish, 132
    as unable to express the nature of things,
        116, 141–2
Lanier, Emilia, 150, 196
Lawson, William, 22, 99
Le Blanc, Vincent, 73
Le Clerc, Jean, 114 n. 22, 131
Leigh, Edward, 75–6, 82, 169, 194, 195
Leonardo da Vinci, 39
Levellers, 68, 107, 108–9, 113
libertines, 48, 170–1
Lightfoot, John, 48, 89, 166
Lilburne, John, 107
Lloid, Lodowick, 79, 114, 187
Lloyd, William, 86
Locke, John, 104, 107–8, 116, 142
Loredano, Giovanni, 12, 15, 28, 46, 79, 82, 87,
    160 n. 101, 154 n. 67, 166, 188, 199, 200
Lovejoy, Arthur, 33–4
Lucidus, Ioannes, 28
Luther, Martin

and Adam's perfect knowledge, 46
and allegorical understanding of Paradise,
    70
and devil, 188
and government, 103
and image of God, 12, 13
and location of Paradise, 74, 75, 79
and marriage, 160, 163
and nakedness, 199
and polygamy, 159
and removal of Adam's rib, 145, 146
and serpent, 183, 184, 187
and sex, 161–2, 163
and subordination of women, 149
and Tree of Life, 191

Mabuse, Jan, 44 n. 62
macrocosm, 28, 40–1, 204, 207–8
man
    and Adamic language, 128–42
    age of on day of Creation, 18–19
    as androgynous, 4–8, 164, 176
    beauty of, 41–2
    and compassion for animals, 123–5
    created outside Eden, 16
    as crown of Creation, 17, 33–41, 64
    and dominion over animals, 11–13, 33–41,
        44, 47, 112, 113–18, 119, 123, 125, 204
    and his ecological responsibilities, 35–6
    and his helplessness at birth, 37–8
    as image of God, 9–11, 11–13, 30–2, 36, 168,
        188, 202
    as microcosm–macrocosm, 39–41
    and nakedness, 37–8, 198–202
    perfect knowledge, 44–8, 54, 114–16
    perfect proportions of, 38–9
    red-skinned, 17–18
    as responsible for corruption of nature, 205
    stature of, 27–32
Marlowe, Christopher, 51
marriage, 18, 148–9, 155–61
Maxwell, John, 105, 107
McColley, Diane K., 110, 156, 196
Meager, Leonard, 92
Mede, Joseph, 180, 182, 186, 194, 195
Melancthon, Philipp, 48, 63, 82, 87
Methuselah, 19
microcosm, 28, 39–41, 66, 204, 207–8
Milles, Thomas, 12, 31, 34, 46, 79, 87, 184, 207
Milton, John
    and Adam as gardener, 101
    and Adam's guilt, 190
    and Adam's perfect knowledge, 48
    and animals as carnivorous, 118
    and animals in Eden, 110, 111

Breinigsville, PA USA
02 January 2010
252469BV00006B/16/P